T0327730

The Making of China's Post Office

Harvard East Asian Monographs 468

The Making of China's Post Office

*Sovereignty, Modernization, and
the Connection of a Nation*

Weipin Tsai

Published by the Harvard University Asia Center
Distributed by Harvard University Press
Cambridge (Massachusetts) and London

Published by the Harvard University Asia Center, Cambridge, MA 02138

The Harvard University Asia Center publishes a monograph series and, in coordination with the Fairbank Center for Chinese Studies, the Korea Institute, the Reischauer Institute of Japanese Studies, and other faculties and institutes, administers research projects designed to further scholarly understanding of China, Japan, Vietnam, Korea, and other Asian countries. The Center also sponsors projects addressing multidisciplinary and regional issues in Asia.

Library of Congress Cataloging-in-Publication Data

Names: Tsai, Weipin, 1974– author.
Title: The making of China's Post Office : sovereignty, modernization, and the connection of a nation / Weipin Tsai.
Other titles: Harvard East Asian monographs ; 468.
Description: Cambridge : Harvard University Asia Center, 2023. | Series: Harvard East Asian monographs ; 468 | Includes bibliographical references and index. | English, with some words and phrases in Chinese. | Identifiers: LCCN 2023037222 | ISBN 9780674295889 (hardcover)
Subjects: LCSH: China. Hai guan zong shui wu si shu—History. | China. You chuan bu—History. | Postal service—China—History—19th century. | Postal service—China—History—20th century. | China—History—1861–1912
Classification: LCC HE7285 .T735 2023 | DDC 383/.4951—dc23/eng/20231006
LC record available at https://lccn.loc.gov/2023037222

Index by Alexander Trotter
∞ Printed on acid-free paper

To Tom

Contents

Figures

Tables

Acknowledgments

I have received so much from so many people in the process of writing this book. First of all, I would like to thank Professors Robert Bickers and Hans van de Ven, for giving me the opportunity to work on the Chinese Maritime Customs Service project as a research fellow. It was such a wonderful project, a pioneering effort in archival research, and it was a great honor for me to be able to take part. Professor Bickers sheltered me for more than two years at Bristol University, and I am very grateful to him for his care and encouragement. I also want to thank Professor Henrietta Harrison for her consistent support; the seeds of my interest in exploring the history of the Chinese postal service were sown in one of our conversations back in 2004.

Special thanks are due for the assistance of the Second Historical Archives of China in Nanjing and the Tianjin Municipal Archives for providing me with materials and help. I particularly thank Mr. Chen Guang, Ms. Lu Jun, and Ms. Yu Jie for their tireless assistance and friendship. During many years of research, I also received help from Professors Song Meiyun and Wu Hongming in Tianjin, as well as Professor Zheng Anguang at Nanjing University. Their warm friendship has enabled me to always feel at home in these two cities. Indeed, the time I spent at the archives in Nanjing was one of the most memorable periods in my academic life, and I remember many happy times together with Drs. Felix Boecking, Federica Ferlanti, and Catherine Ladds.

I would like to express my gratitude to the Special Collections and Archives team at Queen's University Belfast for providing me with support when I was looking through the papers of Robert Hart and Théophile Piry. In particular, I would like to acknowledge the generous support of Ms. Deirdre Wildy; her knowledge, expertise, and advice have consistently led to the most satisfactory results in finding materials. I also want to thank Dr. Aglaia De Angeli, Mr. Robert James Hunter, and Ms. Clare Morrison for transcribing materials for me.

This monograph uses many images and maps. I want to thank Mr. Jamie Carstairs of Bristol University's Historical Photographs of China project for pointing me to some of the most relevant and dramatic images; he also helped me improve the quality of several images used in the book. I am also very grateful for the assistance given by Mr. Gao Tian-tsi and Ms. Tsai Chia-chi of the Specialist Library of the Chunghwa Postal Museum in Taipei. While Mr. Gao gave me access to the library and helped me to allocate some internal publications, Ms. Tsai on many occasions kindly assisted me with important materials and images. I am also very grateful for Mr. Huang Ching-chi and his skill in making the GIS maps that appear in this volume. Additionally, I want to thank Mr. Liao Hsiung-Ming of the Research Centre for Humanities and Social Sciences at Academia Sinica in Taiwan and his team for constructing a GIS map for the military relay courier system.

I wish to thank the Institute of Modern History at Academia Sinica for providing me with wonderful research facilities and excellent archival materials and library resources. My thanks also go to the Chinese Urban History Research Group for hosting my seminar talks and providing me with very useful feedback, and to Professor Lai Hui-min for opening my horizons on the history of trade and mobility in Mongolia; I am very grateful for her input and inspiration.

Let me also express my gratitude to Professors Wu Songdi and Zou Zhenghuan of Fudan University, Professor Huang Mei-e of National Taiwan University, Professor Huang Ko-wu of the Institute of Modern History at Academia Sinica, and Professor Maurizio Marinelli of the University of Sussex. Additionally, Dr. Yu Po-Ching of National Chung Hsing University gave his time and assistance in many ways, and I am very grateful. Thanks also to Mr. Chan Ho-Yan and Ms. Chang Tzu-Ning for collecting materials for me.

I am so fortunate in having been able to establish contact with teachers and friends from various philatelic groups in China and Taiwan; because of them I have been able to explore postal history from very different perspectives. I want to thank my teacher Mr. Zheng Hui in Ningbo, for sharing his knowledge on private letter hongs. My deep gratitude also goes to the late Professor Michael Mao-hsin Lin for sharing materials with me and for publishing my articles in the philatelist journal *Youshi yanjiu* (Postal history research). I want to thank Mr. Tsai Ming-Feng for his countless discussions about individual stamps, letter covers, postage chops, and specific resources. Mr. Tsai, who has authored several books on Chinese postal history, has shared his knowledge with me most generously, and I am very grateful.

My thanks go to the Chiang Ching-Kuo Foundation, Universities' China Committee in London and the British Academy for sponsoring me in this project.

Thanks also to the Department of History at Royal Holloway, University of London, for supporting my research efforts, not least through administrative support, sabbatical time, and assistance with grant applications, which together made my many research trips and long periods spent writing much easier to manage. In particular, for their encouragement and input I want to thank Professor Sarah Ansari, former editor of the *Journal of the Royal Asiatic Society* and currently the society's president, and Professor Kate Cooper, as well as Ms. Penelope Mullens and the School of Humanities administration team, who provided me with excellent support over an extended period. I also want to thank the staff of the Library at Royal Holloway for the service they provided in helping me access materials from far and wide.

My special thanks also go to Ms. Virginia Rounding for her work in editing the manuscript.

I would like to thank Ms. Kristen Wanner of Harvard University Asia Center, and Ms. Angela Piliouras of Westchester Publishing Services, for their guidance, professionalism, and most of all their patience during the book's production stage.

I can't conclude these acknowledgments without thanking my family—in particular, my late father and mother, Tsai Rong-tsan and Tsai Huang Ching-hsiu. Finally, deepest thanks to my husband, Tom, who patiently shared my exciting discoveries and acted as a sounding board; he challenged my many thoughts and read through the drafts many times while also cooking numerous suppers as I deliberated on the actions and motivations of individuals long dead yet whose legacy is used by millions on a daily basis. I am very grateful for his help and input.

THE OLD IMPERIAL
POST OFFICE, PEKING.

INTRODUCTION

On March 20, 1896, Emperor Guangxu issued an edict instructing his foreign ministry, the Zongli Yamen 總理衙門 (Office in Charge of Affairs concerning All Nations), to relay a message of approval for the creation of a Western-style Imperial Post. The intended recipient of this message was Robert Hart (1835–1911), the inspector general of the Chinese Maritime Customs Service (CMCS; 中國海關). When the message reached him a few days later, Hart also learned that he would be the person tasked with the creation and administration of China's first truly national postal service. On April 9, Hart communicated this "definitive and Imperial" decision in an inspector general's circular to his Customs commissioners in all treaty ports, from Niuzhuang (present-day Yingkou) in northeast China, down to Yadong at the western border between Burma, Sikkim, and Tibet, and as far south as Mengzi at the border between Indochina and Yunnan Province.[1] This new postal service would

1. "Chinese Imperial Post: Inaugurated by Imperial Decree," IG Circular 706 (2nd ser.) / Postal Circular 7, April 9, 1896, in *Docs. Ill.*, 2:42.

soon impact the lives of ordinary people on a scale not experienced with any previous modernization project. In a few short years it would not only come to eclipse the CMCS itself in terms of the size of its workforce but would also penetrate Chinese society in ways few people at that time could have anticipated.

In his circular, Hart linked the postal initiative with his first, highly portentous meeting with Prince Gong Yixin 奕訢 (1833–98), head of the then newly formed Zongli Yamen, and Wenxiang 文祥 (1818–76), a senior Qing statesman. That meeting, held in 1861, just after the Second Opium War (1856–60), was a significant event in Hart's life: it was the moment when he set out his stall as candidate for inspector general of the CMCS, and it was also his opportunity to establish a long-term relationship with the high officials at the center of power in Beijing. His success in both set in motion a sequence of events that was to have enormous repercussions over the coming decades—both for Hart personally and for the Qing administration he was to serve for the remainder of his long career. The meeting turned out to be auspicious for all three men. While on some level Hart could be viewed simply as the man foisted on the Qing government by the British legation to run the nascent CMCS, both the intense and zealous Prince Gong and the reserved but profoundly intelligent Wenxiang were intrigued—as we shall see—by Hart's vision, though they were also aware of the limits of what might be achievable within the existing political framework.

Hart's meeting with Prince Gong coincided with the beginnings of the Self-Strengthening Movement, initiated by the prince earlier in 1861. With the end of the Second Opium War, it was a time of many new ideas and projects. In light of China's comprehensive defeat by Japan in the First Sino-Japanese War (1894–95) at the tail end of this period, the judgment of history has not been kind to these efforts. Nevertheless, the notion of "self-strengthening" in response to the arrival of new kinds of foreigners was an idea very much current among Chinese officials of the time, framing both political and practical intent and indeed providing something of an emotional backdrop to the period.

The historiography of the period owes a particular debt to John King Fairbank (1907–91), who correctly framed many of the emotions of those Chinese officials engaged in the Self-Strengthening Movement. Nevertheless, Fairbank's "impact and response" approach to the wider processes of change in China is facing reexamination and challenge as, over the past decade, since the 2010s, scholarship has begun to revisit and reinterpret the period.[2] In their studies on the history of coal mining and the utilization of natural resources, respectively, Peter B. Lavelle and Shellen Xiao Wu demonstrate that, rather than a one-sided flow of ideas, there was extensive knowledge exchange on multiple levels between the Chinese and foreigners. Their studies also identify an ambivalent quality both in the mindset of Qing officials and their practical approaches toward "modernization" as they sought to ground and contextualize the changes they were experiencing and in which they played a variety of roles.[3] Elisabeth Köll and Anne Reinhardt observe a similar dynamic in their studies on railways and shipping, respectively; their work presents fresh perspectives on nationalism, seen as taking form in a reimagining of national space arising from the impact of new forms of transportation.[4] The same observation can also be found in Stephen Halsey's study of the Qing government's attempt to craft a modern state through the introduction of new transportation and communications infrastructure, as well as through experiments in military modernization and administration.[5] Collectively, the new scholarship paints a complex, hybridized picture of modernization that allows for a great deal more fluidity and agency among local Chinese, as actors far more autonomous and empowered than previously allowed for.

In this light, the unique situation of the Post Office provides us with a fresh case study that further elucidates the unsettling and dynamic nature of Chinese modernization and its accommodation of both local voices and foreign visions. This monograph closely examines the creation of the Post Office within the wider historical context, making a conscious effort to go beyond straightforward institutional history though engaging with the character and motivations of the people involved. This monograph provides examples that show the energy of the key actors, as well as frustration in many quarters in manifesting desired change. The book

2. Ssu-yü Teng and Fairbank, *China's Response*, chap. 1.

3. Lavelle, *The Profits of Nature*; Shellen Xiao Wu, *Empires of Coal*.

4. Köll, *Railroads and the Transformation of China*; Reinhardt, *Navigating Semi-colonialism*.

5. Halsey, *Quest for Power*.

will also present evidence illuminating what modernity and sovereignty actually meant for both lower-ranked postal staff and everyday customers through their participation in the establishment of a national post office.

Of the numerous schemes initiated by Hart or falling under his jurisdiction, the creation of the Post Office was the one in which he took the keenest interest. Although it began as an offshoot of the CMCS, it then took a divergent path that was, in some ways, part of its very design, an aspect largely overlooked in existing postal-related scholarship. In this monograph, I emphasize the importance of grounded, localized elements—from local staff operating in local dialects to postal branches and agencies embedded in the fabric of cities, towns, and villages—in the establishment and expansion of the Post Office and argue that early on, the postal service adopted a very different approach from that of the CMCS, with the clear aim that it should be a Chinese institution for the benefit of the wider Chinese public.

Postal Services around the World

Was there an actual need in China for a modern postal service? To answer this question, it is useful to examine the global context. The nineteenth century witnessed many fundamental changes in political realignment, as well as a technology revolution that had a direct and significant impact on the demands for communication. New forms of integrated information networks that brought together the printing industry, postal service, telegraph, railways, and steamers were emerging across the United States and major European countries, not just in their home territories but also connecting colonies and other dependent territories.[6] In Great Britain, which had a Royal Mail service available to the general public as far back as 1635, the Uniform Penny Post was introduced in January 1840. In May of the same year, the world's first postage stamp, soon nicknamed the Penny Black, was introduced. From the early 1860s onward, the Royal

---

6. Osterhammel, *The Transformation of the World*, 712–24.

Mail also worked in close coordination with railway companies, and together with the widespread growth of telegraph services, this led to a rapid expansion in information circulation across Britain.[7]

In continental Europe the word *post* had been in use to describe mail services in northern Italy from the late fourteenth century onward. Between this time and the sixteenth century, merchants and bankers required reliable postal networks to be built up between European cities, as well as with major ports in the Mediterranean. The famous postal system established by the Taxis (Tasso) family in 1490 served the court of Holy Roman Emperor Maximilian I before branching out more widely to reach both the nobility and subjects of Hapsburg territories across Europe.[8] A portion of the Tasso postal service evolved into the Imperial Reichspost for the Holy Roman Empire, becoming the Thurn und Taxis Post at the turn of the nineteenth century. In the first half of the nineteenth century, both France and Prussia developed modern, state-run postal services, reflecting public demand. In 1849 France adopted postage stamps, while around the same time Prussia began using rail services to transmit mail and combined its telegraph network with the state postal service.[9] The Thurn und Taxis Post was incorporated into the postal system of the Prussian kingdom in 1867.

Postal services in the United States were a federal responsibility from the country's earliest days of nationhood, having their roots in the Second Continental Congress of 1775, when Benjamin Franklin was appointed postmaster general. Establishment was formalized in 1792 with the passing of the Postal Service Act, and the post remains one of relatively few federal functions explicitly mentioned in the nation's constitution.[10] By the early 1830s the size of the American postal system was significantly larger than that of either Britain or France, and the existence of such an extensive postal network, together with significant government subsidies, resulted in a flourishing print industry.[11] Stamps based on the

---

7. Campbell-Smith, *Masters of the Post*, 133, 165–67.

8. Migliavacca and Bottani, *Simone Tasso*, 56, 96, 132, 144.

9. Melius, *The American Postal Service*, 15.

10. Melius, *The American Postal Service*, 18; US Constitution, Article I, Section 8, Clause 7; John, *Spreading the News*, 25.

11. John, *Spreading the News*, 5–7.

British model were adopted in 1847.[12] In 1867 the United States Postal Service was expanded to Shanghai, with Pacific mail going through Hyogo and Nagasaki.[13] The transpacific mail service played a role in Japan's Westernization in the run-up to the Meiji Restoration. In 1871, following a visit to Britain and closely observing the British model, Maejima Hisoka 前道密 (1835–1919) set up the Imperial Japanese Post. Maejima had two priorities: to be in a position to request that foreign postal services withdraw from Japan, and to accomplish the incorporation of existing domestic courier services (*hikyaku* 飛脚).[14] In short, the global trend by the mid-nineteenth century was clear: initiatives to centralize and standardize domestic mail services were becoming widespread. This went hand in hand with the extension of mail services to colonial possessions overseas and to other international destinations. A consequence of the latter was the establishment of the General Postal Union in 1874 in Bern, Switzerland, renamed the Universal Postal Union in 1878.[15]

Returning to the Chinese context, it is remarkable to note similarities between China and Japan in the early history of modern postal services. At the Chinese treaty ports, the British and Hong Kong postal services had been established before the First Opium War (1839–42).[16] The local post office of the Shanghai Municipal Council was established in 1863, while France and the United States also introduced their postal services to China in the same decade, followed later by Russia (1870), Japan (1876), and Germany (1886).[17] The presence of foreign postal operations in China increased further during the Boxer Rebellion in 1900 because of the need to support the allied troops. On the whole, the combination of available postal services worked adequately for foreign communities in China.

---

12. Melius, *The American Postal Service*, 19.

13. Koffsky, *The Consul General's Shanghai Postal Agency*, 4.

14. Hunter, "A Study of the Career of Maejima Hisoka," chaps. 1–2; Maclachlan, *The People's Post Office*, 38–41.

15. Universal Postal Union, *Convention of Paris*, 3.

16. Li Songping, *Ke you wai shi*, 19–23.

17. Zhang Yi, *Zhonghua youzhengshi*, 121–24.

Existing Chinese Postal Systems

The Chinese, meanwhile, had their own courier systems: the military relay courier system (*yizhan* 驛站) and the private letter hongs (*minxinju* 民信局). Surviving written records dating as far back as the Western Zhou period (1045–771 BCE) suggests the existence of government-managed roads for messengers and travelers. During the Spring and Autumn period (770–476 BCE), there was an organized relay courier system and a network of travel lodges.[18] Extensive military relay courier systems can also be seen in records of the Han dynasty (202 BCE–9 CE; 25–220 CE) and later the Tang dynasty (618–907 CE), reflecting active exchanges across multiple cultures and kingdoms.[19]

In the mid-thirteenth century, the Mongols' military expansion resulted in hundreds of yam stations—small camps providing support for official travelers and emissaries—in a network covering Eurasia; there were also official postmen.[20] When the Mongols established the Yuan dynasty (1271–1368), they created a hybrid system that combined their military relay courier system (*zhan chi* 站赤; Mongolian: *jamči*) with elements that remained from the Song dynasty, and in particular the military express courier (*jidipu* 急遞鋪).[21] As for the Ming dynasty (1368–1644), even with a much smaller territory, the military relay courier system exercised an important function in consolidating the power of the early Ming emperors. In addition to military purposes, as Hsi-yuan Chen's study of a Yangtze River map of the Ming dynasty suggests, decisions on the location of important elements of public utilities, including the siting of the military relay courier system, fishery tariff stations, and patrol and inspection stations, as well as the allocation of walled towns and investment in bridges and ports, were carefully taken by the central administration with a view to the maintenance of social order and economic control. Chen further stresses that the distances shown between the relay stations

---

18. Lou, *Zhongguo youyi fadashi*, 36–39; Bai, *Zhongguo jiaotongshi*, 23–34.
19. Zhang Yi, *Zhonghua youzhengshi*, 19–27.
20. Favereau, *The Horde*, 128.
21. Zhang Yi, *Zhonghua youzhengshi*, 206–9; Vér, "The Postal System of the Mongol Empire," 30.

on the map were calculated as radiating out from the direction of the emperor's palace in the capital, a small but illuminating signifier of sovereign power flowing out from the center to all corners of the empire.[22]

The relay system in the Qing dynasty was inherited from the Ming, though it was much improved over time in support of Qing imperial expansion, particularly at the northwest periphery. For the Qing rulers, when it came to governing such a massive territory, one of the first tasks was to set up a reliable system of information transmission. One important reform introduced in the management of the military relay courier system was to discharge imperial subjects from direct requirement either to provide food and shelter to imperial couriers or from a duty to operate as couriers themselves. Instead subjects paid taxes to local governments for horses to be kept and stablemen and couriers to be hired. This change, which began in the second year of Emperor Shunzhi's reign (1645), ideally should have released ordinary people from what was frequently a heavy burden, but some local governments continued to pass on the burden, and the reform was still an ongoing battle even as late as the reign of Emperor Yongzheng in the early eighteenth century. Accompanying this reform were further changes in regulations for the military relay courier system: first, tightening the allocation of postal permits (*youfu* 郵符), and second, setting up an information system to record the granting of permits, allocation of courier funds at each station, and usage of horses, carts, and boats. After being recorded by local officials, the audited information was required to be submitted to provincial governors at the end of each season.[23]

Not all reports from local governments were allowed to be sent via such a system, which was supposed to be used only for information classified as urgent; and not all memorandums to the emperors in the Qing period were viewed as official or related to public affairs. In fact, the majority of messages to the Qing court consisted of private business, recommendations, or information about local culture and customs; these were helpful for the gathering of information about the empire, but seldom time-critical communications. Because they were not treated as of-

---

22. Chen Hsi-yuan, "Changjiang tu shang de xiansuo," 269–358.
23. Liu Wenpeng, *Qingdai yichuan*, 171–74, 227, 237. See also Zhuang, *Qingchao zouzhe zhidu*, 136–37.

ficial documents, memorandums in this category were required to be sent using messengers arranged by local officials themselves.[24] By the early nineteenth century it was apparent that, on top of inefficiency, corruption within the system had become notorious. In this context, Robert Hart saw good reason for the introduction of a national post office, and he believed the largest impediment to its creation was the substantial network of private letter hongs.

By the mid-nineteenth century, private letter hongs—or family-owned courier firms—had long proved their usefulness for merchants and ordinary people in the transmission of information, money, and gifts.[25] For more than a century prior to the establishment of the Imperial Post Office (IPO) in 1896, private letter hongs had provided the country's largest communications network. Thus, they were deeply woven into the fabric of Chinese society. In the late eighteenth century, if not earlier, private letter hongs began as a humble means by which letters and parcels were transported in individual locales. Their services eventually extended to transmission across routes far from a sender's home province, achieved through collaboration among hongs distributed across multiple regions, including Chinese migrant communities overseas.[26] In his *Chinese Sketches*, published in 1876, Herbert A. Giles writes, "In any Chinese town of any pretensions whatever, there are sure to be several 'letter offices,' each monopolizing one or more provinces, to and from which they make it their special business to convey letters and small parcels. The safety of whatever is entrusted to their care is guaranteed, and its value made good if lost."[27] Writing as a private individual, Giles praised the service provided by the letter hongs but, if anything, understated their reach and importance; even an institution as resourceful as the CMCS, which had its own mail and courier services in the early 1880s, had to regularly rely on private letter hongs in some locations.[28] As chapters 4

24. Zhuang, *Qingchao zouzhe zhidu*, 109–15; Liu Wenpeng, *Qingdai yichuan*, 184–85.

25. Peng Yingtian, *Minxinju fazhanshi*; Xu Jianguo, *Cong xingsheng dao shuaibai*.

26. Benton and Hong Liu, *Dear China*, chaps. 2–3; Harris, "Overseas Chinese Remittance Firms."

27. Giles, *Chinese Sketches*, 59.

28. Weipin Tsai, "Yi Chongqing he Chengdu," 37–38.

and 6 will show, the hongs continued to operate after the establishment of a national postal service and were its most important rival.

But the ubiquity of the private letter hongs raises an important question: Why replace them if they appeared to be working well? True to his roots as a British subject of the Victorian era, Hart believed an effective, modern, integrated communications network was part and parcel of a modern state, and a national post office was a crucial component of his vision. This sentiment was not necessarily shared by his Chinese colleagues in the Qing government, nor by all of his senior staff in the CMCS. As we shall explore in some of the later chapters, the postal project was regarded by some as an imposition due to its impact on workload, funding, and, indeed, on the required degree of senior-level attention. But there were other reasons Chinese officials eventually came on board, ranging from worries about the decaying of the military relay courier system to revenue-raising aspirations; there was also a strong desire within the Qing administration to project its presence and authority at the ground level—not just near borders or in areas where sovereignty was challenged in some way but more generally across the empire.

Postal History: Scholarship and Key Questions

Scholarship in the Chinese language has examined the postal history of China from a broad perspective, covering the period from antiquity to the second half of the twentieth century. Four representative publications are *The History of the Postal Service, Telecommunications and Air Transportation in China* (*Zhongguo youdian hangkongshi* 中國郵電航空史, 1928), by Xie Bin 謝彬 (1887–1948); *The History of the Development of the Chinese Postal Courier Service* (*Zhongguo youyi fadashi* 中國郵驛發達史, 1940), by Lou Zuyi 樓祖詒 (1901–74); *The Developing History of the Chinese Postal Service* (*Zhonghua youzheng fazhanshi* 中華郵政發展史, 1994), by Yanxing 晏星 (Pan Ansheng 潘安生; 1947–); and *History of the Chinese Postal Service* (*Zhonghua youzhengshi* 中華郵政史, 1996, by Zhang Yi 張翊 (1917–2012).[29]

---

29. Xie Bin, *Zhongguo youdian hangkongshi*; Lou Zuyi, *Zhongguo youyi fadashi*; Yanxing [Pan Ansheng], *Zhonghua youzheng fazhanshi*; Zhang Yi, *Zhonghua youzhengshi*.

While these publications primarily examine communications systems in China from the earliest period of recorded history, each also addresses the development of the modern postal service. To some extent, all explore the role of Hart and the CMCS in the establishment of the postal service, but their attention is focused on other themes such as the activities of foreign postal services in China, the impact of unequal treaties and foreign privilege, and the role of postal communication during the Second Sino-Japanese War (1937–45). In writing this book I have benefited from this long-standing Chinese scholarship on two fronts: first, it filled gaps in my knowledge; and, second, it provided significant insight on account of the identities of the authors, who were either professionally involved in politics or were employees of the Chinese Post Office and therefore steeped in its institutional culture. These works have, over time, become important historiography, shaping the organization's institutional history.

In the English language, two works of scholarship addressing modern Chinese postal history more broadly are Ying-wan Cheng's *Postal Communication in China and Its Modernization, 1860–1896*, published in 1970, and Lane J. Harris's 2012 PhD thesis "The Post Office and State Formation in Modern China, 1896–1949." In the former, Cheng first examines the history of the military relay courier system, the presence of foreign postal services, and the role of private letter hongs. She then traces the development of the Customs Postal Service, and finally chronicles the establishment of the IPO in 1896.[30] Due to the limited sources available at the time, Cheng's work relies heavily on selective collections of official records of the Qing government. Harris's dissertation forms a natural continuity with Cheng's book in terms of a timeline. Using much wider sources, Harris examines the role of the Post Office in the formation of the modern state from the final years of the Qing empire to the communist takeover in 1949. He argues that despite the transition between political regimes, the Post Office was one of the most important state institutions created in the period.[31]

Building on this scholarship, I pose two central questions in this book: How could such an enormous, nationwide institution as the Post Office successfully come into being at the very sunset of a dying empire

---

30. Cheng, *Postal Communication in China*.
31. Harris, "The Post Office and State Formation," ii.

and survive essentially unscathed into the new republic? And why did the postal service emerge in the form that it did, at the moment that it did, and not earlier or later? I investigate these questions by moving away from established tropes that have essentially labeled all large projects in the late Qing period as functioning within the orbit of the Self-Strengthening Movement and driven by a central or elite leadership. I offer a fresh perspective by showing that, on the contrary, fundamentally different methods were employed. This book will demonstrate the unique place of the Post Office at this point in Chinese history.

One important lesson for Hart after launching the Customs Postal Service in the northern treaty ports in 1878 was the necessity of establishing a balance between adopting modernized approaches on the one hand and accommodating local customs and expectations on the other. The learning curve associated with the Customs Postal Service, out of which the IPO was established nearly two decades later, demonstrates that in the processes of modernization, standardization, and globalization, there was always a need for flexibility. Among the local practices and considerations that Hart needed to be mindful of were the long opening hours of postal branches and the long working hours of postal staff; the cultivation of native staff and their promotion over time into senior roles; the need for postage rates to be set at affordable levels, mindful of competition from the private letter hongs; monetary standards in bookkeeping, reflecting exchange rates between silver and local copper currencies; and the recruitment of established businesses as local agents. Hart and his postal team carried the experience they had gained from the successes and failures of these early postal efforts all the way through to the early republican era.

Another key factor that would contribute to the success or failure of the IPO was the choice of people Hart tasked with establishing and managing it. During his leadership of the CMCS, Hart brought in many foreign experts. But his approach to postal matters was different. Rather than hire experienced men from abroad with existing knowledge of postal service operations—for example, from the General Post Office in Britain—Hart preferred to task existing Customs commissioners with managing the project, both centrally and at the local level. Although the Customs commissioners were also foreigners, each would have been living in China for at least a decade, and in most cases longer, before promotion to such a position. Each would have acquired Chinese language skills, as well as familiarity with local customs and experience in dealing with Chinese officials. This approach—prioritizing language skills, cultural awareness, and existing relationships with officialdom over the specifics of postal operations on the Western model—provides a useful perspective on Hart's thinking in relation to the postal project. The downside, however, was that Customs commissioners did not have prior experience running postal services. Those tasked with the job had to learn as they went along, relying heavily on improvisation and personal judgment. Even with the best of intentions, things did not always run smoothly.

The IPO was the first national project launched after China was defeated by Japan in 1895. While the timing of the decision to proceed was in many ways just as significant as the rationale for the project's approval, an exploration of the reasons for the delay greatly illuminates the nature of Qing politics during the previous three decades. As I will show, the long gestation lies in a heady mix of court affairs, practical and financial considerations, and political maneuvering at all levels, from the local to the international.

This book also covers operational procedures and mechanisms within the postal service. My rationale is to try to bring practical historical realities as close as possible to the reader's imagination, allowing an appreciation of the effort involved in modernization efforts. By examining the details of daily operations, particularly at the level of the local postal branch, I attempt to step back from the grand themes of modern Chinese history and engage with the nitty-gritty of operational service design and the ground-level work of postal staff. Critical historical events, such as the Boxer Rebellion, the launch of the New Policies in 1902, the Chinese Revolution of 1911, and calls for independence for Outer Mongolia and Tibet, are discussed in terms of how they directly affected postal service planning, operations, and personnel. I blend this effort consciously with a microhistorical and storytelling narrative approach, when possible, to allow the voices of individuals participating in or impacted by this drama to be heard. There were also important individuals who played a part in halting or delaying the project.

The Cast of Characters

The key players in this groundbreaking activity—the book's dramatis personae—fall into four different groups. First, in his own singular category, is Robert Hart, the instigator of the project as well as the brains behind it. The next group comprises those senior officials, both Han Chinese and Manchu, who were actively involved in the project of modernization after the Second Opium War and whose concerns, both political and practical, helped shape the direction of Qing policy. Most of them worked directly with Hart in some way on different topics, and their careers overlapped to a large degree. While some raised their voices in support of Hart's postal proposal, others caused difficulty at various levels of the administration. At different times, some of them did both.

A third and vitally important group in initiating postal service activities on the ground was Hart's core team of Customs commissioners, who were asked to take charge of aspects of the postal project alongside their daily responsibilities. They wrote regular, detailed reports to Hart on their progress, and they actively involved him in problem solving. Some of them were sent abroad to attend meetings of the Universal Postal Union; others were sent to Britain or the United States to study postal management. At a lower level of the hierarchy, we have the postal inspectors and clerks. After gaining experience in established treaty port locations, a select group of postal inspectors—predominantly foreigners, at first—were sent to explore new territories for postal expansion. As expansion proceeded, more senior Chinese postal clerks were also sent to evaluate potential new routes and in addition conducted the hands-on work of setting up branches and transportation infrastructure from scratch. In the process they gained experience that proved particularly important when the service came eventually to expand to locations at frontiers or deep into China's sparsely populated interior. In my research for this monograph, reports produced by both foreign and Chinese postal staff proved highly illuminating in my understanding of institutional thinking as I was examining decisions on expansion and logistics; these reports also provided invaluable firsthand insight into the detailed work of setting up postal services both in heavily populated regions and in virgin territory far inland.

Finally there are the perspectives of lower-ranked local officials, as well as individuals associated with private letter hongs. These groups offer the most direct and local responses to the arrival of the national Post Office. Their views were frequently at odds with the assumptions and intentions of both Hart and his postal secretaries in Beijing.

The largest body of materials used for the book are the reports and writings of the employees of the CMCS, the IPO and later the Chinese Post Office. The majority of these records are from the Second Historical Archives of China (Zhongguo dier lishi danganguan 中國第二歷史檔案館) in Nanjing and the Tianjin Municipal Archives (Tianjinshi danganguan 天津市檔案館). Hans van de Ven, in his book on the history of the CMCS, details how the materials relating to this service became available in the Second Historical Archives.[32] Because Tianjin was one of the largest treaty ports prior to 1949, and home to the initial experimental Customs Postal Service in 1878, the Tianjin Municipal Archives has substantial collections on the postal service. But questions remained as to how I could best use the available materials to bring multiple perspectives on the establishment of the Post Office, and how I could present the voices of native Chinese in their many guises, including the voices of those inside and outside the Qing administration and those working within the CMCS and the Post Office at different ranks. Even among the foreign-born Customs commissioners, there were strong and different views about the overall direction and response to emerging challenges. Although many of the reports referenced were produced for internal consumption, their authors were able to express their own authentic voices and perspectives.

Because information about how local Chinese (both officials and members of the public) responded to the arrival of the Post Office is both patchy and rare, the reports written by Customs commissioners at treaty ports or by staff sent out to establish new postal branches and routes are particularly valuable. In comparison to more centrally generated materials, these reports provide us with a diversity of viewpoint and a perspective on specific challenges at the local level that we would struggle to find in any other sources. Many of them are extremely detailed, and the drama and confrontation of the exchanges with the locals that they recorded is

32. Van de Ven, *Breaking with the Past*, 17–18.

not only fascinating at the human level but also illuminating in terms of the overall project. In the latter part of this book, particularly from chapter 5 onward, voices reflecting the experience of Chinese communities come to the fore.

In terms of high politics, we have sources that capture the differing perspectives of key Qing officials—those in favor of moving forward with a postal service, those opposed, and those who were ambivalent. These sources include diaries, correspondence, memorandums, and newspapers. Many of the writers knew Hart personally. In this group we can almost detect the movement of the collective psyche of the Qing court over time, particularly as it tracks the impact and aftermath of major political events.

Finally we have Hart's own writings, including his diaries; letters to his London-based secretary, James Duncan Campbell (1833–1907); and instructions to Customs commissioners, which when taken together serve as the basic framework for tracking the development of the postal project. In addition to his steady reflections on the progress of the postal project, Hart's writings also provide us with a notable amount of information on Qing politics and on the status of his relationships with key statesmen and members of the court.

Chapter Conspectus

There are nine chapters in the book, essentially arranged chronologically. Chapters 1 and 2 set out the quite dramatic context underlying late Qing politics and sketch character profiles of Hart, Prince Gong, Wenxiang, and to a lesser extent Li Hongzhang 李鴻章 (1823–1901) and Thomas F. Wade (1818–95). After reexamining well-known events with the specific aim of understanding the personalities, states of mind, and at times the desperation of Prince Gong and other officials, we can start to see why Hart (and not any other Briton) held such an attraction for them. This has indeed been a great historical puzzle. Chapter 2 addresses the modernization plans of Hart and Wade and how they came into conflict with vested interests in the military relay courier system and with the traditional values held by Chinese officials; the chapter also explains why the

Self-Strengthening Movement, under the somewhat weak leadership of Prince Gong and Wenxiang, was not able to push forward Hart's modernization agenda. The chapter, alongside chapters 3 and chapter 4, outlines the reasons why it took so long for the Qing government to decide to set up a national post office, even as a considerable amount of postal-related experimentation and innovation was taking place.

Chapters 3 and 4 bring Li Hongzhang to the foreground and illuminate the ways in which Li became the primary blocker of Hart's postal plans. In addressing the turning point for Hart's postal proposal—namely, the long-awaited edict establishing the IPO in the spring of 1896—no previous publication has managed to provide a satisfactory account of the reasons underlying such a transformational change. Existing scholarship has so far provided a broad but somewhat commonplace perspective emphasizing national shame, the rise of nationalism, and a new wave of national strengthening. Going beyond these, the second part of chapter 4 fully explains why and how Hart's postal proposal was finally approved after so many years. The most important factors were the return of Prince Gong to the center of power, the downfall of Li Hongzhang, and the rise of Weng Tonghe 翁同龢 (1830–1904), who was Emperor Guangxu's teacher.

Chapters 5 and 6 explore how postal expansion was conducted in two stages. Chapter 5 details how the IPO reached beyond the treaty ports to appeal to local officials and local people but then saw postal expansion halted by the Boxer Rebellion. In the aftermath, largely unremarked upon in current scholarship, the IPO and Hart were publicly criticized by powerful provincial governors who openly demanded that the central government either disband the IPO or withdraw from inland areas. Among these officials was Zhang Zhidong 張之洞 (1837–1909), who had been known for passionately advocating for the establishment of the Post Office after the First Sino-Japanese War but who dramatically changed his view four years later. Chapter 6 documents how this opposition was faced down in a new wave of expansion and how the IPO's public presence was shaped to meet Chinese perceptions. On the launch of the New Policies in 1902, the central government tightened its control at the provincial level and local governments were ordered to support postal expansion. Facing strong competition from the private letter hongs, the IPO adopted a series of measures to compete.

As part of its New Policies initiative, the Qing government reorganized its administrative structure in preparation for constitutional monarchy. Chapter 7 explores how subsequent unprecedented modernization of the management of transportation and communications had an impact on the IPO; the chapter also discusses the development of postal logistics, with increased use of railways, day-and-night operations, and portions of the military relay courier system. The Post Office made a striking visual impact on city, town, and even village landscapes, with new signboards, letter boxes, and grand post office buildings. Collectively these helped project a new image for the Qing empire.

Chapter 8 deals with three breakups. First was the bitter but relatively little-known split between the IPO and the CMCS in May 1911, which led to acrimony between Hart's successor and his Post Office counterpart. The second occurred when the IPO survived the 1911 revolution and transformed itself, renamed the Chinese Post Office, for the new republic. The third concerns the ending of the postal connection to Tibet. The short but rather intense history of the provision of postal services in Tibet illuminates the impact of the 1911 revolution and the challenges to sovereignty that faced a new China.

Chapter 9, the concluding chapter, addresses the making of history by the people who were directly involved in the work of China's national post office. The chapter reviews the creation of institutional myths and legends by Hart himself, as well as by others involved in the Post Office's early history; it also explores how the next generation of Chinese postal staff began to write their own postal history, imbuing events with a strong sense of sovereignty and nationalism. But some later staff, including those who went to Taiwan after 1949, subsequently expressed perspectives on foreign involvement that challenged their colleagues' straightforward nationalist narrative. A further discourse, a source of ambivalence for some, is represented by a romantic tale of postal achievement, captured for posterity as part of the Post Office's twenty-fifth anniversary celebrations. This text records the construction and completion in 1918 of what was, at the time, the longest overland postal route in the world, covering postal territories from Beijing to Outer Mongolia. The narrative reflected China's desire in the early 1920s for the postal service to be seen as an institution strongly responsible for consolidating sovereignty across its entire territory.

THE OLD IMPERIAL
POST OFFICE, PEKING.

CHAPTER ONE

A Long Gestation

In the circular that Robert Hart sent to his Customs commissioners on April 9, 1896, communicating the decision that the new postal service was to go ahead, he recalled that he had first proposed this idea on his first visit to Beijing in June 1861.[1] On that trip he had met for the first time Emperor Xianfeng's half-brother, Prince Gong Yixin, and the vice president of the Board of Revenue (Hubu 户部), Wenxiang, who together had set up the Zongli Yamen that January. This initial encounter, as we shall explore, proved to have lasting impact on all of them.

The Second Opium War (1856–60) provided both a political context and a collaborative opportunity that brought together these three men in what was ultimately to become a situation, at least for a time, of mutual trust, cementing Hart's position in relation to the Qing administration and over the long term providing him with a platform where his postal service efforts could come to fruition. By the late 1850s, the Qing empire

1. "Chinese Imperial Post: Inaugurated by Imperial Decree," IG Circular 706 (2nd ser.) / Postal No. 7, April 9, 1896, in *Docs. Ill.*, 2:42.

was in the midst of a traumatic reorientation as it dealt with the shock of two unprecedented upheavals: the Taiping Rebellion, which began in 1850 and was still ongoing, and the Second Opium War, which broke out in 1854 and was drawing to a destructive close as China slowly moved forward with the Treaty of Tianjin (involving Britain, France, Russia, and the United States) and subsequent agreements—notably, the Convention of Beijing, certified in October 1860. Prior to this the imperial capital had suffered the humiliation of the looting and burning of the Summer Palace, the smoke and flames from which could be seen from the other end of the city. The chaos between June and October 1860 brought Prince Gong to the heart of power. Forming an alliance with Wenxiang, he established a new institution that would reform the management of foreign affairs—the Zongli Yamen. It was in the Zongli Yamen's offices, situated on a narrow lane on the east side of the imperial city, that Hart and Prince Gong first met.[2]

The timing of Hart's visit was opportune because the conclusion of the war was creating urgent new issues for China. In Beijing the absence of the emperor and the destruction of the Summer Palace shaped a traumatic psychological situation for Prince Gong, Wenxiang, and the wider Qing administration. Hart, still only twenty-six years old, was by this time acting inspector general of the Chinese Maritime Customs Service (CMCS), but this was his first opportunity to present himself at the core of power. Fluent in his hosts' spoken language, and having given obvious thought to the problems faced by the Qing government, Hart eased their concerns by offering solutions to questions related to navigation of the Yangtze River, the opening of new Customs Houses, and trade tariffs. He also discussed the issues surrounding modernization in China, and the idea of establishing a modern postal service based on the British model was one of his suggestions, though it was not seen as the most important topic. Although this and subsequent meetings in 1861 did not see the materialization of Hart's post office proposal, nevertheless Hart found patrons who were ready to work with him in effecting change. In turn, Prince Gong, only two years older than Hart but already distinguished on the battlefield, and his mentor Wenxiang, by then

2. *YWSM*, Xianfeng reign, 76:1.

forty-two years old and a highly experienced official, had found a foreigner they could work with.

No doubt China would eventually have established a modern postal service, even without Hart's involvement. But the story of the evolution of the service, from its birth as the Great Qing Imperial Post Office through its first ten years of operation, was very much driven by Hart's personal vision and efforts. While the establishment of the CMCS built on a concept broadly familiar in China, which had a long history of applying tariffs on goods, the notion of a state-run modern post office was a completely alien concept, and without Hart's promotion might well have had to wait until after the Chinese Revolution of 1911. By 1896, when the Imperial Post Office was finally established, Wenxiang was long gone; but Prince Gong, who had been forced out of all formal positions in 1884 during the Sino-French War (1883–85), was once again in favor, returning to the Zongli Yamen and the Grand Council (Junjichu 軍機處) in 1894 by the permission of Empress Dowager Cixi 慈禧太后 (1835–1908) as war with Japan threatened.[3] The aftermath of war was once again a driver for change, and this time Hart's postal proposal was central to China's modernizing response. It is both significant and somehow appropriate that Hart, who had spent three decades advocating this course, should reflect on the events of 1861.

A Fearful Ruler and a Palace in Ashes

For Emperor Xianfeng (1831–61), the Taiping Rebellion might have been experienced as a serious body blow—hugely debilitating, but from which recuperation was possible. By contrast, the military campaign of the Arrow War in 1856 against foreign invaders, and the subsequent resumption of fighting in 1860 in northern China, was experienced more like a serious stroke from which he was never able to recover. Xianfeng started his reign in 1850, not long after he turned eighteen, a tender age at which to inherit both the Taiping Rebellion and the ongoing impacts of relentless pressure from foreign powers. Xianfeng was the fourth son of

---

3. Wu Xiangxiang, *Wan Qing gongting*, 145–46.

Emperor Daoguang, but three brothers had died before he was born, when Daoguang was almost fifty. In under two years, Daoguang gained another two sons, one of them Prince Gong, the emperor's sixth. The emperor's concerns at the lack of sons to continue the dynasty gave way to a situation where there were several options. When Xianfeng was nine years old, his mother passed away and he was placed under the care of another of the emperor's consorts, Prince Gong's mother. The two princes were very close when they were young, but they seemed to have quite different personalities. Xianfeng was reportedly suspicious, indecisive, and physically weak, whereas Prince Gong was brave, active, masculine, and very intelligent. There were rumors that Emperor Daoguang favored Prince Gong for all of his good qualities, and the decision on the succession presented a very difficult choice. Daoguang delayed as long as he was able—until he was sixty-four years old. In the end he picked the prince who exhibited personality traits that were similar to his own.[4] Although Xianfeng was often indecisive, and arguably did not show great intelligence, he was very strongheaded in his feelings toward foreigners: he disliked them and preferred to use military force to keep them at a distance.[5] His personality as emperor was shown clearly in the Second Opium War, particularly in the 1859–60 crisis prior to the burning of the Summer Palace. He failed to grasp that his fate had become entwined with foreign interests because his government had been receiving aid from foreign governments to suppress the Taiping Rebellion, and consequently could not comprehend that foreign contacts would inevitably become even closer in the years and decades to follow.

Emperor Xianfeng might reasonably have thought that once the British Treaty of Tianjin was signed the crisis would be ended. On the contrary, this was just the start of his difficulties with foreign powers. He disliked what Article III of the treaty stipulated on the issue of foreign envoys residing in the capital.[6] But perhaps more important, he was already seeking to be released from Article LVI, which required there to be formal, joint ratification of the treaty in the capital a year later and which

4. Wu Xiangxiang, *Wan Qing gongting*, 25; Mao, *Kuming tianzi*, 13–15. See also Mao, *Tianchao de bengkui*, 170–71.

5. Mao, *Kuming tianzi*, 49–50.

6. For the text of the provisions of Article III, see *Zhong wai jiu yuezhang*, 1:296.

would imply having to receive foreigners in his palace.[7] Article III had two key provisions: the first stipulated the option of foreigners being present and taking up residence in the capital, though it left room for their permanent residency elsewhere; the second firmly stipulated use of equal-footing etiquette. James Bruce, the Eighth Earl of Elgin (1811–63), the British high commissioner and plenipotentiary in China and the Far East, was the main individual determining the content of treaty clauses, and he believed that insisting on the issue of etiquette was asking China to surrender "some of the most cherished principles of the traditional policy" of the Chinese Empire.[8] But just as Elgin was insisting on executing the ratification in the capital, Xianfeng was seeking ways to avoid it, in the process sowing the seeds for further clashes in 1859 and 1860. These actions initiated the chain of events that eventually led to the burning of the Summer Palace and the entry of Prince Gong as an interlocutor in the negotiations that followed.

After the signing of the Treaty of Tianjin, Britain, France, and the United States agreed to meet in Shanghai later in the year to revise tariff rates, and Xianfeng sought to use the meeting as an opportunity to set aside four key provisions of the treaty: foreign diplomats residing in the capital permanently; open ports along the Yangtze River; inland travel permission for foreigners; and the 4 million taels (Tls.) in payment agreed upon toward British military expenditures, in exchange for British troops drawing back to Canton.[9] The first three points were regarded by the emperor as damaging to his pride; on the fourth point, he simply did not want to pay. In his farewell instructions, delivered in person, Xianfeng informed his superintendents for the mission—envoys Guiliang 桂良 (1785–1862) and Huashana 花沙纳 (1806–59), both of Manchu background—that he would be more than happy to offer complete exemption from tariffs in return for negation of these four points, with the aim of keeping the foreigners restricted to the south. He believed this offer was a generous one and that it would be accepted in return for concessions on the four points.[10]

7. For the text of the provisions of Article LVI, see *Zhong wai jiu yuezhang*, 1:311.

8. Hevia, *English Lessons*, 68–69. See also Mao, *Kuming tianzi*, 191–92.

9. *YWSM*, Xianfeng reign, 31:31; Separate Article of the Treaty, in *Zhong wai jiu yuezhang*, 1:311.

10. *YWSM*, Xianfeng reign, 30:43–44.

Before the negotiations had even begun, however, it was already very clear that the emperor's strategy could not work. The foreign powers considered that it was in their own interests for the Chinese government to be able to collect reasonable tariffs, in order to create and maintain a stable system for trade. Precisely for this reason, the Board of Inspectors of the Customs House had been set up in Shanghai in July 1854, working in conjunction with Wu Jianzhang 吳健彰 (1791–1866), the Shanghai circuit intendant (*taotai*) at the time who acted as the superintendent of Customs. The Board of Inspectors was the forerunner of the CMCS.[11] The governor-general of Liangjiang (whose jurisdiction was over Anhui, Jiangsu, and Jiangxi Provinces), He Guiqing 何桂清 (1816–62), was in alignment with the allied countries on the tariff issue. Being a provincial governor who understood the importance of the Customs tariff in contributing to local revenues, particularly at that time with significant military expenses being incurred in suppressing the Taiping Rebellion, he was against the idea of tariff exemption. Unable to enforce his will on the negotiations, Xianfeng criticized He Guiqing for letting him down; he also blamed Guiliang and Huashana for the content of the Treaty of Tianjin.[12]

Collectively, the British, French, and Americans were very firm on the opening of treaty ports along the Yangtze River and on rights for their missionaries and merchants to travel inland. On the issue of diplomats residing in the capital, however, there was room for maneuver. Neither France nor the United States had pursued this, and in the end only the British Treaty of Tianjin text stipulated it as a requirement.[13] Guiliang and Huashana wrote a letter to explain why this was the most problematic issue, humbly asking Britain to be sympathetic about the difficult position the Qing government was in.[14] With the ongoing Taiping Rebellion, and the Nian Rebellion taking place in northern China, Elgin

11. *The Origin and Organisation of the Chinese Customs Service*, 1–3.

12. *YWSM*, Xianfeng reign, 30:46, 31:22.

13. For Articles V and VI of the US Treaty of Tianjin, see *Zhong wai jiu yuezhang*, 1:281. For Article II of the French Treaty of Tianjin, see *Zhong wai jiu yuezhang*, 1:314.

14. Enclosure, "Précis of a Letter from Commissioner Kweiliang, Hwashana, &c., to the Earl of Elgin," in No. 215, "The Earl of Elgin to the Earl of Malmesbury," October 22, 1858, translated by Thomas Wade, in *Correspondence Relative to the Earl of Elgin*, 405–6.

understood that if the Qing rulers allowed British diplomats to reside in the capital—a right that would certainly also be claimed by other foreign countries—this would present a huge difficulty for the Qing central government and place the Chinese high officers "in the dilemma of having either to risk a quarrel or submit to some indignity which would lower the Chinese government in the eyes of its own subjects."[15] At this time Elgin was willing to assist the emperor in keeping face, in order to maintain order in China for trade, and thus was prepared in practice not to exercise Beijing residency rights.

Although he was open to softening his stance on the issue of residence in the capital, Elgin still insisted on two things: first, that the original wording in the treaty should be kept, so that diplomats could travel to the capital when necessary, and second, that the treaty be ratified at Beijing a year later.[16] In his reply to Guiliang and Huashana he noted that if the British envoys were properly received at Beijing the following year for the ratification event, and if the full effect given in the Treaty of Tianjin were exercised, "it would certainly be expedient that Her Majesty's Representative in China should be instructed to choose a place of residence elsewhere than at Pekin, and to make his visits to the capital either periodical, or only as frequent as the exigencies of the public service may require."[17] In an immediate return of favor, Elgin was assisted by the Chinese to sail on the Yangtze River up to Hankou to choose which places should be opened for foreign trade. During the trip he witnessed the devastation of towns and cities that had been caused by the Taiping Rebellion, which brought into focus the need to help the Qing rulers reach a better position so that order could be restored. On the conclusion of the trip, Elgin selected Hankou, Jiujiang, and Zhenjiang to be opened for foreign trade.[18] Xianfeng was furious after learning how the negotiation had gone, and he believed

---

15. No. 216, "The Earl of Elgin to the Earl of Malmesbury," November 5, 1858, in *Correspondence Relative to the Earl of Elgin*, 406. See also Morse, *The International Relations*, 1:536.

16. Morse, *The International Relations*, 1:536–37.

17. Enclosure 4, "The Earl of Elgin to Commissioners Kweiliang, Hwashana, &c.," in No. 216, "The Earl of Elgin to the Earl of Malmesbury," 412.

18. Morse, *The International Relations*, 1:538.

that the results of the negotiation in Shanghai had left him in an even worse situation.[19]

Meanwhile, a new problem was brewing in Canton, which had been occupied by British and French troops since 1857: the new viceroy, Huang Zonghan 黄宗漢 (1803–64), was in favor of using force to eject foreign troops from the city. As tension built between local Chinese and foreigners, Huang recruited a militia without official approval from Beijing and even faked an imperial edict to legitimize his actions.[20] No one could have foreseen this. Elgin demanded Huang be removed and expressed growing doubts on the legitimacy of Guiliang and Huashana's actions. Xianfeng was sympathetic to Huang and his compatriots in Canton, regarding their actions as patriotic, but he used this opportunity to relocate the position of superintendent of trade from Canton to Shanghai, and Huang was dismissed. In Xianfeng's calculation, Shanghai was much closer than Canton to Beijing, so if it became a communications hub, there would be no need for foreigners to come to, and much less stay in, the capital.

At the same time, Xianfeng was becoming increasingly concerned about the prospects of foreigners attending court in Beijing and was beginning to consider resisting this—through force if necessary. Throughout the previous year Xianfeng had regularly received updates from General Sengge Rinchen 僧格林沁 (1811–65) about the progress made with military defenses in the Dagu and Tianjin regions and in the area leading up to the Shanhai Pass at the approach to Beijing. Guiliang was opposed to the transmission of any communication relating to this and, in the hope that he might still be able to do something about it, avoided passing on Xianfeng's threats of violent resistance to his foreign interlocutors.[21]

The lack of a reliable and trusted communications channel with foreigners was another symptom of the general inadequacy of the Qing government at the time. The issue was multifaceted, extending beyond the issue of language to the general difficulty in identifying trustworthy intermediaries. The Chinese also found the Westerners to be unduly aggressive in their behavior. For example, Frederick Bruce (1814–67), who

19. *YWSM*, Xianfeng reign, 32:3–4, 18.
20. *YWSM*, Xianfeng reign, 33:10, 34:3–4.
21. *YWSM*, Xianfeng reign, 33:19–21, 8, 30.

was the brother of Lord Elgin and head of the British delegation in the negotiation of the Treaty of Tianjin, was regarded as not easy to deal with.[22] Bruce relied heavily on Thomas F. Wade and Horatio N. Lay (1832–98) in conducting the actual negotiations due to their language skills. Lay had been appointed as inspector of Customs in Shanghai in 1855, to replace Wade, but during the negotiations for the Treaty of Tianjin he had also acted as interpreter not just for Elgin but also for the American, Russian, and French ministers.[23] Through having already worked with the Chinese officials for years, Lay believed that applying pressure by signaling a hot temper on the part of the Western negotiators would help turn the discussions in the required direction. The result of this was that Lay made a bad impression on the Chinese officials, who described his behavior as bullying, ungrateful, duplicitous, and ultimately as an act of stabbing China in the back.[24]

In the absence of a reliable go-between, individuals like Huang Zhongyu 黃仲畲 (years unknown) were in demand. Huang, who used multiple pseudonyms to protect his identity, had worked for Wade and Harry Smith Parkes (1828–85) in the British Consulate in Canton from 1849 onward. Thanks to his good English, his long-standing connections with the British, and his Canton experience, Huang was regarded by Guiliang as a valuable asset. He was suspected by some of double-dealing; for example, erroneous information he had provided to Ye Mingchen 葉名琛 (1807–59), the viceroy of Guangdong and Guangxi at the time, had led to Ye being captured by the British.[25] Despite a rumor that this had been done deliberately, during the negotiations of the Treaty of Tianjin Huang gained Guiliang's trust and was rewarded with the position of subprefect.[26] At the beginning of 1859 Huang arrived in Shanghai at the earnest invitation of Guiliang, and he was given the task of persuading the British to perform the ratification in Shanghai, as he was viewed as a better person for this job than Lay.[27]

22. *YWSM*, Xianfeng reign, 34:29.
23. Stanley F. Wright, *Hart and the Chinese Customs*, 111, 126.
24. *YWSM*, Xianfeng reign, 27:1.
25. Yuan Zhen, "Liangci yapian zhanzheng," 32–34.
26. *YWSM*, Xianfeng reign, 29:14.
27. Guiliang to Emperor Xianfeng, "Huang Zhongyu zai Hu tanxun yiqing Yingqiu reng jian yu jinjing" 黃仲畲在滬探詢夷情英酋仍堅欲進京 [Huang Zhongyu investigated

By early 1860, plans for the visit to Beijing had been circulating for some time among the foreign communities. Foreign merchants, in particular, welcomed this development. British diplomats declared that they planned to stay in the capital for several weeks, and if they did not achieve this goal, it would be considered a defeat.[28] On learning the hard truth, Xianfeng started to prepare for the worst. He sped up military deployment on the coast, and transferred thousands of men from Heilongjiang and Jilin to Tianjin and nearby areas.[29] But diplomatic efforts continued, and he changed his offer to permit foreign envoys to come to Beijing on the following terms: each envoy was to bring no more than ten assistants; envoys and their entourages were to bring no weapons, and were to follow the etiquette practiced by foreign visitors in the past (they were not, for example, to use sedan chairs or bring a band of musicians); and, finally, they would be required to leave the capital as soon as the ratification was completed.[30] Essentially, the conditions demonstrated that the emperor wanted to continue to apply the rules of the tributary system, and expected foreign diplomats to perform kowtow. It appears that Guiliang did not pass on the emperor's new conditions to the British; this was not the only time that he decided to keep to himself messages that he did not think would be helpful.

Bruce and the newly appointed French envoy extraordinary, Alphonse de Bourboulon, arrived at Shanghai in early June but did not see any point

---

the situation of foreigners in Shanghai and reported that British leaders still insisted on going to Beijing], Xianfeng reign year 9, month 1, day 27 (March 1, 1859), ZYJYD, 01-02-007-01-044.

28. Guiliang to Emperor Xianfeng, "Pulusi [Bruce] fengming wei xin gongshi zhujing dengshi gai an tiaoyue shixing" 卜魯斯奉命爲新公使駐京等事概按條約實行 [Bruce was named as new minister to China, and resident in Beijing will be arranged according to the treaty], Xianfeng reign year 9, month 3, day 9 (April 11, 1859), ZYJYD, 01-02-007-03-005; *YWSM*, Xianfeng reign, 34:28–31.

29. *YWSM*, Xianfeng reign, 36:17–18; Hou Jie and Qin Fang, "Haizhan yu paotai," 282–86.

30. Guiliang to Emperor Xianfeng, "Yi tang jianyu jinjing xu xianzhi renyuan bing bude zuojiao paidui" 夷倘堅欲進京須限制人員並不得坐轎排隊 [If the foreigners insisted on going to Beijing, the size of the group was to be restricted, and sedan chairs and music bands were not permitted], Xianfeng reign year 9, month 2, day 25 (March 29, 1859), ZYJYD, 01-02-007-01-092.

in meeting with Chinese officials.[31] Instead Bruce sent a request to the court for the provision of assistance in Tianjin and Beijing—specifically, for transportation and servants to escort them to the capital. He also asked that a clean and spacious house be provided for them in Beijing. On June 20, the ministers of Britain, France, and the United States arrived in Dagu. At this point, Guiliang was still in Shanghai; he was ordered to return to the capital without delay.[32] At the same time, Xianfeng made another offer: he was willing to adopt Sengge Rinchen's advice that the foreign contingent should disembark at Beitang, thirty *li* (around eighteen kilometers) north of Dagu,[33] away from the military defenses that had been prepared at Dagu along the shore barrier, including obstructions made of iron stakes.

This "friendly gesture" was not, however, communicated to Bruce in time to avoid military conflict. As recorded years later by Hosea Ballou Morse (1855–1934) in his account of the events, Bruce was in an impossible position to prevent an exchange of fire due to the late arrival of instructions on the change of plan. By the time Bruce learned of the change, the ships of Captain James Hope (1808–81) were a great distance away.[34] According to Mao Haijian, however, the so-called miscommunication might actually have been deliberate on the part of Sengge Rinchen.[35] In any case, the Chinese had significantly improved their military equipment and the training of personnel at Dagu since 1857. Britain and France did not deploy a large enough flotilla or sufficient weaponry on this occasion, and as a result, while there were thirty-two Chinese fatalities, altogether ninety-three British and French were killed and more than 350 were wounded, including Captain Hope himself.[36] Britain and France decided to retreat. Meanwhile, John E. Ward (1814–1902),

31. Guiliang to Emperor Xianfeng, "Jueding jinjing huanyue bubian zai Hu xiangwu" 決定進京換約不便在滬相晤 [Foreigners decided to go up to Beijing to ratify the treaty, and refused to meet in Shanghai], Xianfeng reign year 9, month 5, day 18 (June 18, 1859), ZYJYD, 01–02–007–03–068.

32. Morse, *The International Relations*, 1:575–576.

33. The conversion between *li* and kilometers used in this book is 1 *li* 里= 0.619 kilometer. From *Decennial Reports 1892–1901*, 1: n.p.

34. Morse, *The International Relations*, 1:582–83.

35. Mao, *Jindai de chidu*, 348–349.

36. Hou Jie and Qin Fang, "Haizhan yu paotai," 286–87.

the US minister to the Qing empire, went ahead with entry via Beitang and arrived in the capital in a low-key fashion: no sedan chairs but donkey carts, and no meeting with the emperor but with Guiliang instead, thereby avoiding the kowtow problem. After seventeen days in residence in Beijing, ratification was executed at Beitang prior to the Americans' return south.[37]

Britain and France were playing a long game. On the one hand, they continued to assist the Qing government in suppressing the Taiping Rebellion; on the other, they gathered forces once again in northern China the following summer. This time they were prepared for war. Not counting transports and thousands of Cantonese "coolies," the British sent out seventy armed vessels, and the French sent forty. Coordinating with the naval forces, eleven thousand British and sixty-seven hundred French infantry arrived at Beitang on August 1. Both Dagu and Tanggu were taken.[38]

On September 17 a group of thirty people, including Parkes; Elgin's private secretary, Henry B. Loch; Thomas W. Bowlby, a correspondent for the *Times*; and assorted others, including French representatives and Indian cavalrymen, went to Tongzhou to deliver Elgin's letter. The content of the letter was intended to firm up arrangements for the ratification in the capital.[39] Prince Yi Zaiyuan 載垣 (1816–61), newly appointed as the high commissioner to conduct the negotiations, said to Parkes that this could be arranged only if Lord Elgin would perform kowtow; otherwise he would only be permitted to hand in the letter to the high commissioners, as the American and Russian ambassadors had done.[40] To this Parkes answered that if an audience with the emperor was not granted, it would mean China did not really want to talk peace; he then ordered his people to pack up and leave immediately. By this time Xianfeng had already ordered Sengge Rinchen to detain the delega-

37. Mao, *Kuming tianzi*, 200–201.

38. Mao, *Jindai de chidu*, 66–70.

39. No. 84, "The Earl of Elgin to Lord J. Russell," September 23, 1860, in *Correspondence respecting Affairs*, 172–73. For Harry Parkes's early career in China, see Lovell, *The Opium War*, 244.

40. *YWSM*, Xianfeng reign, 62:14–15; No. 84, "The Earl of Elgin to Lord J. Russell," 172–73.

tion at Tongzhou. When they arrived at Zhangjiawan, southeast of Tongzhou, in the mist of confusion, they were ambushed.[41] At the same time, the Chinese also arrested several of the French. The group was taken back to Tongzhou, and Parkes was put in heavy chains and questioned daily.[42]

Within the Qing court there were two main views on managing relationships with foreigners. One party, including Prince Gong himself, as well as Guiliang and Guo Songtao 郭嵩燾 (1818–91), who later became the first Chinese minister to Britain in 1876, preferred to have peaceful, cooperative dealings. By contrast, others, including Prince Yi and Sushun 肅順 (1816–61), argued for adopting tougher approaches.[43] After his teacher Du Shoutian 杜受田 (1788–1852) died, Xianfeng found support from Sushun. Though he was Manchu, Sushun had made his reputation through being very critical toward certain Manchu nobles and was particularly intolerant of officials engaged in corruption. He viewed Han Chinese as more reliable than his fellow Manchus.[44] At critical moments, Sushun spoke up for Zuo Zongtang 左宗棠 (1812–85) and Zeng Guofan 曾國藩 (1811–72), and as a consequence these generals, who were engaged at the time in suppressing the Taiping Rebellion, were spared removal and demotion.[45]

On September 21, 1860, upon learning that their men had not returned, the allied troops arrived at Baliqiao in Tongzhou (the last defensible location before the entrance to the capital) and launched a ferocious attack. After Baliqiao was seized, Xianfeng instructed his brother, Prince Gong, to take over negotiations. He himself fled to his palace in Chengde, Rehe, some distance to the northeast, and took Sushun with him.

41. *YWSM*, Xianfeng reign, 61:24; enclosure, "Mr. Loch to the Earl of Elgin," October 9, 1860, in No. 89, "The Earl of Elgin to Lord J. Russell," October 9, 1860, in *Correspondence respecting Affairs*, 191.

42. Enclosure 1, "Mr. Parkes to the Earl of Elgin," October 20, 1860, in No. 108, "The Earl of Elgin to Lord J. Russell," October 30, 1860, in *Correspondence respecting Affairs*, 231–32.

43. Wu Xiangxiang, *Wan Qing gongting*, 15.

44. Huang Jun, *Hua sui ren sheng an*, 429.

45. Mao, *Kuming tianzi*, 242–44.

Prince Gong Yixin and the Final Negotiations

Prince Gong and Xianfeng had previously been close. Xianfeng spent much time in the Summer Palace, and to show his affection to his brother, he gave one of the beautiful satellite gardens to Prince Gong. Prince Gong's mansion, a very popular tourist site today, was another gift from Xianfeng when the prince turned twenty years old. But the serious illness of Prince Gong's mother, Dowager Imperial Noble Consort Kangci 康慈皇貴太妃, had caused conflict when Prince Gong asked Xianfeng to grant her the title of empress dowager. Despite his initial unwillingness— in part out of respect for his own mother, and also because of past competition between himself and Prince Gong—Xianfeng approved the proposal and granted her the title Empress Dowager Xiaojingcheng 孝靜 成皇后. After she died in August 1855, Xianfeng expressed his anger at having been forced into this situation by stripping Prince Gong of his official positions, including those of grand councilor and presiding controller of the Imperial Clan Court (Zongling 宗令). He also ordered that the nameplate of the Empress Dowager Xiaojingcheng not be placed in the Imperial Ancestral Temple, so she was excluded from having a position within the Qing ancestral worship rites.[46]

Given this history, Prince Gong now sought to show loyalty to his brother. Although he did not have much personal experience dealing with foreigners, he was well informed by his father-in-law, Guiliang. Prince Gong described himself as "a round-necked man without much of an education; but he could give himself credit for being loyal to the emperor and benevolent to the people."[47] He reasoned with the allies that conflict was unnecessary and that the emperor was very kind and forgiving. He also asserted that he would like to continue with peace negotiations, but if allied troops advanced beyond Tongzhou, he was determined to fight.[48]

Lord Elgin sent an ultimatum demanding that the foreign prisoners be released in three days. In return, if the Chinese complied, the allies

46. Wu Xiangxiang, *Wan Qing gongting*, 6; Mao, *Kuming tianzi*, 248–51.
47. *YWSM*, Xianfeng reign, 62:37, my translation.
48. Enclosure 2, "The Prince of Kung to the Earl of Elgin," September 21, 1860, in No. 84, "The Earl of Elgin to Lord J. Russell," 175.

would not advance into Beijing, and if the ratification could be done at Beijing under suitable arrangements, the troops would return to Tianjin and leave the north in the spring of the following year.[49] Prince Gong did not take up this offer, as he did not have confidence in Elgin's promise.[50] Some officials suggested to the emperor that Parkes be executed, but Prince Gong believed that Parkes, who could speak and read Chinese, might be of some use later in the negotiations.[51]

Prince Gong sent Hengqi 恒祺 (1803?–1866) to talk to Parkes, and made some positive gestures: he removed Parkes's chains, transferred him to better quarters, and returned Parkes's personal belongings to him. Hengqi (also known as Hoppo), the superintendent of Customs at Canton, had been appointed assistant imperial commissioner for the negotiations. He was well known to the British, having worked very closely with Hart at Canton Customs. Hengqi asked Parkes to write a letter asking Lord Elgin to withdraw the troops.[52] Parkes initially refused, but Hengqi reminded him that Chinese-style torture might be carried out on him if he refused. Parkes then insisted on writing in English, but no one, including Hengqi, was able to read the message, so it was not sent. Hengqi then visited Parkes again, and this time Parkes wrote in Chinese with a few lines in English. In order to understand the content of those few lines, they identified Huang Huilian 黄惠廉, the assistant district magistrate of Miyun County in northeast Beijing, as an English speaker, and the letter was brought to him. Huang noted that the English text was just

49. Enclosure 3, "The Earl of Elgin to the Prince of Kung," September 22, 1860, in No. 84, "The Earl of Elgin to Lord J. Russell," 175; enclosure 1, "The Prince of Kung to the Earl of Elgin," September 23, 1860, in No. 88, "The Earl of Elgin to Lord J. Russell," October 8, 1860, in *Correspondence respecting Affairs*, 179; enclosure 2, "The Earl of Elgin to the Prince of Kung," n.d. [September 24 or 25, 1860?], in No. 88, "The Earl of Elgin to Lord J. Russell," 180.

50. *YWSM*, Xianfeng reign, 64:8.

51. Emperor Xianfeng declared that he would not be sorry to see the prisoners executed, though he did not insist on execution. *YWSM*, Xianfeng reign, 63:7.

52. Parkes and Loch were removed by the Board of Punishments (Xingbu 刑部) to a temple nearby. They could take exercise in the courtyard, and they were supplied with "essentials as good food, beds, &c., but also with the luxuries of writing materials, soap and towels, &c"; enclosure 1, "Mr. Parkes to the Earl of Elgin," October 20, 1860, in No. 108, "The Earl of Elgin to Lord J. Russell," 239.

Parkes's name and the date, but he added that he did not think the letter would achieve Prince Gong's goal.[53]

Parkes's letter was sent together with Prince Gong's letters to Lord Elgin on October 3, 1860, and Huang's view was proved correct.[54] Parkes wrote again, and Wade wrote back. Wade said that Lord Elgin had repeatedly demanded the release of Parkes and the other captives; on the other hand, he pointed out, if the Chinese did not want to negotiate and release the captives, the allies would have no option but to order the troops into Beijing and burn down the city "from one end to the other." He added, "If Peking falls, of course there is an end of this Dynasty," implying that even the Imperial Palace could be affected.[55] Parkes and others imprisoned in the capital were released, and the British survivors were instructed to produce a statement about what they had experienced. The reports showed they were treated brutally at the beginning of their capture, but later were treated with some kindness due to the change of tactics ordered by Prince Gong.[56]

On October 5 some of the allied troops entered the Summer Palace and were taken aback at the luxury of the emperor's home.[57] Having been stationed at the Shanyuan Temple at the south corner of the Summer Palace since Xianfeng had left, Guiliang, Prince Gong, and Wenxiang abandoned this temporary headquarters overnight. Most officials also deserted the city, and the roads were crowded with people escaping; soon the capital became largely empty of people but began to fill up with newly piled wreckage.[58]

Looking at the thick black smoke obscuring the sky, Prince Gong and Wenxiang wrote, "The barbarians have scattered from north and east two directions and occupied the palace. They burned down the streets in

53. *YWSM*, Xianfeng reign, 64:7–15; Guo Songtao, *Guo Songtao xiansheng*, 1:168.

54. Enclosure 17, "The Earl of Elgin to the Prince of Kung," October 4, 1860, in No. 88, "The Earl of Elgin to Lord J. Russell," 187.

55. *YWSM*, Xianfeng reign, 64:18–20; enclosure 3, "Mr. Wade to Mr. Parkes," October 4, 1860, in No. 108, "The Earl of Elgin to Lord J. Russell," 244–45.

56. No. 89, "The Earl of Elgin to Lord J. Russell," October 9, 1860, in *Correspondence respecting Affairs*, 188–89.

57. Morse, *The International Relations*, 1:606.

58. Wenxiang, "Ziding nianpu shang," 32; Li Ciming, "Yuemantang riji," 2:124; Lovell, *The Opium War*, 262–63.

the neighborhood, horrifyingly and appallingly."[59] In tears and despair, Prince Gong thought about abandoning the negotiations and joining the emperor, but the routes to the northeast were blocked by foreign forces, so they could only move south, until they finally reached Changxindian, near the Marco Polo Bridge, beyond the gate of the capital.

In addition to the witness statements, what became the last straw for Elgin was an imperial edict he was shown that had been left behind when Qing officials fled. Believed to have been issued before Parkes and his men were arrested, it showed that the emperor, rather than being unaware of events as had been claimed, was directly responsible for ordering their arrest. The edict referred to the British as "barbarians" and as greedy and untrustworthy. Elgin himself was painted as "truculent, tricky to the last degree."[60] Elgin felt he had been deceived and insulted. While the Qing court had been communicating its willingness to pursue peace negotiations, the emperor had been exhorting and encouraging his soldiers to cut off the heads of the enemy—Tls. 100 for a white barbarian, Tls. 500 for a chief—with Tls. 5,000 offered for sinking a ship.[61]

Elgin also gained the impression that the Qing court regarded the capture of the British subjects as a positive achievement because it "gratified the resentment of the Emperor." He reflected, "Low as is the standard of morals which now obtains in China on such points, we should in my opinion have still further lowered it if we had not treated the act in question as a high crime calling for severe retribution." Elgin now wanted to leave a mark on China, to punish Xianfeng directly, and to require the Qing government's "absolute surrender." He believed that whatever measure he was considering ought to be the most effective, sending a message to the emperor in response to his "crime" without terrifying Prince Gong to the point that he would no longer feel able to stay to complete the ratification, and also not attacking Beijing or anything within the city directly.[62] A final consideration was that the action should

59. *YWSM*, Xianfeng reign, 64:27, my translation.
60. No. 97, "The Earl of Elgin to Lord J. Russell," October 22, 1860, in *Correspondence respecting Affairs*, 206.
61. Enclosure, "Imperial Edict," in No. 97, "The Earl of Elgin to Lord J. Russell," 207.
62. No. 103, "The Earl of Elgin to Lord J. Russell," October 25, 1860, in *Correspondence respecting Affairs*, 213–14.

be completed very quickly so that it would not interfere with the execution of the treaties.

On October 17 Elgin buried the dead British captives in a Russian cemetery before launching his revenge. General Sir James Hope Grant (1808–75) later remembered vividly that it was a bitterly cold winter's day; in the distance, the hills were covered with snow, and the cold wind from the northeast signaled that a "piercing blast of winter" was on its way.[63] Elgin then selected what were known as the emperor's favorite grounds, and secured Hope Grant's commitment to demolish the Summer Palace.[64] The following day, Hope Grant took around two hundred men with him, entered the Summer Palace, and executed the plan. On being confronted with this news, Prince Gong once again wanted to abandon the negotiations, but the Russian minister, Count Nikolai Pavlovich Ignatiev, persuaded him to stay; otherwise, the occasion might be the end of the dynasty. Since the Crimean War (1853–56), Britain, France, and Russia had found themselves collaborating in China; it was not in any of the parties' interests for the Qing dynasty to be pushed to the point of collapse. In the presence of Prince Gong and the imperial seal, the English versions of the Treaty of Tianjin and the Convention of Beijing were certified on October 24, 1860; the French versions were certified the following day. In order to ensure that the new treaties would be known by people across the nation, and in order to prevent the content of the agreements being concealed by the Qing court, Elgin insisted that the Chinese version of the treaties be printed and displayed in every province before British troops would withdraw from Beijing.[65]

In the end, for all his resistance, Xianfeng was left with a broken capital, a burnt palace, fully ratified treaties, and more indemnities to pay. His loss of face was severe, as he was required in the Convention of

63. Knollys, *Incidents in the China War*, 200.

64. No. 104, "The Earl of Elgin to Lieutenant-General Sir Hope Grant," October 15, 1860, in *Correspondence respecting Affairs*, 218. See also Knollys, *Incidents in the China War*, 203–5.

65. No. 109, "The Earl of Elgin to Lord J. Russell," October 31, 1860, in *Correspondence respecting Affairs*; and enclosure 3, "The Earl of Elgin to Lieutenant-General Sir Hope Grant," October 27, 1860, in No. 109, "The Earl of Elgin to Lord J. Russell," 244–45. As regards displaying the treaty, see Article VIII of the Convention of Beijing, in *Zhong wai jiu yuezhang*, 1:427.

Beijing to openly express his "regret" for actions taken at the Dagu Forts in June 1859 due to his "misunderstanding."[66] On the issue of foreign residence in the capital, Elgin withdrew his offer of November 1858 to soften the impact of the Tianjin Treaty provisions. The situation returned to what was stipulated in Article III regarding British residence, and this was subsequently claimed by other foreign countries.[67] Emperor Xianfeng was too afraid to return to Beijing for the ratification, and left the matter in the hands of Prince Gong.

A famous photograph of the young Prince Gong was taken by the Italian British photographer, Felice Beato, during the ratification in the Hall of Ceremonies in 1860, and the prince was not warned in advance that his photograph would be taken (see fig. 1.1). He and hundreds of Chinese officials had gathered to await the British delegation. When the British arrived, Prince Gong greeted Lord Elgin by bringing his palms together in front of his face. In return, Lord Elgin gave him "a proud contemptuous look" and made a slight bow. To General Hope Grant, Prince Gong appeared to be a "delicate gentlemanlike-looking man." On encountering Elgin's cold greeting the prince was "evidently over-powered with fear." In order to take the required photographs, Beato "brought forward his apparatus, placed it at the entrance door, and directed the large lens of the camera full against the breast of the unhappy Prince Kung." This was done without warning, and not having encountered any machine like this before, the prince was struck with horror; it "looked like a sort of mortar, ready to disgorge its terrible contents into his devoted body."[68] On hearing an explanation of the purpose of the equipment, the blood returned to Prince Gong's face and he allowed his portrait to be taken.

Though scarcely any obvious emotion is visible in the photograph, some undercurrent of Prince Gong's feelings can be detected in the way he holds himself: his forehead is drawn and tense but not knitted; his jaw is also fixed, tense and still; his arms and hands are drawn into the long sleeves of his robes. The prince's face and body are held so tightly that it seems as if he is trying his best to prevent all clues as to thought and feeling from escaping. With undoubtedly vivid memories of the

66. British Convention of Peking, in *Zhong wai jiu yuezhang*, 1:424.
67. Morse, *The International Relations*, 1:614.
68. Knollys, *Incidents in the China War*, 209–10.

FIGURE I.I Prince Gong; photograph by Felice Beato. Source: J. Paul Getty Museum; partial gift from the Wilson Centre for Photography.

events of recent days, and with hundreds of pairs of eyes on him, Prince Gong —affects an expression of strength. It seems as if, in the moment that the photographer's light flashed, he was transformed into a person who was more assured about China's future direction in managing foreign affairs.[69]

69. In his research on the history of the Zongli Yamen, Wu Fuhuan concluded that after going through the whole affair of finalizing and ratifying the treaties, Prince

Soon after the ratification of the treaty with Britain and France, Prince Gong was put under further pressure to sign the Additional Treaty of Peking, in which China ceded a large portion of territory in the northeast to Russia.[70] The entire series of episodes leading up to the catastrophe of 1860 had exposed several critical problems in the structure of the Qing central government with regard to its dealings with foreigners. These included a shortage of experts in foreign affairs, a lack of foreign-language skills, and a lack of direct and reliable communication channels. The Treaty of Tianjin was about to add to this burden. It was clearly necessary to now have an office to manage interactions with foreign nations. Prince Gong, Guiliang, and Wenxiang jointly proposed setting up a new institution, the Zongli Yamen. It was formally founded in January 1861, and it was in the headquarters of this new organization that Hart and Prince Gong had their first meetings.

Prince Gong Builds His Power Base

In order to minimize opposition from Xianfeng and those surrounding him, the Zongli Yamen was conceived from the beginning as led by high princes and staffed by a select group of eight Manchu and eight Han Chinese from the Grand Council and the Grand Secretariat (Neige 內閣). The goal was that members of these important institutions would be directly involved in the business of the Zongli Yamen, and as a result, the emperor would be kept well informed. It was also intended that the Zongli Yamen should eventually be taken over by the Grand Council once foreign affairs were perceived to be under proper control.[71]

Located in the deserted Iron Mint Bureau (Tieqianju gongsuo 鐵錢局公所) in Beijing, the Zongli Yamen represented a new departure in the Qing government's management of foreign affairs. Its formation was

---

Gong and Wenxiang had gained new insights into dealing with foreigners. Wu Fuhuan, *Qingji Zongli Yamen*, 13.

70. *YWSM*, Xianfeng reign, 68:14–15. See also Russia Additional Treaty of Peking, 1860, in *Zhong wai jiu yuezhang*, 1:439.

71. *YWSM*, Xianfeng reign, 71:19. See also Wu Fuhuan, *Qingji Zongli Yamen*, 18–19.

groundbreaking because it demonstrated that the Qing government acknowledged that the existing Court of Colonial Affairs (Lifanyuan 理藩院), which prior to that date managed Mongolian, Russian, and Tibetan matters, was inadequate for the new situation. Its establishment indicated something of a resolution to the two key areas of conflict that had led to the two Opium Wars—namely, China's highly prescriptive approach to trade and its insistence that interstate relations be based on the imperial tributary system. New thinking on trade regulation had already begun to become apparent after the establishment of the Board of Inspectors of the Customs House. Prince Gong advocated that the Zongli Yamen should itself supervise all Customs House–related affairs. He did not want the superintendent of trade in Shanghai to control the business of foreign Customs. Nor did he allow the Board of Revenue to own it unreservedly, though the board was to have rights to audit the collections.[72] The foreign-styled Customs organization in Shanghai was upgraded to become the CMCS in 1861, and Lay was appointed as inspector general.

The birth of the Zongli Yamen was also a decisive move by the Qing court in establishing an essential communications channel with foreign powers. Compliance with the Tianjin treaties also saw foreign diplomats permitted to be stationed in the capital, but this had positive effects for the Qing government in that it enabled the Zongli Yamen to wrest control of foreign affairs from the hands of Han Chinese generals, who together had been collaborating with foreign troops in suppressing the Taiping Rebellion along the Yangtze River. Through its combined control of foreign affairs and the CMCS, the Qing central government took direct charge of foreign-related matters.

The Qing court was physically split into two, with part in Beijing and part in Chengde. Prince Gong now occupied a crucial position directing the Zongli Yamen, and this made him an ideal collaborator for Empress Dowager Cixi in the coup that followed the emperor's death. In his sensational account of the Xinyou Coup, historian Wu Xiangxiang vividly reconstructed how the coup unfolded, from the moment Emperor Xianfeng fell ill in early spring 1861, to the point that order was restored in November of that year, following the ending of the rule by eight re-

---

72. *YWSM*, Xianfeng reign, 72:28; Chen Shiqi, *Zhongguo jindai haiguanshi*, 63.

gents after Xianfeng's death.[73] Sushun and other princes not only prevented the ailing emperor from returning to Beijing but also prevented him from seeing Prince Gong and Wenxiang. Xianfeng appointed eight regents, excluding Prince Gong, to assist his young son. The group of eight, constituted by both Han and Manchu high officials, advocated a harder line toward foreigners.[74]

The ambitious Empress Dowager Cixi, the mother of Xianfeng's only son, was already jealous of the close relationship between the emperor and Sushun. Sushun had apparently criticized Cixi in front of Xianfeng.[75] It was believed that, even without the benefit of having received a full formal education, she had actually been assisting Emperor Xianfeng in reading and organizing memorials, which broke the rules that wives of emperors should be kept away from politics.[76] Taking advantage of the attendance of Prince Gong at the funeral at Chengde, the Empress Dowager Cixi gained his collaboration.

Weng Tonghe 翁同龢 (1830–1904), who later became the young Emperor Guangxu's teacher, was in Beijing during these months, and he personally recorded developments after the death of the emperor. On November 1 the new emperor and the two empress dowagers returned to the Imperial Palace in the early afternoon, where more than two hundred officials had been waiting for them since lunchtime. The officials were dressed in plain gowns with woolen coats, velvet caps, and black collars. The royal sedan chairs were wrapped in black cloth, and when the child emperor arrived, all took off their caps and knelt with their foreheads touching the ground after saying their names and greetings. It was learned that Empress Dowager Cixi and Prince Gong had had meetings, and on the following day, an imperial edict authorizing the arrest and expulsion of the eight regents was promulgated.[77] Sushun was spared from death by "slow slicing" but was executed in public; Prince Yi Zaiyuan and Prince Zheng Duanhua 端華 were permitted to hang themselves, and the remainder of the regents were demoted and sent to the

73. Wu Xiangxiang, *Wan Qing gongting*, 50–58.
74. Fan, *Qingji de yangwu*, 1:109–10.
75. Huang Jun, *Hua sui ren sheng an*, 429–30.
76. Mao, *Kuming tianzi*, 286–7; Wu Xiangxiang, *Wan Qing gongting*, 51–52.
77. Weng, diary entries for November 1–3, 1861, in *WRJ*, 1:145.

interior.[78] Empress Dowagers Cixi and Cian 慈安, who had been appointed guardians for the two imperial seals by Xianfeng, jointly administered national affairs behind the curtain.[79] Prince Gong was appointed prince regent (*yizheng wang* 議政王) to lead both the Grand Council and the Zongli Yamen.

Elgin, formerly dismissive toward Prince Gong, started to see him in a different light. He praised the prince for his liberal spirit following several interviews with him. Both Elgin and Bruce noted that Prince Gong was "much less reserved" and was open to discussion about delicate issues, such as the sending of a Chinese ambassador to Britain. Elgin expressed his concern: "It is, I fear, probable that when the Emperor returns from Jehol [Rehe], with the bad advisers who surround him, there may be a moment of reaction; but if foreign affairs continue under the charge of the Prince of Kung, it may be hoped that the new Treaty will be faithfully carried out."[80]

Hart met Prince Gong in June 1861, five months after the establishment of the Zongli Yamen and two months prior to the death of Xianfeng. When they met, Prince Gong's political status was far from secure. On the one hand, he had to demonstrate that he could continue to manage foreign affairs and trade matters; on the other, he also needed to show his loyalty to his brother. With more treaty ports waiting to be opened on the coast and along the Yangtze River, Qing officialdom in both Beijing and the provinces fell into a state of confusion. In the middle of this difficult situation, Hart was ready to provide his advice.

"Our Hart" and "Seven Plans with Two Reports"

Hart had come to China at the age of nineteen in October 1854 as an interpreter for the British consulate and was posted to Ningbo. Compared with the consulates in Canton and Shanghai, the consulate in Ningbo

78. Weng, diary entry for November 9, 1861, in *WRJ*, 1:149–50, my translation.

79. Wang Kaixi, "Xinyou zhengbian."

80. No. 119, "The Earl of Elgin to Lord J. Russell," November 13, 1860, in *Correspondence respecting Affairs*, 254–55.

was a small one, so Hart had plenty of opportunity for direct contact with the local Chinese officials.[81] He was also in charge of mail matters for the legation. He made a very positive impression there, and in March 1858 was transferred to the consulate in Canton, where he worked as secretary to the allied commissioners. The allied commissioners, made up of British and French officials, was the body that ran the administration of the part of Canton occupied by the allied troops between 1858 and 1861.[82] Hart's manager at the Canton consulate, Rutherford Alcock (1809–97), was impressed by Hart's linguistic skills and personal qualities, and considered him the right person "in building up a new system of intercourse with all the Chinese officials."[83] Alcock, Hengqi, and Lao Chongguang 勞崇光 (1802–67), the Canton governor-general, wanted to establish a new type of Customs House in Canton on the Shanghai model in order to address the growing problem of smuggling, which was severely impacting revenue collection. Hart was invited to set up the Canton Customs House and was appointed as assistant commissioner of Customs in June 1859.

The Treaty of Tianjin had stipulated nine new treaty ports, but know-how became a problem. Wade was sent to Beijing to recommend Lay for the position of running a unified Customs Service for China. Despite the fact that Lay had previously shown the arrogant side of his personality to Chinese and Manchu officials, in the absence of a stronger alternative he got the job, becoming the first inspector general of Customs. Lay himself, however, did not see his new position as one for the long term, as he predicted the Qing empire would not survive for another year due to the Taiping Rebellion, the Nian Rebellion in the north, and many other smaller conflicts across the country.[84] He therefore ignored Prince Gong's request to set up a new Customs House in Tianjin, took sick leave, and returned to England in April 1861. Lay recommended George Henry FitzRoy (1826–68), a former private secretary to Lord Elgin, along

81. Chen Shiqi, *Zhongguo jindai haiguanshi*, 58.
82. Leibo, "Not So Calm an Administration."
83. This was written by Alcock in his letter to Bowring in 1858. The text was quoted by the editors of *Entering China's Service: Robert Hart's Journals, 1854–1863* in *Hart Journals 1854–1863*, 234.
84. Chen Shiqi, *Zhongguo jindai haiguanshi*, 64–65.

with Hart, to jointly cover in his absence, and specifically assigned Hart to go to Tianjin on the mission that he did not want to carry out himself.[85] For Hart, this was not unknown territory as he had previously written a handbook on setting up a new model Customs House at Canton for Lay.

Given that Prince Gong urgently needed the inspector general of Customs at Beijing to guide them through the remaining important issues in establishing the CMCS, neither Prince Gong nor Bruce, the new British minister at Beijing, was happy with Lay's abrupt decision to take leave. Bruce wrote to Hart in May to invite him to come to the capital and stay at the newly opened British Legation. Hart stopped first at Tianjin to make some initial arrangements for setting up the Customs House, and on June 5, he arrived in Beijing for the first time.[86] Hart's reputation had preceded him, and he was described as "tamed and obedient" (*xunshun* 馴順) by Hengqi.[87] Hart fully understood the issues that most troubled Prince Gong and Wenxiang, and he came impeccably prepared. He proved himself very different from Lay, and indeed different from any foreigner the Zongli Yamen had encountered before.

Wenxiang had been born into a humble family in the influential Guwalgiya clan, part of the Plain Red Banner, in Shenyang in 1818. He later recalled that, growing up, he was very often ill. He was a late starter academically, but at age nineteen he married into a family better off than his own. His father-in-law not only purchased a qualification for him so he could obtain entry to the provincial examination but also provided him with financial support over a period of years. At the age of twenty-eight he passed the Metropolitan Examination. He then entered the world of officialdom.[88]

By 1859 Wenxiang had already held various positions and led several projects, including the suppression of large groups of bandits in Shaanxi, Shanxi, and Sichuan. He was also responsible for auditing tribute grain transmitted through Tianjin. He was entrusted with constructing the

85. Stanley F. Wright, *Hart and the Chinese Customs*, 196.

86. Wright, *Hart and the Chinese Customs*, 197–98; editors' commentary, in *Hart Journals 1854–1863*, 240.

87. *YWSM*, Xianfeng reign, 76:22, my translation.

88. Wenxiang, "Ziding nianpu shang," 47–69.

FIGURE I.2 Wenxiang; photograph by John Thomson, ca. 1867. Source: Wellcome
Collection, Attribution 4.0 International.

tombs for Empress Dowager Xiaojingcheng, which was regarded as a high
privilege.[89] Through his many different roles, Wenxiang had acquired
substantial experience and knowledge in governmental administration,
in areas as disparate as military campaigns and finance. Alongside his

89. Wenxiang, "Ziding nianpu shang," 77–96. "Guoshiguan benzhuan" 國史館本傳
[Biography of the Qing dynasty by Academia Historica], in Wenxiang, *Wen Wenzhong
gong (Xiang) shi lue*, 15.

position next to Prince Gong at the head of the Zongli Yamen, he was also a senior member of the Grand Council, and senior vice president of the Board of Revenue, which allowed the discussions on Customs affairs and tariffs to be shared between the Zongli Yamen and the board. Later he was also promoted to be the minister of the Board of War (Bingbu 兵部), the Board of Works (Gongbu 工部), and the Board of Revenue, and the minister of the Imperial Household (Neiwufu 內務府). In 1861 he also organized a new military entity, the Divine Mechanism Regiment (Shenjiying 神機營), which became known as the Beijing Field Force. The idea for this came out of Wenxiang's experience of the chaos when the allied troops pushed into Beijing. The regiment's members were the best among the elite of the Metropolitan Banner Troops, and the force was equipped with the most advanced European-style arms that China could obtain at the time.[90]

Before meeting Prince Gong, Hart spent several days with Wenxiang. The latter was eager to obtain knowledge on trade and tariffs, and on some days their meetings lasted as long as seven hours, beginning at breakfast. Hart rapidly came to realize that, rather than the aging Guiliang or the young Prince Gong, Wenxiang was the brains behind the Zongli Yamen. Foreign diplomats in Beijing, including Wade, shared this view, considering Wenxiang to be Prince Gong's mentor.[91] Building on his experience in Ningbo and Canton, Hart gained further insights into the worldview of the high statesmen in Beijing. He enjoyed his conversations with Hengqi, Wenxiang, and the other officials he met in the Zongli Yamen. The sensation of getting close to the heart of power lifted his mood, and Hart often chatted about the conversations he had with Wenxiang and what he accidently heard at the Zongli Yamen to David Field Rennie, a young surgeon at the British Legation, where Hart lodged. Rennie recorded what he learned from various British diplomats and interesting people passing through the British Legation. Hart did not know at the

90. "Guoshiguan benzhuan" 國史館本傳 [Biography of the Qing dynasty by Academia Historica], in Wenxiang, *Wen Wenzhong gong (Xiang) shi lue*, 25–34.

91. Rennie, *Peking and the Pekingese*, 1:215–16; Mary Clabaugh Wright, *The Last Stand*, 71.

time that Rennie had an intention to publish, and later expressed regret that he had told Rennie so much.[92]

It became apparent from the early days of their acquaintance that Hart admired Wenxiang. He spoke in the "highest terms of his intelligence, application, and clearness of expression." But in addition to these qualities, Wenxiang's personality and his approach to managing issues made a direct, long-term impact on Hart. Thanks to his skills in the Chinese language, Hart was able to understand what Wenxiang wanted him to know about the Chinese way of thinking and the logic in operation at court and in wider officialdom. In their conversations, Wenxiang emphasized reason and logic (*daoli* 道理) in the ways of doing things correctly in accordance with Chinese culture.[93] Hart's ability to perceive *daoli*, though he might not necessarily agree with the practical outcome of its application, brought him to see the importance of *tizhi* 體制 in China, "the principles of a state system, basic institutions, proper orders, the state dignity . . . the myth of the state—specifically the acceptance of the imperial supremacy."[94] More simply, the complexities of *tizhi* can be boiled down to the notion of *face*. In coming to an understanding of the importance of *tizhi* and *face* in China, Hart came to a realization that the Chinese path of modernization would never be a straightforward transplant from Western models. As a consequence, Hart's dealings with Chinese officials, such as superintendents of Customs, and his executions of new projects—for example, the postal service—were very much in alignment with his adopted motto: "modestly and slowly."[95]

Unlike Lay, who thought the Qing empire was close to collapse, Hart considered that it might yet be resurgent, if Nanjing could be recovered from the occupation of the Taiping troops. After his meetings with Wenxiang, Hart held this view even more strongly. On June 15, 1861, Hart finally met Prince Gong, who was accompanied only by Wenxiang. The prince asked a long series of questions on Customs House matters, and

92. Hart, entry for March 2, 1866, in *Hart Journals 1863–1866*, 345–46.

93. Rennie, *Peking and the Pekingese*, 1:261, 247–48.

94. Editors' commentary, in *Hart Journals 1854–1863*, 254, 336.

95. Robert Hart to James Duncan Campbell, letter 1014, March 29, 1896, in *The IG*, 2:1057.

noted that Hart "must think him almost childish asking so many, and such apparently simple questions." Prince Gong asserted that he had known almost nothing about the treaties and Customs-related matters, and with customary Chinese humility added that he had "but little to attend to beyond amusing himself" in his oversight role. Hart found that although Prince Gong demonstrated little specific knowledge of technicalities, his instincts and overall common sense in preferring low tariffs in order to encourage trade distinguished him from Wenxiang's more refined, and yet conservative, bureaucratic mentality in wanting to stick to higher rates.[96]

A few days later, when Prince Gong had an opportunity to be alone with Hart, he observed that since Hart had made the long journey to come to China, he must have passed through several countries, and he asked him whether he had visited the country where certain "inhabitants have their bodies perforated by a hole or tunnel, running through them fore and aft, while in the other [country] their heads are attached to their bodies in a pendulous manner, and are carried by them under their arms."[97] What Prince Gong was likely referring to was something he might have previously read, such as the *Classic of Mountains and Seas* (*Shanhaijing* 山海經) and the *Record of Foreign Lands* (*Yiyuzhi* 異域志), in which the texts describe some strange unknown inhabitants in a place called Hole through Chest Kingdom (Chuan xiong guo 穿胸國).[98] Prince Gong's seeming credulity, mixed perhaps with a degree of childlike curiosity, reflected his unreserved attitude in front of Hart. It was something that was revealed again when Prince Gong talked about Russia; he took out a map and, with great and direct emotion, said, "That is a large country, but it is not enough for them, they came last year and took that from us" as he then pointed his finger at the area beyond the Amur River.[99] Both Prince Gong and Wenxiang considered that Britain, though greedy, was primarily interested in trade and commercial profit, whereas Russia's interests were another matter altogether.

96. Rennie, *Peking and the Pekingese*, 1:216, 220, 248.
97. Rennie, *Peking and the Pekingese*, 1:258.
98. Lu Yilu, *Yiyu, yiren, yishou*, 128–31.
99. Rennie, *Peking and the Pekingese*, 1:259.

Managing the navigation of the Yangtze River up to Hankou and related transit duties clearly exceeded the capability of Prince Gong and Wenxiang and also caused early disagreement between Britain and China as the treaties began to take effect.[100] It therefore became the first occasion when Hart was able to prove his value. Unlike Emperor Xianfeng, Prince Gong did not object to foreign trade on the Yangtze River, as long as the British continued to assist in suppressing the Taipings.[101] Early on in April, a version of the Regulations for British Trade in the Yangtze River was prepared by General Hope Grant and Parkes, but the Zongli Yamen and Bruce could not come to an agreement on the terms.[102] With Hart's assistance, Bruce, Wade, Prince Gong, and Wenxiang met up and made progress. Hart was praised by both parties. In his letter to Earl Russell, Bruce said, "Had it not been for the presence of Mr. Hart I do not think the subject would have been made intelligible to them."[103] But compared with Bruce's simple praise, the words communicated by Prince Gong to Xianfeng about Hart were rather more elaborate. He said that Bruce had been very difficult, but Hart was insistent and pushed Bruce very hard to reach common ground. The prince noted that, despite his being foreign, Hart was quite tamed and tractable, and he talked sensibly. In the same memorandum, feeling the need to explain to Xianfeng Hart's motivation in helping China, Prince Gong said he believed Hart, with his "obedient temperament," had his greedy eye on the high salary of the inspector general, so would push the boat out for China.[104] The Zongli Yamen approved FitzRoy and Hart as officiating inspectors general on June 30.[105]

Prince Gong and Wenxiang once told Hart that there was not a single person they could trust in China, "from one of their red-buttoned

---

100. *YWSM*, Xianfeng reign, 78:22–23.

101. Enclosure 2, "The Prince of Kung to Mr. Bruce," Xianfeng reign year 10, month 10, day 13 (November 25, 1860), in "Bruce to Lord J. Russell," December 2, 1860, in *Further Correspondence respecting Affairs*, 2–3.

102. "Mr. Bruce to Earl Russell," October 26, 1861, in *Papers Relating to the Rebellion*, 77–79. *YWSM*, Tongzhi reign, 1:18.

103. "Mr. Bruce to Earl Russell," October 26, 1861, 79.

104. *YWSM*, Xianfeng reign, 79:21, my translation.

105. "Mr. Fitz-Roy and Mr. Hart Appointed to Officiate Conjointly as Inspectors General," IG Circular 1 (1st ser.), June 30, 1861, in *Docs. Ill.*, 1:1–3.

mandarins down to a *tinckchai* [聽差, personal messenger], or orderly," as hardly anyone in the government would tell the straightforward truth. They said that foreigners, on the other hand, would present them with facts and truth, which was something they were longing for.[106] There was a strong element of Manchu insecurity in this. While valuing the contribution of the Han Chinese provincial generals, Hart detected there was also fear in the circle of Manchu officials that their Han colleagues might collaborate with the British to replace the Manchu rulers, and rumors of such maneuvering were to be found both in the provinces and in Beijing.

Hart knew that his popularity with the Zongli Yamen would go up if he could help to increase revenue to assist the campaign to suppress the Taipings. He set out to do so by proposing to add broker guild fees on opium so that the Zongli Yamen could use the income to purchase ships and weapons. Prince Gong and Wenxiang immediately jumped at this idea, and asked Xianfeng to approve it.[107] What had been condemned as immoral in the 1838 letter from Lin Zexu 林則徐 (1785–1850) to Queen Victoria was no longer an issue by this point. Within a month into his short first visit to Beijing, Hart submitted a total of "seven plans with two reports" (*zhang cheng qi jian bing cheng liang jian* 章程七件稟呈兩件). It is very likely that he had prepared most of this material beforehand.[108] The documents laid down the main principles for what the CMCS could bring in tariffs to the Qing government over the following five decades, and they showed how Hart had thought through the role both he and the CMCS could play, in the process making both indispensable. In the document about expenses of collection, Hart demonstrated that he understood the essentials of managing the operation of Custom Houses— both those already open and those yet to be opened. He clearly listed all

106. Rennie, *Peking and the Pekingese*, 1:260.
107. *YWSM*, Xianfeng reign, 79:18.
108. *YWSM*, Xianfeng reign, 79:21–34. The subjects of these documents were trade on the Yangtze River, costs of foreign ships carrying native produce, transit dues, opium imported at the several treaty ports, salt revenue, drawbacks and exemption certificates, the expenses of collection, the opium committees at Canton, and tea revenue in Canton. For English translation, see "Translation of Memorials and Imperial Decrees of 1861 on Opium; Duty treatment of Native Produce in Foreign Vessels, Transit Dues; Trade on the Yangtze; Drawbacks and Exemption Certificates; etc." in *Docs. Ill.*, 6: 91–103.

the essential costs for each Customs House, such as housing, enforcement boats, and salaries. In the salary category he included amounts for all roles from Customs commissioners to clerks, tidewaiters, and servants.[109] On top of his communication skills, these writings further proved Hart's inestimable value to the Zongli Yamen.

Not all of Hart's ideas were adopted immediately, but he managed to ease some of the more pressing problems of Prince Gong and Wenxiang. The question of a national postal service must surely have been mentioned in one of the many conversations between them, though they did not take much notice at the time. Yet, for Hart, a postal service was part of the big blueprint he had drawn up for China, which was transformed into the document titled "A Bystander's View" and submitted to the Zongli Yamen in late 1865.

As soon as Hart had left for Tianjin at the end of June, Prince Gong praised him in front of Bruce. Referring to Hart as "our Hart" (*women de Hede* 我們的赫德), he also said that, if only they could have a hundred Harts, they would have no problem in doing the right things for China.[110] Lay's two-year absence beginning in April 1861 allowed Hart to make a strong connection with the Zongli Yamen. When Lay returned to Shanghai in May 1863, his relationship with the Qing government went from bad to worse very quickly over a flotilla of gunboats he had arranged the purchase of and which had been intended to assist in suppressing the Taiping Rebellion.[111] The Lay-Osborn flotilla scandal not only ended Lay's career in China but, for Wenxiang at least, also cast doubt on the so-called Western line of modernization for the country. In November, Lay was dismissed by Prince Gong, and Hart was appointed as the inspector general of Customs.

The signing of the Treaty of Tianjin in June 1858 was not the end of the argument but instead the beginning of a series of conflicts between the Qing rulers and the allied countries. Emperor Xianfeng's fear of meeting foreigners for the treaty ratification, the issue of diplomats residing in the capital, and challenges surrounding Yangtze River navigation

109. *YWSM*, Xianfeng reign, 79:45–52.
110. Robert Bruce to Earl Russell, July 7, 1861, in Stanley F. Wright, *Hart and the Chinese Customs*, 221n6; Rennie, *Peking and the Pekingese*, 1:263–64.
111. Van de Ven, *Breaking with the Past*, 43–44.

directly caused the further military conflicts in 1859 and 1860. A toxic mix of poor health and political turmoil ultimately ended with Xianfeng's death in Rehe, a coup, and the rise of Empress Dowager Cixi and Prince Gong. Two years of conflict exposed the Qing empire's weakness in understanding foreign affairs. The administration's supposed "foreign experts" were nothing of the sort, lacking language skills and knowledge of how to handle the realities of modern international trade, tariffs, and finance. Prince Gong and Wenxiang attempted to transform this with the creation of the Zongli Yamen, though the underlying challenges remained. But beside these practical problems, the trauma caused by witnessing the smoke and ashes of the burning Summer Palace had left Prince Gong with an urgent need to lean toward available helping hands, even those of foreigners.

THE OLD IMPERIAL
POST OFFICE, PEKING.

CHAPTER TWO

Political Storms and
Frustrated Reforms

In August 1863, after the arrival of a letter from his mother, Robert Hart told Wenxiang and his Zongli Yamen colleague Dong Xun 董恂 (1810–92) that he planned to go home the following year. It had been nine years since he had come to China, during which time he had not once returned home. Wenxiang said that there would be no objection to this, and on his way out, Hart heard a remark pass between the two Chinese men: "Human nature is much the same everywhere."[1] Nine years was indeed a lengthy period, and Hart reviewed his career progression in material form. He had earned £200 in 1854; £270 in 1855; £500 in 1858; £1,500 in 1858; £2,500 in 1860–61; and £3,300 in 1863. He considered that his career trajectory was "not bad."[2] Good news kept coming, as that November he was formally appointed as inspector general with an annual salary of

1. Hart, entry for August 7, 1863, in *Hart Journals 1854–1863*, 303.
2. Hart, entry for July 25, 1863, in *Hart Journals 1854–1863*, 298.

£4,000. That Christmas Eve, which he deemed "a most lovely night," Hart's stream of thoughts and emotions seemed to run as high as the pale moon and twinkling stars outside his window. He wrote,

> Not a bit proud I am! I am more conscious of defects—I am sensible of more deficiencies than is anyone that chooses to criticize me. . . . I don't fear responsibility, and I am cool and unflustered; but I keep to myself, and am content to be unknown, and I always yield. Now what objects have I to live for, to act for officially in China?
>
> 1°. I must whip the Foreign Inspectorate in to shape. . . .
>
> 2°. I must learn more about Chinese; about the littoral provinces, about taxation, about official duties—all with an eye to being useful, and preserving myself from being "trapped".
>
> 3°. I must try to induce among such Chinese as I can influence a friendlier feeling towards foreigners. . . .
>
> 4°. I must do what I can to prevent any growth of or encouragement to antiforeign feeling on the part of the Imperialists. . . .
>
> 5°. I must endeavor to ascertain what products of our Western civilization wd. most benefit China. . . .
>
> 6°. I must set a good example, in conduct, to all my subs.
>
> 7°. I must assist those who are engaged in the noblest of all works, the preaching of the Gospel, & the teaching of Christianity.[3]

After his appointment as inspector general, Hart decided to delay his return in order to oversee some urgent projects: opening Customs Houses in new treaty ports, forming the inspectorate of the Chinese Maritime Customs Service (CMCS), and introducing new trade rules to align with the implementation of the Treaty of Tianjin and the Convention of Beijing. He also issued guidance that each Customs House was required to follow in order to shape institutional spirit and culture in the direction he wanted. The guidance emphasized that the "Inspectorate of Customs is a Chinese and not a Foreign Service" and that Hart wanted all members of the CMCS to constantly bear this in mind, adding that they should "avoid all cause of offence and ill-feeling."[4] These are principles

3. Hart, entry for December 25, 1863, in *Hart Journals 1863–1866*, 53–54; £4,000 sterling was about Tls. 12,000.
4. "The Customs Service, The Spirit That Ought to Animate It, the Policy That Ought to Guide It, the Duties It Ought to Perform," IG Circular 8 (1st ser.), June 21, 1864, in *Docs. Ill.*, 1:36.

he restated thirty years later when the Imperial Post Office was formally launched.

For all of his efforts within the CMCS, Hart started to become discontented with the seemingly reluctant attitude in the Qing court toward implementing change. While the establishment of the Zongli Yamen initially seemed to offer a certain hope that reform might accelerate, all too soon it became clear that traditional attitudes, together with factional infighting at the center of power, where conservative forces had the upper hand, would prove too great a barrier to the efforts of Prince Gong Yixin and Wenxiang.

Barbarians on "Loose Reins" and the "Bystander's View"

In 1862, order in the Qing court was restored through collaboration between the Empress Dowager Cixi and Prince Gong. The Taiping Rebellion was also gradually subdued, and the greater part of the country returned to government control. It was a relatively peaceful period, but it also brought to the fore the Qing administration's deep-seated attitude toward the foreign question, and toward modernization instigated or promoted by foreign influence: "loose reins" (*jimi* 羈縻; the word *ji* means to halter, restrain, and control; the word *mi* as a noun means "the halter of an ox," or, as a verb, "to tie").[5] The concept of *jimi* can be traced back to *The Grand Scribe's Records* (*Shiji* 史記) of the Western Han dynasty (202 BCE–9 CE), which referred to a policy of avoiding the use of military force and applying instead a diplomatic approach toward coexistence with other powers at the periphery.[6] By the second half of the Tang dynasty (618–907 CE) this policy of loose reins had become a more formal system of indirect rule at the frontiers, where peripheral regimes would

5. Wu Fuhuan, *Qingji Zongli Yamen*, 147–50.
6. "We have heard it said that the Son of Heaven in his treatment of the Yi- and Ti-barbarians should rightfully do nothing more than to halter and yoke them and not allow them to break loose" (*Gai wen tianzi zhi yu yi di ye qi yi jimi wu jue er yi* 蓋聞天子之於夷狄也 其義羈縻勿絕而已); Ssu-ma, "Ssu-ma Hsiang-ju Memoir," 129.

accept investiture from the Tang rulers.[7] *Jimi* policy was generally applied when the main dynastic authorities believed they were not militarily strong and sought to avoid conflict. Evolving from the *jimi* administration of the Tang dynasty, through the Yuan dynasty and ultimately to the Qing dynasty, the native chieftain (*tusi* 土司) system or a variation of it was implemented, providing autonomy to largely self-governing ethnic groups in return for their leaders' recognition of the sovereignty of the central rulers. Whenever the *jimi* policy was applied, the goal, which could be for the long or short term, was also to avoid conflict.[8] Together with the tributary system, this approach supported a Sinocentric worldview throughout the Ming and Qing periods.

The flip side of the *jimi* was the concept of *yi* 夷, meaning "other" or "barbarian." As Lydia Liu has pointed out, the use of the term *yi* was an assertion of cultural superiority, and an attempt to strengthen political sovereignty through this assertion. The word *yi* was commonly used in official documents to refer to the peoples of Britain, France, and other Western countries until the Treaty of Tianjin of 1858 stipulated that this usage should be prohibited in any official communications.[9] But even as *yi* was banned in such communications, *jimi* was not. During the First Opium War, the Qing court clearly had uncertainty about whether they should apply the *jimi* policy when dealing with a new kind of enemy coming from the West.[10] This dilemma continued to be seen during the Second Opium War. But when the Zongli Yamen was established, *jimi* came to be the central concept driving the Qing administration's policy in its dealings with foreigners for at least another three decades.

When Prince Gong, Guiliang, and Wenxiang proposed the establishment of the Zongli Yamen in January 1861 they submitted a proposal and a "Six-Article Memorandum" ("Zhang cheng liu tiao" 章程六條). This proposal stated that suppressing the Taiping and Nian Rebellions was the top priority; second was managing the relationship with Russia, while the relationship with Britain came third. In their efforts to tame both

---

7. Rawski, *Early Modern China*, 33.
8. Herman, "Empire in the Southwest," 73–75.
9. Lydia He Liu, *The Clash of Empires*, 40–47.
10. Mao, *Tianchao de bengkui*, chap. 3 and chap. 6.

Britain and Russia, the Qing leaders advocated a common strategy: to carefully observe the respective treaties with both powers. Two benefits were anticipated in so doing: first, foreigners would have no excuse to cross the line into conflict, and second, China would appear to be promoting sincere, friendly relations with foreign countries while implicitly applying the loose-reins policy (*wai dun xin mu er yin shi jimi* 外敦信睦而隱示羈縻).[11]

Matthew Mosca has provided an illuminating account of why Qing foreign policy failed to see the issues encountered in this period from a sufficiently global perspective. The Qing administration's lack of a grand strategy left it consistently responding in reactive and spontaneous ways to the evolving threat from Western countries. In spite of the fact that a huge amount of information—geographical and otherwise—about other countries had been collected from all corners of the empire, in various languages, this information was held centrally and only available to a very few privileged members of the ruling class.[12] Qing methods for managing frontiers were focused on dividing China's extensive land border into specific, clearly defined pockets, something that actively prevented the development of coherent and unified discourses for frontier policy making. As Mosca notes, "For the Qing state, a 'global' outlook would have to be balanced against bureaucratic routines developed to manage the empire's heterogeneous geopolitical environment."[13]

If we compare Mosca's analysis of the Qing approach to frontiers in the eighteenth century with the loose-reins policy of the Zongli Yamen in the late nineteenth, there is a clear logical continuity. In fact, the CMCS provides us with a good example of a modified version of the native chieftain system: using foreigners to control foreign affairs in treaty ports, which were specially defined zones within China.[14] As the tributary system had demonstrably failed to work in framing China's relationship with Western countries, the Qing government had retreated to the loose-reins

11. *YWSM*, Xianfeng reign, 71:18, my translation.
12. Mosca, *From Frontier Policy to Foreign Policy*, 11–17.
13. Mosca, "The Qing State," 104.
14. John Fairbank has labeled the treaty port system which brought the British, Han officials, and Manchu rulers together to govern jointly as "synarchy." Van de Ven, *Breaking with the Past*, 7–8. See also Horowitz, "Politics, Power and the Chinese Maritime Customs," 564.

policy—something that, on some level, was conceptually familiar. The plaque on the front gate of the Zongli Yamen headquarters bore the phrase "Peace and Prosperity for the Chinese and the Foreign" *Zhong wai ti fu* 中外禔福), and this revealed a wish to avoid further wars with the West. But how could real peace be maintained while adhering to the loose-reins policy? According to Prince Gong and Wenxiang, the answer was "self-strengthening" (*ziqiang* 自強), and the priority was military.[15] Ironically, these two principles, loose reins and self-strengthening, later backfired on Prince Gong and Wenxiang when they sought to introduce wider reforms in accordance with Hart's suggestions.

Before the Inspectorate General was moved from Shanghai to Beijing in the winter of 1865, Hart spent three summer months in the capital each year.[16] While in Beijing he visited the Zongli Yamen almost every day, and often spent hours alone with Wenxiang. Hart also built up a friendly relationship with other senior Zongli Yamen officials, such as Baoyun 寶鋆 (1807–91) and Dong Xun. Both were also senior ministers at the Board of Revenue alongside Wenxiang. Often they chatted for hours about nothing of particular importance. The officials at the Zongli Yamen gradually got used to Hart, and he enjoyed obtaining gossip through this kind of exchange. Hart had a solid Western classical education, and he had also acquired Chinese classical learning in the early 1860s. He was therefore able to engage in some philosophical discussions with the Chinese; though grounded as he was in Christian values and a firm belief in Western progress and technology, Hart was never Sinicized. Hart was interested in comparing the Western system with the Chinese one, and he gradually became humbler toward the latter, while the former he began to see with a more critical eye. In his diary entry for January 20, 1865, he wrote, "Really it is difficult to determine by mere abstract reasoning which of the two systems is the better, ours or that of the

15. "The answer to the origin of the problem is self-strengthening, and the priority method is military" (*Tan yuan zhi ce zai yu ziqiang ziqiang zhishu bi xian lian bin* 探源之策在於自強自強之術必先練兵). This famous quotation appeared for the first time in the Zongli Yamen's "Ten-Article Memorandum," which was an expanded version of the "Six-Article Memorandum." *YWSM*, Xianfeng reign, 72:11, my translation.

16. Hart, entries for October 28, 1865 and November 25, 1865, in *Hart Journals 1863–1866*, 330, 334.

Chinese."[17] He considered that the Chinese as a people were superior to any other and, had they learned Christianity, they would be infinitely beyond the West. Indeed, at this time he considered that he ought to publish an introduction to Christianity in Chinese, before the day came for him to leave China for good.[18]

Meanwhile, the British legation thought that reform was being introduced too slowly.[19] Thomas F. Wade criticized Wenxiang for becoming "timid." His fear was that the ship, as captained by Wenxiang, would "go down in the night."[20] Hart's position was more ambivalent: sometimes he strongly agreed with his compatriots, and at other times he was rather more sympathetic to the Chinese perspective. Wade talked about the "forbearance" of foreign powers in providing assistance to China, and their patience, but Hart considered this train of thought to be rather absurd. He wrote, "The Chinese need not thank us for that; we have forced ourselves into their house, & unless we mean to turn them out, we ought really, as men, to allow the 'give and take' principle to operate."[21] But on another occasion he cried out, "O, these Chinese! these Chinese! When will they learn to do the right thing, in the right way, and at the right time?"[22]

Hart directed this dissatisfaction into a reform proposal and completed a draft of his "Bystander's View" ("Ju wai pang guan lun" 局外旁觀論) in October 1865. This was Hart's blueprint for how China might modernize in both domestic management and foreign relationships.[23] He considered that by doing so China would become open to Christian civilization.[24] During this time, Wenxiang was away for lengthy spells, at first on a military campaign and then on a period of mourning following the death of his wife. He had been instructed to suppress a large group

---

17. Hart, entry for January 20, 1865, in *Hart Journals 1863–1866*, 245.
18. Hart, entry for July 15, 1864, in *Hart Journals 1863–1866*, 154.
19. Hart, entry for August 7, 1865, in *Hart Journals 1863–1866*, 310.
20. Hart, entry for July 20, 1865, in *Hart Journals 1863–1866*, 303.
21. Hart, entry for July 9, 1865, in *Hart Journals 1863–1866*, 299.
22. Hart, entry for September 23, 1865, in *Hart Journals 1863–1866*, 320.
23. Horowitz, "Politics, Power and the Chinese Maritime Customs," 567.
24. Hart, entry for January 28, 1865, in *Hart Journals 1863–1866*, 343.

of mounted bandits in Inner Mongolia around the Shanhai Pass, Rehe Province, and Jilin Province.[25]

This meant that instead of showing his "Bystander's View" first to Wenxiang, Hart revealed it to Baoyun and Dong Xun. Hart suspected he might not be the only one taking advantage of Wenxiang's absence, as both officials were in high spirits and paid noticeably more attention than usual to foreign matters. On hearing the main ideas contained in the draft, Baoyun said Wenxiang no longer had "the pluck he used to have." Dong Xun was struck by the text in front of him, though he considered that Prince Gong might well ultimately shy away from the document's contents.[26] He thought the proposal might "excite suspicion," but he still advised Hart to submit it. Neither Baoyun nor Dong Xun thought Hart's reform ideas would just sail through, as they were fully aware of the difficulties with China's *tizhi* framework (the principles of state dignity and face) and the overall situation of the Qing administration; but they wanted to see what kind of sensation would be created by Hart's proposal.

Hart noted that Wenxiang was not at all missed; on the contrary, work still went on as usual, "if not better—without him."[27] Hart was asked to make a few changes to the proposal, as the Zongli Yamen would then be able to submit it to the throne; after that it would be sent to provincial generals for comment.[28] Hart was very pleased with this development, and had high hopes for the proposal's reception. He submitted a final draft in November.

Rather than presenting the "Bystander's View" to the throne directly, however, the Zongli Yamen held it back without revealing any reason for doing so to Hart. Seeing that Hart's proposal had seemingly gotten nowhere, the British diplomats in China decided to lend a helping hand.

---

25. According to Wei Hsiu-mei, the success of this campaign, though somewhat neglected by historians of the period, was no less important than the suppression of the Nian Rebellion. Wenxiang's military victory brought great relief to the Qing court because the location where the bandits were operating was very close to Beijing, in the home territory of the Manchus. See Wei Hsiu-mei, "Wenxiang zai Qingdai."

26. Hart, entry for October 11, 1865, in *Hart Journals 1863–1866*, 324–25.

27. Hart, entries for October 17, 1865, and October 18, 1865, in *Hart Journals 1863–1866*, 326–27.

28. Hart, entry for October 28, 1865, in *Hart Journals 1863–1866*, 329–30.

Soon after Hart had completed the first draft in October, Wade read it and liked it very much. He took a copy away and brought it to the notice of the prime minister, Lord Russell.[29] In 1865, Rutherford Alcock succeeded Frederick Bruce as the envoy extraordinary, minister plenipotentiary, and chief superintendent of British trade. He also took actions to make sure Hart's proposal would be read by the throne. Alcock was a familiar face to British residents in China, having been British consul in Fuzhou and Shanghai from 1844 until 1858, when he was posted to Japan.[30] It was his idea to set up the foreign-led Board of Inspectors of the Customs House in 1854, and he was one of the figureheads of what Hans Van de Ven has called "muscular liberalism": committed to the promotion of a healthy trading environment of benefit to both Britain and China and prepared to get tough with British merchants when they broke regulations in China's territory.[31] Alcock's attitude toward China reflected a shift by the British away from an attitude of paternalism toward what Mary C. Wright has described as "the Co-operative Policy."[32] Notably, this shift did not go down well with British residents in China. They saw British diplomats defending China's interests better than the Dagu Forts could, and they complained that the diplomats were not sufficiently diligent in presenting the claims of British citizens against the Chinese government.[33]

This change in policy toward China was closely connected with developments in British politics and with the country's wider foreign policy concerns. British diplomacy had still not recovered from its defeat at the Schleswig-Holstein conference in London in 1864. Facing the rise of Prussia in Europe, on top of financial constraints that had followed from the expense incurred in the Crimean War, the general mood of the British diplomatic circle, at home or abroad, was against any expansionist action.[34] The appeal of "the Co-operative Policy" might not have been quite so apparent to the Chinese, but both Bruce and Alcock acted in the spirit of this approach; therefore, their priority was to render foreign

29. Hart, entry for October 27, 1865, in *Hart Journals 1863–1866*, 329.
30. "Obituary: Sir Rutherford Alcock."
31. Van de Ven, *Breaking with the Past*, 31–33.
32. Mary C. Wright, *The Last Stand*, chap. 3.
33. Mary C. Wright, *The Last Stand*, 39.
34. Otte, *The Foreign Office Mind*, 23–25.

assistance to help the Qing government institute a program of reform. Alongside Hart and Wade, other foreign representatives, such as the American diplomats Anson Burlingame (1820–70) and Samuel Wells Williams (1812–84), saw themselves as facilitators working to further the common interests of their own governments and that of China.[35]

In this wider context at home and abroad, Alcock saw Hart's "Bystander's View" as in line with Britain's best interests. Alcock might also have seen Hart as his protégé; after all, he had given his unreserved support to Hart's appointment at the Canton Customs House and later as inspector general. On concluding that there was no action being taken by the Zongli Yamen regarding Hart's "Bystander's View," Alcock sought to nudge things along. Aware that the Zongli Yamen would have to respond to any communication coming from him, he sent a letter, together with Wade's "Brief Discussion of New Proposals" ("Xin yi lue lun" 新議略論).[36] Alcock's strategy worked, and a consultation process was initiated. The memorandums were forwarded to provincial governors and superintendents of trade.

By this time Hart had already left China for Europe on his long-delayed trip. He took Binchun 斌椿 (1804–71), a sixty-three-year-old Manchu official, and three students from Tongwen College (T'ung Wên Kuan 同文館) with him.[37] Tongwen College was intended to fulfill one of the founding goals of the Zongli Yamen—to provide a cohort of Chinese with knowledge of foreign languages, better able to engage with foreigners in matters of diplomacy, trade, and technology. It was founded in August 1862 after Prince Gong submitted his "Six Proposed Regulations for the Newly Established Tongwen College" (Xin she Tongwenguan zhuo ni zhangcheng liutiao 新設同文館酌擬章程六條).[38] Hart hoped that this first official visit would lead to the establishment of a Chinese embassy in England. Although this hope did not come to fruition, the trip saw him develop relationships with two people who were to become very important in his life: Hester Jane Bredon (1848–1928), who would become Hart's wife, and James Duncan Campbell (1833–1907). Campbell had originally been recruited by Horatio N. Lay in 1863, but returned

35. Mary C. Wright, *The Last Stand*, 39.
36. *YWSM*, Tongzhi reign, 40:24–37; Fan Baichuan, *Qingji de yangwu*, 1:154–55.
37. *YWSM*, Tongzhi reign, 39:1–2.
38. *YWSM*, Tongzhi reign, 8:31–35.

FIGURE 2.1 *Hart Family, Ireland ca. 1866,* photograph by Shawn Day. Robert Hart is third from the right. First on the right is Hart's brother James, who joined the CMCS in 1867 and was sent to Darjeeling to work on the Sikkim mission in 1898, which led to the opening of Yadong Customs House (see chapter 8). Source: Digital Exhibitions at Special Collections and Archives, Queen's University Belfast.

to London in the wake of the Lay-Osborn flotilla scandal after only a brief stay in China. Campbell's position in the CMCS suffered through association with Lay.[39] During Hart's trip to London, they formed a close bond, and Campbell subsequently became Hart's long-term secretary, based in London. He came to play a major role in the development of the postal service.

Significantly, Hart's and Wade's memorandums were the only two documents pressing for a wider reform program to be submitted to the emperor by the Zongli Yamen in its entire forty-year history before it became the Ministry of Foreign Affairs (Waiwubu 外務部) in 1901. It is worth examining these proposals in some detail. Hart's "Bystander's View" echoed the view expressed in his diary on January 20, 1865, and proposed two essential pillars for Chinese modernization: externally, to build friendly relationships between China and the West and, domestically, to bring in the products of Western science and technology. In the latter category Hart envisaged the widespread adoption of steamships, railways, the telegraph, and a postal service based on the Western model. Regarding international relations, he encouraged China to engage with the world as a player in the new international order. He advocated the holding of audiences for foreign representatives and the establishment of Chinese embassies abroad. With reference to the *Elements of International Law*, Hart reiterated the importance of treaty observation in order to maintain a good trading environment and friendly relations with foreign countries.[40]

In domestic affairs Hart provided a full reform program and pointed out that China's problems with foreign powers typically resulted from its bureaucratic system: military commanders often lacked courage, while civil officials often lacked integrity, despite their extensive education in the Chinese classics. As a direct result of actions taken by officials, critical information was often covered up at local level and failed to reach the central administration. Hart also identified a number of areas for administrative reform, based on adoption of Western models: armed forces, minting of coinage, land taxes, salt administration, transportation, and message transmission (specifically, steamships, railway, postal

39. Robert Ronald Campbell, *James Duncan Campbell*, 7–10.
40. *YWSM*, Tongzhi reign, 40:17.

services, and the telegraph).[41] In Hart's view, a unified coinage and extensive railway and telegraph systems would bring great service to this enormous country, but the post also loomed large. This document is where Hart first put his idea of a Western-style postal service in writing. Building on his belief in modernization, his blueprint not only challenged the existing military relay courier system but also called for a wider perspective on communications, to include their integration with mass transportation.

Having previously seen the "Bystander's View," Wade in his memorandum focused on two issues: China's unsatisfactory bureaucratic system and the benefits of collaborating with Britain and France. He encouraged the Qing government to make more use of foreigners and to send Chinese diplomats abroad.[42] Taken together, the two memorandums proposed a significant move away from the original framework set up by the Zongli Yamen in 1861; neither was a good fit with the loose-reins policy or with the military focus of the Self-Strengthening Movement. Nevertheless, the Zongli Yamen's ministers were clearly interested in seeing what kind of response would come back from their colleagues in the Qing administration. An exploration of the memorandums' reception follows later in this chapter, but first, it is important to address the situation of the military relay courier system.

The Military Relay Courier System

In his study *Empire and Information*, C. A. Bayly explores the Indian experience in order to demonstrate the critical role played in the modern era by information networks in the management of large territories.[43]

---

41. Robert Hart, "Ju wai pang guan lun" 局外旁觀論 [Bystander's view], in *YWSM*, Tongzhi reign, 40:18–21. Hart wrote, "There are a lot of useful and convenient innovations in [Western] foreign countries. It is impossible to list them all. For example, transportation on water routes and railways, machinery for the textile industry, post office, telegraph, coinage, and arms and military methods, they are all extremely exquisite" (author's translation).

42. *YWSM*, Tongzhi reign, 40:24–37.

43. Bayly, *Empire and Information*.

James Hevia takes the exploration further, examining how the acquisition and codification of knowledge and intelligence, in the form of reports, route books, maps, and, ultimately, substantial archives were critical elements in the building of the British Empire in Asia.[44] For the Qing government, the management of information tied closely with the military relay courier system. Beijing, the capital, was the ultimate destination for information, and Zhili Province, in which Beijing was situated, acted as the main hub (see fig. 2.2).[45] It comprised five main trunk routes: to the far reaches of northeast China; to the southeast through Shandong to Jiangsu, Fujian, and Canton Provinces; to the middle south through Baoding, Zhengding, and other places to Henan and Hubei, and further dividing to reach either Canton or Guizhou and Yunnan; to the southwest through Zhengding to Taiyuan in Shanxi Province, branching off both north and south, to either Shannxi, Gansu and Xinjiang, or Sichuan; and finally to the northwest through the Great Wall and important passes along the wall to reach either Outer Mongolia or Xinjiang.[46] Many relay stations, particularly on the western and northern routes, continued to be important and were later incorporated into the system of the Imperial Post Office.

All major administrative provinces and areas, excluding Northeast China, Xinjiang, Mongolia, and Tibet, were expected to contribute a certain amount toward the running costs of the military relay courier system. Most provinces paid considerably more than what was spent within their locality. The surplus was transferred to support those areas that were exempted from making a financial contribution; these included Mongolia, Qinghai, Tibet, and Xinjiang. On average, the annual budget of the military relay courier system was around 3 million taels (Tls.). For example, in Emperor Kangxi year 29 (1690), the expenditure was around Tls. 3.07 million.[47] By the time of the late Qing period,

44. Hevia, *The Imperial Security State.*

45. References used in the making of this GIS map include "Supplementary Cases to the Collected Statutes of the Qing Dynasty" (Da Qing huidian shili 大清會典事例), *juan* 688–89, in *Collected Works on Geography from the Xiaofanghu Studio* (Xiao fang hu zhai yu di cong chao 小方壺齋輿地叢鈔) and the database of the project "Chinese Civilization in Time and Space" of Academia Sinica, Taipei.

46. Liu Wenpeng, *Qingdai yichuan*, 45–46.

47. Liu Wenpeng, *Qingdai yichuan*, 252–54.

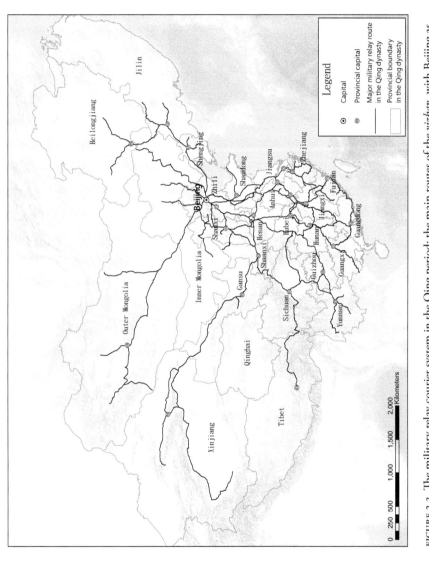

FIGURE 2.2 The military relay courier system in the Qing period: the main routes of the *yizhan*, with Beijing as the central information hub. Source: Produced for the author by the Center for GIS, Research Center for Humanities and Social Sciences, Academia Sinica.

expenditure had expanded to around Tls. 4 million.[48] These were huge sums, even for a state as wealthy as China. Excluding grain collection, in the middle of the Emperor Kangxi period from the late seventeenth to early eighteenth century, the annual revenue raised by the Chinese state was around Tls. 30 million, rising to around Tls. 40 million by the middle of the Emperor Qianlong era, in the latter part of the eighteenth century, before falling off again in the Emperor Daoguang period due to war and uprisings—for example, in Daoguang year 22 (1842) the state revenue was around Tls. 37 million. This constrained financial situation continued through the remainder of Daoguang's reign.[49] From the Emperor Xianfeng period onward (1850), the Qing government started to expand its revenue collection to meet the extra expenditure. In 1852, around the start of the Taiping Rebellion, while reducing the land tax in a show of goodwill toward the peasant class, the *lijin* system was introduced and became an important income stream for the local governments.[50] In this period, Customs revenue also started to make a substantial impact on the Qing administration's finances.[51] By 1880 the revenue picture was significantly expanded. For example, annual revenue in 1885 was around Tls.77 million, reaching Tls. 105 million in 1903, Tls. 235 million in 1908, and Tls. 297 million in 1911. But the expenditures in these four years were around Tls. 73 million, Tls. 135 million, Tls. 237 million, and Tls. 339 million, respectively.[52]

Against this increase in state expenditure, complaints about the inefficiency and corruption of the military relay courier system were already commonplace by the end of the eighteenth century, and concerned voices grew ever stronger as the nineteenth century progressed. Criticisms

48. "Feng Guifen cai yizhan yi" 馮桂芬裁驛站議 [Feng Guifen on abolishing the military relay courier system], in *QXWTK*, 375:16; "Youchuanbu hui zou" 郵傳部會奏 [Memorial from the Ministry of Posts and Communications], in *QXWTK*, 376:17.

49. Ren, "1850 nian qian hou." See also Shen Xuefeng, *Wan Qing caizheng*, 30–31.

50. Zhou Zhichu, *Wan Qing caizheng jingji*, 68–71, 76–80. *Lijin* 釐金 was originally a tax levied on goods in transit at route checkpoints through provinces and collected by local governments. Shortly after, such a system was extended to shops.

51. Zhou Zhichu, *Wan Qing caizheng jingji*, 139–46. Different sources state different results in the proportions of land tax, salt tax, Customs tax, and *lijin* contributing to the overall government revenue structure. See Shen Xuefeng, *Wan Qing caizheng*, 232.

52. Shen Xuefeng, *Wan Qing caizheng*, 31, 40.

included mail not being dispatched as promptly as it should be and local officials using resources for their personal benefit or overclaiming expenses. The relay officials and teams were also accused of harassing locals when passing through.[53] Nevertheless, despite widespread awareness within the Qing administration of the increasingly poor performance of the relay system, Hart's "Bystander's View" failed to gain a positive reception at court.

A Political Storm

It soon became apparent that the timing of these reform proposals could not have been worse. Antireform voices had come to surround the young emperor and Empress Dowager Cixi, and the empress's relationship with Prince Gong, who had come to her aid during the coup three years previously, was deteriorating rapidly. On March 30, 1865, Cai Shouqi 蔡壽祺 (1816–88), the official responsible for keeping a diary of the emperor's movements, impeached Prince Gong for corruption, abuse of power, and nepotism. This impeachment tipped power decisively toward Empress Dowager Cixi and clipped the wings of Prince Gong. An eight-man committee was formed, comprising members of the Grand Secretariat, the Board of Punishments, and the Board of Revenue. Several men on this committee, such as Woren 倭仁 (1804–71) and Zhou Zupei 周祖培 (1793–1867), were members of an inner circle close to the emperor and Empress Dowager Cixi. Zhou Zupei, who disliked Sushun, had been in support of the coup back in 1861. He was also one of the officials who suggested that the two empress dowagers should "reign behind a curtain." Woren, a Manchu official, acquired his fame as a prominent figure in neo-Confucianism. Both Woren and Zhou came from Henan Province, and they were close friends; they were leading members of the Grand Secretariat, a prestigious group whose members were styled "grand scholar" (*daxueshi* 大學士). The Grand Secretariat was responsible for drafting imperial decrees, overseeing the state examinations, and keeping the

53. "Youzheng yizhan" 郵政驛站 [Postal service, military relay courier system], in *QXWTK*, 374:15.

state papers. Woren was also a member of the Board of Revenue. In 1862 Zhou had recommended Woren as a teacher for the six-year-old Emperor Tongzhi. Woren became the young emperor's principal teacher, and was the person who spent most time with him, making substantial efforts to acquire suitable materials for teaching purposes.[54]

Woren kept a diary for many years, but it was not a straightforward record of daily routines; rather, entries were often structured as essays reflecting his thoughts and his areas of study. He regularly showed his diaries to close friends in his neo-Confucianist group in order to receive their critique. Although generally regarded as one of the officials who were advocates for reform, Zeng Guofan also became close to Woren through his participation in this circle.[55] Tracing back to the philosophy of Cheng Yi 程頤 (1033–1107), Cheng Hao 程顥 (1032–1085), and Zhu Xi 朱熹 (1130–1200) in the Song period (960–1279), Woren believed that *li* 理, which for the neo-Confucianists meant rational principles derived from the natural order, would show the way for humanity in the secular world. For Woren and his fellows, the fundamental reason for the weakness of the Qing dynasty lay in the minds and attitudes of people who had moved away from *li*. It was time for the government, along with China's intellectuals, to reassert social responsibility through the promotion of the old classics in order to direct society back on the right path.[56] Holding several important positions in the government, Woren became a central figure in the anti-Westernization clique at the heart of the Qing court.

Once the investigation began, Cai Shouqi admitted that he had no firm evidence against Prince Gong, only rumor or hearsay. But even with this admission, the committee, led by Woren, chose not to drop the case and instead escalated it. The emperor—or, rather, the Empress Dowager Cixi—initially sought to strip Prince Gong of all his positions, including his roles on the Grand Council and in the Zongli Yamen.[57] Upon this development, memorials arrived from all directions to express opinions on Prince Gong's future. Prince Chun Yixuan 奕譞 (1840–91), Prince Dun Yicong 奕誴 (1831–89), Wenxiang, and others spoke up for him, while

54. Li Xizhu, *Wan Qing baoshou sixiang*, 137–38.
55. Li Xizhu, "Woren jiaoyou shulue," 104–8.
56. Li Xizhu, *Wan Qing baoshou sixiang*, 127–29.
57. Weng, entry for April 3, 1865, in *WRJ*, 1:379–80.

Woren and other officials pushed in the other direction.[58] Woren said that even though there was no evidence to prove Prince Gong guilty on all counts, the rumors nevertheless showed that his behavior must have incited jealousy; the prince should therefore engage in reflection and improve his self-discipline.[59]

The final decision fell to Empress Dowager Cixi. Constrained somewhat by family ties and under pressure from Prince Gong's supporters, she felt she had to close the case by adopting more gentle measures than some were pushing for.[60] On May 9, 1865, Prince Gong was called in to see the emperor and the two empress dowagers to hear the final verdict. He was reported to have presented himself as very ashamed, in tears, with his knees and chest on the ground to show deep regret for his conduct and gratitude for the rulers' mercy. Empress Dowager Cixi allowed Prince Gong to keep his official positions on the Grand Council and the Zongli Yamen but took away his honorary title of prince regent.[61]

Prince Gong's impeachment had a significant political impact, and Hart's "Bystander's View" was a casualty of it. Empress Dowager Cixi used the opportunity to put distance between herself and Prince Gong and to establish an even stronger grip on the affairs of the court. Even though Prince Gong survived the turbulence, his influence diminished considerably. During these months Hart was traveling between different treaty ports and was not in Beijing. While he had heard about specific events as they unfolded, he did not initially comprehend the seriousness of the situation.[62] When Hart finally had a chance to be alone with Wenxiang that summer, Wenxiang warned him not to even mention the matter as it was a sore spot for him, and he also claimed he had forgotten everything that had happened in those two months.[63]

The affair resulted in a major reversal for those in the Qing administration who favored reform. Although Baoyun and Dong Xun liked many of the ideas presented by Hart and Wade, collectively the Zongli

58. Li Xizhu, *Wan Qing baoshou sixiang*, 164–65.
59. Weng, entry for April 7, 1865, in *WRJ*, 1:381–82.
60. Wu Xiangxiang, *Wan Qing gongting*, 101–12.
61. Weng, entry for May 9, 1865, in *WRJ*, 1:390–91.
62. Hart, entry for May 7, 1865, in *Hart Journals 1863–1866*, 259.
63. Hart, entry for August 17, 1865, in *Hart Journals 1863–1866*, 313.

Yamen kept a safe distance from the two proposals. When presenting them to the throne during Hart's absence from China, the Zongli Yamen's comments on the content of both proposals were unfavorable, and the tone of the response to Wade's document was particularly critical, noting that the proposal included "harsh words, threats and intimidation."[64]

No one wanted to risk expressing support. Although the majority of feedback from provincial officials had been in favor of exploring the issue of opening embassies and introducing audiences for foreign diplomats, their responses consistently referred back to the loose-reins policy and stayed closely in line with the military-focused Self-Strengthening policy. Chonghou 崇厚 (1826–93), now superintendent of trade for the three ports (Niuzhuang, Tianjin, and Yantai) and vice president of the Board of War, agreed to adopt the ideas presented on military training and explore the question of foreign audiences, but he did not like the proposals on transportation, and particularly those on railways.[65] Guanwen 官文 (1798–1871), grand scholar and governor-general of Hubei and Hunan, wrote that the proposals were intended to instill fear and that the government should not be patronized in this way. He reminded his colleagues that China's policy for managing foreigners had long been based on the loose-reins principle (*Zhongguo fu yi ben shu jimi* 中國撫議本屬羈縻), and saw no need for change. He argued that suggestions on mechanized transportation were a front for malicious intent, and that the proposals were designed to benefit foreign companies. Guanwen also questioned whether it remained necessary for the country to have foreigners in its service now that the Taiping Rebellion had been suppressed.[66] Liu Kunyi 劉坤一 (1830–1902), governor of Jiangxi Province, was of the same opinion, and insisted that China needed to adhere to the loose-reins policy rather than give in to the proposals. On the issue of the poor quality of civil servants in the administration, Liu said this was not caused by too much focus on Chinese classics but rather was because officials did not fully understand the political-economic subjects within those Chinese classics. He also believed that China's trade routes and military relay courier system were sufficient to meet the needs of the country and considered that the in-

64. *YWSM*, Tongzhi reign, 40:10.
65. *YWSM*, Tongzhi reign, 41:18–21.
66. *YWSM*, Tongzhi reign, 41:41–42.

troduction of railways and the telegraph would only expose inland China to unnecessary risk, allowing foreigners to exchange information more easily.[67] Ruilin 瑞麟 (1809–74), the governor-general of Guangdong and Guangxi, and Jiang Yili 蔣益澧 (1833–74), the governor of Guang-dong, considered the questions of the post and the telegraph to be very trivial, categorizing them as "skill arts" (*ji yi* 技藝), a dismissive term.[68] Similarly, Ma Xinyi 馬新貽 (1821–70), the governor of Zhejiang Prov-ince, scorned the proposals on the telegraph and the mint as vulgar and unimportant.[69]

Zhang Guoji, in his study of the reigns of Emperor Jiaqing (1796–1820) and Emperor Daoguang, pointed out that in this period there were two top-down principles of governance that had significant impact on the sociopolitical situation: the promotion of agriculture alongside the suppression of industrial production, and a focus on moral principles that amounted to a policy of indoctrination of the populace. In the first cat-egory, activities such as the manufacture of handmade goods, mining, and industrial activity were discouraged, in parallel with a discourse that Western technology was to be regarded as nothing more than clever con-trivance. Both emperors also promoted a discourse encouraging the ap-plication of moral standards, though without this being associated with a focus on legal sanctions for those falling short of the ideal.[70] From the high provincial officials' responses to the two proposals, a case can cer-tainly be made that demonstrates the continuity of these principles. Even individuals such as Zuo Zongtang 左宗棠, who later set up the Fuzhou Arsenal and Naval College (福州船政學堂 Fuzhou chuanzheng xuetang) in 1866, openly echoed the discourse of loose reins and did not see any point in doing more than was required by the foreign treaties. Zeng Guofan was reluctant to support mining.[71] In what appears to be a survival

67. *YWSM*, Tongzhi reign, 41:43–44.
68. *YWSM*, Tongzhi reign, 42:63, 45:32. For the evolution of the term *ji yi* and how it became connected to Western technology in the late nineteenth century, see Hailian Chen, "Technology for Re-engineering the Qing Empire."
69. *YWSM*, Tongzhi reign, 45:32.
70. Zhang Guoji, *Qing Jiaqing Daoguang shiqi*, chap. 2. For a discussion on Em-peror Yongzheng's stress on the importance of agriculture, see Li Ta-chia, "Cong yi shang dao zhong shang," 7–8.
71. Fan, *Qingji de yangwu*, 1:443–44.

of attitudes from the previous Jiaqing-Daoguang era, railways, commercial steamships, and telegraph services were regarded as unnecessary and a nationwide postal service was never seriously considered.

Yet in contrast to the reactions displayed by his colleagues toward their proposals, Wenxiang said to Hart and Wade that it was not as if the Chinese did not understand the utility of railways and other innovations, but China did not have the money, and the government did not want to use either foreign money or foreign people to build them. Quite apart from the lack of capital, face was also a concern. According to Hart, Wenxiang said, "Give us face; if you don't give us face, we can do nothing."[72] It was clear, therefore, that despite the fact that key figures in the Zongli Yamen might have wanted to move away from military-focused modernization and the loose-reins policy, the wider political climate meant that this was not possible. Moral teaching derived from classical learning continued to be regarded as the foundation for the betterment of officialdom, and this discourse reached a peak over the controversial matter of Tongwen College.

"Inspector General of Everything"

The impeachment of Prince Gong showed that anti-Westernization forces had come to the fore and indeed were embedded at the center of power in the person of Empress Dowager Cixi. The officials who acted in support of the impeachment of the prince were the same individuals who had been in favor of the coup back in 1861, but now they disagreed with Prince Gong on the kind of reform that China needed. Meanwhile, the Zongli Yamen was preoccupied in dealing with the legacy of the ratification of the Treaty of Tianjin and the Convention of Beijing. This included enacting the various treaty provisions agreed upon with various Western countries; handling follow-up matters with Russia; mediating in many conflicts that arose in the treaty ports between local governments, local Chinese, foreign merchants, and missionaries on both the coast and along

---

72. Hart, entry for July 20, 1865, in *Hart Journals 1863–1866*, 303–4. See also Hart, journal entry for January 17, 1867, SQBH.

the Yangtze River; and, last but not least, handling the matter of property and land for foreign missions as they sought to establish their presence in the treaty ports and inland.

On experiencing the treatment received by his "Bystander's View," Hart concluded that if he wanted to move ahead with any modernization projects, he had to rely on resources that were directly available to him. Fortunately, just such a source of funding was available: tonnage dues, seven-tenths of which from 1868 were permitted to be retained by the CMCS. Collected from the ships at the treaty ports, tonnage dues were introduced in the Treaty of Nanjing and extended in the Treaty of Tianjin mainly for the purpose of the improvement of harbors and the building of lighthouses to make coastal navigation safer.[73] Additionally, Hart spent his allocation of tonnage dues on introducing revenue cruisers and harbor police on coasts and rivers. In 1868, using the same source of funding, the Marine Department (Chuanchao bu 船鈔部) was established, under which specialist functions for harbor engineering, harbor master operations, and coastal lighting were set up.[74] Around this time Hart also contemplated setting up meteorological stations at each treaty port, a function that was formally added in 1869.[75]

Through these projects Hart's reach progressively extended far beyond the remit originally envisaged when the CMCS was established. In his own words, Hart fancied himself the "Inspector General of Everything," though Johannes von Gumpach, who fell out with Hart over his position at Tongwen College, phrased it less charitably, noting that Hart "will have his finger in every pie."[76] While being unable to formally support his "Bystander's View," Hart believed that the Zongli Yamen was happy to keep throwing him something to "nibble at," and this included the

73. "Tonnage Dues, Seven-Tenth of, to Be Received Monthly and Remitted Quarterly," IG Circular 2 (1st ser.), March 13, 1868, in *Docs. Ill.*, 1:85–86; "Memorandum concerning the Application of Moneys Collected as Tonnage Dues from Foreign Shipping by the Chinese Government," March 21, 1871 (1st ser.), in *Docs. Ill.*, 1:213–20; Stanley F. Wright, *Hart and the Chinese Customs*, 295.
74. "Marine Department, Organization of," IG Circular 10 (1st ser.), April 25, 1868, in *Docs. Ill.*, 1:86–94; Bickers, "Infrastructural Globalization."
75. Bickers, "Throwing Light on Natural Laws," 179–200.
76. Regarding "Inspector General of Everything," see Hart, journal entry for August 5, 1867, SQBH; and Von Gumpach, *The Burlingame Mission*, 21.

matter of Tongwen College.[77] Education was one of the issues Hart had stressed in the "Bystander's View," and Tongwen College became an obvious target for Hart to seek to exercise his influence. Yet while the issue of the "Bystander's View" was largely a victim of internal Qing court politics, resistance over Tongwen College came from a much wider circle.

Tongwen College was supported by the three-tenths portion of tonnage dues collected by the CMCS and transferred directly to the Zongli Yamen.[78] The original focus was to train students in the English, French, and Russian languages, but Hart did not believe this was sufficient. He wanted to transform the college from one based around languages into a much more broad-based institution of learning by rapidly expanding the curriculum to include chemistry, engineering (including fortification design), artillery, and natural philosophy.[79] With a desire to educate young Chinese men in order to "make China the chief among nations," Hart was enthused to further expand the curriculum over time into a twelve-year one by including more subjects, such as international law, political economy, surgery, military science, astronomy, and more mathematics.[80]

Prince Gong and Wenxiang were prepared to support Hart's plan, in spite of the fact that the agitation caused by the impeachment was still fresh. Before seeking permission from the emperor, they had already given Hart instructions to recruit suitable teachers when he was in Europe. But instead of introducing multiple subjects at once, as Hart had proposed, they focused on astronomy and mathematics. In January 1867 Prince Gong submitted "Six Regulations on Learning Astronomy and Mathematics at Tongwen College" (Tongwenguan xuexi tianwen suanxue zhangcheng liutiao 同文館學習天文算學章程六條) to make his case. Those qualified to enroll in the new curriculum at the college included young and promising candidates who had not already passed provincial exams but held a senior licentiate position by imperial favor, as well as those who already passed either provincial or central exams and

77. Hart, journal entry for July 12, 1867, SQBH.
78. "Tonnage Dues, Yamen's 3/10ths of, to Be Remitted through the Inspector General," IG Circular 21 (1st ser.), August 22, 1863, in *Docs. Ill.*, 1:33.
79. Hart, entry for July 28, 1864, in *Hart Journals 1863–1866*, 164.
80. Hart, journal entry for February 4, 1867, SQBH.

were under the age of thirty; enrollment was open to those who currently held any official position below the fifth rank and also to those who were not holding official positions. Students were to be paid a salary during their fellowship.[81]

Anticipating possible arguments against such an expansion, in his long memorial Prince Gong used Emperor Kangxi's enthusiasm in these two subjects to strengthen the case. He also stressed that the Qing court had no reason to shy away from these subjects and refuse to bring them to Tongwen College because provincial officials such as Li Hongzhang and Zuo Zongtang had already set up schools in Shanghai and Fuzhou, respectively, and hired foreigners to teach there. Finally Prince Gong pointed out that Japan had already sent people to Britain to learn its language and knowledge, and he believed Japan would be able to make its own ships sooner rather than later and might even come to compete with the West. If a small country like Japan could do this, it would be disgraceful if China refused to change and continued to smear Western technology as "worthless craft."[82]

A Crippled Ministry

Behind the scenes, the issue of Tongwen College touched a very sensitive nerve for officials, the vast majority of whom had climbed the career ladder through the traditional route of the *keju* 科舉, the state examination system. The debate over the college was not an isolated matter; on the contrary, it was wrapped in long debates on how China should respond to the new challenges of the age. The debate over Tongwen College helps shed light on the historical context, and why the kinds of reform proposed by Hart, including the national postal service, were not possible at the time.

What Hart referred to as something for him to "nibble at" actually touched upon a highly sensitive matter: a fundamental crisis of identity that was challenging deeply held beliefs, undermining existing value

---

81. *YWSM*, Tongzhi reign, 46:3–4, 43–48.
82. *YWSM*, Tongzhi reign, 46:43–48.

systems, and ultimately challenging the structures of power, status, and wealth in the Qing empire. For Qing officials, their intellectual learning provided a holistic perspective that encompassed all aspects of humanity, the natural world, and the wider universe. Intellectual learning was therefore about developing personal qualities, including personal morality, in order to achieve total harmony with the external world. The state examination was the mechanism by which the whole system was held together. Both Hart and the Chinese officials sought guidance from their respective traditions and cultures, but while Hart could separate physics, chemistry, and mathematics from Christianity or constitutional law, the Chinese did not have sufficient space or permission to separate their system of knowledge and learning from traditional holistic perspectives of morality and values in the Confucian epistemological system.

Officials from both the provinces and the capital wrote to express their deep concerns about the new curriculum at Tongwen College. Woren not only had a private conference with the two empress dowagers to express his concerns, but also submitted a memorial expressing his view.[83] The discourse employed in attacking Tongwen College reforms were not just about the specifics of the proposals; rather, it was escalated to the level of accusing and shaming individuals for abandoning the basic values of Chinese culture and society. The antiforeign sentiment of Woren was in alignment with his focus as teacher of the Tongzhi emperor. He sought to cultivate the emperor so that he might become the ideal Confucian king. The ten-year bond between the teacher and student seemed to run very deep, and when Woren died some years later, in 1871, the emperor appeared to be quite affected.[84] As Hart's personal Chinese writer Li informed him, Woren "is the chief of the literati; the senior teacher of the Emperor. . . . His opposition, therefore, is enlisting all the literati against the T'ung Wên Kuan."[85] Although the Tongwen College experiment went ahead that year, recruitment was unsatisfactory, as the conflict affected perceptions negatively.[86]

83. Li Xizhu, *Wan Qing baoshou sixiang*, 169.
84. Li Xizhu, *Wan Qing baoshou sixiang*, 145–46.
85. Hart, journal entry for July 2, 1867, SQBH.
86. Li Xizhu, *Wan Qing baoshou sixiang*, 173.

Feeling isolated and unsupported, on July 15, 1867, Hart complained about Wenxiang to Alcock: "I alternate between hope and despair: after leaving Wên [Wenxiang], I always feel that things look well, so kindly is his manner, and so taking his talk; but when I cool and reflect a little, I begin again to see that nothing is done; and that, apart from an ardent desire to possess powder and pistols, his mind is set upon but little else."[87] Around two weeks later in his diary, Hart remarked that Wenxiang was like an "old woman" and "he fears his own shadow, won't step out of himself, and sits growling like a 'dog in the manger!'"[88] He felt his contact was restricted to only a few officials at the Zongli Yamen, and he believed that behind the "smiling face" of Wenxiang and his colleagues toward himself was "a bitter hatred" toward foreigners.[89] In fact, it appeared that Hart's suspicions might well have been the result of a trap set by Woren, who had been recently added as a member of the Zongli Yamen. Perhaps aware that Burlingame, the US minister, was friendly with Hart, Woren had told him that things were not always what they seemed, and although Wenxiang and two or three other members of the Zongli Yamen were friendly to foreigners' faces, they were, as Burlingame dutifully reported to Hart, "quite the reverse when they get among the other set."[90]

Meanwhile, Hart found a way to experiment with his ideas for a postal service. He had already introduced a rigorous reporting system as officiating inspector general, with carefully designed forms for data collection.[91] As the CMCS expanded along with the number of treaty ports, Hart extended this practice and controlled the service by acquiring a steady flow of information through networks that permeated the whole institution and beyond based largely on regular correspondence. He enjoyed reading all kinds of information, including interesting intelligence and the "sayings or doings of individuals" at each locality fed to him by

87. Hart, journal entry for July 15, 1867, SQBH.
88. Hart, journal entry for July 28, 1867, SQBH.
89. Hart, journal entry for July 12, 1867, SQBH.
90. Hart, journal entry for May 25, 1867, SQBH.
91. "Collection and Expenditure, Quarterly Returns of, to Be Made Out in New Form, English and Chinese, Enclosed," IG Circular 9 (1st ser.), February 16, 1863, in *Docs. Ill.*, 1:24–27.

his commissioners at treaty ports.[92] In its early stages, this Customs mail service was far from being a united and coherent system across Beijing, Tianjin, Shanghai, Yantai (Chefoo), and Zhenjiang, particularly because foreign steamships were often unable to run along the icy coast all the way from Shanghai to Tianjin. To accommodate this information exchange, a mail service for internal purposes was put in place by the end of 1866 after Hart returned from Europe.

As a result of the Treaty of Tianjin, Britain, France, and the United States were granted the privilege to set up their own postal services in the treaty ports. The Zongli Yamen was responsible for the security of mail transmitted to and from their respective legations should these mail services fail to perform as required.[93] Seeing Hart had an internal postal service running, the Zongli Yamen was happy to pass on this responsibility for foreign mail to the CMCS, no matter how primitive the new service might be. There were certainly teething problems. On January 8, 1867, Hart recorded, "The *Ting-chai* [聽差, personal messenger] carrying the mails to the English and French Legations was thrown, & the pony bolted with the Mail Bags; the bag for the French Legations was recovered, but the others cannot be found." The next day he wrote, "Recovered the thrown bags containing English Legation's mails; one was broken, but we got its contents from the neighboring houses."[94] Shortly afterward, the CMCS extended access to the mail service to the wider public in both Beijing and Tianjin; according to the announcement, payment from individuals could be organized either as a season subscription, or by a cash payment per item for nonsubscribers.[95] Nevertheless, despite this additional workload, in practice the service remained principally for internal Customs use.

Aside from the Tongwen College question, the negotiations conducted between 1867 and 1869 over revision of the Treaty of Tianjin, as well as the missionary massacre in Tianjin in 1870, put the proreform

92. "Semi-official Correspondence with IG," IG Circular 15 (1st ser.), April 10, 1874, in *Docs. Ill.*, 1:329–30; Ladds, *Empire Careers*, 38–39; Van de Ven, *Breaking with the Past*, 76–82.

93. Cheng, *Postal Communication in China*, 63–65.

94. Hart, journal entries for January 8, 1967, and January 9, 1867, SQBH.

95. Robert Hart to Thomas Dick, Tianjin Customs commissioner, March 4, 1867, in *Zhongguo haiguan yu youzheng*, 1. See also appendix B, "Tientsin Customs Post," in *Report* (1921), 105.

camp under further attack. The Tianjin Massacre stirred up huge anti-foreign sentiment, and the violence was directed not only toward French residents in Tianjin but also toward Russians, other foreigners, and Chinese Christian converts.[96] In the presence of the two empress dowagers, the high officials were once again divided over the issue. There were outspoken calls for foreigners to be expelled, and Prince Chun, who had supported Prince Gong during the impeachment, was now behind an antiforeign movement in Zhili Province and also openly criticized the Zongli Yamen and its approach to foreign affairs. Zeng Guofan, by now in charge of managing the fallout of the Tianjin Massacre, was criticized for not being tough enough with foreigners.[97]

Almost three decades after the First Opium War there were, perhaps, already some signs indicating violence prior to the Tianjin Massacre as resentment toward foreigners built up. During the negotiation for the treaty revision, Wenxiang warned Alcock against pressing China too hard for reform, or "loss and danger" might occur.[98] Wenxiang's warning was almost certainly heard by Hart as he assisted in the negotiations all the way through. He agreed with Wenxiang, and outlined his own perspective in a long piece which appeared in the *North China Herald*. Hart clearly wanted to convey a strong message that China should be left to do things at its own pace:

> Nothing but complete ignorance of China could have permitted the public to assume that the vast changes now looked for are regarded as necessary, and longed for by China herself, and nothing could well be more unreasonable than to suppose that such changes—even if felt by China to be called for—could be hurried forward. . . . However advanced the Chinese may be in civilization, it is not to be forgotten that their civilization is not a Christian civilization; they are Asiatics, too, and there is a pride of race about them that leads them to tread upon the neck that bends, rather than to lift the head that touches the dust, when its owner is an alien.[99]

96. Weng, entries for June 23, 1870, and June 27, 1870, in *WRJ*, 2:775–77.

97. Weng, entries for July 23, 1870, August 17, 1870, and August 27, 1870, in *WRJ*, 2:784–85, 790, 792.

98. Sir R. Alcock to the Earl of Clarendon, March 18, 1869, in *Correspondence respecting the Revision*, 328.

99. Hart, "Note on Chinese Matters," *North China Herald*, November 9, 1869.

While the impact of the Tianjin Massacre was still playing out, arguments for and against reform were put aside temporarily when Taiwan was invaded by Japan in May 1874. In what was recognized as a time of national crisis, there was some reflection on what China had or had not learned since the end of the Second Opium War. Noting the harm that Japan could inflict on China, Prince Gong reviewed the progress made by the Self-Strengthening Movement. He stressed that, after the tremendous shock in 1860, the government had had no choice but to adopt the policy of loose reins in order to gain time for reform. He took the opportunity to cast blame on those who had attacked both him and the Zongli Yamen for failing to understand the challenges they faced.[100] It is not known for certain, but it would be unsurprising if this memorial, like many others, was coauthored with Wenxiang. But we also have Wenxiang's own words summarizing his perspective: "There is no one who does not talk about self-strengthening, but in over ten years little has been accomplished. The causes lie in the fact that those who despise and disregard foreign affairs rely on empty words, having nothing practical [to offer], [and] those accustomed to the peace are anxious that nothing happens for fear of arousing suspicion. There may be some people who devote themselves to the careful study of current affairs, but owing to the lack of funds, nothing can be achieved or developed."[101]

Wenxiang was on two months' sick leave, but he obviously wanted to make his thoughts on the topic clear to all. His use of the phrase "empty words" referred to the group around Woren and Prince Chun, while "lack of funds" alluded to the huge financial resources directed to repairing the Summer Palace by order of the emperor a year earlier, which had caused another serious clash between Prince Gong and the emperor. Wenxiang's assessment invited others to express ideas for further reform, and the voices of Han Chinese provincial officials were particularly prominent as they were directly involved in the Taiwan crisis. Among them, Li Hongzhang claimed leadership. Indeed, while the Zongli Yamen's reform ideas were caught up in the politics of the capital, Li had been busy elsewhere

---

100. *YWSM*, Tongzhi reign, 98:19.
101. Wenxiang, "Guoshiguan benzhuan," 38–39, translated in Cheng, *Postal Communication in China*, 68.

cultivating his own ideas. He supported Shen Baozhen 沈葆楨 (1820–79) in submitting a plan for expanding the Fujian Shipyard, and he also backed the plan of Ding Richang 丁日昌 (1823–82) to strengthen the Chinese naval force on China's coasts.[102] Following the Taiwan crisis, these plans finally received proper attention at court. It was at this point that Li went a step further and submitted his own memorandum, which set out a grander scheme.[103]

Li Hongzhang was fully aware of Hart's "Bystander's View," having read it back in July 1867 when he came to Beijing. According to Hart, Li had been impressed by it and had asked to take a copy away with him. Hart had complied, hoping that Li might "do or suggest something useful."[104] Hart and Li were not strangers to each other. They had worked together as far back as the late 1850s on the supply of weapons to suppress the Taiping Rebellion, and in the 1860s they had cooperated against the Nian rebels. There was common ground, and Hart saw Li as an ally.[105] He had wished Wenxiang could be as brave as Li, and in one diary entry in October 1868, Hart recorded a meeting with Li. Sharing cigars and liqueur, they talked about the good old days and mutual acquaintances when they were working on the Taiping war together. Hart and Li also appeared to be on the same page on issues related to railways, the telegraph, and Tongwen College.[106] Sharing his views regarding the failure of reform, Li joined Prince Gong and Wenxiang in pointing a finger at those who only provided empty words.

Unlike his colleagues, who rejected mining, railways, steamships, the telegraph, and a postal service, Li was an advocate for their introduction, and this allowed him to mark out his territory for the next two decades. He revealed himself as even more ambitious in introducing Western technologies than Zeng Guofan, whom he regarded as his teacher in many

102. *YWSM*, Tongzhi reign, 98:24–27. See also Chen Yue, "Shen Baozhen, Li Hongzhang," 16–18; and Hou Jie and Qin Fang, "Haizhan yu paotai."

103. For Li Hongzhang's long proposal, see *YWSM*, Tongzhi reign, 99:12–34.

104. Hart, journal entry for July 16, 1867, SQBH.

105. Hart, journal entry for February 16, 1867, SQBH.

106. Hart, journal entry for October 12, 1868, SQBH; Richard J. Smith, "Li Hungchang's Use of Foreign Military Talent," 6.

ways.[107] Li's expansive proposal covered military matters, mining, transportation, communications, and education; these topics were to take center stage in the later phase of the Self-Strengthening Movement from the mid-1870s until the First Sino-Japanese War. Here we see the entry of a powerful local general who had steadily, through careful actions and many battles, climbed the political ladder beginning in the late 1850s. His skill both in cultivating foreign advisers and in managing his superiors had shaped his success. On account of his positions as viceroy of Zhili and superintendent of trade for the northern ports, Li's office in Tianjin was by that time the most important stop for Western envoys on their way to Beijing. According to W. A. P. Martin (1827–1916), then president of Tongwen College, Li Hongzhang was a relative giant among his compatriots at six feet two who had established himself as "a friend of progress" and as very accessible to foreigners. Describing Li's characteristics, Martin noted, "His thunder is usually followed by a burst of sunshine, and no man knows better how to intersperse the light and shade, but he is deficient in that polished self-restraint which marks the well-bred mandarin."[108]

Emperor Tongzhi died in January 1875. Empress Dowager Cixi adopted her three-year-old nephew as her son, and put him up as the new emperor; and so ended the Tongzhi Restoration period. In the prevailing climate of conservatism in court politics, the influence of the Zongli Yamen was somewhat less than China's situation warranted. Each minister of the Zongli Yamen occupied several official positions, and they were overloaded with responsibilities, as well as highly constrained by political infighting.[109] Although Hart's "Bystander's View" hinted at the potential of a modern communications network for China, all he could manage at this stage was a small-scale, internally focused Customs mail service, connecting treaty ports with Beijing and Shanghai.

The Taiwan crisis became a turning point for reform, and Li Hongzhang established his leadership for a new phase of the Self-Strengthening Movement to include steamships, the telegraph, and mining. Meanwhile, neither merchants nor the Qing government were particularly concerned

107. Fan, *Qingji de yangwu*, 1:319–23.
108. Martin, *A Cycle of Cathay*, 349–51, 353.
109. Wu Fuhuan, *Qingji Zongli Yamen*, 57–58.

about postal matters. This was partly because they did not see any profit to be made from a postal service and partly because the country's needs for postal communication were perceived as being essentially met by the several existing mail services available in China at the time. Ultimately, the first real impetus to move ahead with the provision of public postal services did not arrive until the negotiations over the Margary Affair, twelve years after the "Bystander's View."

THE OLD IMPERIAL
POST OFFICE, PEKING.

CHAPTER THREE

The Customs Postal Service

On May 26, 1876, Robert Hart made the following entry in his diary:

> Wên Hsiang is dead!
>
> Whatever his faults or failings, he had wonderful qualities; quick intelligence—clear insight—able powers of debate—genial manners—immense mastery of detail—wonderful power of work— . . . and self-sacrificing patriotism. From lowly position—the son of a poor cotter in Manchuria, he rose to be the first man in the Empire: now he is gone at the early age of 57! If there is any man I have known I shall be glad to meet in a better world, it is Wên Hsiang. Peace to his ashes![1]

By the time of his death, Wenxiang had been ill for more than two years, but the crisis following the Japanese invasion of Taiwan in 1874 had encouraged him, together with Prince Gong Yixin, to voice disappointment and dissatisfaction at the progress of the central government's reform program in the period after 1861. With the support of several

---

1. Hart, journal entry for May 26, 1876, SQBH.

provincial officials over the Taiwan crisis, as was discussed in chapter 2, a new wave of reform began to take shape. This, together with the rise of Li Hongzhang, an increasingly assertive voice for change who held the positions of viceroy of Zhili and superintendent of trade for the northern ports, strengthened the position of Prince Gong.[2] Behind the palace walls, planning had begun to secure the succession. For the Qing court at this time there was no immediate threat from abroad except for some looming difficulties caused by the death of Augustus Raymond Margary in February 1875, a young British diplomat who was killed on the border between Burma and Yunnan Province. His murder provoked a strong reaction from the British minister, Thomas F. Wade, which sparked a lengthy negotiation that eventually resulted in the signing of the Chefoo Convention in August 1876.

For the most part, Wenxiang left the talks to the management of Prince Gong, with help from Hart and Li Hongzhang, but shortly before his death he contributed to the decision to agree to the setting up of a Chinese embassy in London and to select Guo Songtao as the first Chinese minister to be sent to the West. This was a milestone in late Qing politics, and Guo's first task was to deliver the emperor's regrets for the murder of Margary.[3] Guo, from a wealthy merchant family, had not had a smooth career, having been an outspoken figure for reform since the 1850s, but he had enjoyed a long-term relationship of mutual admiration with Li Hongzhang.[4]

In response to Margary's murder, Wade was determined to teach China a lesson once again on how to treat foreigners, just as James Bruce, the Eighth Earl of Elgin had in 1860. Having been more than merely Elgin's interpreter at the time, Wade recalled only too well the circumstances of how the Summer Palace was burned down in order to send a direct message to Emperor Xianfeng over the capture and treatment of Harry Smith Parkes and his companions, as well as the emperor's forced

2. Robert Hart to James Duncan Campbell, letter 119, February 10, 1875, in *The IG*, 1:187.

3. "Zongshu zou qing pai zhu Yingguo gongshi pian" 總署奏請派駐英國公使片 [Zongli Yamen memorial on sending diplomat to station in Britain], Guangxu reign year 1, month 9, day 28 (August 28, 1875), in *Qingji waijiao shiliao*, 1:46.

4. Jia, "Li Hongzhang yu Guo," 20–25; Zhong Shuhe, "Lun Guo Songtao," 135–36.

public expression of regret for China's actions in the Dagu Forts conflict in June 1859. In 1875 Wade's approach was to require a similar act of contrition, and in the process, he took advantage of the opportunity to push the British position in a range of other matters, including the issue of the Chinese embassy in London, exemption from *lijin* for foreign commodities in inland China, and the opening of Beihai, Wenzhou, Wuhu, and Yichang for trade. Moreover, Wade's rather fierce negotiating stance allowed Hart to enter into and play a significant role in the talks, which led to a revival of the idea of a national postal service.

The experimental postal service that arose from this proved to be a seminal learning experience for the Chinese Maritime Customs Service (CMCS), as it encountered major issues requiring serious consideration if the ultimate goal was to be the creation of a national post office. The timing of the postal experiment was not ideal, as Hart took a second period of leave and returned to Europe with his wife and children in March 1878, and some months were spent in connection with the Universal Exposition in Paris. Prior to Hart's departure, Gustav Detring (1842–1913), the commissioner of Customs at Tianjin, had been assigned to the postal project. With no one in the CMCS having any real prior knowledge of running postal services, Detring could only improvise while pushing forward as best he could. Unfortunately, on his return in May 1879, Hart rapidly found out that the fledgling postal service had endured some rough moments and had even become associated with scandal.

Li Hongzhang, Thomas F. Wade, and the Margary Affair

Thomas F. Wade's personality and career are something of a conundrum. Coming from a military background, he first arrived in Hong Kong in 1842 during the First Opium War. By 1843 he was working as a translator in increasingly important roles before taking up his first diplomatic position as vice consul in Shanghai in 1852. There he soon found himself involved in efforts to restore order to the management of foreign Customs efforts that had essentially collapsed due to the Taiping Rebellion, as part of a three-man commission that was the precursor to the CMCS. He subsequently served in many diplomatic roles, and at the time of the Margary Affair held the position of envoy extraordinary and minister plenipotentiary and served as chief superintendent of British trade in China, a position he held until his retirement in 1883. Wade's contribution as a Sinologist was immense; throughout his career in China he was prolific as a writer, covering topics as diverse as the structure and command system of the Chinese Army, Chinese language learning, and the translation of the works of Confucius into English. On retirement from the diplomatic service Wade returned to Britain, becoming the first professor of Chinese at his alma mater, Cambridge University, in 1888. It was a position he was well prepared for, having taught young diplomats arriving at the Beijing legation, and he donated to Cambridge many volumes he had collected over four decades.[5] In James Hevia's view, Wade was "an exemplary imperial nomad, an almost perfect frontier agent" for the British empire.[6] And yet, for all of his knowledge of and sensitivity to Chinese culture and customs, as a diplomat dealing with the Qing administration he could be ruthless—and indeed, sometimes reckless—in furthering British interests, with an arrogant streak and an impatience that did not always endear him to his hosts.

It was apparent from the beginning of the negotiations that there was very little trust between Wade and the Zongli Yamen. Wade was clearly upset by the death of Margary, who had been a favorite student; indeed, Wade once said Margary was one of the most promising among the staff of the British legation.[7] Fundamentally, Wade had no faith in the Qing government's investigation into Margary's murder, either before or after any conclusion was reached. He considered China as having failed to "act with *bonā fide* effort."[8] He was also becoming exasperated with what

5. Cordier, "Thomas Francis Wade."
6. Hevia, "An Imperial Nomad," 3.
7. Kwan, "Fanyi zhengzhi ji Hanxue," 19–20. Wade to the Earl of Derby, March 12, 1875, in *Correspondence respecting the Attack*, 2; Wade to the Prince of Kung, March 27, 1875, in *Correspondence respecting the Attack*, 12–13.
8. The issue of *bonā fide* was a concern of Wade, and on several occasions he raised it in his correspondence with Qing officials and his reports to the Earl of Derby. Wade, "Memorandum for the Information of his Excellency the Grant Secretary Li," enclosure of Wade to the Earl of Derby, August 26, 1875, in *Correspondence respecting the*

he saw as the backwardness of the Qing administration and sanguine about its possible replacement with some alternative. For the Zongli Yamen, Wade's hasty manner and his inconsistent and changing demands during the negotiations presented a big puzzle. It was the lack of faith between the two parties that gave Li Hongzhang and Hart an open door to intervene.

In March 1875 Wade threatened to cut off all relations with Prince Gong and withdraw the British legation to Shanghai if his demands were not met. Faced with this threat, Prince Gong quickly agreed to the demands as presented. But Wade subsequently abandoned his initial position and came up with several wholly new requests.[9] Prince Gong and Wenxiang turned to Li Hongzhang for a solution. It was known that Li shared similar views with Prince Gong and Wenxiang on many subjects relating to reform, and his political status was secure after his successful management of the Tianjin Massacre and the Taiwan crisis. Li had gained a reputation for being something of a foreign expert after dealing with several incidents involving foreign Christians.[10] When Wade passed through Tianjin in August, Li was instructed to meet with Wade and to attempt to soften his position. In order to pacify Wade and reduce the risk that the conflict might escalate into a military one, Li suggested sending Chinese officials to England to explain China's situation; it was this proposal that ultimately delivered a permanent Chinese embassy in London.[11]

In June 1876 Wade once again halted negotiations, packed up and left Beijing, and again his action caused bewilderment. Wade's own rationale was that his sense of dignity had been offended at his treatment

---

Attack, 51. Wade to the Earl of Derby, July 14, 1877, in *Correspondence respecting the Attack*, 127. Being aware of this, Zongli Yamen had to issue clarifications, for example, Prince Gong to Wade, September 22, 1875, in *Correspondence respecting the Attack*, 77.

9. Exchanges between Wade and Prince Gong on March 28–29, 1875, in *Correspondence respecting the Attack*, 16–18.

10. Su Mei-fang, "Li Hongzhang ziqiang sixiang," 199–200.

11. "Zongshu zou Yingshi zai Jin xiang Li Hongzhang tichu Dian'an liutiao jieduan yaoxie pian" 總署奏英使在津向李鴻章提出滇案六條籍端要挾片 [Memorial from Zongli Yamen on the British minister proposing to Li Hongzhang in Tianjin a six-clause demand to settle the negotiation for the Yunnan incident], Guangxu reign year 1, month 7, day 28 (August 28, 1875), in *Qingji waijiao shiliao*, 1:41–42.

by the Qing court, and by extension, he had been offended at the treatment of Britain. He told Li Hongzhang, "Officials are acting as if they were cajoling children . . . you only provide empty words and treat Britain like a small country such as Ryukyu and Korea. I was no longer able to stomach such wrongness so I decided to leave the Capital."[12] Li was once again concerned that Wade would present an unfavorable report on the situation, which would result in a misunderstanding with the British government. Rumors of war were everywhere in the British community in China. William Nelson Lovatt, who at the time worked for the CMCS as a tidewaiter, even welcomed war. He felt for China's own good that it ought to be punished in a "motherly way" by Britain. He was rather disappointed on finding out no war would come, and blamed Wade for not been aggressive enough.[13]

Yet, in his report to the Zongli Yamen, Li seemed to accept what the French and American ambassadors had told him: that despite his hot temper and desire always to keep "face," Wade was actually a very pleasant and kind man.[14] Noting that Wade was still in a state of uncertainty about what demands he should make, Hart observed of his old friend, "what he is in search of is that *ignis fatuus* [lit. foolish fire, or a will o' the wisp]; a something that shall guarantee the future!"[15]

Beyond this, Wade was also influenced by politics closer to home. On the one hand, he was grateful for Hart's assistance and publicly praised him for his contribution, bringing mutual benefit to China and to foreign countries; but on the other, as negotiations dragged on, he desired less of Hart but more of the Chinese ministers.[16] Sensing that Hart was getting close to having his post office, Wade withdrew his support for the

---

12. Li Hongzhang, "Yu Yingguo Wei shi da wen jielue" 與英國威使答問節略 [Interview with British Ministry Wade, extract], Guangxu reign year 2, month 5, day 29 (June 20, 1876), in "Yi shu han gao" 譯署函稿 [Correspondence with the Zongli Yamen], *juan* 5:18, in Li Hongzhang, *Li Wenzhonggong quan shu*, my translation.

13. Patterson, *William Nelson Lovatt*, 67.

14. Li Hongzhang, "Lun Dian an weixian" 論滇案危險 [On how the Yunnan incident case was about to fall apart], Guangxu reign year 2, month 4, day 21 (May 14, 1876), in "Yi shu han gao," *juan* 5:8–9, in Li Hongzhang, *Li Wenzhonggong quan shu*.

15. Robert Hart to James Duncan Campbell, letter 150, May 12, 1876, in *The IG*, 1:220, emphasis in the original.

16. Zhang Zhiyong, "Hede yu Zhong Ying Dian'an."

postal idea and quietly left it out, together with the mint project, from the final agreement of the Chefoo Convention. When asked by US minister George Seward why he had not included these in the agreement, Wade said he did not realize the Chinese government wanted them.[17] Later, in his final report on the Margary Affair, Wade wrote, "Near the end of my negotiations, it was suggested that I might engage the Government to establish a mint and a postal service. Of the two latter I will say that I half regret the loss of the opportunity. Neither a mint nor a postal service, however, appeared to me to find a fit place in any of the three Sections of my Agreement."[18]

To Hart, Wade's declared reasoning appeared false. He even shared this thought with Li Hongzhang, and said to Li that he believed that their more than twenty-year friendship had gone through a change during the negotiations to settle the Margary Affair.[19] Two months after the signing of the Chefoo Convention, in one of his letters to James Duncan Campbell, Hart wrote, "He [Wade] walked into my library in the usual way the day before, but our relations have lost the cordiality they once had. I cannot congratulate him on his treatment of 'the Margary affair.' . . . He was offered a *Mint* and *Postal establishment*, but he decided not to have them—or forgot about them!"[20] Hart later heard from Seward that Wade had told him the reason he did not support moving forward with mint and post was that he did not want Hart to have "too much power and too much patronage."[21]

In 1886, in a letter to Henry Kopsch (1845–1913), the Customs commissioner at Ningbo who would later become the first postal secretary for the Imperial Post Office (IPO), Hart claimed he had obtained prior

17. "No. 57: Mr. Seward to Mr. Fish," October 3, 1876. Office of the Historian, US Department of State, https://history.state.gov/historicaldocuments/frus1877/d57.

18. Wade to the Earl of Derby, July 14, 1877, in *Correspondence respecting the Attack*, 147.

19. Li Hongzhang, "Shu Yantai chu yi" 述煙臺初議 [On the initial negotiation at Yantai], Guangxu reign year 2, month 7, day 4 (August 22, 1876), in "Yi shu han gao," *juan* 6:2, in Li Hongzhang, *Li Wenzhonggong quan shu.*

20. Robert Hart to James Duncan Campbell, letter 158, November 17, 1876, in *The IG*, 1:228, emphasis in the original.

21. Robert Hart to James Duncan Campbell, letter 184, October 25, 1877, in *The IG*, 1:252.

agreement from the Zongli Yamen and the superintendents of trade to connect the post office and mint with the resolution of the Margary Affair. This meant that the Chinese government had been happy to use the opportunity to have these two projects written into the treaty in order to reduce potential opposition either from other officials or from the general public. With the government's assent, Hart was able to go to Wade and ask him to include them in the draft agreement.[22] When the IPO would finally be established in 1896, the year following Wade's death, Hart remained unable to let the matter go and described Wade's attitude toward the postal question as "a conspiracy of silence."[23] Such a view has been the institutional belief of the CMCS, as well as the post office itself, and Wade has been seen in a negative light in the context of modern Chinese postal history.[24] But is this fair? There are alternative versions of events that indicate that Wade's account might be true, at least in part. The role of Li Hongzhang is central to this question.

When Hart was asked by the Zongli Yamen to draft a plan as a counteroffer to settle the affair, he came up with a proposal covering the opening of more ports, the imposition of tariffs on native products and foreign goods, transit duties, *lijin*, and the establishment of a postal service and a central mint. On the latter two Hart proposed himself as best placed to take them forward.[25] His proposal was seen by the Zongli Yamen and forwarded to Li Hongzhang. In a letter to Shen Baozhen, Li revealed that the Zongli Yamen had agreed to go along with most of the points, with the exception of the mint and a post office. On these the Yamen had instructed Li to make the decision.[26] It is at this point that Hart may have

22. Robert Hart to Henry Kopsch, March 17, 1886, SHAC, 679 (1) 14907.

23. "Postal: Enclosing Chinese Version of Regulations and Yamên Memorial," IG Circular 709 (2nd ser.), April 30, 1896, in *Docs. Ill.*, 2:55.

24. Morse, *The International Relations*, 3:62; Cheng, *Postal Communication in China*, 72; Weipin Tsai, "Breaking the Ice," 7–8. The author's view on the role of Li Hongzhang in Hart's postal project has changed since 2013.

25. "Zongli Yamen zou Zhong Ying jiaoshe buneng yuliao qing zhengdun jiang hai fang zhe" 總署奏中英交涉不能預料請整頓江海防摺 [Zongli Yamen on the negotiations, that Britain is not predictable, and suggests the government should proceed to prepare military defense on coasts and rivers], Guangxu reign year 2, month 5 day 23 (July 14, 1876), in *Qingji waijiao shiliao*, 1:106.

26. Li Hongzhang, "Zhi Shen Youdan zhijun" 致沈幼丹制軍 [To General Shen Youdan (Baozhen)], Guangxu reign year 2, month 5, day 20 (July 11, 1876), in "Peng liao

misunderstood the Zongli Yamen's intention and mistakenly believed that it had also approved his plans for a mint and a post office.

In the same letter to Shen Baozhen, Li said he did not want Hart, as a foreigner, to get involved in the matter of the mint. Later, in his reports to the Zongli Yamen, Li expressed concerns about both the post office and the mint and noted that these concerns were shared by other officials involved in the negotiations. There was a general fear that it might leave Hart with too much power and that it would become too difficult to remove him at some future date should it become necessary (*Ling zong shuiwusi zhuan shan qi quan zhi cheng wei da bu diao zhi huan* 令總稅務司專擅其權致成尾大不掉之患).[27] What lay behind this concern was that, in Qing legal practice, a treaty carried the status of law, and consequently, a breach of a treaty was seen as a violation of that law. This had been repeatedly emphasized since the early 1860s.[28] Conversely, for Hart, the best guarantee available to him to ensure that the Qing government would commit to the postal project was to have that commitment included in the treaty. Li also noted that he had said to Wade that he could not understand why the latter would want to support a post office, as there was no profit to be had in it for British merchants. Li could only imagine that perhaps Wade wanted to use the post office question in order to reward Hart for his assistance.[29]

Hart and Li Hongzhang subsequently met up several times to go through his proposal. On July 10, 1876, Hart once again pressed the topics of the post office and the mint. He was confident that the mint project could be completed in two years. As for the post office, he assured Li that he would only start with the treaty ports, and only deliver mail, not silver or parcels, and therefore would not damage the business of the private letter hongs. Li sensed Hart's passion and tenacity on this matter,

han gao" 朋僚函稿 [Correspondence with friends and colleagues], *juan* 16:16, in Li Hongzhang, *Li Wenzhonggong quan shu*.

27. Li Hongzhang, "Lun Hede quan jie Dian an tiao yi lun" 論赫德勸結滇案條議論 [On Hart suggesting to settle the agreement for the Yunnan case], Guangxu reign year 2, intercalary month 5, day 15 (July 6, 1876), in "Yi shu han gao," *juan* 5:28–29, in Li Hongzhang, *Li Wenzhonggong quan shu*.

28. Enclosure 2, "Prince Kung to Sir F. Bruce," June 19, 1863, in *Copy of Prince Kung's Answer*, 2.

29. Li Hongzhang, "Lun Hede quan jie Dian an tiao yi lun," 5:29–30.

and was rather struck by Hart's manner as he kept putting down the key points of the discussion in his "foreign-styled notebook" (*yang biji* 洋筆記). In the end Li agreed to go along with the postal project, but was still reserved about the mint.[30]

Following these meetings, in Hart's mind, the mint and the post office were in the bag. But Li Hongzhang's account of the final stage of the negotiation is very revealing on this matter, and suggests that the contrary was the case. Li recalled that neither he nor Wade had mentioned either the mint or the post office when drafting the Chefoo Convention, nor did they consider Hart's counterproposal. Only after the draft agreement had been produced did Wade finally bring up the mint and the post office, saying he believed that these two projects would benefit China. Wade said he had heard that the Chinese government had already agreed to approve these projects, and asked for a written confirmation from Li. Li said he would support the post office project, as he saw no harm in it to China; however, the matter of the mint would require much more consideration. Li did not provide Wade with any written confirmation, and two days later they met up again to sign the convention, then went their separate ways.[31]

In the end, Hart's effort to win the go-ahead for these projects came to nothing. The mint proposal was soon dropped altogether, in the face of huge opposition from Customs superintendents and local officials; Li Hongzhang preferred to keep any mint under direct Chinese control rather than ceding it to the inspector general's discretion. Hart did come away with a small victory when Li and the Zongli Yamen let him proceed with an experimental overland postal service, among the northern treaty ports to start with, using the CMCS budget. Li Hongzhang envisaged that one day he would himself establish a national post office for China, to sit alongside his growing brief that embraced railways, telegraph services, and steamships. He promised Hart that "as soon as it [the experimental

30. Li Hongzhang, "Yu He zong shuiwusi wenda jielue" 與赫總税務司問答節略 [Interview with Hart, the inspector general of Customs, extract], Guangxu reign year 2, intercalary month 5, day 19 (July 10, 1876), in "Yi shu han gao," *juan* 5:34–35, in Li Hongzhang, *Li Wenzhonggong quan shu.*

31. Li Hongzhang, "Lun zhu yin guan ju" 論鑄銀官局 [On the central mint], Guangxu reign year 2, month 9, day 10 (October 26, 1876), in "Yi shu han gao," *juan* 6:30, in Li Hongzhang, *Li Wenzhonggong quan shu.*

postal service] should be found to be a success, he [Li] would 'father it' officially and have it converted into a National Post Office."[32]

At the beginning of 1877 Hart embarked on preparations for the postal experiment, which would start the following year, linking Niuzhuang (Yingkou), Beijing, Tianjin, Yantai (Chefoo), Shanghai, and Zhenjiang (Chinkiang). He called on his Customs commissioners at the treaty ports to study and report back on their local postal situations, including the established private letter hongs and any foreign postal services in operation.[33] He also decided that Tianjin should be the base for the experiment and assigned Detring to take charge. Detring had joined the CMCS in April 1865 at age twenty-three; he was made a commissioner in March 1872, and transferred from Yantai to Tianjin in 1877.[34] From his experience in Yantai, northern ports were not alien to him. He had already assisted Li Hongzhang over the Margary Affair in Yantai, and had become a close associate.[35] Indeed, their friendship only ended with Li's death in 1901.[36]

On being asked to take forward the project, beginning with the establishment of overland postal routes from Tianjin, Detring quickly built up relationships with local merchants and important officials. These contacts proved invaluable for the management of the postal routes project. Given that Detring did not know much about postal services at the start of his assignment, he used the year 1877 for learning and preparation, studying the local situation of the treaty ports involved and the experience of various foreign countries. His work in the first three years in the role foreshadowed efforts to come almost two decades later in the creation of a national postal system, and Detring quickly encountered what were to be some of the most challenging issues in the future, including the planning and logistical operation of routes, conflict with local officials, and collaboration with local Chinese merchants operating as postal agents.

32. Robert Hart to Kopsch, March 17, 1886.

33. Chen Ling-chieh, "Qingmo haiguan yu Da Qing youzheng," 48.

34. Robert Hart to Gustav Detring, September 26, 1877, SHAC, 679 (2) 1898. See also *Service List (1877)*, 2.

35. Rasmussen, *Tientsin*, 76.

36. "Postal Service," IG Circular 90 (2nd ser.), December 22, 1879, in *Docs. Ill.*, 1:402.

Customs Postal Couriers and Early Routes

In the run-up to a public opening, Detring had only a year to put things in order. On March 23, 1878, the route between Beijing and Tianjin was formally inaugurated; it was the first day the experimental postal service was offered to the general public.[37] At this point there were no stamps available, but there was a degree of confidence that things would eventually come together. There were three substantive issues which required immediate attention: stamps, couriers, and route design. Of the three, the issue of stamps was the most straightforward. Detring contacted Campbell in London regarding postal regulations in Britain and France and the cost of stamp-making machines in the former. He also asked Campbell to find out prices for stamp printing in England.[38] Campbell had previously worked in the postmaster general's office in London, and his knowledge and assistance in the CMCS postal project would prove useful.[39] He took the question to the postal printing company De La Rue, but his efforts came to nothing.[40]

Under the pressure of time and budget, Detring decided to proceed with local assistance and had the stamps printed by the CMCS's own printing department. In May 1877 he had begun to collaborate with Benet Palamountain, the manager of the printing office of the Customs Statistical Department in Shanghai. They used a Chinese artisan to engrave a stamp design on copper. Detring wanted the five-candarin stamp to be yellow, the three-candarin stamp red, and the one-candarin stamp blue, but in the end green was used for the one-candarin stamp instead.[41] The

37. "Tientsin Customs Post," Appendix B, in Report (1921), 105.

38. Gustav Detring to James Duncan Campbell, March 5, 1877, in *Qingmo Tianjin haiguan youzheng*, 21–25; James Duncan Campbell to Robert Hart, Z/53, May 11, 1877, in Hart and Campbell, *Archives of China's Imperial Maritime Customs Confidential Correspondence*, 1:272.

39. Robert Ronald Campbell, *James Duncan Campbell*, 92.

40. Reisz, "An Issue of Authority," 11–15.

41. Gustav Detring to F. Hirth (Acting Statistical Secretary), June 15, 1878, in *TYS*, 1:202; Juan Mencarini, "Note on the Postage Stamps of China, 1878–1905," Appendix E, in Report (1905), lxi, lxiv. It was once suggested by German philatelist Herbert Munk and then quoted by Chinese philatelist Chen Tse-chuan that Hosea Ballou Morse was the designer of the first stamp of the Customs Postal Service, but there is at

designs for these three values were essentially retained until 1894, though the size of the stamps themselves were reduced in 1885. Notably, these early batches of Customs-made postage stamps were very close in design to those of the Shanghai Local Post Office that had been issued in 1865.[42] Known as Shanghai Large Dragon stamps, this first batch of stamps had also been printed locally, albeit from engraved wood blocks in a some-what primitive fashion while waiting for permanent-issue postage stamps to arrive from England in early 1866.[43]

Although this was just an experimental project, Detring was bold enough to include the Chinese characters for "Great Qing Post Office" and the image of a five-clawed Chinese dragon, which symbolized the Qing emperor. All three of the stamps shared this dragon image in the middle, with "Great Qing" (Da Qing 大清) characters above it, "Post Office" (Youzhengju 郵政局) characters on the right side, and the value of each stamp on the left side (see fig. 3.1). The stamps became available for the public to purchase in July but were met with some resistance, as reg-ular customers were used to a bookkeeping system and were reluctant to switch.[44]

The charge for a letter of under one-half ounce from Tianjin to Bei-jing was three candarins, which equaled forty-eight cash (copper coins); the charge for a letter to Niuzhuang, Shanghai, or Yantai was five canda-rins (eighty cash).[45] The candarin (also written as *candareen*), was a weight measurement used in China and other countries in East Asia at the time;

---

present no evidence to support this view. Morse, in his third year in the CMCS, was working for Detring in 1877 in Tianjin with the rank of fourth assistant A. As a junior assistant, he was in charge of organizing incoming and outgoing mail for Tianjin Cus-toms. In his writing on the Margary Affair and the history of the Customs Postal Service in *The International Relations*, Morse did not claim involvement in designing the first postage stamp. See Seal, "Translation from Kohl's Handbook," 27; and Chen Tse-chuan, "Haiguan shouci dalong youpiao," 5.

42. Reisz, "An Issue of Authority," 16–17.

43. "Shanghai Stamps," *Times* (London), February 14, 1927. The new postage stamps that arrived from London were designed and printed by Messrs. Nissen and Parker.

44. Gustav Detring to C. L. Simpson (Customs Commissioner at Yantai), July 29, 1878, in *TYS*, 1:207; Gustav Detring to Ls. Rocher (Assistant Chinese Secretary), Au-gust 8, 1878, in *TYS*, 1:212–13.

45. "Postal Notification," May 1, 1878, in *Zhongguo Qingdai youzheng tuji*, 14. The stipulations in the notification were implemented from May 15 onward.

FIGURE 3.1 Customs Postal Service stamps for three values: one, three, and five candarins. The chops on these postage stamps read "Postage is paid, no further request for payment" (*Xin li yi fu, wu suo wu gei* 信力已付 勿索勿给). Source: Tsai Ming-feng, *Ru shi wo ji*, 37, courtesy of the Chunghwa Postal Museum, Taipei.

according to the measurement standard of the Qing period, one tael (*liang* 兩) was ten mace (*qian* 錢), and one mace was ten candarins (*fen* 分); hence, one silver tael was one hundred silver candarins in weight.[46] In 1877, when Hart and Detring decided on the values for the postage stamps, they opted for this traditional unit, but based on Haikwan (Customs) taels (Hk. Tls.). This compared with charges for a letter carried by private hongs, which ranged from fifteen to as much as two hundred cash

46. Burger, *Ch'ing Cash*, 1:16.

in Tianjin or even more depending on the distance. (Postal charges are discussed in detail in chapter 6.)

It is worth explaining the background to the Haikwan tael, the virtual currency used as a unit of account by the CMCS. After the opening of the original five treaty ports in 1842, a uniform rate for the payment of tariffs became an urgent issue. China lacked a uniform currency, and the five treaty ports each had their own local copper cash coinages, each with a different shape, weight, purity, and conversion rate to silver coinage. Different silver coinages, too, were in use—both local and foreign. There was, therefore, an immediate requirement for a common standard, a tael of account to be used across all five ports, "the pure silver value of which should be clearly established in comparison with local taels and foreign dollar coins."[47] Calculated using established commercial conversion rates between Chinese catties and European measures, the weight assigned to the Haikwan tael was 583.20 troy grains of silver one thousand fine.

Transportation was another important issue for Detring to resolve. In spring, summer, and fall, mail was delivered via steamship around the coast and along the Yangtze River. With only a limited budget available, Detring secured the collaboration of the China Merchants' Steam Navigation Company on a temporary basis to deliver mailbags between the northern ports and Shanghai free of charge.[48] Founded in 1873, the company was a joint venture between the Qing government and private merchants that had emerged from the Self-Strengthening Movement. Li Hongzhang was the prime mover behind its foundation. Meanwhile, Li Hongzhang also ordered the Chinese navy to inform the Niuzhuang and Tianjin Customs Houses of the departure schedules of their ships, so that they could also transport mailbags.[49] Detring secured similar assistance from John Swire and Sons' China Navigation Company.[50]

In addition to the coastal routes, it was essential to set up overland lines, especially from December to March, when iced-up ports made reliable transportation by ship impossible. Right from the beginning, nei-

---

47. Stanley F. Wright, *China's Struggle for Tariff Autonomy*, 27–28.
48. Gustav Detring to Tang Tingshu, July 17, 1878, in *TYS*, 1:204.
49. Chen Ling-chieh, "Qingmo haiguan yu Da Qing youzheng," 39–40.
50. Gustav Detring to the IG [Inspector General], September 30, 1878, SHAC, 679 (2) 1930.

ther Detring nor Hart wanted to adopt a method of delivery based on the stagecoach, which was an approach common to the systems of the British General Post Office and the US Post Office Department.[51] Rather, the approach of the military relay courier system was their model for overland delivery. There were four overland lines to organize: Tianjin to Beijing, Tianjin to Niuzhuang, Tianjin to Yantai, and Tianjin to Zhenjiang. Among these four, the Tianjin–Beijing route was the shortest and most straightforward, and it was the first to be established. This line was about 230 *li* (around 140 kilometers) long, and the work to develop the infrastructure and the procedures to bring it into service provided very valuable learning for the creation of the longer routes to follow. The main challenges were associated with personnel, logistics, and, in particular, scheduling in such a way as to meet expectations for the speed of the service. The Tianjin–Zhenjiang line, at two thousand *li* (around 1,240 kilometers), was the longest of the four and faced additional challenges. The following sections focus on the development of these two lines.

Tianjin to Beijing

In order to make a start, Detring turned to Hu Yongan 胡永安, a contracted office porter of the existing postal department.[52] This was a low-ranking role: the postal department belonged to the "Miscellaneous" section within the Revenue Department of the overall CMCS structure, and the *Staff List* in the 1870s and 1880s did not even include "porter" as a listed rank under native staff.[53] Nevertheless, Hu Yongan's prior experience in delivering mail for the CMCS was a useful asset to be retained.

The overland route between Beijing and Tianjin was already familiar to Hu and his men. In continuing to use it, his couriers not only retained the benefit of this familiarity but also had access to the inns and teahouses with which the existing service had built relationships. Issues

---

51. Duncan Campbell-Smith, *Masters of the Post*, 102–5; John, *Spreading the News*, 93–95.

52. Gustav Detring, "Memorandum—Courier Relay Line Tientsin–Peking," enclosed with No. 39/IG, March 26, 1878, SHAC, 679 (2) 1930. Gustav Detring, "Overland Mail Service 1879–80," 15 January 1880, SHAC, 679 (2) 1931.

53. "Memorandum on the Memo of Service," IG Circular 23 (2nd ser.), October 1, 1874, in *Inspector General's Circulars, First Series, 1861–1875*, 527.

with variations in trip time became apparent fairly quickly, however, with major factors being the condition and availability of horses and the state of the roads. The original plan was that Hu's courier team would deliver up to forty catties (eighteen kilograms) of mail within twelve hours when weather conditions were favorable. It soon proved that this level of service was not achievable, and within two months of the service launch, performance was deemed unsatisfactory.

To assess the situation himself, Detring made a dry run on the route to Beijing in February, though during the daytime and without carrying mail.[54] Detring was fond of horse racing, and made a significant contribution to the Race Club in Tianjin from the 1880s onward.[55] But even with his great passion for riding, he found that the planned schedule did indeed prove almost impossible to meet. The reality was that the couriers were having to travel sections of the journey during the night, in the dark, and in the process losing their way more than once. One story involved an experienced hand carrying mail to Beijing. He fell off his horse into a ditch near Caicun, about forty kilometers northwest of Tianjin. He picked himself up and rode on—toward Beijing, he thought. It was four hours before he realized he had been traveling in the wrong direction, arriving back at Yangcun, where he had originally picked up the mail before his fall. His explanation was that the road conditions had rapidly changed from his previous journey along the route, as peasants had plowed the fields and changed the landscape. Solutions were attempted, including changing around the animals in use, to horses in the daytime and donkeys at night, but the whole trip still routinely took seventeen hours, not the twelve originally envisaged.[56]

Learning from these experiences, and from his own dry run, Detring saw that it was necessary to adopt a formal relay system, setting up stations to keep horses dedicated for service use and to provide accommodation for riders; this, of course, meant spending money. On this short line, three relays were set up, in Yangcun, Hexiwu, and Zhangjiawan.[57]

54. Gustav Detring to the IG, June 7, 1878, SHAC, 672 (2) 1930.
55. Rasmussen, *Tientsin*, 78.
56. Detring to the IG, June 7, 1878.
57. "Memorandum—Courier Relay Line Tientsin–Peking," enclosed with No. 39/IG, March 26, 1878, SHAC, 679 (2) 1930.

These three locations were already important in terms of traffic and administration, as they were on the main overland routes and also on the northern section of the Grand Canal system (see fig. 3.2).[58] The combined costs to run these stations comprised (in local silver) fifteen taels per month for rental of premises, seventy-two taels per month salary for twelve couriers, and ninety-six taels in overall expenses for provision of sixteen horses.[59] Couriers were required to wear uniforms that included an official hat and a "black waistcoat with red border and white breast shield" with the Chinese characters for "Tianjin Maritime Customs Postman" (*Jin haiguan xinchai* 津海關信差). Each courier was required to carry a passport (*huzhao* 護照) issued by Detring.[60]

Tianjin to Zhenjiang

Lessons were learned from the setting up of the Tianjin–Beijing line, and a relay system with stations under Customs control was part of the planning from the beginning. The Tianjin–Zhenjiang route was nine times longer than the Tianjin–Beijing line and stretched through three provinces. In geographical terms, the landscape was varied, and included the northern Chinese plains, a mountain range, and complicated water routes including parts of the Huai River, the Yellow River, and the Grand Canal system. This complexity certainly required multiple types of transport. Moreover, as the route covered three provinces, its planning and operation met with considerable political difficulties.

From the time that the CMCS started to transport letters for legations, as well as its own correspondence, the Zhenjiang Customs House had been the location used to consolidate mail bound for the north, which came from Shanghai, from south of Shanghai, and from the Yangtze River. At the same time, all the mail sent from the north through Tianjin to Shanghai and beyond was transmitted to this port before being dispatched to its final destination. While the CMCS postal department had, under less strict time pressure, been able to cope with the task in the previous decade, it was clear that a serious overhaul would be required

58. *Tianjin jianshi*, 27, 57–59.
59. Detring to the IG, June 7, 1878.
60. "Memorandum—Courier Relay Line."

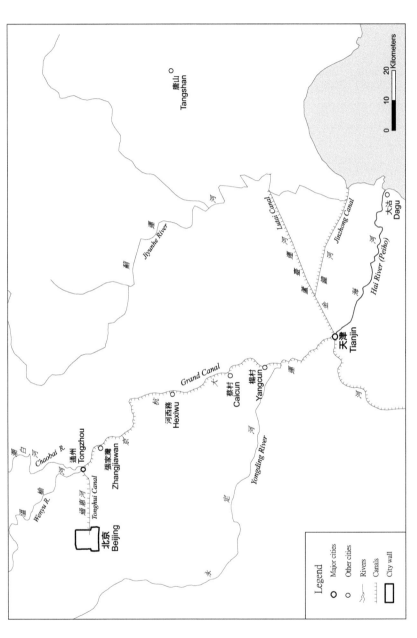

FIGURE 3.2 The postal route between Tianjin and Beijing, 1878. The relay stops were Yangcun, Hexiwu, and Zhangjiawan. Map © Weipin Tsai; cartography by Huang Chingchi.

before the service on this line could be extended to the general public. The route also had to rely to an even greater extent on collaboration with Chinese firms, which ended up running postal branches on the CMCS's behalf and whose activities were, as we shall see, to lead to some embarrassment for the service.

From a logistics and route-planning point of view, the line was divided into five long sections. The first section was from Tianjin to Dezhou, with ten relay stations; the second was from Quliudian to Taian, with eight relays; the third was from Chijiazhuang to Yizhou, with seven relays; the fourth was from Lijiazhuang to Zhongxingji, with seven relays; and the final section was from Yugou to Guazhou, with ten relays (see fig. 3.3). This complex arrangement was organized by Tong Zaitian 佟在田, who had been a low-grade military guard in Tianjin but who had some useful local connections. Each section of the line was placed in the charge of one designated Chinese, recruited by Tong. The first trial batch of mail was handed over in Zhenjiang on December 16, 1878, and arrived in Tianjin after twelve days; the second trial batch was sent on December 19, and took eleven days. Tianjin Customs also made three dispatches to Zhenjiang around the same time, and they took between thirteen and seventeen days to arrive.[61] While the relay seemed to work well for the first few runs, very soon the mail from Tianjin to Zhenjiang was being confiscated by Shandong officials, which disrupted the arrangements for the line. The reasons for the mail confiscation were twofold: the obstructive attitude of the local officials toward the postal project and the unstable nature of the collaboration between the CMCS and local merchants.

Scandal and the Customs *Po-ssu-ta*

From the very beginning of his work, Detring had formed the view that it was necessary to work with private letter hongs for the transmission of mail.[62] In June 1878 he wrote, "My chief study has been and is still, the

61. Gustav Detring to the IG, February 15, 1879, SHAC, 679 (2) 1931.
62. "Memorandum in Reply to IG's Memorandum concerning Postal Scheme," March 1877, in *Qingmo Tianjin haiguan youzheng*, 47–48.

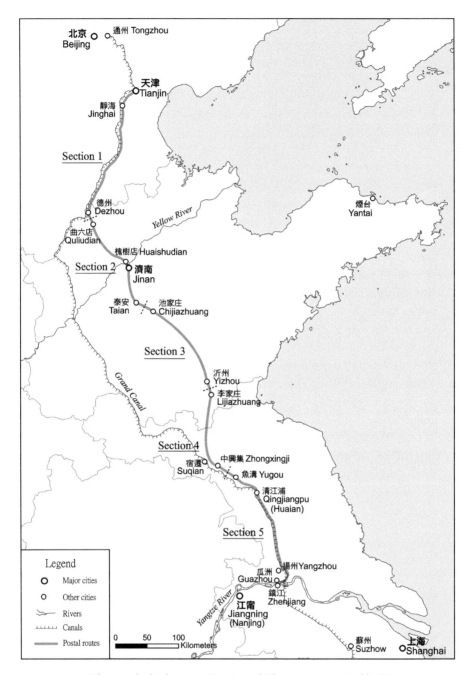

FIGURE 3.3 The postal relay between Tianjin and Zhenjiang, organized by Tong Zaitian, 1878. The route was divided into five sections; Jinan was included in section two. Map © Weipin Tsai; cartography by Huang Chingchi.

treatment of Chinese mail matters; my object being to bring, by agreement, under our control the existing private postal establishments, and make them act as collectors and distributors of mail matters of Chinese origin."[63] When Hu Yongan's team encountered difficulty in running the Tianjin–Beijing line due to lack of sufficient manpower and horses, Detring quickly engaged a private mail courier, Decheng letter hong (德成信局), to take over the delivery work while Hu put his house in order.[64]

At the same time, Detring, through a member of the CMCS staff, Wu Huan 吳煥, brought the collaboration between the CMCS and local merchants to another level with the creation of a new type of enterprise styled as the Chinese-Foreign Postal Agency (Hua yang shu xin guan 華洋書信館) (see fig. 3.4). Branches were opened in several northern cities covered by the CMCS overland postal service. Wu Huan, a writer within the CMCS, was transferred from Yantai to Beijing to assist the postal project in October 1877.[65] Wu had worked for Detring when the latter was in charge of Yantai, and it would seem likely that he was trusted by Detring. He turned out to be an ideal middleman to talk to Chinese counterparts and, acting as Detring's representative, he was sent to initiate postal discussions in Beijing, Shanghai, Tianjin, and Yantai. He was also a key individual in creating the Chinese-Foreign Postal Agency scheme.[66]

Detring's postal project rapidly became known to the locals in Tianjin, and he was soon approached by Dachang 大昌, a long-standing commercial firm in the city. The firm already had branches in Beijing, other northern ports, and Shanghai, and would also be willing to set up a new branch in Niuzhuang. According to Detring, Dachang's manager, Liu Guifang 劉桂芳, was "a man of good intelligence and understands the

63. Detring to the IG, June 7, 1878. During the winter season, letters from other Yangtze River ports were also instructed to be sent to Zhenjiang for transmittal to the north; see Gustav Detring to Commissioners of Custom at Ningpo, Hankow, Wuhu, Kiukiang, November 23, 1878, TMA, W2-2.

64. "Memorandum for Postal Department IG of Customs," Gustav Detring to the IG, May 29, 1878, TMA, W2-2.

65. *Service List (1877)*, 39; *Service List (1880)*, 42.

66. Detring to the IG, June 7, 1878; Gustav Detring to James Hart, Customs Commissioner of Shanghai, November 22, 1878, in *TYS*, 1:223.

回信仍送前門打磨廠西頭
路北玉隆店內華洋書信館

FIGURE 3.4 Two designs of the many franking marks used by the Chinese-Foreign Postal Agency at different branches. On the left is a chop for a branch in Tianjin, bearing the details of year, month, and date in the Chinese calendar. On the right is a chop that carries the text for an instruction that letters in response should be delivered to the same agency and gives its location. Source: Padget, *The Postal Markings of China*, 26.

importance of the postal scheme."[67] Detring agreed to enter into a close collaboration with Dachang, based on the following principles: first, the postal shops set up by Dachang in the specified locations would bear the name Chinese-Foreign Postal Agency. Second, the costs of opening the branches would be borne by Dachang itself. Third, the postage rates would be set by Dachang, on a provisional basis, in order to compete with local private letter hongs, and for domestic letters there was no insistence on the use of postage stamps—the public would be

67. Detring to the IG, September 30, 1878.

permitted to pay on the same basis as with private letter hongs. Fourth, the mail items collected by the Chinese-Foreign Postal Agency were to be packed separately, but would be transported together with mail collected by the Customs Postal Service and have access to services by steamship from those companies that had entered into partnership with the service. In return, the Chinese-Foreign Postal Agency would transmit to local recipients the Chinese letters delivered to their locations by the CMCS postal couriers. Finally, postage fees collected by the Chinese-Foreign Postal Agency would be retained by them until further changes were announced.[68] The scheme was initially put into operation in Beijing, Shanghai, Tianjin and Yantai in June 1878; it was extended to Niuzhuang in July.[69] What this collaboration actually meant in practice was that the Chinese-Foreign Postal Agency became the CMCS's own private letter hong and it opened branches in multiple locations. The close relationship between the CMCS and the agency was in evidence on the mailbags that were used in different ports: the bags carried the English words "Chinese Postal Service Customs House" and the Chinese characters for the Chinese-Foreign Postal Agency.[70]

Tong Zaitian, who put together the Tianjin–Zhenjiang line, was in fact, a friend of Liu Guifang's son and had been recommended to Detring by Liu Guifang and Wu Huan. What had not been revealed, however, was that Tong had a bad record, including cases of being involved in physical violence. Detring only found this out when he asked Li Hongzhang to issue five passports for the couriers, and the news came as a surprise. But instead of insisting on calling a halt to the arrangements installed by Tong, Li supported moving forward and expressed the hope that Tong might use this opportunity to prove his trustworthiness.[71] Unfortunately, in late December 1878, problems arose. Mailbags were

68. Detring to the IG, September 30, 1878. For steamship companies also delivering the mail collected by the Chinese-Foreign Postal Agency, see Detring to Commissioners of Custom at Shanghai, Yantai, Niuzhuang and Tianjin, August 6, 1878, in *TYS*, 1:209–11.

69. Gustav Detring to G. Hughs (Customs Commissioner of Niuzhuang), July 20, 1878, in *TYS*, 1:205.

70. Gustav Detring to Commissioners of Custom at Shanghai, Yantai, Niuzhuang and Tianjin, August 6, 1878, in *TYS*, 1:210.

71. Gustav Detring to R. Bredon (Deputy IG), January 4, 1879, in *TYS*, 1:240–41.

confiscated at Taian, a town south of Jinan, the provincial capital of Shandong, and the couriers were detained. Tong Zaitian disappeared. The Shandong authority questioned the right of the couriers to wear uniforms, use flags, and carry weapons during the night. They also challenged whether the couriers should be allowed to use horses as a means of transportation.[72]

A large part of the Tianjin–Zhenjiang line went through Shandong Province, but it had not occurred to Detring to smooth the relationship with the Shandong governor and other local officials before charging ahead with the service.[73] Neither had he realized that the introduction of the Chinese-Foreign Postal Agency would be seen as the creation of a new, direct competitor by private letter hongs. This situation was not helped by the poor relationship between Li Hongzhang and the Shandong governor, Wenge 文格 (1822–93); Li had not informed Wenge about the postal plan in advance on account of their mutual antipathy.[74] Even though the mailbags were later released, the Chinese-Foreign Postal Agency was expelled from Jinan.

Li Hongzhang was displeased by Wenge's actions, and believed them to have been made out of ignorance. One of the reasons given by Wenge for seeking to forbid access to the Customs Postal Service was to prevent foreigners from becoming too well informed about inland China. Li thought this a wholly ridiculous reason, as he believed there was no way to prevent foreigners from acquiring such information. That said, Li also blamed Hart for not having provided a detailed report on the plan before going on leave. Li repeated what he had already said to the Zongli Yamen—that, after Hart's return, the government should think about extending the role of the superintendents of trade for both northern and southern ports to include supervision of the postal service; of course, that would mean that he himself should be involved in the decision-making.[75]

72. Gustav Detring to the Customs Superintendent Zheng [Zaoru], January 13, 1879, in *Jin haiguan mi dang*, 9–10.

73. Detring to the IG, February 15, 1879.

74. Gustav Detring to R. Bredon (Deputy IG), January 5, 1879, in *TYS*, 1:241–42.

75. Li Hongzhang, "Fu Jin haiguan Zheng guancha" 復津海關鄭觀察 [Response to the Superintendent of Tianjin Customs Zheng Yuxuan], Guangxu reign year 4, month 12, day 19 (January 11, 1879), in "Peng liao han gao," *juan* 18:25–26, in Li Hongzhang, *Li Wenzhonggong quan shu*.

An interesting aside is the fact that Customs postal couriers continued to run the service throughout this time; no one seemed to want to directly pull the plug on the service or to question the use of the name printed on the postage stamps, Great Qing Post Office.

Detring decided to close the route put together by Tong Zaitian and set up his own through centralizing the other three postal lines under his supervision. He introduced a hierarchical structure with three levels of responsibility: courier chief (*zong xinchai* 總信差), stationmaster (*xunyi* 巡役), and courier (*xinchai* 信差). He appointed Hu Yongan as courier chief to lead all couriers of the four postal lines. It was Hu's job to put teams together and be responsible for their conduct. In order to reconstruct the Tianjin–Zhenjiang connection, as well as to replace their lost base in Jinan, Detring and Hu found alternative locations so that logistics could be replanned. They identified Jinghai and Qihe.[76]

Jinghai, sixty *li* (around 37 kilometers) south of Tianjin, was a river town set against the Grand Canal and the Ziya River, one of the five major tributaries of the Hai River system in northern China. While Tianjin acted as the hub for the Tianjin–Beijing and Tianjin–Niuzhuang routes, Jinghai shared the burden of administration and became the secondary hub for the two south-facing lines, Tianjin to Yantai and Tianjin to Zhenjiang. After the original postal operation had to leave Jinan, Qihe was its replacement. Qihe was on the northwest side of the Yellow River and therefore well positioned to oversee mail crossing the river in both the Yantai and Zhenjiang directions. After crossing the Yellow River, the mail was carried by donkey, mule, or pony to Qingjiangpu (Huaiyin today) in northern Jiangsu Province. From Qingjiangpu to Zhenjiang, small, fast boats were used.[77] Mail from Tianjin to Zhenjiang was dispatched at noon on Tuesday, Thursday, and Saturday. Light mail from Zhenjiang to Tianjin was dispatched on Monday, Wednesday, and Saturday. Heavy mail delivery would be scheduled when mail from Europe arrived via Shanghai. The whole line was maintained by three Customs porters and thirty-nine couriers (fig. 3.5).

76. "Overland Mail Service 1879–80 Organization, Estimated Expenditure," Gustav Detring to the IG, January 15, 1880, SHAC, 679 (2) 1931.

77. In "Overland Mail Service 1879–80," Detring made a mistake in stating that Qihe was east of Jinan.

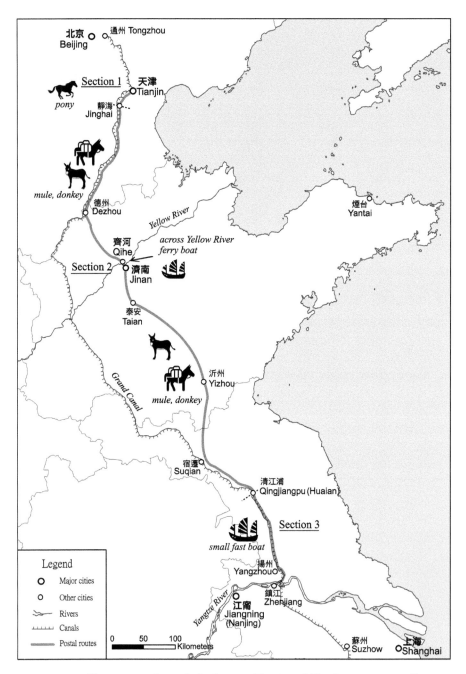

FIGURE 3.5 The reorganized postal relay between Tianjin and Zhenjiang, 1879–1880. Due to the variation in the landscape, ponies, donkeys, and mules were employed as well as small, fast boats. Following the interruption in Jinan the previous winter, a new station was set up in Qihe. Map © Weipin Tsai; cartography by Huang Chingchi.

Table 3.1. Four routes' comparison, overland winter mail service, 1879–1880

	Tainjin to Beijing	Tianjin to Niuzhuang	Tianjin/Jinghai to Zhenjiang	Qihe to Yantai
Distance in *li* (kilometers)	250 (155)	1,200 (743)	2,000 (1,238)	850 (526)
Service months in winter	3	4	3	3
Transit time	Around 20 hours	8 days	Light mail: 12 days Heavy mail / mail from Europe: 16 days	6–7 days
Dispatch days	Daily	From Tianjin: varied, depending on arrival of mail from Europe. From Niuzhuang: every Saturday noon.	From Tianjin: Tuesday, Thursday, Saturday noon. From Zhenjiang: Monday, Wednesday, Saturday.	Wednesday (both locations)
Dispatch runs over the whole winter season	n/a	32	30 (Tianjin to Zhenjiang) 40 (Zhenjiang to Tianjin)	22
Estimated expenditure (in Hk. Tls.)	492	384	1,400	110

Source: Information extracted from "Postal Notification—Overland Winter Mail Service, 1879–1880" and "Overland Mail Service 1879–1880 Organization, Estimated Expenditure," enclosures in Gustav Detring to IG, January 15, 1880, SHAC 679 (2) 1931.

In addition to the broken relay system, problems encountered in the collaboration with the Chinese-Foreign Postal Agency also required a major rethink as the matter escalated into a national scandal. A report from the commissioner of Customs at Zhenjiang, James Twinem, outlined the situation, noting that the conditions under which the collaboration between Dachang and Detring had been agreed were not always faithfully observed. For example, rather than using the funds of Dachang, Wu

Huan set up a Chinese-Foreign Postal Agency branch in Zhenjiang within a large building rented by the CMCS. The upper part of the building was used as accommodation for a married tidewaiter of the CMCS, and the lower part was, during the winter courier season, used as an office and divided into two parts, with one handling foreign mail and one handling Chinese mail. The same tidewaiter was assigned to manage foreign mail during the winter courier season, while some Chinese were employed by Wu to manage the Chinese mail. In addition to the question of housing, the courier system of the Chinese-Foreign Postal Agency soon showed that it was inadequate, not least in the provision of horses. The situation forced Twinem to request assistance from the superintendent of Customs and the couriers of the Zongli Yamen, in order to deliver mail for Beijing.[78]

When Hart returned to Europe with his family in 1878, he took the opportunity to attend the Universal Exposition in Paris. On that occasion he was asked about postal services in China, and the likely moment when China might join the Universal Postal Union. Knowing that the CMCS had only recently started to bring postal services to the general public, Hart took the firm view that China was not yet ready to join the union. On his return to Beijing after the first winter postal experiment, it was time for Hart to reflect on what had and had not worked. His first challenge was to manage Detring, who told him that he had received no thanks but only criticism. Insisting that he had "nothing to hide, nothing to regret," Detring nonetheless added that he did not want to become a source of embarrassment for the service and would be happy to step down from the management of postal affairs.[79] But instead of removing him from postal responsibilities, Hart formally appointed Detring as his commissioner for postal matters and entrusted him with regulating the working of the postal departments at the various Customs Houses.[80]

Detring decided to cut off all connection with the Chinese-Foreign Postal Agency. He made a public notification of this decision and gave the CMCS postal departments a rather creative Chinese name, keeping

78. James Twinem, "Reply to Queries concerning Postal Service," July 14, 1879, SHAC, 679 (2) 674.
79. Detring to the IG, February 15, 1879.
80. IG Circular 89 (2nd ser.), December 22, 1879, in *Docs. Ill.*, 1:401–2.

the sound of "post": *po-ssu-ta* 撥駟達, which literally means "to dispatch a four-horse carriage to reach destinations swiftly."[81] The Customs' rapid separation from the Chinese-Foreign Postal Agency meant that Customs staff had themselves to take on the tasks not only of delivering mail between the northern treaty ports and Beijing but also of delivering letters to recipients, as far as was possible, within those cities. For the inland mail in areas where they had no reach, they would need to work with selected local private letter hongs.

Despite Detring's decision to end all association with the Chinese-Foreign Postal Agency, the latter had already made a substantial impact on the postal market and its activities had long passed out of his control. Detring had entered into collaboration with Liu Guifang's Dachang firm in 1878 with the intention of taking the Customs Postal Service into the Chinese market in a fairly limited way. He claimed he did not realize at the time that his assistant Wu Huan had a far larger business opportunity in mind. Wu, acting as Detring's representative, used the Chinese-Foreign Postal Agency to attract funds from the public. Hart was not pleased to learn that the CMCS had become attached to an entrepreneur's commercial venture.

Public Confusion and a Mess to Clean Up

Wu Huan had gone far beyond his original remit, turning the Chinese-Foreign Postal Agency into his own—increasingly substantial—business. He achieved this by promoting his business in the five treaty ports and along the Yangtze River through emphasizing its association with the CMCS. On July 22, that year, *Shenbao*, the most popular daily newspaper in the Chinese language at the time, printed an advertisement to announce the opening of the Chinese-Foreign Postal Agency in Shanghai, and declared that a shareholding company had been set up. The advertisement said the company was the forerunner of the Chinese Post Office, and that it already had branches in the five northern treaty ports.

---

81. "Haiguan Po-ssu-ta gaobai" 海關撥駟達告白 [Postal notification], January 11, 1880, in *TYS*, 1:275–77, my translation.

It announced that a new branch was to be opened on the "third road" in Shanghai, close to many newspaper presses, teahouses, and hotels. It also forecast that detailed postal regulations would be published in the near future.[82]

Sure enough, on September 4, a long article titled "Preface to the Regulations of the Chinese-Foreign Postal Agency" ("Hua yang shuxinguan zhangcheng xu" 華洋書信館章程序) was published, providing a narrative intended to strengthen the agency's position as a patriotic and nationalistic enterprise to protect China's postal rights. Claiming to have Detring's support and Li Hongzhang's authorization, the article reported that the Chinese-Foreign Postal Agency would eventually expand to the Yangtze River area, inland China, and Southeast Asia. It claimed the new establishment would not hurt the business of the private letter hongs and expressed the belief that the agency would benefit the future establishment of China's national post office.[83] In its notification on the postage rates for various distances, the agency differentiated itself from other private letter hongs by imitating the style and content of the narrative used in the Customs Postal Service. For example, for the Tianjin–Zhenjiang line, there were twenty-two stops with forty-four stables and eighty-eight horses; the relay for this line should complete each sixty *li* in four hours, and complete the whole trip in ten days, whatever the weather.[84]

A week later, *Shenbao* published an editorial on its cover page to promote the Chinese-Foreign Postal Agency, which deliberately raised the firm to semiofficial status. The article, "On the Benefit of the Establishment of the Chinese-Foreign Postal Agency," carefully painted this commercial postal opportunity as part of a government and merchant joint venture by adopting Western methods. It also asked questions intended to provoke a patriotic reaction from its readers: If Japan could have a Western-style post office, why should China not have one, too? Why should China not have a postal establishment that would allow the gen-

82. "Xin she Hua yang shuxinguan" 新設華洋書信館 [On the newly established Chinese-Foreign Postal Agency], *Shenbao*, July 22, 1878.

83. "Hua yang shuxinguan zhangcheng xu" 華洋書信館章程序 [Preface to the regulations of the Chinese-Foreign Postal Agency], *Shenbao*, September 4, 1878.

84. "Hua yang shuxinguan xin she ma di xiangxi zhangcheng" 華洋書信館新設馬遞詳細章程 [Detailed regulations for the horse-run delivery service of the Chinese-Foreign Postal Agency], in Sun Junyi, *Qingdai youchuo zhi*, 56.

eral public to become its shareholders? Why should the mail courier business be dominated by a few wealthy Ningbo and Shaoxing merchants?[85]

The initial target for capital fundraising was Hk. Tls. 100,000, divided into one thousand shares, with individuals able to purchase up to one hundred shares each. After a person had purchased fifty shares, he or she was permitted to nominate a person to work for the Postal Agency. It was noted that the initial capital was intended to support around one hundred branches, and further waves of fundraising might be launched for later expansion.[86] It is unclear whether Detring was aware of the commercial plans of the Chinese-Foreign Postal Agency and that both his own and Li Hongzhang's names were being used to promote the selling of shares. It had been apparent from the Shandong incident that Detring did not at that point shy away from his association with the agency and indeed had defended it as a "beneficial establishment."[87] But this does not necessarily imply complicity in the broader commercial venture. According to the content of an apologetic letter from Wu Huan to Detring in 1881, it appears that Detring had been in the dark about this aspect and found out about it from newspapers.[88]

Wu Huan played a big part in the scheme, and managed to persuade Twinem to support him by claiming that Hart, Detring, and Li Hongzhang had already approved the share-offering plan. With Twinem's acquiescence, Wu gained support from the Customs superintendent of Zhenjiang, and later asked Shen Baozhen, who was the superintendent of trade in the southern ports at the time, to approve the share-offering plan so the company could set up branches at the treaty ports in the Yangtze River area. Hart learned about the proceedings not from any of these parties but from the acting deputy commissioner at Jiujiang Customs House, E. T. Holwill. Hart was astonished, and he ordered a full investigation.[89]

85. "Lun chuang she Hua yang shuxinguan zhi li" 論創設華洋書信館之利 [On the benefit of establishing the Chinese-Foreign Postal Agency], *Shenbao*, September 11, 1878.

86. "Hua yang shuxinguan zhaoshang rugu," 3–4.

87. Detring to the IG, February 15, 1879.

88. Wu Huan to Gustav Detring, April 11, 1881, TMA, W1-9-2138.

89. "Hua yang shuxinguan" 華洋書信館 [Chinese-Foreign Postal Agency], in *TYS*, 1:333.

Detring was on leave when Hart found out about the affair. Colin Jamieson and H. E. Hobson, Customs commissioners who were deputizing for Detring, instigated the investigation on Hart's behalf. It was discovered that Liu Guifang of the Dachang company had dropped out of the scheme in 1879, and the whole of the franchised business had been placed under Wu Huan's management. Although Detring had indeed terminated the formal institutional connections between the CMCS Postal Service and the Chinese-Foreign Postal Agency, both institutions still transmitted letters for each other between Beijing and Tianjin daily, and mailbags used by the agency still bore the words "Chinese Postal Service, Customs House."[90] Acting on Hart's instruction to clean up the mess, Hobson told the manager of the Chinese-Foreign Postal Agency at Tianjin, Qiu Lansun 邱蘭孫, to close down the CMCS's account and asked him to return all mailbags. He also told Qiu to remove the English words "Post Office" from the board hanging in the agency's doorway. At the same time, Tianjin Customs put out a large notice at the front entrance to declare that it had no connection with the agency.[91] Wu Huan was ordered to close all Chinese-Foreign Postal Agency branches in other cities, and it turned out that the agency had run up debts amounting to Hk. Tls. 7,900. The CMCS agreed to reimburse Hk. Tls. 2,000, but not more, and Wu Huan was dismissed by the end of 1882.[92]

After ending the trouble associated with the Chinese-Foreign Postal Agency, Hart turned his focus internally to the CMCS's postal departments. He kept what Detring and Hu Yongan had put together for the courier relay system on those routes, and he also unified rules for using funds for postal matters, announcing a series of regulations on the use of postage stamps and on the operation of a franking system for both Customs mail and letters from the general public. Hart applied new ethical practice requirements on all staff dealing with letters, including imposition of restricted access to letter boxes, and introduced a prohibition on employees communicating "to any person other than his official superiors any knowledge which he gains in the doing of his work, either as to

90. "Hua Yang Shu Hsin Kuan," Colin Jamieson to Robert Hart, July 26, 1882, SHAC, 679 (2) 1932.

91. H. E. Hobson to Robert Hart, November 8, 1882, SHAC, 679 (2) 1932.

92. "Hua yang shuxinguan," in *TYS*, 1:334; *Service List (1883)*, 118.

the names of the writers and addresses of letters or as to any other matter."[93] The letter box placed at CMCS postal departments was to be accessible daily from 7:00 a.m. to 7:00 p.m. for all who wished to post letters, and the postal officer was to be available daily, except Sundays, from 11:00 a.m. to 5:00 p.m. to sign chit books, register letters, sell stamps, and answer inquiries.[94] Knowing Chinese customers were used to the practice of private letter hongs, for which recipients often paid either all or half the postage on delivery and had concerns that affixed postage stamps might be removed en route, Hart required that a chop be stamped on all Chinese letter covers reading "the postage is paid, no further request for payment" (*xin li yi fu wu suo wu gei* 信力已付 勿索勿給; for stamps bearing these marks, see fig. 3.1).[95]

After Hart cut off all connections with the Chinese-Foreign Postal Agency, the Customs Postal Service at the treaty ports continued to work with local private letter hongs, but without setting up joint franchises. The Customs Postal Service also quietly expanded from the original realm of five treaty ports and the lower Yangtze River area farther south, to Wenzhou.[96] In addition to Detring, Customs commissioner Henry Kopsch also expressed interest in postal matters. Alongside Hart and Detring, over the following decade Kopsch was to become a key figure in the push for a national post office.

One thing worth noting is that the Customs Postal Service was not the only communications-related project that followed from the Margary Affair. A new government-led, treaty-port-based communications system was also launched, known as the Wenbao bureaux (Wenbaoju, 文報局). Chapter 4 will explore how the establishment of this service intensified a sense of competition between Hart and Li Hongzhang and how it impacted efforts to establish a national post office.

93. "Customs Post Offices," enclosure, in IG Circular 202 / Postal No. 3, November 21, 1882, 5, TMA, W2-1-2833.

94. IG Circular 202 / Postal No. 3, December 23, 1882, in *Inspector General's Postal Circulars 1–89*, 5, TMA, W2-1-2833.

95. Hart wrote, "Each cover or article of Chinese mail matter distributed should be marked with a stamp showing that postage is paid and that no fee or gratuity is to be paid to the letter-carrier." IG Circular 205 / Postal No. 5, December 22, 1882, in *Inspector General's Postal Circulars 1–89*, 8, TMA, W2-1-2833.

96. IG Circular 204 / Postal Circular 4, December 22, 1882, 6.

THE OLD IMPERIAL
POST OFFICE, PEKING.

CHAPTER FOUR

All Eyes on the Prize

When Japanese troops landed in Taiwan in 1874 in what was effectively an act of war, it became very clear to the Qing government that a telegraph system was needed.[1] This awareness, shared by both the Zongli Yamen and provincial governors, underpinned a series of projects on telegraph and railways from the second half of the 1870s onward. Building on existing efforts of the China Merchants' Steam Navigation Company, a key figure in this development was Li Hongzhang. Indeed, while Robert Hart patiently worked to establish the so-called Customs Po-ssu-ta (Customs Postal Service) from the late 1870s onward, Li was chief among his competitors to claim the prize of establishing a national post office. Although there was still no immediate plan for abolishing or replacing the military relay courier system (because there was no clear alternative), the broader issue of communications was beginning to as-

---

1. Baark, *Lightning Wires*, chap. 5; Yongming Zhou, *Historicizing Online Politics*, 23–31; Halsey, *Quest for Power*, 220–22.

sert itself as an important topic for both central and local governments. Li's reservations around giving Hart responsibility for both the postal service and the mint, shown in his letters to both Shen Baozhen and the Zongli Yamen during the negotiations following the Margary Affair, hint at his efforts to clip the wings of British influence, efforts that extended into the 1880s and became more apparent as time went on.

The prime of Li's influence came in the late 1870s and reached its peak in the run-up to the First Sino-Japanese War (1894–95). Although Li was not one of the Zongli Yamen ministers during this period, major issues related to military training, large industrial projects, and important questions relating to foreign affairs required consulting Li, and his views mattered—in some cases carrying even more weight than those of the Zongli Yamen.[2] He held the position of the viceroy of Zhili for twenty-five years, apart from a period of one hundred days of mourning when he was on leave. Li skillfully maintained a friendly but equal distance from both Prince Gong and Prince Chun and did not get involved in competition between the two brothers. Although he was against Emperor Tongzhi's plans for repairing the Summer Palace in 1873, Li expressed this opposition very delicately, in such a way that it did not harm his relationship with Empress Dowager Cixi; in fact, the latter's trust in Li only increased over the years that followed.[3] While Prince Gong was stripped of his official positions in both the Grand Council and the Zongli Yamen by Empress Dowager Cixi in 1884, Li was entrusted with negotiations over the Sino-French War.

The death of Shen Baozhen in 1879 transferred the weight of naval development from south to north, and this brought Li closer to Germany, while his distance from Britain increased.[4] Li became very friendly with Gustav Detring, who was his "right-hand man in all foreign and not a few native affairs." Observing the intimate relationship between these two men, Paul King, an established Customs commissioner who spent a lot of time with both men early on in his career,

2. Tsai Chen-feng, *Wan Qing waiwubu*, 44–46.
3. Xie Shicheng, *Li Hongzhang ping zhuan*, 226–32.
4. Chang Ken-ming, "Cong renshi dao rentong," chap. 4; Liu Zhenhua, "Li Fengbao, Xu Jianyin."

noted, "It was an open secret that the I.G. [Inspector General Hart] was not too well pleased with the limitation of his autocratic power which resulted from the Viceroy's ægis over Detring. . . . Both he [Detring] and the Viceroy were fond of playing at politics and many were the 'all night' sittings, at the Yamen, to which the Tientsin Commissioner was summoned."[5] In the race between Britain and Germany to sell military equipment and ships to China from the mid-1870s onward, Li also developed a close association with the German minister, Max von Brandt (1835–1920). These developments were to have an impact on Hart's postal plans.

Hart needed to tread carefully at the edge of a realm increasingly shared between Li and the Zongli Yamen, while at the same time the Zongli Yamen had to balance its own inclinations with those of Li. The First Sino-Japanese War brought about a change in the political climate that impacted the popularity of Li as well as the fortune of Hart's postal proposal. A year after the signing of the Shimonoseki Treaty that ended the war, the Great Qing Imperial Post Office (IPO) was formally established. But this outcome was far from preordained. Between the launch of the Customs Postal Service in 1878 and that of the IPO in 1896, various parties were active in discussions or exchanges of memoranda exploring various differing perspectives on a national post office and this phenomenon marked a significant change from the previous rejection of the idea by Qing officials in the 1860s after reading the "Bystander's View." Another sign of change was that Li, working with other provincial governors, initiated a postal experiment quite separate from Hart's initiative. This initiative was known by the name Wenbao bureaux (Wenbaoju, 文報局). *Wenbao* had, for centuries, been the name given to official correspondence; appending *ju* added the meaning "office." The setting up of Wenbao bureaux, taken together with the activities of foreign post offices, the private letter hongs, the Customs Postal Service, and, of course, the military relay courier system meant that China found itself in an era that saw the coexistence of multiple postal systems, each with its own focus but with many areas of overlap and even competition.

5. King, *In the Chinese Customs Service*, 72, 74.

The Wenbao Bureaux

Wenbao bureaux is a loose term for the semiofficial mail service that started in 1876 and ended around 1912 with the complete abolition of the military relay courier system.[6] There was no centrally controlled organization, and in most cases, local governments were the main initiators of the bureaux in their provinces. Within this thirty-five-year history, there were four types of Wenbao bureau. The first type was initially set up in Shanghai and Tianjin to handle communications with Chinese embassies abroad. The second began to open at major treaty ports and provincial capitals from the 1880s onward, handling official mail between local and central administrations and also enabling local administrations to communicate directly with one another.[7] Not all provinces had Wenbao bureaux, and the term *bureau* was merely a label used by people at the time to refer to the mail system. The bureaux themselves tended to be attached either to offices of the China Merchants' Steam Navigation Company or to local shops.

The third type is exemplified by the bureaux opened in Taiwan, initially for military purposes, in the year 1877. The fourth type focused on China's periphery. Starting in 1907 in the northeast provinces, this type of Wenbao bureau was rapidly adopted across both Outer Mongolia and southeast China, notably in Guangdong, Guangxi, Guizhou, and Yunnan.[8] The key reason for the establishment of Wenbao bureaux in these areas was to retain the original military relay courier system budget within these provinces while at the same time combining traditional relay methods, largely dependent on horses, with telegraph and railways.[9] A significant

6. While most Wenbao bureaux ceased operation following abolition of the military relay courier system, they continued in Northeast China until 1914. Zhang Yi, *Zhonghua youzhengshi*, 174.

7. Wang Menghsiao, "Qingdai moye zhi wenbaoju," 2; Yanxing [Pan Ansheng], *Zhonghua youzheng fazhanshi*, 221.

8. Zhang Yi, *Zhonghua youzhengshi*, 171–73.

9. Zhao Erxun 趙爾巽, "Feng sheng wenbao yi di zhe," 奉省文報驛遞摺 [Memorial on Wenbao bureau and relayed mail in Fengtian Province], Guangxu reign year 33, month 4, day 8 (May 19, 1907), in *ZJYS*, 185–86; Xu Shichang 徐世昌, "Feng sheng xian

volume of mail from these bureaux was handed to the IPO where the latter had a presence locally.[10]

In most existing scholarship on Chinese postal history, the Wenbao bureaux system has been collectively described as a contingent project brought in to remedy the broken functioning of the military relay courier system. The consensus has largely been that the initiative was a misplaced or mistaken scheme, doomed to failure.[11] While these views have validity, there are nevertheless important aspects of the scheme that reveal much about the mindset of the Chinese officials who created the Wenbao bureaux and their overall intent for the broader communications framework at the time, and it is clear that their efforts largely fulfilled the purpose for which they were designed. Rather than adopting the Customs Postal Service, the Wenbao bureaux system was the specific invention of Chinese officials, intended to accommodate their needs by instituting a better system of information exchange for both official and personal mail between administrative hubs, and between these hubs and Beijing. The Wenbao bureaux integrated multiple postal systems, and in relation to the Customs Postal Service became both competitors and collaborators.

The bureaux system was not—and was never intended to be—a replacement for the military relay courier system, as right from its origin, the bureaux's function included transmission of officials' private letters (which were not allowed to be transmitted through the military relay courier system) and there was provision in the budget to support this purpose. In 1876 Guo Songtao proposed to the Qing government the setting up of a system for Chinese diplomats abroad to be able to communicate with the homeland. In his six-clause regulation proposal, one critical point related to private mail: Guo stated that the Shanghai Wenbao bureau would hand family letters to trustworthy private letter hongs and that the bureau should absorb the cost of postage of under one thousand cop-

ji sheli wenbaoju" 奉省現既設立文報局 [Memorial: Fengtian Province has set up Wenbao bureau], Guangxu reign year 33, month 7, day 27 (September 4, 1907), in *ZJYS*, 191–93.

10. *Jiaotongshi youzheng bian*, 1:27.

11. Yanxing [Pan Ansheng], *Zhonghua youzheng fazhanshi*, 223. Zhang Yi, *Zhonghua youzhengshi*, 173.

per cash for each letter.[12] The costs of running a bureau were included in the budget of each Chinese embassy abroad, and this was ultimately funded from Customs revenue.[13] The ministers had the right to nominate people to work in the bureau.

Wenbao bureaux were closely involved with the China Merchants' Steam Navigation Company, which had been transmitting mail for officials on the coast prior to 1876. Guo Songtao nominated Huang Huihe 黃惠和, an employee of the company who enjoyed the personal trust of Li Hongzhang, to take charge of the task.[14] Huang had previously studied in England and spoke English well. In 1878, at the suggestion of Li, the Shanghai Wenbao bureau was expanded to manage mail matters for Chinese diplomats in Germany, Japan, and the United States.[15] Monthly expenditure reports illustrate which items were included in the parcels to embassies abroad, with postage paid for both Chinese and foreign steam companies: telegraph messages and the newspapers *Shenbao*, the *News* (*Xinwenbao* 新聞報), *A Review of the Times* (*Wanguo gongbao* 萬國公報), and occasionally the *Peking Gazette* (*Jingbao* 京報).[16] Itemized lists made by the office of Chen Shutang 陳樹棠, the commercial agent (*shangwu weiyuan* 商務委員) to Seoul, Korea, reveal very clearly that a substantial volume of mail that went through the Shanghai Wenbao bureau consisted of private letters. For example, on the list for the Emperor Guangxu reign year 10, month 4 (May 1884), there were six items of official correspondence and nineteen letters to various individuals. From one of the itemized lists in the Emperor Guangxu reign year 10, month 7 (August 1884),

12. Li Hongzhang, "Shanghai sheli dong xi yang wenbao zongju zha wen" 上海設立東西洋文報總局札文 [Memorial on setting up Shanghai Wenbao bureau for oversea mails], in *Huangchao zhanggu, juan* 18, 1624–34.

13. "Zongli Yamen zou qing pai yuan" 總理衙門奏請派員 [Zongli Yamen's memorial on sending representatives], in *Huangchao zhanggu, juan* 18, 1608–10.

14. Li Hongzhang, "Shanghai sheli dong xi yang wenbao," 1624.

15. Li Hongzhang, "Shanghai sheli dong xi yang wenbao," 1624–34.

16. Huang Huihe, "Cheng bao di ji gongwen han jian wuxu zifei zhifu qingxing" 呈報遞寄公文函件無須資費支付情形 [Report on no payment required on official mail and approval requested], Guangxu reign year 4, month 12, day 23 (January 15, 1879), ZYJYD, 01-40-001-02-012.

there were thirty-five letters altogether, of which only seven were classified as official.[17]

Zhang Shusheng 張樹聲 (1824–84), the viceroy of Guangdong and
Guangxi, set up a Wenbao bureau in Canton in 1883 after having briefly
been acting viceroy of Zhili during Li's one-hundred-day mourning leave.
Zhang was a close ally of Li; both were from Hefei in Anhui Province,
and Zhang had first joined Li when he was recruiting for the Hui Army
back in 1861 to suppress the Taiping Rebellion.[18] Funded by provincial
budgets, the goal of the Canton Wenbao bureau was to deliver qualify-
ing officials' correspondence that fell outside the purview of the military
relay courier system and to connect with bureaux at other locations.[19]
A report written by Louis Rocher, the Customs commissioner at Canton
in 1891, provides us with the basic structure of this bureau and its network. There were four staff members at the Canton Wenbao bureau: two
managers, one secretary, and one writer. Rocher noted, "Official covers
only are received for transmissions, and mails are exchanged with similar departments established in Foochow [Fuzhou], Amoy [Xiamen],
Tainan, Swatow [Shantou], Shanghai and Tientsin [Tianjin]."[20] In es-
sence the Canton Wenbao bureau processed and distributed mail for
final delivery by other organizations such as the Customs Postal Service.
For dispatches to Chinese legations in foreign countries, mails were passed
on to relevant agencies such as the Consular Postal Agency at Shamian.
The Wenbao system at Fuzhou was managed by the China Merchants'
Steam Navigation Company, whose representative also looked after the

17. "Yu Shanghai wenbaochu wanglai shuxin cun juan" 與上海文報處往來書信存卷
[Records on correspondence with Shanghai Wenbao bureau]. Guangxu reign year 9,
month 11—month 12 (December 1883–January 1884), ZYJYD, 01-41-015-01. See also
itemized mail list number 5, received on Guangxu reign year 10, month 4, day 11
(May 5, 1884); and itemized mail list no. 13, received on Guangxu reign year 10, month
7, day 3 (August 23, 1884). The bundle normally took nine or ten days to travel between
Seoul and Shanghai.

18. Xie Shicheng, *Li Hongzhang ping zhuan*, 67.

19. Zhang Shusheng, "Guangdong tianshe lunchuan wenbaoju ji qing sihou
yangwu zhongda shijian gai you dianbao zhuanda" 廣東添設輪船文報局及請嗣後洋務重
大事件概由電報轉達 [On setting up steamship Wenbao bureau and request all foreign-
related important matters should be communicated through telegraph], Guangxu reign
year 9, month 8, day 26 (September 26, 1883), ZYJYD, 01-24-008-01-015.

20. "Canton, 1882–1891," in *Decennial Reports 1882–91*, 573.

telegraph station at that port.[21] Such a small but effective operation could easily be duplicated in Shantou and Xiamen. Because no formal Wenbao bureaux were set up in Hankou, Nanjing, or Zhenjiang along the Yangtze River, the China Merchants' Steam Navigation Company performed essentially the same functions at these locations.[22] Taking advantage of the opportunity presented by Yuan Shikai's posting to Korea in 1885, Li also set up a Wenbao bureau in Yantai.[23]

The 1880s witnessed a boom in interport communications through the widespread expansion of shipping, telegraph, and postal services in mainland China, Hong Kong, and Taiwan. Lin Yuju's study on Chinese merchants' correspondence clearly demonstrates the interconnectedness between treaty ports and nontreaty port locations.[24] Working from a similar perspective, Zhu Marlon's work shows that a significant volume of information circulated in this area through the transfer of mail, printed materials, and commodities, and via telegraph.[25] The role of the Wenbao bureaux in these information networks not only indicates the awareness of officials regarding the demand for information exchange but also cuts across both official and private communications, as the line between the two became increasingly blurred.

After Wenbao bureaux were established in Shanghai and Tianjin, for military reasons Taiwan also acquired a bureau. Under the supervision of Ding Richang, the governor of Fujian Province, the telegraph station at Fuzhou was connected with Anping, Tainan, in Taiwan in November 1877.[26] The following year Ding set up a Wenbao bureau in Tainan.

21. "Foochow, 1892–1901," in *Decennial Reports 1892–1901*, 2:111; "Min Zhe zongdu Bian wen" 閩浙總督卞文 [Letter from Governor General of Fujian and Zhejiang Provinces Bian], February 19, 1891, in Guo Tingyi and Li Yushu, *Qingji Zhong Ri Han*, 5:2877.

22. "Chinkiang, 1892–1901," in *Decennial Reports*, 1:459; Zhang Yi, *Zhonghua youzhengshi*, 170.

23. Li Hongzhang, "Zhu Han Yuan dao qing yi Cheng Yunhan banli wenbao lian" 駐韓袁道請以程雲翰辦理文報立案 [Regarding Yuan Shikai, the Chinese minister to Korea, requesting the appointment of Chen Yunhan to organize mail matters for him], Guangxu reign year 13, month 4, day 20 (June 11, 1887), ZYJYD, 01-25-023-01-012.

24. Lin Yuju, "Tongxun yu maoyi," 175.

25. Zhu Marlon, "Waijiao qingbao yu gangji baoye."

26. H. E. Hobson, "Takow Trade Report for the Year 1877," February 13, 1878, in Huang Fusan and Lin Man-Houng, *Qingmo Taiwan*, 1:331; Lü Shih-Chiang, *Ting Jih-Chang*, 257–58.

The combination of telegraph and Wenbao bureaux was a critical element of Ding's strategic plans. In 1881 the governor of Taiwan, Cen Yuying 岑毓英 (1829–89) expanded the bureaux network to Jilong in northern Taiwan, and then to Taipei. A steamship was designated for the line between Jilong and the mainland cities of Mawei and Fuzhou, reducing the journey time for mail from thirty-six to nine hours. Jilong replaced Tainan as the most important destination for official mail.[27]

More steamships were acquired by Cen Yuying and Liu Mingchuan 劉銘傳 (1836–96) to travel between the Chinese mainland and Taiwan; the ships carried official and private mail, passengers, and trade commodities.[28] In 1887, while Liu was in office as governor of Taiwan, Taiwan's status was upgraded to become a province of China. After noting a lack of communication between mainland China and Taiwan during the Sino-French War, Liu put considerable energy into constructing telegraph lines and railways, providing support for the development of the mining industry. Liu, another Hefei native, had also joined Li Hongzhang's Hui Army in his early twenties through the recommendation of Zhang Shusheng. Despite his lowly background, Liu proved himself in military campaigns and became one of Li's most capable leaders.[29]

In 1886, to capitalize on the rise in trade, the Formosa Trading Company (Taiwan shangwuju 台灣商務局) was set up with the backing of Liu Mingchuan by a group of merchants and officials. Notably, the founders of this company were Sheng Xuanhuai 盛宣懷 (1844–1916) and Ma Jianzhong 馬建忠 (1845–1900), the two senior managers of the China Merchants' Steam Navigation Company at the time.[30] Under this new trading company, two steamers were brought in to connect Singapore, Hong Kong, Sai Kung, Taiwan, and Shanghai.[31] According to the report of the commissioner of Customs at Danshui, Edmond Faragó, the steam-

27. Cao, *Zhonghua youzhengshi Taiwan bian*, 72–74.
28. "Hangyun" 航運 [Shipping], in *Taiwanshi*, 455.
29. Xie Shicheng, *Li Hongzhang ping zhuan*, 68.
30. "Sheng Xuanhuai, Ma Jianzhong shang Liu Mingchuan bing" 盛宣懷、馬建忠上劉銘傳稟 [A joint report of Sheng Xuanhuai and Ma Jianzhong to Liu Mingchuan], Guangxu reign year 11, month 12, day 21 (January 25, 1886), in *Lunchuan zhaoshangju*, 229–31.
31. "Hangyun," in *Taiwanshi*, 455.

ers of the Formosa Trading Company sailed under the German flag.[32] The reasons for this are not clear from the sources, but it is a fair assumption that it had to do with the eligibility of foreign-flagged firms to pay one-off transit dues rather than being required to pay *lijin* at multiple ports along their chosen route. Liu also extended his attention to a postal scheme. In the spring of 1888, without obtaining approval in advance from Beijing, the Taiwan Post Office (Taiwan youzheng 台灣郵政) was set up, headquartered in Taipei. Liu transformed the existing military relay courier system in Taiwan into a new postal service for the general public.[33] As part of this initiative, he had modern-style postage stamps printed by the Bradbury Wilkinson Company in London. The design was based on pairing a traditional dragon and phoenix image with another image, the money horse, which was often used in a business context; this was a traditional combination at the time of the Chinese New Year. The postage stamps were not ready for the launch of the post office, however, and woodblock-printed postal tickets (*Youzheng shang piao* 郵政商票) were made for the purpose instead (see fig. 4.1).[34] The postage stamps ended up being used as train tickets between Jilong and Taipei (see fig. 4.2).[35]

The postage rate was based on the number of stations an item needed to pass through. Liu appointed Zhang Weiqing 張維卿, the chief of telegraph operations at Taipei, to set up the postal project.[36] From the start, the intention was to use the military relay courier system and Wenbao bureaux resources to accommodate both official and private mail so that income from private mail would help offset the costs. In the proclamation for the establishment of the Taiwan Post Office, it was clearly indicated that the founder Liu Mingchuan did not shy away from competing with private letter hongs, it being stated that the new entity intended to follow the practice of hongs in providing both mail services

32. Edmond Faragó, "Tamsui Trade Report for the Year 1886," January 18, 1887, in *Qingmo Taiwan*, 2:715.

33. Cao, *Zhonghua youzhengshi Taiwan bian*, 83–84.

34. Ho, "1888 nian xiaolong," 55–65; Cao, *Zhonghua youzhengshi Taiwan bian*, 114–17.

35. J. L. Chalmers, "Tamsui Trade Report, for the Year 1888," in *Qingmo Taiwan*, 2:792.

36. Cao, *Zhonghua youzhengshi Taiwan bian*, 87–88.

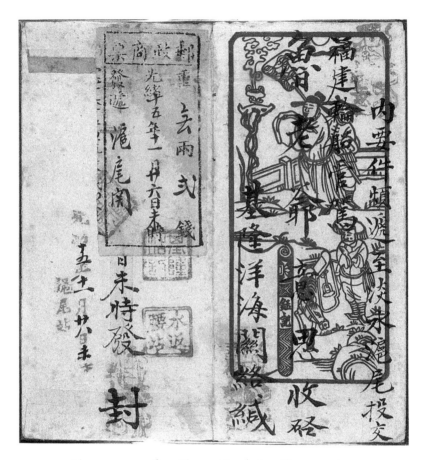

FIGURE 4.1 A letter cover sent from Jilong to Danshui, on Guangxu reign year 15, month 11, day 26 (December 18, 1889). The box affixed on the top left is the postal ticket. Source: *Youzhan xuancui* 郵展選粹, 208.

and silver delivery to mainland China and Hong Kong.[37] The Tainan and Taipei Wenbao bureaux were designated as the chief post offices, and the mail service linked up with the Customs Postal Service at Fuzhou, Shanghai, and Xiamen.[38] When mail arrived from mainland China through

37. Luo, *Liu gong Mingchuan*, 2:951–52.
38. "Youzheng" 郵政 [Postal service], in *Taiwanshi*, 457.

FIGURE 4.2 A Formosa postage stamp, with a dragon above and a horse below, used as a train ticket from Taipei to Xikou (Songshan 松山), as the chop shows. Source: *Youzhan xuancui* 郵展選粹, 219.

the private letter hongs, the hongs also gradually began to use the Taiwan Post Office for local distribution.[39]

The development of Wenbao bureaux on the coast and along the Yangtze River indicated substantial demand for a modern communication method among officials for their correspondence—official and private, urgent and nonurgent. In working closely with the China Merchants' Steam Navigation Company, the bureaux had a great advantage over the Customs Postal Service, whose transportation arrangements were restricted to a small number of treaty port destinations. This contrasted with the scale and flexibility of the connections provided by such a substantial shipping company, which serviced many additional treaty and nontreaty port destinations on both the coast and the river. The Wenbao bureaux enabled Li and the other officials involved in their creation to establish a solution that was under their control. The flexibility, entrepreneurial flair, and practical problem-solving demonstrated by these officials is striking, as is their avoidance of the difficult topic of a national

39. Cao, *Zhonghua youzhengshi Taiwan bian*, 60.

post office: the Wenbao bureaux existed to perform a specific function, and appear to have performed it well.

As exemplified in the close working arrangement with the China Merchants' Steam Navigation Company, an important characteristic of the Wenbao bureaux was successful integration of the logistics of mail delivery with modern transportation systems. An important collaborator of Li in implementing this approach was Sheng Xuanhuai. Deeply involved in the development of steamship transportation, the telegraph, the railway, and mining in the late Qing period, Sheng was in Li's inner circle.[40] He later became minister of Posts and Communications 郵傳部 (Youchuanbu) in 1911. While scholars have examined Sheng's writings on steamship transportation, the telegraph, the railway, and mining, in 1881 Sheng had in fact also drafted a proposal on organizing postal systems nationwide. Noting the significant increase in the volume of mail carried by the private letter hongs, as well as corruption in the military relay courier system, including its illicit use for transmitting personal letters, Sheng suggested that provincial governments should introduce a levy on mail, split into two categories: light mail and heavy mail. He estimated that, on average, each province would have between 4.5 and 4.6 million items of mail daily, and by applying his rates, each province would raise 2 million taels (Tls.) annually from light mail and Tls. 170,000 from heavy mail.[41] By treating mail as a commodity, Sheng's proposed levy was similar to transit dues: once a tariff had been paid at the departure point, fees would not be charged again when the item passed through subsequent tariff stations.

Sheng Xuanhuai's plan indicated that he was one of a number of individuals thinking about the future of the postal market in China. It is clear that his plan was an aggressive one, however, and Li did not act on it. Instead some rather delicate moves were carried out on his behalf by the German minister, Max von Brandt. The next section will explore the actions of various parties with an interest in China's postal affairs, and the response of Hart and the Zongli Yamen.

40. Xia, "Lun Sheng Xuanhuai," 57, 62.
41. Sheng Xuanhuai, "Shang Li Hongzhang tiao chen" 上李鴻章條陳 [Memorandum to Li Hongzhang], Guangxu reign year 7, month 11 (November 1881, specific date unknown), Shanghai Municipal Library Archives, Sheng Xuanhuai Collection, SD 088440.

Other Interests

In 1881, while Hart was working to put the Customs Postal Service's house in order, he heard gossip that Robert Wilson Shufeldt (1822–95), an American naval office and diplomat, was taking on a role in postal affairs. He wrote to James Duncan Campbell,

> Postal: This is hanging fire—as far as I am concerned. The high officials would willingly see my experiment succeed and then father it: but they will not help it with either Orders or funds. On the other hand, they are meditating putting it in American [Shufeldt's] hands with the orders and funds they withhold from me. . . . I expect one of these days to find Detring named Director General of Posts and Telegraphs. Li believes in Germany because France got thrashed . . . he's fond of big-sized men—so he likes Clayson, Johnston, and Detring; and he's again fond of flattery and sycophants and so he prefers Americans to Englishmen.[42]

Shufeldt was sent to East Asia in 1880 to make a formal trade agreement with Korea. He originally turned to Japan for assistance, but it was a fruitless effort, as Japan was not pleased at the US attempt to push into Korea. He then went to Li Hongzhang. From the perspective of China's assertion of the traditional suzerainty of Korea in relation to the Qing empire, Li was more than willing to bring in US interests to counter Japan's rising influence on the Korean Peninsula. Shufeldt returned to Tianjin in July 1881 with his daughter with high hopes that negotiations with Korea would begin soon, but this was not the case. There followed a frustrating period of waiting through the summer and autumn, during which he kept hoping Li would offer him a formal role as an aide to the Chinese Navy, similar to that taken up by a number of fellow countrymen who were working as official consultants to the Meiji government.[43] Li seemed to want to avoid making such a commitment, however, while still often consulting Shufeldt informally on naval matters and adopting

---

42. Robert Hart to James Duncan Campbell, letter 336, August 8, 1881, in *The IG*, 1:380–81. For Robert Wilson Shufeldt's business in China, see Paullin, *Diplomatic Negotiations*, 305–6.

43. Su Ran, *Yuandong guoji guanxishi*, 89–91, 75.

his suggestions. Li also arranged several high profile visits for Shufeldt to naval bases, warships, and arsenals, which taken together fed rumors that Shufeldt might be being positioned for a major role in the north of the country.[44] Gossip about Shufeldt taking on a role in postal affairs may have been a consequence of the far-reaching conversations between him and Li Hongzhang during this long waiting period in Tianjin, but in the end the rumored role did not materialize, and the issue disappeared with Shufeldt's departure.

Less than a year later, another drama arose. In December 1882 the German minister, Brandt, submitted a memorandum to the Zongli Yamen on postal matters. He suggested that China should consider joining the Universal Postal Union (UPU) and send a delegation to attend its next congress, which would be held in Lisbon, Portugal, in 1884 (though in fact the congress was not held until 1885).[45] Brandt explained that the invitation originated from Germany's state secretary of the post, Heinrich von Stephan, and he believed that by joining the UPU, the Chinese government would benefit from increased postal revenue. No doubt there were positive motives behind the invitation, but it also came at a moment when Germany was seeking to expand its influence in Chinese affairs and at the same time to reduce British influence. In his long text, Brandt stressed that Germany understood it was currently impossible for China to join the UPU on a full national basis but that it could be possible to make a start through connecting the treaty ports. He also gave examples of countries and territories that were not yet formal members but had expressed an intention to join, and explained that UPU benefits were available to these entities as long as the regulations were followed and access fees paid.

The Zongli Yamen was obliged to respond to such a formal diplomatic communication and sent a Chinese version, translated by Tongwen College, to both Li Hongzhang (the viceroy of Tianjin and superintendent of trade for the northern ports) and Zuo Zongtang (the viceroy of

44. Paullin, *Diplomatic Negotiations*, 305–6.

45. Max von Brandt to Zongli Yamen, "De shi zhao qing pai yuan ru wanguo youzhenghui you" 德使照請派員入萬國郵政會由 [Germany ministry invited China to send people to attend the Universal Postal Union], Guangxu reign year 8, month 10, day 23 (December 3, 1882), ZYJYD, 01-07005-01-001.

Anhui, Jiangsu, and Jiangxi and superintendent of trade for the southern ports) for comment.[46] Long-term tension between these two officials was a matter of public knowledge by this time.

The context of the Zongli Yamen's action lies in the developing consensus of the Qing government toward commerce at the time, as there was a gradual transition from constraining commerce to promoting it. According to Li Ta-chia, the process of change was evident when Li Fan 李璠, the provincial censor for Hubei and Hunan (湖廣道監察御史) argued in 1878 that the government should be bolder in bringing commerce into policy making and use the development of trade to help resist Western invasion.[47] The shift to an overtly entrepreneurial approach can be seen in many facets of policy in the period, whether on the topic of Wenbao bureaux or—to return to the matter at hand—the response of Li Hongzhang's camp to Brandt's memorandum.

Li instructed the Tianjin Customs superintendent Zhou Fu 周馥 (1837–1921), and Wu Tingfang 伍廷芳 (1842–1922) to look into the question before he went on mourning leave. Their report acknowledged that, while the military relay courier system transmitted only official mail and the postage charged by private letter hongs for other sorts of mail was considered high, it would be a drastic move for China to adopt a Western-style national post office at the present time. Nevertheless, the potential of postal services to generate revenue was attractive, and the report's conclusion was to recommend experimenting with the development of modern-style postal services at treaty ports in order to ascertain the response of the general public. Yet instead of making the venture completely state-sponsored, the model Hart always had in mind, the report suggested that the postal experiment be run at treaty ports using a "government-supervised merchant undertakings" approach, which would align with the structure of both the China Merchants' Steam Navigation Company and the Imperial Chinese Telegraph Administration. The report also rec-

---

46. Zongli Yamen to Brandt, "Youzhenghui shi ying xing nanbei dachen he fu bing jiang yangwen songhuan you" 郵政會事應行南北洋大臣核復並將洋文送還由 [Regarding the Universal Postal Union matter, will consult the superintendents of trade for the southern and northern ports, and return the German version of correspondence], Guangxu reign year 8, month 12, day 30 (February 7, 1883), ZYJYD, 01-27-005-01-002.

47. Li Ta-chia, "Cong yi shang dao zhong shang," 18–22.

ommended that the government should consider attending the next Postal Union Congress. This view was echoed in its entirety by Zhang Shusheng, by this time the acting viceroy of Zhili.[48]

In contrast to his northern colleagues, Zuo Zongtang could only bring himself to agree on sending a delegation to the congress. Echoing the reservations he had expressed toward Hart's "Bystander's View" in 1865, Zuo strongly opposed the idea of establishing a national post office, as he was deeply concerned not to deprive private letter hongs of business, which implied that he was equally unenthused at the idea of running an experimental postal service at the treaty ports.[49] As a result, nothing came of Brandt's proposal.

Despite their divergent views, however, there was some common ground: none of these officials appeared concerned at the presence of foreign post offices. Neither the existence of a handful of post offices in treaty ports from Britain, France, and the United States; Russia's postal connection with Beijing; nor the existence of a municipal post office in Shanghai seemed to influence their thinking in any particular direction. Notions of postal privilege and nationalism, ideas that became burning issues at a later date, were not yet a consideration for Qing officials—partly because of the relatively small scale of foreign operations, and partly because they believed most native Chinese were well served by the private letter hongs, but mostly because the wider discourse surrounding unequal treaties and its associated terminology did not develop until after the turn of the century. On the contrary, with multiple and sometimes overlapping systems available—the military relay courier

48. Zhang Shusheng, "Ju Zhou dao deng suo ni sheli youzheng ge jie huo xian shixing yu tongshang ge kou huo zhan you chushi dachen pai yuan wang guan zai shang ban you" 據周道等所擬設立郵政各節或先試行於通商各口或暫由出使大臣派員往觀再商辦法由 [The outlines made by Tianjin circuit intendant Zhou Fu regarding setting up post offices at treaty ports and sending a delegation to attend the Universal Postal Union to observe first], Guangxu reign year 9, month 3, day 5 (April 11, 1883), ZYJYD, 01-27-005-01-004.

49. Zuo Zongtang, "Youzhenghui shi ju Su Song taidao bing cheng ni qing jian yuan qianwang pangguan ticha qingqing zai xing ding zhi you" 郵政會事據蘇松太道稟稱擬請揀員前往旁觀體查情形再行定止由 [The report of the Shanghai circuit intendant (Shao Youlian)] regarding sending a delegation to attend the Universal Postal Union to observe before making a decision], Guangxu reign year 9, month 6, day 19 (July 22, 1883), ZYJYD, 01-27-005-01-006.

system, Wenbao bureaux, foreign postal services, private letter hongs, and the telegraph—these officials thought China's communication needs were well provided for.

Hart was certainly conscious of Li Hongzhang's double-dealing on postal matters. He saw that, on the one hand, Li had supported the Customs postal plan but that, on the other, Li himself was also exploring ways in which he personally might find a way to move forward with a national post office, even though at no point did he submit a memorandum to the central administration solely on this topic. When, after the sudden death of Harry Smith Parkes in 1885, Hart had the opportunity of taking on the role of British minister to China, he noted that Li would be happy to see him move on from the CMCS, while the Zongli Yamen would be pleased for him to remain.[50] Should Hart move on, there was a rumor that Detring might be the next inspector general.[51] On another occasion, Detring hinted that Li would prefer an American take on the role of inspector general, either Edward B. Drew or Hosea Ballou Morse, who were both Customs commissioners.[52] After some soul-searching, Hart decided to stay, noting his reasons in a letter to Campbell: "I fear am just now a key-stone: if I move, the Customs' arch bids fair to tumble down, and in the general interest, I must give up the Legation and its greater dignity and promise of better things in order to look out for the safety of my flock on the meadow below."[53]

Noting the growing interest in postal matters from various quarters, in 1884 Hart had Henry Kopsch prepare a postal proposal. Kopsch, the Customs commissioner at Ningbo, had previously shown interest in postal developments when he was Customs commissioner at Jiujiang. In May 1877 he had drafted a postal proposal in Chinese for Hart, in which he addressed the currently available postal services in China, and asked why China should not have its own national post office. The proposal

50. Robert Hart to James Duncan Campbell, letter 538, September 12, 1885, in *The IG*, 1:606.

51. Detring told Hart that some people at the court asked him if he would fancy being the next inspector general. Detring's response was that he would "rather be with Li above than with Yamen where there are so many chiefs etc." Hart, journal entry for March 30, 1886, SQBH.

52. Hart, journal entry for July 22, 1885, SQBH.

53. Hart to James Duncan Campbell, letter 533, July 31, 1885, in *The IG*, 1:602.

went into specific details on postage rates for parcels, letters, and newspapers.[54] After his transfer to Ningbo, he met a very capable Customs writer, Li Gui 李圭 (1842–1903). Li was originally from Nanjing, and more than twenty of his family members, including his mother, wife, and young daughter, had been killed by the rebels when they entered the town during the Taiping Rebellion. Li Gui was captured and later worked for the Taiping camp as a writer. He eventually ran away, arriving in Shanghai, where he met some foreigners. He was recruited by the then Customs commissioner of Ningbo, H. E. Hobson, and joined the CMCS in June 1865.[55] On Detring's recommendation, he was assigned to accompany the CMCS delegation to the Philadelphia Centennial Exposition in 1876.[56] The group traveled to Japan, the United States, England, and Europe. When the delegation group arrived in London, it went to the CMCS's London office, where Li met Campbell; he also met up with Customs commissioner F. W. White, who was on leave at the time. Li noted that they had had an excellent working relationship in Ningbo for four years, when White was stationed there, and it was a great pleasure to have such a reunion.[57]

On his return to China, Li Gui was given a year's leave to write up his travels, subsequently published as *New Records of Travels around the World* (*Huanyou diqiu xinlu* 環游地球新錄). Li Hongzhang wrote the book's preface, and recommended it to the Zongli Yamen, which sponsored the publication of three thousand copies.[58] In the publication Li recorded the operations of the post offices of various countries he had visited (for more on the work, see chapter 7). Given his language skills and their shared interest in postal services, Kopsch engaged Li in 1885 to translate the *Hong Kong Postal Guide*. When Xue Fucheng 薛福成 (1838–94) was the Ningbo circuit intendant (*taotai*), Li Gui was assigned to be his

---

54. Henry Kopsch, "Ban she tongshang ge kou guan xinju jie lue" 辦設通商各口官信局節畧 [An outline for establishing official post offices at the treaty ports], in *Tianjin haiguan dangan*, 2:21897–903.

55. Zhong Shuhe, "Li Gui de huanyou," 172.

56. Li Hongzhang, "Xu."

57. Li Gui, *Huanyou diqiu xinlu*, 87; a short biography of Li Gui appears in a footnote in "Postal: Enclosing Chinese Version of Regulations and Yamên Memorial," IG Circular 709 (2nd ser.), April 30, 1896, in *Docs. Ill.*, 2:56.

58. Zhong Shuhe, "Li Gui de huanyou," 172.

foreign affairs consultant, while still maintaining his position at the CMCS. Over his career, Xue worked for Zeng Guofan and then Li Hongzhang, and gained a reputation as a keen modernizer. Xue, together with Li and Kopsch, prepared a memorandum in late 1885 that advocated for a national post office; it was formally submitted by Zeng Guoquan 曾國荃—the new superintendent of trade for the southern ports and brother of Zeng Guofan—to the Zongli Yamen.[59]

Hart felt the whole thing had become very promising: "So 'Behind the clouds, is the sun still shining!'"[60] In that warm early spring, with lilacs ready to burst into bloom in his garden, Hart was ready to act: he started to prepare a postal plan for the Zongli Yamen with his personal Chinese writer.[61] He asked Campbell to talk to the postal printing company De la Rue about postage stamps, and he transferred Kopsch to Shanghai, detaching him from normal Customs duties in order to work on the postal project. At this time, Hart also thought Shanghai should house the future postal headquarters, and considered that, in future, the role of postal secretary should be combined with that of statistical secretary.[62] There were even conversations between Kopsch and F. G. Machado, the British postmaster of Shanghai, about potentially taking over the staff and facilities of the General Post Office there.[63]

The Zongli Yamen's response to these developments requires some attention. Several important works of historiography for late Qing history, such as the *Draft History of the Qing Dynasty* (*Qingshigao* 清史稿) and the *Encyclopedia of the Historical Records of the Qing Dynasty* (*Qingchao*

59. Zongli Yamen, "Yi ban youzheng" 議辦郵政 [On establishing a postal service], Guangxu reign year 22, month 2, day 7 (March 20, 1896), in IG Circular 709, 2:57–60.

60. Hart, journal entry for February 6, 1886, SQBH. Hart is quoting a line from the poem "A Rainy Day" by the American poet and educator Henry Wadsworth Longfellow (1807–82).

61. On March 22, 1886, Hart recorded, "Began the Postal dispatch to Yamen." The next day he wrote, "Worked with Li on postal dispatch," and on the following day he wrote, "Again worked with Li on postal dispatch. Still windy." On March 26 he wrote, "Finished draft of Postal dispatch." Hart, journal entries for March 22, March 23, March 24, and March 26, 1886, SQBH.

62. Hart, journal entry for February 27, 1886, SQBH.

63. Henry Kopsch to Robert Hart, January 12, 1886, in *Zhongguo haiguan yu youzheng*, 40–45.

xu wenxian tongkao 清朝續文獻通考), wrongly record that the Zongli Yamen
did not respond to the request initiated by Zeng Guoquan, supplemented
by Hart's proposal, until 1890, with the decision to allow the Customs
Postal Service to expand to other treaty ports as long as this would not
harm the interests of the private letter hongs.[64] This commonly shared er-
ror originated in an important memorandum submitted by the Zongli
Yamen to the throne in March 1896; however, the Zongli Yamen was
wrong in its recording of history.[65] Rather than 1890, it was in 1886 that
the Zongli Yamen reached a conclusion, swiftly followed by action. In
early April it let Hart know that it would refer the issue to Li Hongzhang, and on May 2, Hart was notified by the Zongli Yamen that his
postal experiment could be extended to other treaty ports, but only
this; no further expansion was agreed upon, and certainly no national
post office.[66]

Back in 1876, in the middle of the negotiations following the Margary Affair, Hart had told Campbell, "In China, one has generally to talk
ten years before accomplishing anything!"[67] Ten years on, he was able to
move one step further, expanding the Customs Postal Service to additional treaty ports. But it would be yet another ten years before his goal
of a formal postal establishment would become reality.

Court Politics and the Sino-Japanese War

In 1892 Kopsch was once again in Shanghai, transferred back to run the
Customs Statistical Department while also acting as Hart's eyes and ears
for any possible turbulence that might interfere with his postal strategy.
On the one hand, Hart did not believe foreign post offices in China were
a real threat to his own agenda; on the other, he was very happy to use

64. "Jiaotong si—Youzheng" 交通四—郵政 [Transportation part four—Postal
service], in *Qingshigao*, *zhi* 127, *juan* 152. See also "Youzheng," in *QXWTK*, 377:18.

65. Zongli Yamen, "Yi ban youzheng," 2:58.

66. Hart, journal entries for April 5 and May 1, 1886, SQBH; Robert Hart to James
Duncan Campbell, letter 574, May 8, 1886, in *The IG*, 1:638.

67. Robert Hart to James Duncan Campbell, letter 146, March 16, 1876, in *The IG*,
1:216.

their activities for his own purposes.[68] When he heard that the Shanghai Local Post Office, run by the Municipal Council of the International Settlement, might join the UPU, he decided to ring the alarm with the central administration. Referring to the Municipal Council's plan as "a tremendous bit of cheek," he used the issue to reopen discussions on postal matters with the Zongli Yamen and also sent Campbell to Bern, Switzerland, to kill the idea.[69]

Li Hongzhang, as well as Liu Kunyi, superintendent of trade for the southern ports at that time, confirmed to the Zongli Yamen that they had also heard rumors that the Shanghai Local Post Office planned to expand into more treaty ports. Given these developments, in August 1893 Hart told Kopsch that the Zongli Yamen wanted him to submit the postal proposal again.[70] On February 13, 1894, Hart told Kopsch that he believed the Zongli Yamen was at its last consultation stage "before making the final plunge."[71] But another six months passed without any conclusion. By August 17 Hart told Kopsch that the opponents to his postal proposal were stronger than its supporters, but that the matter would be resolved. The only regret he felt was that although special postage stamps had been made for the Empress Dowager Cixi's sixtieth birthday, the Japanese military campaign might have spoiled everyone's enthusiasm.[72]

Facing pressure from the encroaching Japanese military, China formally declared war with Japan on August 1, 1894, in the name of the Guangxu emperor.[73] The war took place on two fronts: on land, in Korea and its borderlands with China, and in the northern part of the Yellow Sea. This was the moment for Li Hongzhang to demonstrate what his northern fleet, largely equipped with battleships and cruisers procured

68. Robert Hart to Henry Kopsch, December 15, 1892, MS Chinese 4.

69. "Hart raised the issue again and said that if we still don't establish a Post Office, it would give foreigners excuses to further complicate the situation"; Zongli Yamen, "Yi ban youzheng," 2:58, my translation. See also Robert Hart to James Duncan Campbell, letter 871, December 18, 1892, in *The IG*, 2:915; and Robert Hart to James Duncan Campbell, letter 876, February 12, 1893, in *The IG*, 2:920.

70. Robert Hart to Henry Kopsch, August 21, 1893, MS Chinese 4.

71. Robert Hart to Henry Kopsch, February 13, 1894, MS Chinese 4.

72. Robert Hart to Henry Kopsch, August 17, 1894, MS Chinese 4.

73. "The War—Declaration of War by the Emperor of China," *North China Daily*, August 3, 1894.

from Germany, was truly made of. When the war started, the perception shared by many foreigners who lived in China, including Hart, was that China had the military advantage.[74] Although the real situation was initially hidden from the populace through the dissemination of misleading reports, the Qing court was soon in more or less constant receipt of reports outlining China's defeat in one battle after another. Only one month after the declaration of war, the likelihood of China's defeat had become apparent. Li Hongzhang's military campaign was severely criticized by Li Hongzao 李鴻藻 (1820–97), a grand councilor and grand scholar. Li Hongzao (no relation) even accused Li Hongzhang of deliberately slowing China's military deployment.[75]

At the urging of many court officials, Empress Dowager Cixi overcame her reluctance and asked Prince Gong to return to the Grand Council and the Zongli Yamen; he was also asked to direct the military campaign.[76] Hart was summoned to see Prince Gong on October 7, 1894. He wrote to Campbell, "I believe I am to see Prince Kung this afternoon—it's about 11 or 12 years since we last met, and now over thirty-three since our first talk. How quickly the time flies—how full each moment seems and how important for the moment—and how quickly a gone second and a done work loses its interest and its importance: what motes in the sunbeam we are!"[77]

It was a difficult winter at court, as the bad news kept coming. For example, in November several battles in Lüshun Bay ended disastrously for one of the Qing commanders in chief, Constantin von Hanneken (1855–1925), who led a force of one hundred thousand men with twenty-five hundred foreign officers.[78] On November 8, Weng Tonghe, now

74. Weipin Tsai, "The First Casualty," 149.

75. Weng, entry for Guangxu reign year 20, month 8, day 18 (September 17, 1894), in *WRJPY*, 4:1905–6.

76. Weng, entries for Guangxu reign year 20, month 8, day 28 (September 27, 1894) and Guangxu reign year 20, month 9, day 7 (October 5, 1894), in *WRJPY*, 4:1907–8, 1910.

77. Robert Hart to James Duncan Campbell, letter 947, October 7, 1894, in *The IG*, 2:991.

78. Robert Hart to James Duncan Campbell, letter 950, November 4, 1894, in *The IG*, 2:994; Weng, entry for Guangxu reign year 20, month 10, day 9 (November 6, 1894), in *WRJPY*, 4:1917. Hanneken later married Detring's daughter Elsa in March 1895;

teacher of the twenty-four-year-old Emperor Guangxu, noted that the food supply to the military in Lüshun at the time could only last for a half month, and on November 24, he recorded that a telegram had arrived saying Lüshun was gone, leaving him alarmed and frightened.[79] In December, as birthday celebrations were held for Empress Dowager Cixi, the idea of negotiation was put on the table by the US minister to China, Charles Denby, and by the Chinese New Year season at the end of January 1895, the military campaign had spread south to Weihai, in the coastal area of Shandong Province.[80] By February 1895 it had become clear that China could not afford to prolong the war and would have to look for solutions through negotiation.

A sense of humiliation soon grew across the country, reaching an unprecedented level. Li Hongzhang's personal reputation fell precipitously both before and after his signing of the Treaty of Shimonoseki. Still recovering from a gunshot wound after an assassination attempt, he was on the receiving end of stinging criticism from all corners over the loss of Taiwan as well as the loss of the war itself. The Qing court removed him as viceroy of Zhili—a position he had held for a quarter of a century—and kept him in Beijing.[81] At this time, Weng Tonghe was in the ascendant and about to reach his maximum point of influence. Also on the rise was Zhang Zhidong, viceroy of Anhui, Jiangsu, and Jiangxi and superintendent of trade of the southern ports. The shake-up at the Qing court following the war with Japan was profound, and with this came the opportunity for ideas long frustrated to start to move forward—not least, a national post office.

Weng Tonghe's father, Weng Xincun 翁心存, had been one of the teachers of Emperor Tongzhi, and was a close friend of Woren. As was

<hr>

see Robert Hart to James Duncan Campbell, letter 965, February 24, 1895, in *The IG*, 2:1010.

79. Weng, diary for Guangxu reign year 20, month 10, day 11 (November 8, 1894) and for Guangxu reign year 20, month 10, day 27 (November 24, 1894), in *WRJPY*, 4:1918, 1921.

80. Robert Hart to James Duncan Campbell, letter 955, December 9, 1894, in *The IG*, 2:1000; Weng, entries for Guangxu reign year 21, month 1, days 2–6 (January 27–31, 1895), in *WRJPY*, 4:1928, 1935.

81. Weng, entry for Guangxu reign year 21, month 7, day 9 (August 28, 1895), in *WRJPY*, 4:1971–72.

noted in chapter 2, Woren was Tongzhi's leading teacher and had had many clashes with Prince Gong and Wenxiang. Nevertheless, despite being well aware of this history, over time Weng Tonghe moved away from Woren's views on modernization and on the making of an ideal king. In his study on Weng Tonghe, Hsiao Kung-chuan argues that, although Weng Tonghe had a rather inconsistent approach to foreign affairs, the more contact he had with foreigners, the more pragmatic were the views he came to adopt. In 1887 Weng received sixteen books on varied topics regarding modernization from Zeng Guoquan, and he soon began to share these reform ideas with Emperor Guangxu. In 1889 Weng also suggested that the emperor read Feng Guifen's *Essays of Protests from the Jiaobin Hut* (*Jiao bin lu kang yi* 校邠廬抗議), a collection of arguments for reform. A month later he also presented a copy to Empress Dowager Cixi.[82]

Zhang Zhidong had been working since the mid-1860s to develop a good relationship with Weng Tonghe, even though he was his junior. Zhang's talents in classical literature had been well known since his teens, and through his relationship with Weng's nephew—both passed the state exam the same year—Zhang was able to make an impression on Weng in informal situations. He also expended significant effort in acquiring rare paintings and calligraphy in order to capture the attention of Weng, a prestigious court scholar long before Zhang's own rise to influence.[83] Although the relationship between Weng and Zhang became distant in the late 1880s, their long-term dissatisfaction with Li Hongzhang and the new Shimonoseki Treaty brought them closer once again.[84] Zhang did not always see eye to eye with Li Hongzhang, and during the negotiation of the treaty he became involved in efforts to discredit him through the leaking of details.[85] One of several mutual acquaintances who subsequently became allies was Kang Youwei 康有為 (1858–1927), who was to

---

82. Hsiao, *Weng Tonghe yu wuxu*, 16–18, 14–15.

83. Wang Weijiang, *"Qingliu" yanjiu*, 195–98.

84. Hsiao, *Weng Tonghe yu wuxu*, 40–41.

85. Mao, *Wuxu bianfa de lingmian*, 7–8. Mao, *Wuxu bianfa shishi kao*, 36–41, explains how the efforts of Kang Youwei and Liang Qichao in leading petition efforts criticizing Li Hongzhang's conduct in the negotiations in April had come about as a result of some officials intentionally acting to leak details of the draft treaty wording. At this time Zhang Zhidong was close to Kang Youwei.

be the main brain behind Emperor Guangxu's Hundred Days' Reform program in 1898.

On May 11, 1895, three days after the ratification of the treaty at Yantai, Emperor Guangxu issued an edict to explain to the country what had just transpired and what the implications of the treaty were. He advocated revenue increases in order to further reform. Two months later, another edict was released, directly naming areas for reform: railways, the mint, mining, mechanization, taxation and *lijin*, the military, education, and a post office. Together with this edict, nine memorials authored by different officials on various reform programs were sent to local governors for comment. Among these reform programs, the one proposed by Hu Yufen 胡燏棻 (1836–1906), the Guangxi provincial juridical commissioner, in June 1895 was regarded as the most important by Emperor Guangxu, and presumably Weng Tonghe thought the same.[86] Among other important issues, Hu argued strongly for the benefits of having a national post office in his proposal.[87]

Prince Gong's health had not been good since he returned to power, but he continued to meet regularly with Weng Tonghe and other officials. Shame over defeat by Japan and the loss of Taiwan are reported to have led these officials to heated arguments and reduced them to tears on several occasions.[88] Memorials, recommendations, and petitions poured into the court, and Weng recorded in his diary that during this period he was overwhelmed digesting these documents. But according to Hart, there was "no central initiative, or control, or plan!" At Prince Gong's request, Hart sent in yet another reform proposal, with eighty suggestions for the emperor to consider.[89] Other foreign residents in Beijing—the British, French, Germans, and others—also saw a unique moment to exert their influence. For example, Timothy Richard (1845–1919), a British missionary with long-standing connections to China, was very active in talking to Weng Tonghe and Zhang Zhidong, providing

86. Zhang Hairong, "Jiawu zhan hou," 70–72, 75.
87. Hu Yufen, "Bianfa ziqiang shu," 284–85.
88. Weng, entries for Guangxu reign year 21, month 3, day 10 (April 4, 1895), Guangxu reign year 21, month 3, day 12 (April 6, 1895), and Guangxu reign year 21, month 3, day 24 (April 18, 1895), in *WRJPY*, 4:1947, 1949.
89. Robert Hart to James Duncan Campbell, letter 981, August 4, 1895, in *The IG*, 2:1027.

them with his reform ideas.[90] In one meeting where Prince Gong, Richard, Weng, and several other Chinese officials were present, Nicholas R. O'Connor, the British minister to China, said he could see the beginning of China's fall and noted that many foreign countries wanted to have a slice of it. He asked why China was still so deeply asleep.[91]

Weng Tonghe was by this time a strong supporter of reform, which was evident in his diary by spring 1895, when it became clear that China was going to lose the war. In April 1895 Weng presented his student, Emperor Guangxu, with writings by the modernizers Chen Chi 陳熾 and Tang Zhen 湯震.[92] Weng joined the Zongli Yamen in August 1895, and while he certainly had less prior experience in dealing directly with foreigners, he clearly demonstrated that he desired a good working relationship with Hart. They met very regularly to discuss issues related to loans; revenue raising and methods, including changes in stamp duties to increase revenue; and the issues around the management of new treaty ports. More than once they had long discussions, not always directly related to practical matters. For example, one day in September 1895, Hart, Weng, and Zhang Yinhuan 張蔭桓, another minister of the Zongli Yamen, met to talk about how the adoption of the silver standard would affect the repayment of loans. The conversation got sidetracked, and they drifted into a discussion about philosophy that focused on Mencius 孟子 (372–289 BCE) and Mozi 墨子 (470–391 BCE). Reflecting on the conversation, Weng recorded in his diary that it was "incredible." After several intense conversations with Hart in the aftermath of the war, Weng came to the same conclusion Wenxiang had arrived at in 1861: that Hart could be very useful for China, though he seemed to forget that only a few months earlier he had recorded that Hart was rather a "hateful man" when the latter reduced the size of a loan intended to support the ongoing war effort from £5 million to £3 million.[93]

90. Mao, *Wuxu bianfa de lingmian*, 451–63.

91. Weng, entry for Guangxu reign year 21, month 9, day 14 (October 31, 1895), in *WRJPY*, 4:1982.

92. Weng, entry for Guangxu reign year 21, month 3, day 23 (April 17, 1895), in *WRJPY*, 4:1949.

93. Weng, entries for Guangxu reign 21st year, 7th month, 24th day, and 8th month, 4th day (September 12 and 22, 1895) and for Guangxu reign year 20, month 12, day 26 (January 21, 1895), in *WRJPY*, 4:1975, 1974, 1932.

Weng's approach to reform involved making connections with individuals already in the field, and particularly those who had worked for Li Hongzhang and Zhang Zhidong.[94] Wu Tingfang, who had previously been instructed by Li Hongzhang to explore the possibility of setting up post offices at treaty ports by applying the "government-supervised merchant undertakings" approach, found his way to Beijing. In September, Wu tried to impress Weng by talking up potential projects on the railways, in banking, on the mint, on stamp duties, and on the postal service.[95]

In early December, Hart made observations on what had been going on at court in these months, and noted that a coup d'état would not astonish him, as officials were grouping themselves behind either Emperor Guangxu or Empress Dowager Cixi. He noted that Weng was very close to Timothy Richard and Gilbert Reid, a US missionary, and that the two Westerners were providing the emperor's teacher with all sorts of reform ideas. Hart's view on these "two Rs" was that they were "worthy people both, but the idea of their reforming China, remodeling its institutions, and, in short, carrying on its government, is too delicious!"[96] Perhaps Hart had some premonition of the Hundred Days' Reform of 1898 and regarded any ideas that were more radical than his own as doomed to failure. Yet he would certainly have been pleased that the general atmosphere at the Qing court was favorable to his postal scheme.

On December 27, 1895, Zhang Zhidong sent three memorials to the central government regarding new military training, railways, and a national post office. The Emperor's response was agreement to proceed with the first two proposals, but with regard to the post office he pointed out that the Zongli Yamen had looked into it.[97] The atmosphere at the court at this time was favorable: Prince Gong was back at the center of power,

94. Hsiao Kung-chuan, *Weng Tonghe yu wuxu weixin*, 37.

95. Weng, entry for Guangxu reign year 21, month 7, day 25 (September 13, 1895), in *WRJPY*, 4:1974.

96. Robert Hart to James Duncan Campbell, letter 1000, December 8, 1895, in *The IG*, 2:1044.

97. Zhang Zhidong, "Qing ban youzheng pian" 請辦郵政片 [Memorial on establishing a postal service]. Guangxu reign year 21, month 11, day 12 (December 27, 1895), in Zhang Zhidong, *Zhang Zhidong quanji*, 2:1057–58.

Weng Tonghe was eager to facilitate modernization and had a certain trust in Hart, and Li Hongzhang's wings had been clipped.

Timing was everything. The Zongli Yamen had been waiting for the right moment to strike, and this arrived when Li was appointed to lead a delegation to attend the coronation of Czar Nicholas II in Russia.[98] On February 28, 1896, Li said his farewells to Empress Dowager Cixi and, three days later, appeared at the Zongli Yamen to choose gifts for foreign leaders: jade, porcelain, and bronze.[99] He then traveled south to Shanghai in order to catch the French mail boat on April 2.[100] Writing on March 15, Hart expressed his frustration that the Zongli Yamen had not yet presented its final post office memorandum to the emperor, even though it had been ready a week earlier: "Yamen is exasperating: they— the riders—rush their horses and then themselves refuse the jump!"[101] Five days later, on March 20, the Zongli Yamen presented the long-awaited proposal to the emperor, who approved it the very same day.[102]

The Imperial Post Office

Hart could now return to his old diary entry from 1867 and add a national post office to his list of responsibilities as "Inspector General of Everything." In the inspector general's circular that followed the impe-

98. Weng, entry for Guangxu reign year 21, month 12, day 27 (February 10, 1896), in *WRJPY*, 4:2000.

99. Weng, entry for Guangxu reign year 22, month 1, day 19 (March 2, 1896), in *WRJPY*, 4:2006–7.

100. Li Hongzhang's journey to Russia involved taking the French mail boat from Shanghai to Port Said; taking a Russian steamer from Port Said to Odessa via Constantinople; and taking the train from Odessa to Moscow. After Russia he would visit Berlin, Paris, and London. Robert Hart to James Duncan Campbell, letter 1008, February 16, 1896, in *The IG*, 2:1051.

101. Robert Hart to James Duncan Campbell, letter 1012, March 15, 1896, in *The IG*, 2:1055.

102. Robert Hart to James Duncan Campbell, letter 1013, March 22, 1896, in *The IG*, 2:1056; "Chinese Imperial Post: Inaugurated by Imperial Decree," IG Circular 706 (2nd ser.), April 9, 1896, in *Docs. Ill.*, 2:42; Zongli Yamen, "Yi ban youzheng," 2:57.

rial edict, he thanked Gustav Detring for his work in organizing the Customs Postal Service, which had been running since 1878; thanked Henry Kopsch for his study of postal matters, which he noted had been very beneficial in the drawing up of postal regulations; and recognized the excellent work done by Li Gui.[103] Kopsch was appointed postal secretary, in addition to his role as statistical secretary, and based in Shanghai. He had ten months to prepare before the IPO was scheduled to open to the general public on the Chinese New Year the following year.[104] Even so, after more than three decades of lobbying, now that the moment had arrived Hart sought to introduce the new service at a cautious pace. In the circular he wrote,

> Notwithstanding the fact that the sanction is both definitive and Imperial, a very modest beginning will still be made, and the system will be both introduced quietly and developed slowly; but while procedure will be so planned as to avoid friction in respect of whatever might hurt deserving people's livelihoods by unnecessary interference with existing institutions or embarrass and occasion difficulties for officials and governments, it is confidently expected that some future day will see the Imperial Post functioning widely and fully appreciated, the people finding in it and its developments an everyday convenience and the Government a useful servant and, in this populous, industrious, and letter-loving country, a perennial source of revenue.[105]

There were two reasons for Hart to take a slow approach: first, he wanted to avoid overburdening the Customs staff with too much work at the outset, as they were the only available human resource at this point; second, his team needed time to build up knowledge of running a postal service, learning through doing, while refraining from unnecessary

103. IG Circular 709, 2:56.
104. IG Circular 755 / Postal No.21, December 9, 1896, in *Inspector General's Postal Circulars 1–89*, 72, TMA, W2-1-2833. The official inauguration day for the IPO was set for Guangxu reign year 23, month 1, day 19 (February 20, 1897), which was also Hart's birthday. But in the local operations, the initial days were varied during the Chinese New Year month of 1897; see "Enclosure—Chinese Imperial Post Office," IG Circular 767 / Postal No. 28, February 13, 1897, in *Inspector General's Postal Circulars 1–89*, 104, TMA, W2-1-2833.
105. IG Circular 706, 2:42.

expenditure, as the IPO was to be funded through CMCS revenue.[106] Regarding the role of postal secretary, Hart did not want to bring in any new expertise from England because he felt any new man "would be worse than useless." While acknowledging that the IPO would have to work up to foreign requirements, key to its success was a chief who would be able to "conciliate Chinese feeling and dovetail with Chinese methods, possibilities and exigencies—three things no new-comer would understand or stand!"[107]

Kopsch was one of H. N. Lay's recruits, and had joined the CMCS in 1862. He rose to the rank of Customs commissioner in 1868, and served at many treaty ports. He was a member of the Eastern Bimetallic League, situated at the Shanghai Bund, and he published a brochure titled *Brevities on Eastern Bimetallism* in 1896.[108] In their postal plan of 1886, Hart and Kopsch had concluded that the statistical secretary should also be the postal secretary. There was a strong rationale for combining these roles: the statistical secretary acquired highly detailed and specific knowledge of the work of the treaty ports through the collation and publication of statistical reports from each of them across the whole of the Customs operation; this included responsibility for the preparation and processing of a large variety of forms covering assets, revenues, and expenditures, an overview of which would be essential in setting up the new postal administration. Kopsch's hot temper was known in the service: he had been on the receiving end of lectures by Hart on several occasions over his abrupt manner with Chinese officials and for overstepping his authorization.[109] But in comparison with handing the role to an entirely new person just landed from abroad, Kopsch's experience in China was a big advantage.[110]

106. "Postal Secretary Appointed: His Position Defined," IG Circular 873 (2nd ser.), January 3, 1899, in *Docs. Ill.*, 2:174.

107. Robert Hart to James Duncan Campbell, letter 1014, March 29, 1896, in *The IG*, 2:1057–58.

108. For the career of Kopsch, see the note in "Postal: enclosing Chinese Version of Regulations and Yamêm Memorial; Previous Action Recorded," IG Circular 709, 2:56. See also Kopsch, "Brevities on Eastern Bimetallism," 1–34.

109. Robert Hart to Henry Kopsch, April 30, 1869; Robert Hart to Henry Kopsch, January 5, 1874. MS Chinese 4.

110. Hart to Campbell, letter 1014, 2:1057–58.

Hart understood that the IPO would have to rely on native letter hongs to transmit mail to inland locations and that it would be sensible to maintain a harmonious relationship with them for as long as possible. In order to avoid a situation in which the fledgling organization would be in direct business competition, he left native letter hongs to fix their own postage rates and practices.[111] Both the Zongli Yamen and Hart wanted to leave the hongs unchallenged at this early stage to avoid public resistance.[112] The framework and general practice of the native postal industry in China can be glimpsed from the 1882–91 *Decennial Reports* of the CMCS (see table 4.1). Some treaty ports did not provide any information about letter hong activity, and although the majority of them did, it is likely that the information gathered in many places was incomplete. Nevertheless, the collated information is sufficient to demonstrate the scale of private letter hong activity.

The cautious approach adopted by Hart reflected the reality of the situation of the service as it existed at the time. It became apparent that existing postal arrangements focused on treaty ports would not be able to operate at the substantially larger scale that would soon be required. He requested that each Customs House update him on current local postal arrangements and provide a view as to whether and how they might meet demand once the IPO was officially opened to the general public the following year. The responses from Customs commissioners provide us with a useful account of the situation at the ground level.

On June 19, 1896, the acting commissioner of Tianjin Customs, Francis A. Aglen (1869–1932), responded to the inspector general's query. The Customs Postal Service in Tianjin was the most established station, as it has been the headquarters of the larger Customs Postal Service since 1878. H. D. Summers, a second-class tidewaiter, was in charge of postal operations, and he had two foreign outdoor staff to assist him as necessary. There were also a Chinese candidate clerk and twelve Chinese letter carriers. The Shanghai Local Post Office was not present in Tianjin at this time, and all foreign mail, with the exception of that coming from

---

111. "Enclosure—Chinese Imperial Post," in IG Circular 706, 2:46–48.

112. "Fan you minju rengjiu kaishe bu duo xiaomin zhi li" 凡有民局仍舊開設不奪小民之利 [The existing native letter hongs will remain running; we would not deprive ordinary people of their profit]. Zongli Yamen, "Yi ban youzheng," 2:59.

Table 4.1. Survey of private letter hongs at treaty ports, 1882–1891

City	Number of hongs	Headquarters	Areas covered	Postage price in cash (文)	Commissioners' notes
Yantai	5	Shanghai	Beijing, Niuzhuang, Shanghai, Tianjin; other southern places via Shanghai	80–200, or above	Owned by Ningbo merchants; postage based on distance, not weight
Chongqing	16	Chongqing, Hankou	Gansu, Guizhou, Shaanxi, Sichuan, Yunnan; other treaty ports via Hankou	Rate by distance: 60/letter to Hankou; 300 per parcel per catty (1.10 pounds)	3 of 16 specialized in Chongqing-to-Hankou route
Yichang	3	Hankou	Hankou, Sichuan	16 to Shashi; 48 to Chongqing (overland); 24 from Chongqing (water route); 24 to Hankou	Prepayment required to distant places
Hankou	27	n/a	Almost all provinces	200 to Beijing; 80 to Ningbo and Shanghai; 100 to Hong Kong and Canton; 24 to Changsha; 30 to Jiujiang	12 hongs using overland couriers; 15 using steamers
Jiujiang	14	Hankou, Shanghai	Jiangsu, Jiangxi	20–120 letters and light parcels	Agencies rather than branches; one agent in charge of several hongs
Wuhu	15	Shanghai	Along Yangtze River; other inland places	Rates varied by weight, distance, and competition	Armed agencies to handle merchandise
Ningbo	15	Ningbo	Other ports, inland places	30–400 by distance (e.g., 70 to Shanghai, 200 to Tianjin, 400 to Beijing)	Excellent service at excessive price

Wenzhou	9	Ningbo	Other ports, inland places, many through Ningbo	100 to Shanghai, 70 to Ningbo	6 days to Ningbo, overland couriers; 3.5 to Ningbo, "day and night" courier; combined letter discount applied
Fuzhou	8	n/a	All treaty ports; also inland locations	30 to Amoy; 50 to Shanghai; 100 to Taiwan; 200 to Hong Kong, Ningbo, other Yangtze ports	Exceeded 600 cash to Guizhou, Sichuan, Yunnan
Tainan	5	n/a	Treaty ports and Hong Kong	100 collected prior to delivery	Before the departure of a steamer, a messenger was sent around to collect mail from the offices' constituents
Xiamen	23	Half in Shanghai	Other treaty ports; also inland places, Southeast Asia	30 to Fuzhou; 100 to Hankou and Tianjin	Terminology: *pijiao* (批郊): to Southeast Asia, remittance was a large part of business; *xinju* (信局): mainly in China; *uenshuguan* (文書館): worked with the Customs Postal Service to transmit letters locally by foot messengers
Shantou	19	Some at Shanghai	Other treaty ports, inland places, and Southeast Asia (i.e., Malacca, Saigon, straits between Canton, Hong Kong and Taiwan)	30 to Xiamen and Hong Kong; 50 to Shanghai and Fuzhou; 80 to Niuzhuang, Yantai, and Hankou; 100 to Tianjin and Beijing	Two groups, Chaozhou agencies and Ningbo agencies; remittance was a large part of business; rates to northern ports doubled in winter

(continued)

Table 4.1. (continued)

City	Number of hongs	Headquarters	Areas covered	Postage price in cash (文)	Commissioners' notes
Canton	Macao–Hong Kong letter hongs (港澳信局): "considerable number"	Canton	Hong Kong, Macao	15–20 to Macao and Hong Kong	Exact number of letter hongs not given, but likely greater than 10
	Steamship letter hongs (輪船信局): 5–6	Canton	All ports in China reached by steamers; inland places	200 to Tianjin; 400 for farther northern places	Registered mail, extra fees applied
Qiongzhou	1	Qiongzhou	Hong Kong; other treaty ports in China	20 to Hong Kong; 30 to Canton; 200 for places north of Hong Kong	A local hotel took official and military mail
Beihai	0	Engaged with private steamers based in Canton	Canton; other ports	15 to Canton overland (12 days)	Used steamers and junks
Longzhou	0	Messengers from Beihai and Nanning	Guangdong, Guagnxi	30–100	No large packages
Mengzi	0	n/a	A traditional bank delivered mail and newspapers for the CMCS to Chongqing, Hankou, and Shanghai		At the provincial capital Yunnanfu (sent-day Kunming), two postal hongs to and from the Yangtze River, the coast, and Chongqing for 250 cash per 1 catty (1.10 pounds) mail matter

Source: Compiled from Decennial Reports, 1882–91.

Germany and Japan, was handled by the Customs Postal Service. Summers's daily duty started at 7:00 a.m. and continued until 5:00 p.m.; his busiest days were those when foreign steamships arrived. Aglen indicated that, under current arrangements, they would only be able to cope for a few months once the IPO was opened to the general public.[113] Summers, who was British and joined the CMCS in 1891, was later praised as a "capital man" for his excellent service during the Boxer Rebellion.[114] Despite starting from a less than prestigious position as an outdoor tidewaiter, Summers had a rather successful career in the postal service. He was promoted to postmaster for the Tianjin District in 1906, and later worked as postmaster in Beijing and other locations.[115] He was one of the senior foreign staff of the Chinese Post Office after 1914.

On June 20, the acting Customs commissioner of Ningbo, F. S. Unwin, also responded to Hart's query. At that time the post office in the city was managed by an assistant examiner and a second-class tidewaiter. In contrast to the high demand for postal services in Tianjin, on average the postal officer at Ningbo worked only two to three hours a day. Unwin estimated that, once the IPO was opened to the general public, the current arrangement would be insufficient and he might have to engage private letter hongs. He noted plans to recruit a Chinese assistant for two hours each morning and evening, and for longer when foreign mail arrived. Three letter carriers would also be required initially. He stressed that more space was needed for post office activity. Besides that in the city of Ningbo, Unwin proposed a plan to set up a postal branch at Zhenhai, a busy town north of Ningbo. Two staff members, one foreign and one Chinese, would be required in order to execute the plan.[116]

It is clear that service provision was at the time very uneven. The report on the situation in Nanjing from the Zhenjiang Customs commissioner, Walter T. Lay, revealed a very different picture to that of Ningbo or Tianjin. The Zhenjiang Customs commissioner was also in charge of the opening of an IPO office in Nanjing. Although Nanjing was one

113. Francis A. Aglen to the IG, June 19, 1896, SHAC, 679 (2) 1936.

114. This was noted by the postal secretary, Jules A. van Aalst. "Postal Secretary's Office Mr. van Aalst's Memo to Successor," October 10, 1901, SHAC, 679 (1) 14908.

115. *Service List (1907)*, 176.

116. F. S. Unwin to the IG, June 20, 1896, SHAC, 679 (2) 1336.

of the treaty ports named by the French Treaty of Tianjin in 1858, it was not opened for foreign trade until the spring of 1899.[117] For this reason, in contrast to the situation at the other two ports, the Customs Postal Service presence there was almost nonexistent, as what limited services were needed there were outsourced. For domestic letters, a private letter hong was engaged to manage all mail requirements inside the city. For foreign mail, an agent of the China Merchants' Steam Navigation Company was assigned to collect and transport all mail to and from steamers. Lay believed it would be wise to establish a formal contract with this agent, as he provided a service to nearly all bund frontages and enjoyed a monopoly on boats. If the CMCS was able to formally secure his services in the near future, it might be able to avoid disadvantageous terms later on. Space to set up IPO premises was also an issue in Nanjing, and Lay had recently sent a man out to look for a suitable building with land for expansion. But aside from this, he believed there was no need to spend money until business began to increase.[118]

Two months later, Lay wrote again. An IPO branch had been duly set up, and this had attracted no resistance from either the private letter hongs or the general public. He had held a meeting with some representatives of the local private letter hongs to explore future collaboration. With assistance from the same private letter hong agent, Lay had also assigned D. Mullen, a British second-class tidewaiter, to take on the main postal duties. (We will return to Mullen's career in chapter 6.) Lay noted that when the IPO was opened on the Chinese New Year, there had been very little to do. But on the following day he wrote, "We were besieged by people who were anxious to buy stamps, to enquire if they could post letters to all parts of the empire, and in particular if they could transmit money."[119]

These examples are indicative of the wider situation for the Customs Postal Service in the run-up to the formal launch of the IPO, running at

---

117. "Nanking, 1892–1901," *Decennial Reports 1892–1901,* 1:405.

118. Walter T. Lay to the IG, December 9, 1896, SHAC, 679 (2) 680. Walter T. Lay was the brother of Horatio Nelson Lay. See note of IG Circular 432 (2nd ser.), in *Docs. Ill.,* 1:591.

119. Walter T. Lay to the IG, February 10, 1897, SHAC, 679 (2) 680. For D. Mullen's record, see *Service List (1895),* 34.

a small scale or even barely functioning. Working hours varied widely depending on locations and seasons, and there was a mix of individuals engaged: Customs outdoor staff of the Revenue Department along with some local Chinese contracted for specific activities. These arrangements, reflecting tight budgetary control of postal-related activity, continued into 1897.

In preparation for the launch, Customs commissioners were instructed to display a notice to inform the public about the establishment of the IPO, and private letter hongs were required to register with it before the Moon Festival of 1897. In the places where the IPO was to have an established initial presence—in treaty ports, with the exception of Chongqing, Longzhou, and Mengzi—the hongs were also required to hand in their collected mail to the IPO in sealed packages for transmission.[120] This new rule created a clash between the IPO and the hongs; repeated conflicts along these lines were to become a significant part of Chinese postal history in the years that followed, as we shall explore in later chapters.

In order to make the IPO accessible to the general public without requiring too much initial investment, the IPO worked with shops to set up letter boxes. For example, in Tianjin, after identification of suitable, trustworthy Chinese shops in the city and its suburbs, their premises would be supplied with a letter box along with stamps for sale to the public. The letter box was to be placed in a convenient location inside each shop, with an accompanying sign in Chinese displayed outside:

A Notification from the Post Office

Be aware that postage stamps of the Post Office have been entrusted to [name of shop] for sale; a letter box is also set up inside the premises. With the exception of parcels and other objects, all residents and travelers may insert letters for any destination with postage stamps affixed into this box. The Post Office will collect mail accordingly every day. This rule applies to all; please follow and do not disobey it.[121]

---

120. "Enclosure—Chinese Imperial Post," 2:50.

121. "Youzhengju yu" 郵政局諭 [A notification from the post office], enclosed in Louis Rocher to Francis A. Aglen, October 18, 1897, TMA, W2-4. My translation.

Louis Rocher, by now the Customs commissioner at Shanghai, also worked with selected shops, located in both the International Settlement and the French Concession. In his notification, in addition to a message similar to the one being displayed in Tianjin, the text also emphasized that the service was available to "people of all colors and races" to ease the minds of native Chinese.[122]

Despite Hart's stated intention of avoiding competition with private letter hongs at this early stage, the hongs at treaty ports felt the impact straightaway. Relations were immediately set on edge due to requirements for registration and initiatives on working with local shops, and tensions rose immediately in Shanghai over the Chinese New Year period of the IPO's formal opening. There were sixteen hongs registered with the IPO in Shanghai, and during the holiday season, they worked at different speeds; this became the background to a conflict between them. The letter hong named Quantaisheng 全泰盛 reportedly handed its mail collections into the IPO more rapidly than anyone else, and this led to panic among the rest. The hongs at Shanghai decided to hold a meeting in a local restaurant but, unexpectedly, two to three hundred people showed up. These extra people were mainly from the hongs operating along the Yangtze River, as they were facing similar competition from the IPO and were not happy with the new rules. The crowd quickly turned into a mob, and they held the Quantaisheng manager responsible for their difficulties. They tore off his fox fur jacket and beat him up, and they also destroyed the restaurant's furniture (see fig. 4.3). The local police arrested some of them; afterward, Kopsch and Rocher promised to look into the matter and come up with some solutions.[123]

In addition to the relationship between the IPO and the native letter hongs, Hart and Kopsch had to face another important matter: China's membership in the UPU. Their divergent views on this topic were to lead to a parting of the ways soon after the birth of the IPO.

---

122. "Fan zhu se ren deng yi ti zun zhao" 凡諸色人等一體遵照 [The rule applied to people of all colors], appendix 2, in Rocher to Aglen, October 18, 1897. My translation.
123. "Xinju zhao shi" 信局肇事 [Letter hongs caused trouble], *Shenbao*, February 8, 1897.

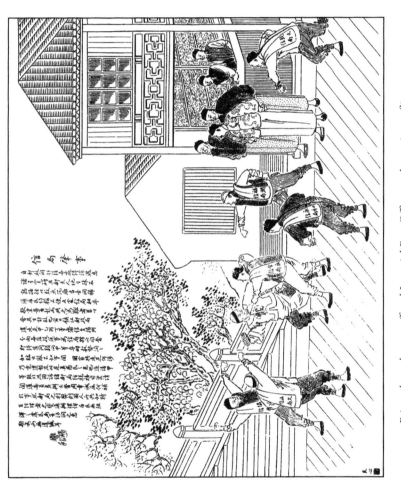

FIGURE 4.3 Private letter hong staff and Imperial Post Office employees in conflict at a restaurant. The hong staff are angry with the IPO, which is depriving them of business. Each figure is marked with a hong's name; the exception is the third figure from the left, marked in the center of his chest by two Chinese characters signifying "Post Office." Source: *Dianshizhai Pictorial (Dianshizhai huabao* 點石齋畫報), issue 10, February 10, 1897.

The Universal Postal Union and France

In his work on the history of the International Telegraph Union and the UPU, taking China and Japan as examples, Douglas Howland uses the concept of "administrative internationalism" as a framework for exploring interactions between nations in the late nineteenth century. In making a distinction between administrative internationalism and sovereignty-based diplomacy, Howland argues, "Where the sovereign state became the preferred unit of international society in the course of the twentieth century, international administrative unions presented a different mode of international order in the nineteenth century."[124] Prior to the establishment of the League of Nations after the First World War, international cooperation was based either around multilateral treaties or on cooperative organizations under the broad category of administrative internationalism. The Geneva and Hague Conventions are examples of the former, and the Red Cross and the UPU of the latter.[125]

When Japan set up its national post office in 1871, it hoped the post offices of Britain, France, and the United States would withdraw from Hyogo, Nagasaki, and Yokohama. This did not happen automatically, however, and even when Japan tried to force the issue through treaty renegotiation, it still failed. Japan turned to the UPU for a solution, and hoped the administrative power of the union would apply pressure on those nations that had their own postal services in Japan. It formally joined the UPU in 1877, and the British General Post Office withdrew from Japan in 1879, with the French postal service leaving the following year.[126]

Hart did not think Japan's case was applicable to China, even though China also had foreign post offices in its territory. Notably, when China was invited to join the International Telegraph Union in 1885, Li Hong-

124. Howland, "An Alternative Mode of International Order," 162.
125. Howland, "Japan and the Universal Postal Union," 23–39. See also Howland, "Telegraph Technology and Administrative Internationalism," 184–87.
126. Yabuuchi and Keisuke, *Nihon yūbin hattatsushi*, 116–24.

zhang and Sheng Xuanhuai both rejected the idea.[127] When an invitation arrived from the Swiss Federal Council of the UPU to become a new member, Hart requested that the Zongli Yamen inform the council of China's intention of eventual membership but noted that this membership would not take full effect until the IPO branches at the treaty ports were in good working order.[128] Hart had embraced the idea that he did not want China to join the union too soon, complaining that both France and Germany wanted to bully China into joining the UPU prematurely.[129]

Hart's stipulations regarding international mail were as follows: first, foreign mail arriving in China should be transmitted by the IPO rather than by foreign post offices in China; second, the IPO should observe the rules and rates set up by the UPU, even without acceding to membership.[130] Hart believed that voluntarily observing the rules of the UPU at the current stage would be sufficient for the IPO to operate according to international standards without being forced to comply straightaway with all international obligations. His plan was that the IPO should negotiate its own arrangements with the post offices of Hong Kong, Russia, and Singapore, while conversations with the post offices of French Indochina and Taiwan were already underway. The IPO was also working on securing bilateral agreements with key foreign post offices and the Shanghai Local Post Office.[131] Bilateral agreements were later reached with the British and French postal services.

Although Hart had insisted that the Zongli Yamen decline full membership of the UPU, he wanted China to attend the Postal Union Con-

127. Li Hongzhang, "Zi ju Sheng dao Xuanhuai xiang cheng Zhongguo dianxian ru hui you sun wu yi qingxing you" 咨據盛道宣懷詳稱中國電線入會有損無益情形由 [On Sheng Xuanhuai's claims that there is no advantage but damage to gain if China were to join the International Telegraph Union], Guangxu reign year 12, month 1, day 1 (February 4, 1886), ZYJYD, 01-09-010-01-001.

128. IG Circular 743 / Postal No.18, September 23, 1896, in *Inspector General's Postal Circulars 1–89*, 63, TMA W2-1-2833. The document was issued in the name of Prince Gong.

129. Robert Hart to James Duncan Campbell, letter 1065, May 23, 1897, in *The IG*, 2:1119.

130. "Enclosure—Chinese Imperial Post," 2:51.

131. Robert Hart to F. E. Taylor, H. F. Merrill, and Bruce Hart, Postal Congress, Washington, No. 1, March 25, 1897, MS Chinese 5.

gress, to be held in Washington, DC, in 1897.[132] China's delegation comprised Wu Tingfang, now the Chinese ambassador to the United States; Francis Edward Taylor, the statistical secretary and deputy postal secretary; Robert Hart's son Bruce, who worked at the London office of the CMCS; and Henry F. Merrill, the Chinese secretary of the CMCS, who was on a special mission to the congress.[133]

Merrill, an American, was instructed to stay in the background in order to make connections with all the necessary parties in managing postal collaboration with Japan and the United States. Merrill's mission also included initiating talks on individual mail arrangements between China and its neighbors.[134] During the six-week-long congress, there were many group meetings, and the delegation was often asked, "When will China join the Union?"[135] The meetings privately arranged between Bruce Hart, Merrill, and one Captain Brooks, the superintendent of foreign mail for the US Post Office Department, were the most fruitful. These three met on several occasions over the following few months, and the discussions resulted in an understanding between the two post offices, including rates, routes (via Japan on the Pacific routes), and carriage by steamship companies.[136]

Behind the scenes, there was another reason for Hart's reservations about moving to full membership in the UPU: France's interest in the new service. As soon as the IPO was established, the French minister to China, Auguste Gérard, had asked that the Zongli Yamen be "fair" when recruiting foreign staff for its new IPO. In response to this query, Hart had explained to the Zongli Yamen that, for the foreseeable future, there would be no need for fresh recruitment as he would use existing Cus-

132. The conversation with the UPU was kept alive, mainly through Campbell, for a number of years. Before formally joining the UPU in 1914, China sent delegations to attend important meetings, including Postal Union Congresses in Washington in 1897, Paris in 1900, and Rome in 1906. Collectively these meetings provided opportunities for China to glean useful postal knowledge and to conduct useful networking.

133. Hart to Taylor, Merrill, and Hart, March 25, 1897. As usual, Hart gave lengthy instructions on the key tasks for this mission and referred to several critical postal communications in the past so that the delegation would be well prepared beforehand.

134. Robert Hart to H. F. Merrill, August 15, 1897, MS Chinese 4.

135. H. F. Merrill to Robert Hart, June 24, 1897, MS Chinese 5.

136. H. F. Merrill to Robert Hart, November 15 and December 6, 1897, MS Chinese 5.

toms staff to support the IPO's activities. He said to the Zongli Yamen that the IPO was China's own business, and that foreign countries should not get involved, let alone insist on the use of French consultants.[137]

At the heart of the so-called Scramble for China in 1898, pressure from France to push the Qing government to use Frenchmen for the IPO increased, alongside urgent issues on new loan arrangements, the lease of Guangzhou Bay, and the construction of the Indochina-Yunnan Railway. France successfully extracted a promise from the Zongli Yamen that, when China's IPO left the custody of the CMCS and became independent, China would accept France's recommendation for its directorship.[138] Hart wrote to Campbell, "The P.O. too has to be pushed on a bit, but I go at it in a half-hearted way knowing the French want it as soon as it is on its legs and independent."[139]

Clearly Hart wanted to keep the IPO under his protection, and was reluctant to expand it too soon to avoid straining CMCS finances, as well as keeping it away from France. He therefore had a very different view from Kopsch regarding the timing of UPU membership. Their argument over UPU membership can be traced back at least as far as 1889, and this became a reason, though not the only one, for Kopsch's resignation.[140] But ultimately the division between the men was one of approach: Kopsch

137. Zhang Yi, *Zhonghua youzhengshi*, 311–12. Along the same lines, years later in a letter to Campbell, Hart wrote, "We must hold on to it as a Customs department—otherwise it [the IPO] will become French and cease to be Chinese and cosmopolitan"; Robert Hart to James Duncan Campbell, letter 1331, June 12, 1904, in *The IG*, 2:1416.

138. Pierre René Georges Dubail, "Zhong Fa tielu zujie ji youzhengju shi" 中法鐵路租界暨郵政局事 [On the railways, concessions and postal service matters between China and France], Guangxu reign year 24, month 3, day 19 (April 9, 1898), ZYJYD, 02-02-012-01-001; Stephan Jean Marie Pichon, "Pinyong Fa yuan shi" 聘用法員事 [Employing French people], Guangxu reign year 24, month 8, day 28 (October 13, 1898), ZYJYD, 002-02-012-01-002.

139. Robert Hart to James Duncan Campbell, letter 1119, October 23, 1898, in *The IG*, 2:1175; Stanley F. Wright, *Hart and the Chinese Customs*, 675.

140. Hart was also dissatisfied with the way Kopsch organized stamps and postal regulation for money orders, and said he regretted making Kopsch the postal secretary. Robert Hart to James Duncan Campbell, letter 1062, April 18, 1897, in *The IG*, 2:1115. In another letter Hart wrote, "As to the Postal matter I do not want China to enter Union until work can be properly done and as our hands have been these last two years, and are still, too full of much more important work, I am in no hurry to make any advance." Robert Hart to Henry Kopsch, June 18, 1889, MS Chinese 4.

wanted to build the IPO from the top down, and to that end thought early membership of the UPU would assist in a process of modernization. Hart, however, sought to apply more of a bottom-up philosophy and "perfect the domestic system" first.[141] He said to Kopsch, "The Union cannot help me to eject the others and adherence to it would saddle us with all sorts of reciprocal obligations and special responsibilities for not one of which are we ready! First get the offices all opened and in good working order—crawl, walk, trot, gallop—that's my plan: and you must take your time from me!"[142]

Kopsch, a long-term partner of Hart on postal matters, took leave in May 1897, and never returned to the CMCS. He found his life elsewhere, and his thirty-eight-year service to the CMCS officially ended in January 1900, when Hart accepted his resignation. He gave Kopsch £1,000 as a farewell gesture to thank him for his work on the postal project and the Statistical Department.[143] The departure of Kopsch meant that Hart's bottom-up approach to the IPO's development would have to be carried out by someone else. The question of joining the UPU would not be settled until 1914.

141. Robert Hart to James Duncan Campbell, letter 1062, April 18, 1897, in *The IG*, 2:1115.

142. Hart quoted what he wrote to Kopsch in his letter to Campbell; Robert Hart to James Duncan Campbell, letter 1057, March 14, 1897, in *The IG*, 2:1109.

143. Hart, journal entry for January 2, 1900, SQBH; IG Circular 783 / Postal No. 37, May 12, 1897, in *Inspector General's Postal Circulars 1–89*, 118, TMA W2-1-2833.

CHAPTER FIVE

"Crawl, Walk, Trot, Gallop"

Local Politics and the First Stages of Postal Expansion

The end of the First Sino-Japanese War sparked the beginning of a new political storm. Between June and September 1898, the Guangxu Emperor's Hundred Days' Reform proceeded chaotically, ending in bloodshed. Even as it began, Robert Hart had already noted how febrile the situation was. On May 29 he recorded, "Prince Kung dead," and on June 19, in a letter to James Duncan Campbell, he captured an unexpected development at the center of power as Weng Tonghe was dismissed; for Hart, this was the Empress Dowager Cixi's revenge for how Weng had treated her favorite, Li Hongzhang: "It seems that Wêng's own fussy conservatism, perhaps lending itself to a palace plot to put power in the Empress Dowager's hands, has been the chief cause of the cruel Edict the Emperor threw out at him. It is said there is more to follow . . . and possibly the old lady, finding that the blood she has tasted does no harm, may go in for a deeper libation."[1] But as things turned out, it seems apparent that Weng had a lucky escape, as he would surely have been caught up in the brutal coup that ended the Hundred Days' Reform.[2] The first wave of postal expansion began in the aftermath of these events.

Initial Trials for Postal Expansion

On September 12, 1898, the Zongli Yamen ordered Hart to accelerate postal expansion and prepare to take over the workload of the military relay courier system. The apparent trigger for this was a plea to the Zongli Yamen from a low-ranking scholar, Shen Zhaohui 沈兆禕, in Beijing. Shen, who held the relatively modest official title of senior licentiate (*yougong* 優貢), claimed that people who had experienced the workings of the Imperial Post Office (IPO) were impressed and pleased; therefore, he suggested it should open more branches beyond those in the capital and the treaty ports. This plea from a member of the literati was not interpreted as a one-off but rather as representing a wider view shared by many in the country. No doubt part of the enthusiasm of the central government stemmed from hopes for a fresh revenue stream, as well as the potential to save money on the military relay courier system. The Zongli Yamen used the opportunity to ask Hart to work on postal expansion on two fronts: first, to open more postal branches in Beijing and the treaty ports; and second, to introduce postal services to inland prefectures, at the level of provincial capital (*fu* 府), subprefecture (*ting* 廳), department (*zhou* 州), and district (*xian* 縣).[3] Looking beyond immedi-

---

1. Hart, journal entry for May 29, 1898, SQBH; Robert Hart to James Duncan Campbell, letter 1112, June 19, 1898, in *The IG*, 2:1169.

2. Mao, *Cong jiawu dao wuxu*, 380–83, points out that in order to reduce his own risk when the Hundred Days' Reform became contentious, Weng Tonghe changed some of the content of his diaries with the aim of covering up his involvement with Kang Youwei.

3. Zongli Yamen to IG, Guangxu reign year 24, month 7, day 27 (September 12, 1898), enclosure, in "Postal Secretary Appointed: His Position Defined," IG Circular 873 / Postal No.44, January 3, 1899, in *Docs. Ill.*, 2:176.

ate expansion, the Zongli Yamen also wanted to know how the IPO might replace the military relay courier system and Wenbao bureaux in providing a service to local governments.

Hart complained about the Zongli Yamen's expectations to Campbell, noting that "the Zongli Yamen is urging me to push on with Postal extension, Stamp-duties, etc: but is not even giving me the *soap* with which to blow the bubbles."[4] Responding to the Zongli Yamen, Hart reminded them that, so far, the central government had not yet set up a specific budget to fund the IPO; therefore, with the only resources available being the moderate funding coming from the Chinese Maritime Customs Service (CMCS), the IPO could not be expanded overnight. Despite his protestations over funding, Hart went on to outline three areas of focus for expansion. First was a clear commitment that, within six months, clusters of postal branches were to be gradually extended from their existing locations in the treaty ports and new post offices opened progressively in the direction of the interior. Second, referring back to his postal plan of 1893, Hart proposed a widespread opening of post offices attached to train and telegraph stations, and he asked the Zongli Yamen to render support by ordering the managers of relevant companies to offer suitable rooms either within their premises or nearby for the IPO to use. Alongside this, Hart requested that railway companies be obliged to permit IPO employees to travel along with mail items for a reasonable charge and that telegraph companies be obliged to allow the IPO to send messages at reduced fees. Hart stressed it was important that the three utilities should work together closely in the interests of the state, and he hoped the Zongli Yamen would put its weight behind this.

By this time, combining postal services with railway and telegraph systems was no longer a fresh idea. It had first been formally proposed in Hart's "Bystander's View," and discussion of the issue had been going on for some time among some Chinese elites. Recording his thoughts on traveling to Europe with Binchun and Hart in 1865, Zhang Deyi 張德彝 (1847–1918) had been impressed at how trains operated in France. He noted that telegraph and postal facilities had been set up at train stations

4. Robert Hart to James Duncan Campbell, letter 1121, November 13, 1898, in *The IG*, 2:1177, emphasis in the original.

to help provide timely service.[5] When Wang Tao 王韜 was in Cairo and London in 1867, he, too, was impressed by communications systems that brought together steamers, trains, and postal services.[6] While these writings did not gain much traction in the 1860s, by the late 1870s and early 1880s similar discourses had begun to pop up in various places, urging public support for a series of railway and telegraph projects. Among the people who promoted these schemes were Guo Songtao, Ma Jianzhong, and Xue Fucheng, all of whom were in favor of the establishment of a modern post office (see chapter 4), and would be posted to Europe as diplomats at different stages of their careers.

The third element of Hart's postal expansion plan concerned the military relay courier system, and how the IPO might assist it by sharing some of its workload. Knowing this was a sensitive subject, Hart avoided engaging directly in questions of its abolition, declining to offer any sort of plan or timetable and recommending that the Zongli Yamen discuss the future of the military relay courier system with the Board of War before making any drastic changes. At this early stage, Hart's view was that the IPO might be able to offer its support in collaborating with the governors of most provinces in the transmission of official mail if this could be sent to the main offices of the IPO at one of the treaty ports. This was not, of course, possible in provinces where there were no treaty ports, such as Gansu, Henan, Shaanxi, Shanxi, and Xinjiang.[7]

All three of Hart's areas of focus for expansion came to be very important in driving the growth of the service. The establishment of new clusters in coordination with railway and telegraph services became central activities in postal route planning, while coordination and collaboration with the military relay courier system became progressively more important at a later stage, as the IPO expanded to frontiers. The principal mechanism in operation at this time of postal expansion was a combination of cluster-based and path-shaped approaches. The former was "based on extremely dense centers with sparser surroundings," and the latter "based

5. Zhang Deyi, *Hanghai shuqi*, 43.

6. Wang Tao, *Manyou suilu*, 78, 113.

7. IG reply to Zongli Yamen, Guangxu reign year 24, month 8, day 4 (September 19, 1898), enclosure, in "Postal Secretary Appointed: His Position Defined," IG Circular 873 / Postal No. 44, January 3, 1899, 2:184.

on a specific route, not on a group of neighboring centers."[8] These two approaches were not mutually exclusive; indeed, they were often complementary. The cluster method dominated planning in cities, from the selection of trustworthy shops as postal agencies to positioning letter boxes outside hotels or respectable residents' properties, while path-driven planning relied heavily on (often interprovince) steamship and rail routes and on the creation of long-distance routes to China's frontiers.

Jules A. van Aalst (1858–191?) was Henry Kopsch's replacement.[9] Van Aalst's knowledge of postal matters was not as comprehensive as Kopsch's, and Hart had to spend a considerable amount of time coaching him, while his appointment resulted in a change to Hart's original plan to have the postal secretary based in Shanghai acting jointly as statistical secretary. The postal secretary from this point onward was based in Beijing. Van Aalst was Belgian, and had joined the CMCS in 1881 as an outdoor staff watcher in Canton.[10] When he was transferred to Beijing in 1883, he was assigned to postal work.[11] Hart was delighted to have this bright young man alongside him in Beijing, not least because Van Aalst was an excellent musician, playing piano, flute, and oboe. Hart, himself an amateur violinist and cellist, was soon asking Campbell to send him the latest sheet music; there were several other musicians in their circle, and many Saturday nights were soon given over to concerts.[12] Hart appointed Van Aalst to attend the International Health Exhibition in London in 1884 and proposed that he write a book on Chinese instruments for the exhibition. Van Aalst compiled an introductory book

8. Segal, "Communication and State Construction," notes that one of the principal mechanisms in operation in Germany's main period of postal expansion was a combination of cluster-based and path-shaped approaches. This mechanism proved useful in conceptualizing the construction of postal networks in China.

9. IG Circular 783 / Postal No. 37, May 12, 1897, in *Inspector General's Postal Circulars 1–89*, 118, TMA, W2-2833; IG Circular 801 / Postal No. 40, September 29, 1897, in *Inspector General's Postal Circulars 1–89*, 121, TMA, W2-2833.

10. *Service List (1881)*, 33.

11. Van Aalst joining as a watcher was not mentioned in the institutional short biography attached to "Postal Secretary Appointed: His Position Defined," IG Circular 837, January 3, 1899, 2:174.

12. Robert Hart to James Duncan Campbell, letter 395, January 7, 1883, in *The IG*, 1:429; Robert Hart to James Duncan Campbell, letter 429, August 11, 1883, in *The IG*, 1:480.

titled *Chinese Music*, which was published by the Statistical Department
of the CMCS. In his introduction, Van Aalst observed that, rather than
getting into debates with those who might regard Chinese music as "de-
testable, noisy, monotonous [and] hopelessly outrages our Western notions of music," he wanted his volume to show "the contrast or similarity
between Western and Chinese music, to present abstruse theories in the
least tiresome way, to add details never before published and to give a short
yet concise account of Chinese music."[13]

Van Aalst brought fresh energy to the execution of postal expansion.
He noted that suboffices would need to be opened in order to increase
the density of connections between cities, towns, and villages. Two kinds
of suboffices were envisioned: the first type would function as postal
branches, with their work involving both the reception and distribution
of mail; the second type would simply sell postage stamps and receive
postal matter. The second type was more like a postal agency (discussed
in detail chapter 6).[14] It was the district postmasters' responsibility to
identify locations for new branches, but they were to follow a clearly stipulated process for extending the service:

> It is, in each district, from the Head Office as a starting point and with
> the Head Office for terminus, to and from the interior, that develop-
> ment is to be planned. The first sub-Office of any line must be con-
> nected with the District Head Office, the second sub-Office with the
> first, the third with the second, and so on, and each sub-Office must
> have its own local staff and its own set of Couriers to run no further
> than from their station to the next. The fifth station must not be opened
> till the first, second, third, and fourth have been established.

Regarding the selection of premises for new post offices, temples were
seen as the best option, and particularly those with large courtyards and
several rooms for hire; otherwise, shops in central parts of cities were also
to be considered, with thought given to space for future enlargement. One
or more signboards with white backgrounds and black Chinese characters

13. Van Aalst, "Introduction," in *Chinese Music*, iii.
14. IG Circular 877 / Postal No. 45, January 9, 1899, in *Inspector General's Postal Circulars 1–89*, 144, TMA, W2-2833. Later, Van Aalst clarified the first type as postal branches; see "Inland Extension," Postal Circular 23, June 26, 1899, in *Postal Secretary's Circulars 1–134*, 178, TMA, W2-2833.

reading "Great Qing Post Office" (Da Qing youzhengju 大清郵政局) would be hung in prominent places, and offices were to be neat and respectable. There should also be a small reception room with simple Chinese-style furniture to receive local officials or respected customers. Each proper suboffice would have its own staff, in the roles of clerk, sorter, and carrier, and in order to reduce friction with local private letter hongs, any of the staff who showed interest in working for the IPO should be given priority in the hiring. This principle was particularly to be observed in inland areas in order to take advantage of individuals who possessed good local knowledge and had previous experience in postal work. In inland stations, "strangers, i.e. men not of the locality, should not be used . . . except temporarily to initiate the work."[15]

Van Aalst distinguished private letter hongs in inland areas from those on the coast that had come to rely on steamships—"coast postal hongs" (*lunchuan xinju* 輪船信局).[16] He believed particular care should be taken to foster collaboration with inland letter hongs, where the IPO had far fewer resources. In order to gauge the effort involved in establishing offices inland, a formal trial was conducted. Deng Weifan 鄧維藩, a Chinese assistant postal clerk from the Beijing Post Office, was sent to open a series of suboffices between Beijing and Jinan. This was a successful case study for the IPO, as through it the IPO was able to identify and consolidate those practices that worked well. Deng's experience provided the IPO with much useful information on how to interact with both local governments and the general public, and his initiative also inspired the IPO to work even more closely with local shops.

Deng Weifan's mission covered eight locations across Zhili and Shandong, and they were a mixture of provincial capital, prefecture, subprefecture/department, and district locations. Listed in chronological order of opening, these were Baoding, Hejian, Xianxian, Dezhou, Qihe, Dongguang, Cangzhou, and Jinghai (see fig. 5.1). After arriving in each place, the first tasks for Deng were to find a suitable place to rent and to hire or assign staff to run the branch and provide a courier service to carry mail

15. Postal Circular 23, June 26, 1899, 178–79.
16. Van Aalst used the phrase "coast postal hongs" for 輪船信局, although the literal translation of this term is "steamship letter hongs"; Postal Circular 23, 178–79. His usage was widely accepted in the IPO communications.

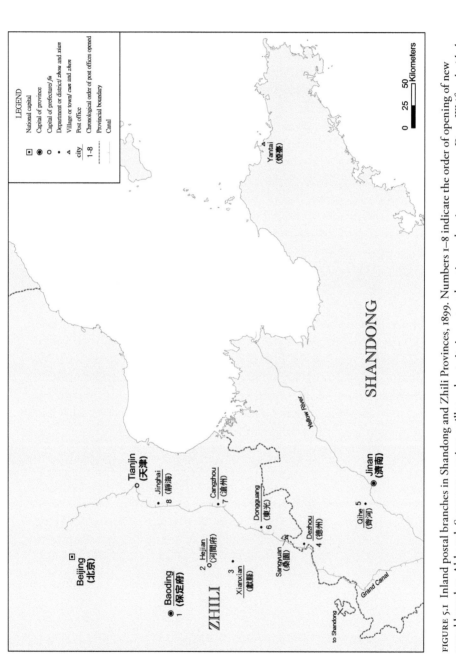

FIGURE 5.1 Inland postal branches in Shandong and Zhili Provinces, 1899. Numbers 1–8 indicate the order of opening of new postal branches. Although Sangyuan was just a village, due to its important location and active commerce, Deng Weifan decided to open a branch there. Map © Weipin Tsai; cartography by Huang Chingchi.

between the new branch and two or sometimes three other branches. Location was the most important consideration, and Deng established his eight branches in a mixture of temples, churches, and shops. In Baoding, the provincial capital of Zhili, a temple to the Red Emperor Guan 紅關帝廟 was rented. This temple, which had eleven rooms and was situated in the middle of the city, was only three *li* (1.9 kilometers) from the railway station (see fig. 5.2).[17]

Baoding shared characteristics with many towns in northern China. Streets and lanes were narrow, and its widest street would most likely have been able to accommodate just one horse-drawn cart at a time.[18] Deng had the rooms refurbished, and also had the main gate repaired, above which he placed the official signboard. He also posted notifications at the entrances to several streets to advertise the new postal service. These notifications opened with a line that emphasized that the IPO had been set up by the inspector general by order of the Guangxu Emperor with the aim of introducing a service beneficial to commerce and to the general public (see fig. 5.3).[19] These messages also included information on the location of the post office and its opening hours, which were 8:00 a.m. to 5:00 p.m. The Baoding branch received many inquiries, as the town had a sizable number of resident merchants and officials. There were already five or six private letter hongs serving the town, with an estimated combined daily throughput of around thirty letters. In a very short period, the business of the post office exceeded the performance of the hongs, receiving more than one hundred mail items daily.[20]

The next stop was Hejian, around 208 *li* (around 129 kilometers) from Baoding. Hejian was home to around two thousand Muslim households, as well as a large Christian community. Deng Weifan rented some rooms from Shengshitang 勝世堂, a Roman Catholic organization with a printing workshop. Although Hejian had the status of a prefecture, there were scarcely any wealthy people there, and the daily collection was only of two or three letters; it is therefore logical to assume that the location of

17. Deng Weifan report, enclosure, in "The Peking-Chinan Line," *Postal Circular* 25, September 25, 1899, in *Postal Secretary's Circulars 1–134*, 186, TMA, W2-2833.

18. Wang Qingcheng, "Wan Qing Huabei cunluo," 19.

19. Jules A. Van Aalst to the Postmaster at Tianjin, March 6, 1899, TMA, W2-5.

20. Deng Weifan report, 186.

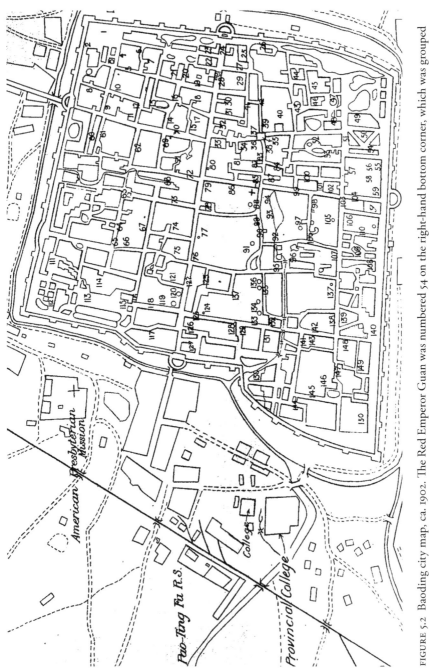

FIGURE 5.2 Baoding city map, ca. 1902. The Red Emperor Guan was numbered 54 on the right-hand bottom corner, which was grouped with other temples. The railway station, "Pao-Ting Fu R.S.," was located just outside the city wall on the left-hand side. Source: Used by permission of the British Library.

大清郵政官局揭曉

旨飭令

照得前經奉

總理衙門轉飭總稅務司設立

大清郵政官局並次第推廣以便商民而收利權茲於

本府城內紅關帝廟街關帝廟內添設郵政局每

日自早八點鐘至午後五點鐘收發各項信件其

資費辦法即請到局探詢先特宣布眾知

光緒二十五年正月二十七日

FIGURE 5.3 Post Office notification displayed in Baoding, Zhili Province. Source: Enclosed in J. Van Aalst to the postmaster at Tianjin, March 6, 1899, TMA, W2-5.

a postal branch there was an IPO decision made at least in part to serve the local churches, as well as to provide a useful link in the postal chain. The third stop was Xianxian, south of Hejian. Again, despite the fact that this was a very poor county, a postal branch was opened on a church property, and in addition, a letter box was set up in a shop inside the city.

Deng placed notifications at another three shops outside the city to advertise the service.[21]

Dezhou, on the Grand Canal at the border between Shandong and
Zhili, was Deng's fourth stop. Although Dezhou had been an important
relay station for the Customs Postal Service since 1878, it had never previously been home to a post office branch. The new branch was opened
on a commercial street near the south gate of the city, and Deng predicted
it would be busy, as the city had an active commercial community. After
Dezhou, Deng traveled on to Qihe, which had been a relay station for
the Customs Postal Service that was close to a major crossing point of
the Yellow River, and it deserved a proper post office to work in conjunction with the one at Dezhou.

Deng's final three stops were at Dongguang, Cangzhou, and Jinghai, each also on the Grand Canal. At Dongguang it was very difficult
for Deng to secure premises, but after ten days he found some near the
city's north gate. The district magistrate (*zhixian* 知縣) of Dongguang
was very curious about the IPO and asked Deng many questions. While
establishing the Dongguang office, Deng's attention was drawn to the
town of Sangyuan, which in comparison to Dongguan had a more active commercial community, although it had a lower position in the
administrational hierarchy. He therefore decided to set up an additional
postal station there. Deng then made his way to Cangzhou, and discovered that the town suffered from recurrent violent clashes between the
Manchu military and the Muslim community. He requested assistance
from the Cangzhou departmental magistrate (*zhizhou* 知州) responsible for the area. Like his colleague in Dongguang, the magistrate in
Cangzhou knew nothing about the IPO and asked many questions. In
the end he agreed to arrange regular patrols to protect the post office
site and also to publish notifications to explain the government-
controlled nature of the IPO to the general public. Unfortunately, Deng
had less luck with the district magistrate of Jinghai, despite the fact that
the county had also been one of the relay stops of the Customs Postal
Service since 1878. This magistrate refused to see Deng because he did
not have the right paperwork.[22]

21. Deng Weifan report, 187.
22. Deng Weifan report, 188.

On completing his tour, Deng summarized his experience and made a number of recommendations. Some of these proved to be very valuable and were incorporated into the general guidelines for future practice, such as procedures for furnishing premises as well as guidance on interacting with local communities. As Deng's trip was the first attempt by the IPO to open branches outside the familiar treaty port environment, the biggest unknown factor was how the service would be received by both local residents and local officials. Deng noted a considerable degree of ignorance about the establishment of the IPO even among local officials, let alone among ordinary people. He and his colleagues did their best to hide the fact that the IPO was managed by foreigners and, to reduce any possible suspicion, avoided showing any documents or forms containing English in front of customers or officials. They also put notifications outside the post office, by the city gates, and at the entrances of main streets to explain the postal regulations and assure the populace that the IPO was a Chinese organization.[23] Although some governors at treaty ports had issued proclamations to inform people that the new postal service was indeed opening under imperial sanction, people at large were slow in grasping this fact.[24] This meant that the work of promoting the IPO to the general public mainly fell on the shoulders of the IPO staff.

In some respects, this is puzzling. It had been three years since the imperial decree announcing the national postal service, so why were local administrations not engaged in its rollout and promotion? Deng's experience took the IPO deep into the treacherous area that was to prove the biggest challenge in executing inland postal expansion: local politics.

Postal Expansion and Local Officials

As is shown in Fei Xiaotong and Wu Han's work on the structure of traditional Chinese society, the bureaucracy and local gentry at the department and district levels were positioned between emperors and the common

---

23. Deng Weifan report, 189.
24. Walter T. Lay to IG, "Post Office Fracas at Yangchow," March 29, 1897, SHAC (2) 680.

people. An emperor did not communicate directly with either the local gentry or the common people but instead through the local bureaucracy, who were his servants and the executors of his will. Bureaucracy and the gentry were deeply intertwined with one other, the common thread being the exam system. Between them they controlled knowledge, land, and wealth, and held great sway over public opinion. Within this structure, if an emperor did not have the support of both the bureaucracy and the local gentry, his legitimacy was threatened.[25] The influence of the local gentry has already been illustrated by the actions of Shen Zhaohui in pleading with the central government to expand the postal service.

Sharing a similar perspective, Tung-Tsu Ch'u, in his study on the local political system of the Qing dynasty, points out that all administrative units, from the province to the department and the district, "were designed and created by the central government, which financed their budgets, appointed their officials, and directed and supervised their activities." Magistrates of department and district were agents of the central government, and they carried out the policies of the state in taxation, jurisdiction, public works, education, and civil defense. The magistrate of a district held the lowest jurisdiction, and no other form of government existed below this. Because a magistrate was never a native of his jurisdiction, he heavily relied on local gentries for information and allowed them to have "informal power" in ruling.[26] In his study on rural China, Kung-chuan Hsiao notes the tightly woven links between clan leaders, rural headmen, and gentry in the implement of social order at the lower administrative level—particularly in villages.[27] Collectively these studies argue that given the structure of Chinese society and politics in the late Qing period, local officials and members of the gentry

25. Fei, "Jiceng xingzheng de jianghua," 338–40; Wu Han, *Huangquan yu shenquan*, 2–9, 41–50.

26. T'ung-tsu Ch'u, *Local Government in China*, 1, 15–16, 168–82. See also Wei Hsiu-Mei, *Qingdai zhi huibi zhidu*, 8–15. The Qing government imposed a strict system to prevent nepotism, applied to most officials with some exceptions. The principle was to post officials outside their native province. A distance of five hundred *li* (around 310 kilometers) was originally used; it was reduced to three hundred *li* (around 186 kilometers) in 1908.

27. Hsiao, *Rural China*, 264–74.

remained among the most important channels for implementing central policies.

In Deng Weifan's report, the seeming lack of awareness of the postal project among local officials in Zhili and Shandong, the two provinces closest to the capital, signaled either a state of broken communications between the central power and its local administrations—or, alternatively, if local officials were feigning ignorance, an effective deprecation of state policy. In either case the attitude of local officials toward the IPO was significant in three aspects. The first aspect was how the IPO, in its very early stages of establishment, would be perceived at the grassroots of Chinese society. This was related to whether or not local officials would be willing to create a friendly environment for its arrival and actively work to minimize local hostility, including providing protection to staff and premises. The second aspect was how the arrival of the IPO disturbed the existing sociopolitical order, which was constituted by the local merchants, gentries, and even magistrates' subordinates who tended to stay behind after local magistrates were transferred to other places.[28] The third aspect was that, given that local officials, from prefects to magistrates, were obliged to carefully receive and observe orders from their superiors, specifically provincial governors (*xunfu* 巡撫) or governors-general (*zongdu* 總督), the attitude of these senior officials toward the IPO was most critical to the success of its expansion. Sitting between the local magistrates and the central government, provincial governors and governors-general had significant influence on magistrates concerning transfers, retention of positions, and recommendations for preferment and promotion.[29] The governor was the highest authority (both civil and military) in a province, subordinate only to a governor-general, who would typically oversee two or three provinces. Both provincial governor and governor-general were well informed about the decisions and policies of central government, and they had the responsibility of passing on new orders to subordinates in their jurisdiction and of making sure these orders were carried out.[30]

28. For the relationship between magistrates, who moved from place to place either by transfer or promotion, and their subordinates, who had been local residents for generations, see Feng Xianliang, *Ming Qing Jiangnan*, 480–81.

29. Watt, *The District Magistrate*, 46–47.

30. Ch'u, *Local Government in China*, 6–7.

Deng Weifan's somewhat uneven experience with local magistrates was echoed by that of other senior postal staff. The experience of Hosea Ballou Morse at Longzhou was a good example. Longzhou was in Guangxi Province, on the border with French Indochina, and had become a treaty port in 1887. When Morse arrived in 1896 he found "everything quiet, and no questions even raisable." He believed that the best thing he could do after his arrival was to "sit tight and do no spurring." But within a week, he had already met the magistrate (*taotai* 道台) twice. He found that the magistrate was interested in only two things: the post office and opium, the two items that he considered might attract income. The magistrate had previously received a dispatch from the governor communicating the Zongli Yamen's memorial on the launch of the IPO, as well as operational details set out by Hart. Subsequently, the governor also directed the magistrate to appoint a deputy (*weiyuan* 委員) to assist in postal matters. Although it was common, indeed necessary, for the local governor, who was sometimes also the Customs superintendent at a treaty port, to have a deputy to act as his right-hand man and as a go-between with the Customs commissioner, such a position was not required for postal work. Having some suspicions about the unusual attitude of the magistrate, Morse asked to read the dispatch from the governor. After digesting its contents, Morse considered he needed to clarify some issues. First, he stressed that the business of the IPO was a concern for the whole empire rather than something to be dealt with at the provincial level. Second, he emphasized that postal rules would be made by the IPO rather than by local officials.[31] Morse had hoped that, after these clarifications had been given, the magistrate would step back and let IPO personnel proceed according to their own practice. But the magistrate still went ahead and appointed a deputy, instructing him to lease premises for the post office. His view was that the sooner the post office opened, the quicker a profit could be made. In the end Morse had to communicate that there was no rush to open a post office until detailed instructions had been issued, and when the time came, the post office would be opened at the Customs House.[32]

31. Hosea Ballou Morse to Robert Hart, June 10, 1896, MS Chinese 3.
32. Hosea Ballou Morse to Robert Hart, June 24, 1896, MS Chinese 3.

Later Morse had a somewhat different experience in dealing with officials when he was posted to Yuezhou to open a brand new Customs House and post office there. Originally Hart wanted to send Julius Neumann; however, the viceroy, Zhang Zhidong, objected to Neumann, as the German was reputed to have a bad temper and to be unsuited to such a delicate task.[33] On his arrival, Morse encountered a completely opposite attitude from the local magistrate. In contrast to the overenthusiasm he had encountered in Longzhou, in Yuezhou the magistrate was very reluctant to enter into any specific discussion about either Customs House or post office. After one dinner, the magistrate made it very clear to Morse that he was Zhang Zhidong's nominee, and until he had settled affairs with the viceroy and the newly appointed provincial governor, he would prefer not to give his personal opinion.[34] The situation, however, shifted rapidly after the magistrate received orders from the viceroy, and he demanded the post office be opened "at once."[35] Post office premises were subsequently established in Yuezhou, Changde, and Changsha. These examples indicate that provincial governors acted as gatekeepers for the transmission of policy initiatives between central government and local officials at department and district levels. In the progress of the extension of IPO services to the interior, in the absence of direct communication between the Zongli Yamen and local magistrates, the attitudes of governors toward the IPO was decisive.

As a general principle, the staff of both the CMCS and the IPO, from high-ranked officials to the general workforce in front-line service, were required to see themselves as employees of the Qing government, empowered to carry out the state's policies. This was a long-term institutional principle established by Hart back in the 1860s. Many ranks within the CMCS, whether "indoor" or "outdoor," were required to rotate between different treaty ports. This deliberate practice of transferring staff to a new location every few years was intended as a mechanism to keep them fresh and engaged in local affairs and to broaden their experience within the Qing empire. The practice also helped to unify procedures across the

33. Robert Hart to Hosea Ballou Morse, April 13, 1899, MS Chinese 4.
34. Hosea Ballou Morse to Robert Hart, June 13, 1899, MS Chinese 3.
35. Hosea Ballou Morse to Robert Hart, July 27, 1899, MS Chinese 3; and Hosea Ballou Morse to Jules A. Van Aalst, July 27, 1899, MS Chinese 3.

service.[36] Of the various ranks, the most frequently rotated were commissioners at the Customs Houses, although there were some exceptions, such as Gustav Detring, with his long tenure at Tianjin.

Through being stationed at multiple treaty ports, Customs commissioners acquired experience in dealing with local officials, including Customs superintendents and their deputies. In fact, since the service's early years, clear instructions on how to deal with local Chinese officials had already been laid down.[37] Hart also gave individual commissioners specific instructions as particular situations arose. For example, in 1867, he had written to Charles Hannen, the commissioner of the Jiujiang Customs House, to instruct him in how to handle the discipline of Chinese clerks who had connections with the local magistrate. Hart's advice to Hannen was to dismiss a Chinese writer just as he would his own private writer in such a circumstance, but report the dismissal to the magistrate and ask him to find a replacement. If the magistrate was unable to find a replacement, or delayed making an appointment, Hannen should find a new writer himself. He also insisted that Hannen assert his authority: if any Chinese writer refused to act under a foreign one, he was to "dismiss him on the spot: don't ask any one's opinion." If there was a query from the deputies, "just tell them quietly you have dismissed the person for disobedience, and say no more. . . . Be very quiet, very pleasant, and good tempered with them; but be firm, and don't stand any nonsense."[38] Such firmness notwithstanding, Hart believed that friendly relations with local officials was essential, and when his commissioners stepped out of line and created unnecessary difficulties, they were reprimanded. For example, when Kopsch was Customs commissioner at Jiujiang in 1874, he seemed to lose his grip in dealing with a deputy. Hart told Kopsch to shake off his "unreasonable *weiyuan*-phobia" and observe certain inspector general's circulars, where the guidance for maintaining good relations with local officials was laid down.[39]

36. Drew, "Sir Robert Hart," 16.

37. "The Customs Service, the Spirit That Ought to Animate It, the Policy That Ought to Guide It, the Duties It Ought to Perform," IG Circular 8 (1st ser.), June 21, 1864, in *Docs. Ill.*, 1:37–9; IG Circular 25 of 1869, November 1, 1869, in *Inspector General's Circulars*, 231.

38. Robert Hart to Charles Hannen, May 30, 1867, MS Chinese 4.

39. Robert Hart to Henry Kopsch, January 5, 1874, MS Chinese 4.

Morse's interactions with officials in Longzhou and Yuezhou was certainly in alignment with the CMCS's institutional guidelines in avoiding unnecessary conflict with magistrates and deputies. Morse's methods in dealing with them were echoed by John Patrick Donovan (1852–193?) when he went on a tour to inspect postal work in the Yangtze River region. Donovan, who came from a poor Roman Catholic family in East London, had joined the CMCS at a young age, first traveling to China in 1873 at the age of twenty-one. He subsequently spent forty-two years of his life in China. In 1896, the year the IPO was inaugurated, he was appointed as a postal officer in Shanghai. Donovan studied postal systems of other countries, and he helped Kopsch to draw up postal rules and regulations. His inspection reports and his memoir provide an insightful account of how the service was extended to inland China in this early period of expansion. In March 1900 Donovan was ordered to take a tour to inspect postal services between Hangzhou and Hankou in the role of inspecting deputy. The places he visited included the treaty ports and inland towns and counties. The purpose of the tour was to bring uniformity into every detail of postal activity, and to evaluate new locations either for postal branches or for letter boxes through studying the size and layout of specific locations, the area's population, and its primary means of communication—water or overland. He was also tasked with talking to local officials, if they would receive him, and to explain to them the purpose and policies of the IPO.[40]

Donovan spoke good Nanjing-tone standard Chinese, Shanghainese, and several other local dialects. His language skills allowed him to communicate well with local people, and he was able to gather information firsthand by wandering along high streets and spending time in teahouses. Traveling predominately by boat, Donovan encountered both positive and negative responses from the local officials and people. Outside the treaty ports, he found that the situation was almost uniformly difficult. Just like his native Chinese postal colleagues, he reported that inland local officials typically possessed only a very rudimentary understanding of the national postal service, "and some were not aware that it was a Chinese institution owing to its being under foreign control and management."[41]

40. Donovan, "Travels and Experiences in China," 1:24, 194, 195, 202.
41. Donovan, *Yesterday and To-day in China*, 140.

For example, when he arrived in Huangzhou Prefecture, twenty-five miles (around 15.5 kilometers) southeast of Hankou, he was initially not welcome. Huangzhou was notorious for antiforeigner feeling, and the local official declined Donovan's request for a meeting. Donovan persisted, explaining the reasons for his official visit, and insisting on seeing the city; within a short time, an official chair with four "coolies" was sent to bring him to the *yamen*, the local magistrate's official residence and office. During the meeting, he caught sight of the official's female family members peeping from behind screens, but he had to pretend not to notice.[42]

On learning more about the new postal service, not all local officials persisted with their skepticism, though some were more open than others. During his trip, Donovan traveled to Nanchang, a prefecture south of the Jiujiang treaty port in Jiangxi. He journeyed by steam launch in both directions, twelve hours each way. En route, he also noticed a town called Wucheng. Despite having only the administrative status of a large village, Wucheng was substantial in size and was important as a local hub for commerce. Nanchang and Wucheng were connected by the Poyang Lake system, and there were thirteen steam launches operating there, alongside local junks. Nanchang had substantial Christian communities, including Roman Catholics and a Methodist mission.[43] Donovan noted that despite being inland, "the inhabitants were exceedingly friendly" in Nanchang. Both people and officials "were anxious for the establishment of an Imperial Office," as the local native letter hongs were not thought to provide an adequate service, and mail was at that time being sent and received via Jiujiang overland without the use of steam launches. Donovan did not manage to see the magistrate, and he blamed this on the brevity of his visit, as he was able to stay for only one full day. But he submitted his calling card and some copies of the *Imperial Postal Guide* (*Youzheng zhangcheng* 郵政章程). He recommended both Nanchang and Wucheng as places where postal suboffices should be established, and his advice was subsequently followed.[44] These are shown on a 1907 postal map (see fig. 5.4), which features the postal route between Jiujiang and

---

42. Donovan, "Travels and Experiences in China," 1:203.
43. "Kiukiang, 1892–1901," in *Decennial Reports 1892–1901*, 1:342, 360.
44. Donovan, "Tour of Inspection," April 30, 1900, SHAC 137 (1) 7603.

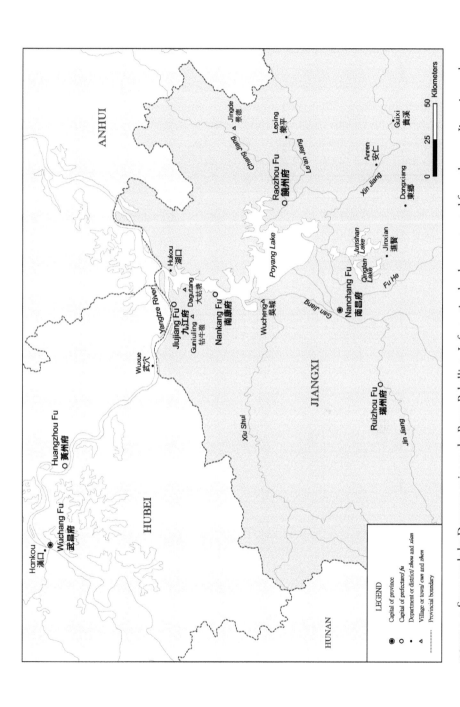

FIGURE 5.4 Stops made by Donovan prior to the Boxer Rebellion. Information has been extracted from the 1907 Jiangxi postal map in *China—Postal Album (Da Qing youzheng yutu 大清郵政輿圖)*, which was produced by the Statistical Department of the CMCS. Map © Weipin Tsai; cartography by Huang Chingchi.

Nanchang, via Wucheng; by this time an important link, it featured a day-and-night service combining water and overland carriers.

Donovan continued his tour and arrived at Ningbo on June 20, 1900. From the Customs commissioner there he learned that the German minister, Baron von Kettler, had been murdered in Beijing. More news soon came from the north that the foreign allies had started to mobilize troops and warships. The Boxer Rebellion was underway. Donovan decided to pause his tour and return to Shanghai.[45] While the Mutual Protection of Southeast China pact managed to keep the fighting away from several provinces in southern China below the Yangtze River, the turmoil caused by the Boxer Rebellion brought postal expansion to a standstill. Northern China fell into months of horror.

The Boxer Rebellion

In the days leading up to the siege, life in Beijing was already badly affected. The telegraph was completely cut off by June 10, and regular postal communication to Tianjin stopped by June 15. On June 13, E. Wagner, a French second assistant and also acting postal secretary during Van Aalst's leave, reported armed rebels patrolling several streets inside the Beijing gates all day long. At night they appeared at the post offices, threatening to burn them and kill the postal staff. Although there were official soldiers on the streets, they did not intervene with the rebels. Some postal staff ran away out of fear.[46] On receiving an ultimatum from the allied troops, on June 19 Empress Dowager Cixi ordered the foreign legations to withdraw themselves within twenty-four hours, before the formal start of hostilities at 4:00 p.m. on June 20. The legations managed to send female family members and children to safety, and proceeded to prepare to defend themselves.[47] Hart sent Edward Drew, the Customs commis-

---

45. Donovan, "Travels and Experiences in China," 1:205.

46. Robert Hart to Zongli Yamen, "Xuanwumen nei jie xi xiao shi da jie quanfei zhi youju" 宣武門內街西小市大街拳匪至郵局 [The rebels arrived at the post office situated in the main street of the western market by the Xuanwu gate], Guangxu reign year 26, month 5, day 17 (June 13, 1900), ZYJYD, 01-14-002-02-011.

47. Hart, "*These from the Land of Sinim*," 19.

sioner at Tianjin, a note via a courageous messenger, believed to be his last communication before joining the British legation for the duration of the eight-week siege that followed. In Drew's memory, the message was written in ink on a small scrap of paper. It said:

> Legations ordered to leave Peking in 24 hours!!!—R.H.
> 19 June, 1900, 4 P.M. Good bye!
> Pay bearer Tls. 100 [one hundred taels]—R.H.
>
> [To] Drew,
> Customs,
> Tientsin.[48]

Hart left his papers and invaluable personal archive of more than fifty years behind and took only "a small roll of blankets and a few clothes" with him. Crouching low at the British legation, he heard "Precisely at 4 P.M. firing began, and rifle bullets were whistling down the Wang-ta Street between Austrian Legation and [the Customs] Inspectorate."[49]

Between Beijing and Taiyuan, the post offices were either burned down or smashed up. Postal branches on the northern stretch of the uncompleted Beijing-Hankou Railway were also affected and were closed for the duration.[50] Allied troops destroyed post office premises in Tanggu, Tangshan, the Shanhai Pass, and other places. As well as destroying the Chinese post offices, they brought in their own field post offices. From the postal officer H. D. Summers's detailed report, as well as Drew's descriptive letters, we are able to get a picture of the impact of hostilities on postal activity in Tianjin and the surrounding areas from June to November, 1900. These records show a devastating loss of personnel, office buildings, and postal infrastructure, as well as material such as postage stamps and mail right across the region, in what in normal times was the busiest postal district in northern China.

The headquarters of the Tianjin Customs Service, as well as the city's post office, was situated in the French Concession. The Tianjin area was worst hit between June 17 and 23. The Qing troops, working together with

48. Drew, "Sir Robert Hart," 27.
49. Hart, "*These from the Land of Sinim*," 20.
50. H. D. Summers, "1900 nian de youzheng gongzuo qingkuang" 1900 年的郵政工作情況 [Report on the postal work of the year 1900], in *TYS*, 2.1:40–41.

rebel forces, moved into the French Concession, killing indiscriminately. Chinese residents of Tianjin suffered particularly badly as they were attacked both by Chinese rebels and by allied troops. Drew reported that French and Russian soldiers in particular behaved violently toward the native population, but that with assistance both from other allied troops and from foreign residents, around three thousand Chinese had been able to leave the town by early July.[51] By early June, most of the Chinese postal clerks at the Tianjin headquarters had already fled, somewhat understandably abandoning their posts without giving notice. Three foreign staff members disappeared, one resigned, and another was killed. By mid-June, all couriers, personal messengers (*tingchai* 聽差) and lower-class staff had also left, and only a handful of foreign staff remained. The majority of those who stayed were either ill or not experienced in postal work, with the exception of Summers himself and H. E. Howard, a British national and third-class postal officer. On June 17, roads were closed, the railway between Tianjin and Tanggu was destroyed, and rebels started to attack foreign concessions with guns and artillery. The headquarters of the Tianjin Post Office was badly damaged, and all doors and windows trashed. The attack did not cease until July 14. The sorting office was bombed while its staff sheltered in the basement. Work had effectively ceased, though Summers personally made some attempt to carry on working in spite of the chaos, alongside Howard and a recent recruit, a German man named Mileck.[52]

No mail arrived at Tianjin for two weeks until the end of June, when one hundred mailbags were delivered by warship, though many of them had already been opened and examined by Russian troops. Almost all of the associated paperwork was lost; hence it was very difficult to organize those mail shipments. With assistance from the British Navy and British Field Post, postal work started to resume on the Tianjin–Beijing and Tianjin–Tanggu lines, though the service was very slow. For protection,

51. Edward Drew to Robert Hart, June 17, 1900, in *Zhongguo haiguan yu Yihetuan*, 83–87.

52. For a description of the postal situation during these months, see H. D. Summers, "Cheng Shanghai shu youzheng zongban di shier hao wen"呈上海署郵政總辦第 12 號文 [Report no.12 to the acting postal secretary in Shanghai], November 7, 1900, in *TYS*, 2.1:32–39. See also *Service List (1901)*, 232.

newly contracted Chinese couriers were allowed to travel together with the British Field Post convoys on Mondays, Wednesdays, and Fridays. Howard accompanied the first courier trip to Yangcun and made the necessary arrangements with the British Field Post commandant there.[53] While the IPO regarded this assistance as welcome at the time, the consequence was that the British Field Post remained in China for several years, as did both German and Japanese post offices. The latter both subsequently expanded their operations across northern China, following the movement of their respective troops, and later opened their services to the general public, becoming rivals to the IPO in the region.[54] From late July onward, order was gradually reestablished in the city of Tianjin, along with regular postal services, but surrounding towns and villages were still in chaos.[55] Months later there were still many instances of interruption to postal activity; some of these were caused by Russian troops, some by other allied troops, and some by local rebels. In Jinghai a Chinese postal clerk was murdered because he was a Christian. In Yangcun a postal courier was attacked by a German soldier and his pony taken away. In Dongguang a Chinese postal clerk came close to being executed by the rebels and was spared only through the intercession of a friend. Many postal branches set up by Deng Weifan the previous year, including those at Dezhou, Hejian, and Qihe, remained closed into November.

After several weeks with no communication, Hart was believed to be dead. A funeral was scheduled for him at St Paul's Cathedral in London, and an assumed "vacancy" for an inspector general became a talking point among provincial governors-general and assorted foreign ministers. Li Hongzhang, now the viceroy at Canton, made an initial move by appointing Paul King as a "sort of Inspector General for the southern ports," with similar discussions taking place in Shanghai.[56] With support from the consular body and Nanjing governor-general

53. J. W. H. Ferguson, "Report on the Postal Communication between Peking-Tientsin and vice-versa," September 29, 1900, SHAC 679 (6) 1296.

54. Summers, "1900 nian de youzheng," 2.1:40–41.

55. Edward Drew to Robert Hart, October 5, 1900, in *Zhongguo haiguan yu Yihetuan*, 90–91.

56. Francis Taylor to Robert Hart, September 7, 1900, MS Chinese 4.

Liu Kunyi, the Customs commissioner for the Statistical Department, Francis Taylor, was ordered to act as temporary inspector general. On July 16 Taylor issued a short inspector general's circular to announce the appointment.[57]

It soon became apparent, however, that Hart had survived the siege. On July 21, he received two letters from the Zongli Yamen, and on the following day, he was able to reply. Communication between the Zongli Yamen and Hart had been reestablished.[58] The Zongli Yamen sent some vegetables, ten watermelons, two blocks of ice, and some white flour to Hart.[59] Communication more generally between Hart in Beijing and the outside world began to resume by the end of July. But the events of this time did not pass without casualties; E. Wagner was killed by a bomb during the siege, and several Customs staff were also badly wounded.[60]

Hart's response to these momentous events was characteristically thoughtful. His mind went back to Wenxiang. Having previously witnessed the Tianjin Massacre, and now surviving the Boxer Rebellion, his instinct was not for revenge or retribution but to reassess the position of Western nations in respect to this ancient civilization. While the young Hart had arrived in China as a by-product of British colonialism, the older Hart had formed his perspective. So while Western newspapers called for punitive measures, Hart suggested the world should ponder the causes of this episode more deeply. His perspective was clear: that sixty years of imposed treaties between China and the West had raised emotions across the country, and the Boxer moment was a volcano-like out-

57. "Inspector General, Officiating: Mr. F. E. Taylor appointed," IG Circular 951 (2nd ser.), July 16, 1900, in *Docs. Ill.*, 2:230.

58. Zongli Yamen to Robert Hart, July 21, 1900, in *Zhongguo haiguan yu Yihetuan*, 23; Robert Hart to Zongli Yamen, July 22, 1900, in *Zhongguo haiguan yu Yihetuan*, 24.

59. Zongli Yamen to Robert Hart, July 27, 1900, in *Zhongguo haiguan yu Yihetuan*, 25; see also Enclosure No. 9, "Zongli Yamen zongban han zhi Zongshuiwusi" 總理衙門 總辦函致總稅務司 [Secretaries of the Zongli Yamen to inspector general] in "Inspectorate General, Peking: Correspondence with Yamên and Proceeding Generally during Siege of Legations in 1900," IG Circular 961 (2nd ser.), October 5, 1900, in *Docs. Ill.*, 2:249.

60. Robert Hart to Zongli Yamen, July 22, 1900, 24. For E. Wagner, see *Service List (1901)*, 230.

let for the inevitable resentment that had built up. Among the treaties, Hart identified the imposition of "transit pass" arrangements and "extra-territoriality" as the issues causing the strongest feelings. The former allowed foreign merchants to sail through China without paying *lijin* to local governments; this put Chinese junk owners at a disadvantage when it came to competition and also reduced the income of local governments. Alongside this, extraterritoriality damaged national pride, as it allowed foreigners to be exempted from Chinese laws and customs, and created an imperium in imperio. Previously Wenxiang had expressed his view to Hart as follows: "Do away with your extra-territoriality clause and your missionaries and merchants may go where they please and settle where they please; if your missionaries can make our people better, that will be our gain; if your merchants can make money, ours will share in the advantage!" Besides transit pass and extraterritoriality issues, Hart understood that there were other reasons why Chinese officials might be sympathetic toward the Boxers and even provide them with support. Many had had unpleasant experiences in their contact with foreigners, whether in Beijing or in the provinces. They had been treated to "language and accompaniments never employed in dealings with the officials of other countries . . . foreign intercourse and its effects had made many foes—some wise men tolerated, but none loved, and many determined to end it."[61] In addition to the ambivalent attitude of the central government toward them, the Boxers also gained political legitimacy through the active support of gentry and degree holders in some northern places. As result, the Boxers were able to put pressure on magistrates to collaborate with them.[62]

After the death of Wagner and before Van Aalst returned to the post in June 1901, Donovan was appointed as acting postal secretary and stationed in Shanghai. The Beijing Post Office finally returned to normal on January 1, 1901, and the Tianjin Post Office managed to do so on March 1.[63] During his leave, with the assistance of Campbell, Van Aalst

61. Hart, *These from the Land of Sinim*, 151, 157, 161, 124, 130.
62. Harrison, "Village Politics and National Politics," 84–86.
63. For the Beijing Post Office, see "Peking Post Office, Postal Circular 38, December 31, 1900, in *Postal Secretary's Circulars 1–134*, 282, TMA, W2-2833. For the Tianjin

visited the General Post Office in London. He paid particular attention to postage stamps, postal materials, and pillar boxes, as well as to the postal collection and delivery systems operating in the city. He also went to Waterlow & Sons, where some of the Chinese stamps were printed. He met several managers of the General Post Office, and took away important documents to study, including a "Memorandum for Statistics," as well as those providing instructions to postmasters. Van Aalst was introduced to Harry Buxton Forman, who was assistant secretary of the General Post Office at the time.[64]

On returning to his post, Van Aalst wrote a long report to Hart to lay out what should be done in the aftermath of the Boxer Rebellion. In this dispatch, Van Aalst identified key issues such as membership in the UPU, competition from foreign post offices in China, and ways in which foreign-owned railways and steamship companies should assist the IPO. He specifically stressed how the service should be further expanded by enlisting the cooperation of provincial governors. Van Aalst noted that it had been more than four years since the imperial decree that had initiated the IPO, but the general public was still largely unacquainted with the service. He believed that now was the time to request the Zongli Yamen to instruct provincial governors once again to communicate about the postal service with their subordinates.[65]

It soon became clear that the political atmosphere had changed after the Boxer Rebellion, however, and the IPO had become a target for senior officials in the southern provinces. Just as Van Aalst was banking on assistance from provincial governors, the last thing he expected was that there would soon be resistance coming his way from precisely this quarter. Two important governors-general, Liu Kunyi and Zhang Zhidong, who had supported the national post office initiative in 1895 and 1896 now asked the central government to revisit the postal project and to halt the growth of the IPO outside the treaty ports.

Post Office, see "Tientsin Post Office," Postal Circular 43, February 9, 1901, in *Postal Secretary's Circulars 1–134*, 289, TMA, W2-2833.

64. James Duncan Campbell to Robert Hart, Z/801, April 5, 1901, in Hart and Campbell, *Archives of China's Imperial Maritime Customs*, 3:546.

65. Van Aalst to Robert Hart, July 21, 1901, SHAC 679 (6) 1297.

Zhang Zhidong Tries to Turn Back the Clock

Before Empress Dowager Cixi was allowed by the allies to return to Beijing, she was required to agree on the necessity for reform. And so she did. Under the name of the Guangxu Emperor, in January 1901 an edict was issued to announce the Qing government's intent. Li Xizhu's study of the role played by provincial governors in the reforms launched after the Boxer Rebellion explores the various ways governors communicated and collaborated in order to ensure their views were heard by the central government. Soon after the edict was issued, the governor of Shandong, Yuan Shikai 袁世凱; the viceroy of Hubei and Hunan, Zhang Zhidong; the viceroy of Anhui, Jiangsu, and Jiangxi, Liu Kunyi; the governor-general of Sichuan, Kuijun 奎俊 (1841–1916); the governor of Shanxi, Cen Chunxuan 岑春煊 (1861–1933); and other governors around the country began to contact one another with unusual frequency. They discussed their views on the present situation, agreed on common positions, and decided whether memorials to the throne should be sent singly or jointly. For these governors, it was extremely important to get the message and tone of their input correct, as no one at this stage really knew how serious Empress Dowager Cixi was about reform and how far she was prepared to go down the path of a Western-style program. On reading the imperial edict, Zheng Xiaoxu 鄭孝胥, who had been lightly involved in the Hundred Days' Reform and a close associate of Zhang Zhidong, believed that it carried "too many empty words, and its real meaning was rather hidden."[66] Besides, the memory of the bloody events which had ended the Hundred Days' Reform was still fresh in the minds of many people.

While some governors sent their memorials individually, Zhang Zhidong and Liu Kunyi had three joint memorials carefully prepared, collectively referred to as the "Three Memorials for Reforms from the Governors-General of Jiangsu and Hubei" ("Jiang Chu huizou bianfa sanzhe" 江楚會奏變法三折). These memorials were to become the foundation for the Qing government's final set of reforms over its last ten years: the so-called New Policies (*Xinzheng* 新政). The three memorials were a

66. Li Xizhu, *Difang dufu yu Qingmo xinzheng*, 57–58, 105, my translation.

significant outgrowth of the framework of the Self-Strengthening Movement and represented a much greater expansion of Hu Yufen's 1896 reform proposal (see chapter 4). One of the memorials, titled "Memorial on Eleven Western Methods for Reform" ("Chouyi bianfa jin ni caiyong xifa shiyitiao zhe" 籌議變法謹擬采用西法十一條折), is particularly relevant in the context of these pages because it touched on postal issues. The memorial was lengthy, and it addressed matters related to education, recruitment for the civil service, constitutional and legal reforms, military reform, agriculture, commerce, mining, industrialization, currency reform, and ways to improve government revenues.

On postal matters, the memorial proposed to drastically reduce the role of the IPO and allow local governments to organize their own postal services. It argued that the IPO had caused upset for private letter hongs and therefore brought trouble and additional workloads for local officials. It also complained that the fees charged by the IPO for remittances and money orders were too high and that the IPO deprived the general public of the convenient service provided by the hongs. The solution proposed was to allow each province to make good use of the existing military relay courier system by permitting it to receive mail from the public. While the funding for the military relay courier system from the central government was to be reduced, provincial governments were to be permitted to keep the income raised through providing mail service to the general public. The memorial stressed that there would be no need to open too many branches, and no need at all to hire foreigners who might interfere in China's domestic affairs. The IPO should be content with serving the treaty ports, as well as controlling the steamers on the coasts and main river routes; transportation on inner water routes should remain under the control of the officials of prefecture, department and district, without any involvement of the Customs commissioners.[67]

Generally speaking, these memorials were well received after being circulated among high officials and foreign diplomats, and they certainly helped shape the New Policies reform. Yet no action was taken by the

---

67. Zhang Zhidong, "Chouyi bianfa jin ni caiyong xifa shiyitiao zhe," Guangxu reign year 27, month 6, day 5 (July 20, 1901), in Zhang Zhidong, *Zhang Zhidong quanji*, 2:1445–47.

central government to implement the recommendations for the postal services, and the IPO soon resumed its expansion program, including opening several branches in Hubei over the course of 1901. *Shenbao* praised this "state owned and self-made" postal service, claiming that merchants and the general public all benefited from it.[68]

Such developments provoked Zhang Zhidong into further action. In December 1901 he sent memorials individually to the Ministry of Foreign Affairs. Earlier that year, as requested by the Boxer Protocol, the Zongli Yamen had been upgraded to become the Waiwubu. Zhang's memorials addressed two specific issues: native Customs and postal matters. In contrast to the relatively calm tone adopted in the previous joint memorial, Zhang wrote in terser language, stating that Hart had too much power. He added that although he appreciated that the government had huge indemnities to pay, foreign powers should not interfere in how the funds should be raised and should not help the Customs commissioner at Hankou to expand his power. He particularly emphasized that it was wrong for the postal service to extend inland, and that if the central government did not do something to constrain matters, Hart would eventually come to control all important interests as well as the governing power.[69]

Two weeks later, Kuijun, the governor-general of Sichuan, sent a memorial to the same office, echoing Zhang's views. He urged the Ministry of Foreign Affairs to order the inspector general to halt all postal expansion outside the treaty ports in Sichuan and to stop attempting to control some native Customs stations in the greater Chongqing area. Kuijun stressed that, previously, the Zongli Yamen had only allowed post offices to be opened in the treaty ports, and if the Customs commissioner tried to set up branches inland, this would reduce the power

68. See, for example, "Tuiguang youzheng" 推廣郵政 [Promoting the postal service], *Shenbao*, December 7 and December 13, 1901.

69. Zhang Zhidong to Waiwubu, "Gekou changguan gui shuisi jianguan deng qing you" 各口常關歸稅司兼管等情由 [On the management of native customs by Customs commissioners], Guangxu reign year 27, month 11, day 3 (December 13, 1901), ZYJYD, 01-14-021-02-076. Regarding Hart's power, Zhang wrote, "Ruo bu ji zao xianzhi Zhongguo zhengquan liquan jiang jin gui Hede yi" 若不及早限制中國政權利權將盡歸赫德矣 [If the power of Chinese government is not restricted soon, it will fall on Hart].

of local officials and disrupt local Customs.[70] Following these two memorials, Liu Kunyi submitted his own to address the point about the
postal service.[71]

To make sure the postal issue could not be quietly ignored by the
Ministry of Foreign Affairs, Liu Kunyi and Zhang Zhidong also expanded
their campaign, engaging with Chinese-language newspapers in Shanghai and accusing Hart of leading far too many projects beyond his core
business of collecting trade tariffs. The newspaper reports that resulted
used quite sensational language, arguing that China had fallen into the
hands of foreigners, that Chinese officials were acting as local guards, and
that Chinese people were effectively slaves. They added that the central
government should immediately put a stop to Hart's postal extension and
allow local provinces to manage their own postal services.[72] It is interesting to note that even though in a strict sense the IPO at this time was
under the supervision of the Ministry of Foreign Affairs, these officials
already considered the postal service as a domestic operation, and they
sought to paint the use of foreigners to run it as an affront to their conception of Chinese sovereignty. This view ultimately came to be reflected
in the reorganization of the central government in 1906, which will be
addressed in chapter 7.

When Hart learned how severely he was being publicly criticized outside Beijing, he was horrified. In what was turning into a political show-
down, Hart decided to spend his sixty-seventh birthday writing to the
Ministry of Foreign Affairs. He laid out a series of facts that would have
been all too familiar both to members of the ministry and to local governors, explaining why the CMCS was set up in the first place, why he

70. Kuijun to Waiwubu, "Fei tongshang kouan kaiban youzheng fenju Jiangbei mu
guan liang shi shuisi bude lanban you" 非通商口岸開辦郵政分局江北木關兩事稅司不得攬
辦由 [Postal branches at nontreaty port areas and native Customs in Jiangbei should
not be managed by Customs commissioners], Guangxu reign year 27, month 11, day 13
(December 23, 1901), ZYJYD, 01-14-021-02-089.

71. Liu Kunyi to Waiwubu, "Youzheng ben shu Zhongguo neizheng deng qing
you" 郵政本屬中國內政等情由 [The postal service by nature belongs to China's domestic affairs], Guangxu reign year 27, month 12, day 13 (January 22, 1902), ZYJYD,
01-14-021-02-113.

72. Robert Hart to Waiwubu, February 20, 1902, in *Zhongguo haiguan yu youzheng*,
103–4.

had become inspector general, why the IPO was established and why it had to expand inland, why the military relay courier system was to be abolished, and why some *lijin* and some native Customs were placed under his control. This recapitulation of institutional history was not Hart's central message; rather, it formed the backdrop to his insistence that either provincial officials should fully accept that postal extension was state policy and get behind the policy rather than causing problems, or he would be happy to return to Britain.[73] For Hart, it is clear that the issue was sufficiently important to be a potential resignation matter.

In its response, the ministry said that when it had received these memorials from the local governors, it had immediately rejected their contents. The ministry even took the step of reminding Zhang Zhidong that he himself had previously recommended giving approval to Hart's postal project back in 1895. The ministry acknowledged Hart's efforts in carrying a heavy burden for the government over many years and expressly stated that it wanted him to stay. Indeed, to emphasize this point, Hart was rapidly granted an audience with Empress Dowager Cixi and the Guangxu Emperor on February 23. In that twenty-minute meeting, Hart was treated to a flattering reception. He was given some presents from the royals: a piece of calligraphy of the word *fu* 福 (fortune), four embroidered screens, two porcelain vases, and four rolls of silk satin.[74] In conversation, the Empress Dowager recalled that Prince Gong had presented Hart's "Bystander's View" to her in the 1860s and said "it would have been better for China if his ideas had been carried into practice at that time."[75] She also emphasized her determination to persist with the planned reforms. Hart expressed in return that he "could not be expected to retain the position for ever. . . . Her Majesty smiled and said change was not desired."[76]

73. Hart to Waiwubu, February 20, 1902, 104–6.
74. "Inspector General: Sir Robert Hart Granted Audience by the Empress Dowager and Emperor," IG Circular 1007 (2nd ser.), February 26, 1902, in *Docs. Ill.*, 2:307–9.
75. "Peking: Imperial Audiences," *North China Herald*, March 12, 1902. In this audience setting, three people were received by order. The first one was Hart, and the other two were two bishops of the Roman Catholic Church in Beijing, Monsignors Favier and Jarlin.
76. "Inspector General: Sir Robert Hart Granted Audience by the Empress Dowager and Emperor," IG Circular 1007 (2nd ser.), February 26, 1902, 2:307.

On the surface it seems strange that fingers should be pointed at Hart and the IPO, and in particular that objections had been raised in such vehement language. Why had powerful individuals like Liu Kunyi and Zhang Zhidong changed their attitude, from supporting the IPO to attacking it? The answer, of course, was money. The Qing government's financial situation had been seriously impacted by the First Sino-Japanese War. In order to manage the indemnity, China had taken three large loans from foreign banks between 1895 and 1898. The third loan, of £16 million, was issued jointly by the Hong Kong and Shanghai Bank and the Deutsch-Asiatische Bank. As projected Customs tariff revenue provided insufficient security for these loans, the Qing government arranged additional fixed quotas from the general *lijin* of Hangzhou, Jiujiang, Shanghai, and Suzhou, along with the salt *lijin* of Datong in Anhui, Hankou, and Yichang.[77] Hart had once pointed out that *lijin* control would hurt the private purse of every Chinese official, and he was right about this.[78] The situation was only to get worse from this point, as further financial difficulties arrived following the Boxer Rebellion. In order to settle the Peace Protocol and Boxer indemnities, the Qing government had to reorganize its revenues, taking away further income from local provinces. The total amount of the Boxer indemnities was Hk. Tls. 450 million, extending over thirty-nine years to more than Hk. Tls. 982 million with interest; each year the payment was not to exceed Hk. Tls. 20 million. The remaining revenues of the CMCS not yet allocated as loan collateral were far below being sufficient to meet this. It was agreed that the tariff should be raised to an effective 5 percent ad valorem rate. Additionally, native Customs revenues within a fifty-*li* (around 31 kilometers) radius of the open ports had to be drawn in to secure the payment, and these revenues were placed under the responsibility of the CMCS. This meant that a significant portion of the income of local governments was removed and redesignated.[79]

77. Chen Shiqi, *Zhongguo jindai haiguanshi*, 297, 302–3; Stanley F. Wright, *Hart and the Chinese Customs*, 665–66.

78. Van de Ven, *Breaking with the Past*, 140.

79. Stanley F. Wright, *Hart and the Chinese Customs*, 745–46; Weipin Tsai, "The Inspector General's Last Prize," 244.

In the end, Hart remained at the helm, and the IPO continued to expand. In the midst of this political drama, Li Hongzhang had been relatively quiet, perhaps because he was preoccupied in negotiating with the allied nations. In early November 1901 he died, just hours after he had signed the final Boxer Protocol. Hart wrote,

> Poor old Li was at work thirty hours before death: wonderful vitality—wonderful determination not to succumb and not to let anybody have a say in things so long as he was to the fore to decide! He died on the 7th and I was in his room just after they closed the coffin on the 8th. The Diplomatic Body visited on the 9th. *Yuan Shih Kai* is to be Viceroy. As I said in my wire, except that Russia loses her man, his disappearance will have no effect, i.e. no bad effect. In fact, it will be all the better for China when the old fogies make room for the coming men: but these latter will, in turn, make just as many mistakes—of another kind![80]

80. Robert Hart to James Duncan Campbell, letter 1222, November 10, 1901, in *The IG*, 2:1289.

CHAPTER SIX

Becoming Chinese

In October 1901, Jules A. Van Aalst was removed from his position as postal secretary. Robert Hart had had concerns for some time over whether Van Aalst was the best man for this position, related in part to his commitment to postal work but also to his hot temper. On his return from Europe, Van Aalst openly disobeyed an official instruction from Hart concerning the treatment of money orders; soon after, Hart decided to replace him.[1] On November 1, Théophile A. Piry (1851–1918) took over as postal secretary. Hart made an effort to ensure a smooth handover: he praised Van Aalst for his "industry and attention to duty" and publicly noted that the change was not a "prelude to change of plan or principle" for the Imperial Post Office (IPO), calling for loyal cooperation from district postmasters and other postal staff in working with Piry "for the

---

1. When dealing with money orders, Hart wanted the postmasters to charge according to the rate of exchange, but Van Aalst told them not to follow Hart's instructions. Robert Hart to James Duncan Campbell, letter 1217, October 6, 1901, in *The IG*, 2:1284.

extension and development of the postal system as a Chinese institution."[2] The appointment of Piry marked the end of a period of uncertainty in the stewardship of the IPO, and Piry held the position of postal secretary until his retirement in 1916.

The restoration of postal services in northern China and the arrival of Piry did mark a new beginning after the upheaval of the Boxer Rebellion. Hart experienced a sudden moment of doubt soon after the appointment, fearing that Piry might plot with the French government to gain control over the IPO, but the air was soon cleared.[3] Hart and Piry's explicit strategy was to maximize the Chinese character of the IPO and to make its services available as widely as possible across the country. Reestablishing the approach that had been in force before the upheaval had intervened, the IPO pushed on with exploiting its monopoly use of trains and steamships in order to move deep into the territory of the private letter hongs. At the same time, the IPO also promoted its Chinese character and branding to the general public, particularly through collaboration with local shops and through the efforts of Chinese postal clerks, who were the face of its front-line services.

A Change in the Political Climate

If there was an ideal place in which to focus efforts to rebuild and repair the physical damage and address the emotional losses suffered by the postal service during the Boxer Rebellion, it was surely Shanxi Province, which had experienced some of the most devastating violence seen during the period. In some ways it was a small thing in the context of the countless broken and devastated souls in the province, but the restoration of postal communication would bring with it a measure of hope.[4] The Shanxi governor, Cen Chunxuan, wrote to Hart to request the

2. IG Circular 988 / Postal No.53, October 31, 1901, in *Inspector General's Postal Circulars 1–89*, 167, TMA, W2-2833.

3. James Duncan Campbell to Robert Hart, Z/1388, August 21, 1903, in Hart and Campbell, *Archives of China's Imperial Maritime Customs*, 3:752.

4. For detailed accounts of the violence, see Harrison, *The Missionary's Curse*, 108–15.

restoration of postal services in the province, and he held out the prospect that if the post office could be restored to how it was before, relations between the Chinese and foreigners could be rebuilt and perhaps even improved. Cen Chunxuan had recently been promoted to this position after protecting Empress Dowager Cixi and the Guangxu Emperor in their flight from Beijing to Xi'an. He wanted a post office to be set up at Taiyuan, and the existing post office at Xinle to be relocated to Zhengding. While both Xinle and Zhengding were on the northern stretch of the Beijing-Hankou Railway, Xinle did not have a train station. The governor acknowledged that there would still be challenges for the postal service, as many rural places in Shanxi were very isolated, and their population, including local officials, very conservative. But he vouched to do his best to persuade people across the province that disagreements should be set aside and relations between Chinese and foreigners rebuilt.[5]

In response to Governor Cen's request, Hart wrote that he was more than willing to open a post office in Taiyuan, but in order to do so it was necessary first to reopen the existing post offices in Baoding and Dingzhou, which had been closed and damaged during the Boxer Rebellion. They were also on the northern stretch of the Beijing-Hankou Railway, situated on the main route between Beijing and Taiyuan, and were needed to provide essential logistical support for Taiyuan. The work to rehabilitate the post offices at Baoding and Dingzhou, and to move the post office from Xinle to Zhengding, would require ten to fifteen days for each task, so Taiyuan would have to wait for around fifty days before the city would have its own post office.[6]

Weeks later Hart wrote again to update the governor on progress. He noted that the IPO had sent a Chinese postal clerk named Deng Weiping 鄧維屏 to Dingzhou and Zhengding, and that postal services had been successfully restored after the railway line between Baoding and Dingzhou had been reinstated. The railway line between Dingzhou and Zhengding was not yet ready, however, and mail would therefore be trans-

---

5. Cen Chunxuan to IG, Guangxu reign year 27, month 3, day 24 (May 12, 1901), enclosure, in IG Circular 975 / Postal No. 52, September 17, 1901, in *Inspector General's Postal Circulars 1–89*, 159–60, TMA, W2-2833.

6. Robert Hart to Cen Chunxuan, Guangxu reign year 27, month 5, day 16 (July 1, 1901), enclosure, in IG Circular 975 / Postal No. 52, 160–62.

mitted between these two places by the military relay courier system.[7] Deng Weiping was one of the senior postal clerks, familiar with the postal regulations, and was also the brother of Deng Weifan, one of the most experienced Chinese postal clerks in the service who had set up postal branches across northern China, as discussed in chapter 5. In the same piece of correspondence, Hart also reported that he planned to send Deng Weifan and two other Chinese postal clerks to Taiyuan; he asked Governor Cen to assign some staff to assist the group after their arrival. Before the departure of these men, the Zongli Yamen issued them with passports to minimize any difficulties with local officials in their journey between Beijing and Taiyuan.[8] Hart also communicated with officials at Dingzhou and Zhengding to ask them to provide protection for the clerks as they passed through.[9]

Hart requested that Governor Cen display notifications in advance at all corners of the city to inform people of the arrival of the post office to allay any concerns that might arise and thus minimize the potential for trouble. Cen issued four notifications; each had a clear headline message, but also detailed text that provided a lengthy explanation of the origins of the IPO and its imperial status. This narrative also stressed the benevolent impacts the IPO was intended to have on society in bringing people of all walks of life closer, no matter where they were living in China or abroad.[10] For all of the prominence of their display, the posters' detailed wording was intended not for ordinary people but for an educated minority in a position to assert authority and status by communicating a message to the wider populace. But while Cen's actions had a practical focus, his effort was also symbolic, intended to encourage and enable

7. Robert Hart to Cen Chunxuan, Guangxu reign year 27, month 6, day 3 (July 18, 1901), enclosure, in IG Circular 975 / Postal No. 52, 162–63.

8. Robert Hart to Zongli Yamen, Guangxu reign year 27, month 6 (June 1901, specific date unknown), SHAC, 137 (2) 304.

9. Robert Hart to department magistrate of Dingzhou, Guangxu reign year 27, month 5, day 13 (June 28, 1901), SHAC, 137 (2) 304.

10. "Zhao lu Shanxi fu buyuan Cen kuochong youzheng gaoshi" 照錄山西撫部院岑擴充郵政告示 [A copy of a notification on the postal expansion, issued by Shanxi Governor Cen], Guangxu reign year 27, month 7, day 25 (September 7, 1901), enclosure, in IG Circular 975 / No. 52, 164.

his subordinates and members of the local gentry to get on board with developments.

In similar fashion, through mobilizing the assistance of local officials working together with Chinese postal clerks, postal services were also extended to Henan and Shaanxi. Deng Weifan, now ranked in the service hierarchy as third postal clerk A, assigned to set up the route between Taiyuan and Xi'an via Pingyang Prefecture, Puzhou Prefecture, and Tongguan Department. Shu Xiutai 舒修泰, who joined the IPO in 1899 and now held the rank of candidate postal clerk B, was entrusted to build a line between Kaifeng and Xi'an, via Henan Prefecture, Shanzhou, and Tongguan.[11] Building on this momentum, the IPO pushed farther north and west. Zhang Hengchang 張恆昌, ranked as a fourth-class postal clerk, led in setting up postal branches in Datong, followed by Guihua (Hohhot), which was already beyond the Great Wall. At the same time, Deng Weiping, ranked as third postal clerk B, was sent to Xinzhou to set up postal stations there so that the new postal branches opened by Zhang Hengchang in Inner Mongolia could also be linked with Taiyuan on the western side. Together with the branch at Zhangjiakou, these new routes connected Beijing, Taiyuan, Xi'an, and Inner Mongolia; they were important for mercantile interests, but also soon became important carriers of official communications (see fig. 6.1).[12]

While the postal extension project in northern China seemed to go from strength to strength, there was bad news coming out of Xiangfu District in the area of Kaifeng in Henan. It was reported that a letter box had been attacked by local malcontents, and despite the intervention of the magistrate, harassment had later spread to several postal branches and one postal branch signboard had been vandalized by a mob.[13] Hart

11. Robert Hart to Zongli Yamen, Guangxu reign year 28, month 7, day 12 (August 15, 1902), SHAC, 137 (2) 304. For the ranks of Deng Weifan (Teng Wei-fan on the *Service List*) and Shu Xiutai (Hsu Hsiu-tai on the *Service List*), see *Service List* (1902), 155, 159.

12. Robert Hart to Waiwubu, Guangxu reign year 29, month 4, day 10 (May 6, 1903), SHAC, 137 (2) 304. For the ranks of Deng Weiping (Teng Wei-ping on the *Service List*) and Zhang Hengchang (Chang Heng-chang on the *Service List*), see *Service List* (1903), 154, 166.

13. "Zhao lu Xiangfuxian gaoshi" 照錄祥符縣告示 [A copy of a notification for Xiangfu District], attachment to Robert Hart to Waiwubu, Guangxu reign year 29, month 10, day 8 (November 26, 1903), SHAC, 137 (2) 304.

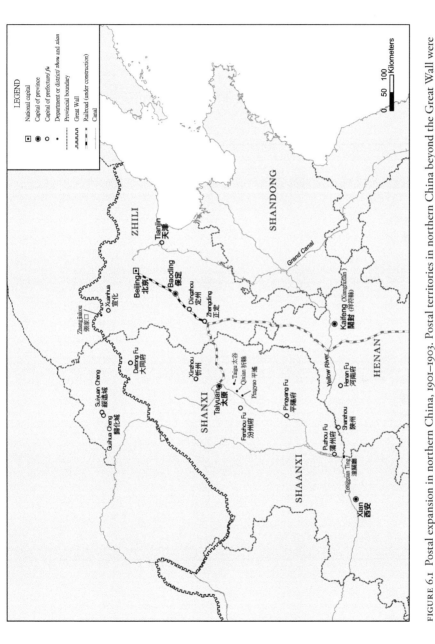

FIGURE 6.1 Postal expansion in northern China, 1901–1903. Postal territories in northern China beyond the Great Wall were connected after the Boxer Rebellion through the efforts of the two Deng brothers and other Chinese postal clerks. Despite holding relatively low status in the administration hierarchy, being at the district (*xian*) level, Pingyao, Qixian and Taigu already had postal branches due to the needs of Shanxi merchants and their families. Map © Weipin Tsai; cartography by Huang Chingchi.

brought the case to the Ministry of Foreign Affairs, which ordered the provincial governor of Henan, Chen Kuilong 陳夔龍 (1857–1948), to act appropriately.[14] In turn, the governor issued an even longer public proclamation than the one posted in Shanxi. Similar in tone to the earlier notification, the governor's notification went further, directly addressing the elephant in the room: the presence of foreigners in the IPO branches. In an effort to allay suspicion, the governor used an analogy from the Spring and Autumn period (770–476 BCE), that the good brains of the Chu state could be put to use by the Jin state. He stressed that there was nothing wrong in employing foreigners, as long as they could bring benefit to the state-owned postal service.[15] Hart considered that this proclamation was well crafted, as it stated the case very clearly and forcibly, so he circulated it widely across postal districts in the hope that it might be usefully shown to officials in other areas.[16]

The active support of provincial governors, as recounted above in Henan and Shanxi, represented a sea change in attitudes within officialdom compared to what had preceded the Boxer Rebellion. Taken together with the central government's rejection of provincial governors' calls to halt postal expansion (as addressed in chapter 5), these cases reflected a growing demand from the central government to assert its authority in an effort to bring about effective change. This was soon seen more widely in a change among less senior, more local officials from a culture of resistance toward the IPO to general support of it. In this period, the final decade of the Qing dynasty's existence, it seems somewhat paradoxical that the mechanisms of the imperial sociopolitical structure were still in reasonably good working order, at least in the case of the IPO: provincial governors transmitted the central government's policy to the lower-level administrations, and in turn the policy was executed by prefects and magistrates; at the same time, we see local gentries and literati playing their role as mediators in communicating and explaining the narrative of policy to the general public.

14. Hart to Waiwubu November 26, 1903.

15. "Zhao lu Henan xunfu lai gaoshi" 照錄河南巡撫來告示 [A copy of a notification issued by the governor of Henan], enclosure, in IG Circular 1134 / Postal No. 75, March 3, 1904, in *Inspector General's Postal Circulars 1–89*, 234–36, TMA, W2-2833.

16. IG Circular 1134 / Postal No. 75, 233.

Noting that the new political situation was friendly toward geographical extension of postal services, Hart decided to secure a monopoly in the transmission of mail by railway and steamships. This meant that the IPO would now compete head-to-head with private letter hongs in a broad swath of the market for postal services, an inevitable stage in making the IPO a truly Chinese institution.

A Competitive Marketplace

If we take 1901 as the starting point of this period of intense competition, there were significant points of difference between the service provided by the hongs and that provided by the IPO. A report produced by W. C. Haines Watson, the acting Customs commissioner at Chongqing, offers useful insight into the general operation of hongs around this time, set alongside what were recorded as the shortcomings of the IPO. It is worth mentioning that most reports produced by Customs commissioners on local private letter hongs were incomplete, as some hongs inevitably escaped notice. For example, on the route between Chongqing and Guizhou, in addition to Maxiangyue 麻鄉約, which is listed in table 6.1, a hong named Rongfahe 榮發合 also provided a service, though it was not included by Watson.[17]

According to Watson's report, there were seven large hongs in the area (see table 6.1 and fig. 6.2).[18] Despite some variation in practical detail, the business model of the hongs at Chongqing was representative of the situation for hongs more widely. Equally, the shortcomings of the IPO operation at Chongqing, as well as the limitations of the network connecting the city, reflected the situation at many other locations, particularly inland. These hongs at Chongqing focused on local, in-province services but also offered services to more distant places—notably, to Hubei, the interior of Sichuan, and Yunnan. This was achieved, for the most part, through interhong collaboration. For example, for a letter to

17. Guozhong, "Lue tan Guizhou jindai," 3:1737. My thanks to Tsai Ming-feng for providing me with this source.

18. "Chunkiang, 1892–1901," in *Decennial Reports 1892–1901*, 1:174–75.

Table 6.1. Private letter hongs based in Chongqing, 1901

Name of hong	Year established	Head office location	Branch offices, and service to which places	Postage price in cash (文)	Time en route (days)	Which days	Remarks
Huyuchang 胡裕昌	1822	Hankou	Hankou	60	8–10	6 times per month for all destinations	By boat
			Shashi	60	7–9		By boat
			Yichang	60	5–6		By boat
			Kuifu	40	3–4		By boat
			Wanxian	30	2–3		By boat
			Chongqing	—	—		—
			Chengdu	40	7–9		Overland
Zengsenchang 曾森昌	1880	Hankou	Hankou	60	8–10	6 times per month for all destinations	By boat
			Shashi	60	7–9		By boat
			Yichang	60	5–6		By boat
			Kuifu	40	3–4		By boat
			Wanxian	30	2–3		By boat
			Chongqing	—	—		—
			Chengdu	40	7–9		Overland
Maxiangyue 麻鄉約	1866	Chongqing	Chengdu	32	8	9 times per month for all destinations	Overland
			Jiading	40	10		Overland
			Luzhou	24	4		Overland
			Guizhou	72	12		Overland
			Dajianlu	100	15		Overland

Hong	Year	Base	Destination			Frequency	Transport
Xiangheyuan 祥合源	1883	Chongqing	Luzhou	24	4	9 times per month for all destinations	Overland
			Xufu	32	6		Overland
			Zhaotong	80	20		Overland
			Yunnan Province	180	50		Overland
Songbochang 松柏長	1823	Chongqing	Luzhou	24	4	6 times per month for the first four destinations; 3 times per month for Qinzhou and Guangyuan	Overland
			Xufu	32	6		Overland
			Zhaotong	80	20		Overland
			Yunnan	180	50		Overland
			Qinzhou	120	13		Overland
			Guangyuan	80	10		Overland
Sanxiangzi 三痲子	1883	Chongqing	Hezhou	24	1–2	6 times per month for all destinations	Overland
			Shunqing	40	4		Overland
			Baoning	48	6–7		Overland
			Tongzhou	56	7		Overland
			Shehong	48	5		Overland
			Miaozhou	56	7–8		Overland
			Suining	48	5		Overland
Leichunlin 雷春林	n/a	Chongqing	Suiding	56	7	6 times per month for both destinations	Overland
			Quxian	48	6		Overland

Source: Operational details of seven private letter hongs, as outlined in "Chunkiang, 1892–1901," in *Decennial Reports 1892–1901.*

Note: There were additional hongs operating in these areas that were not included in the report.

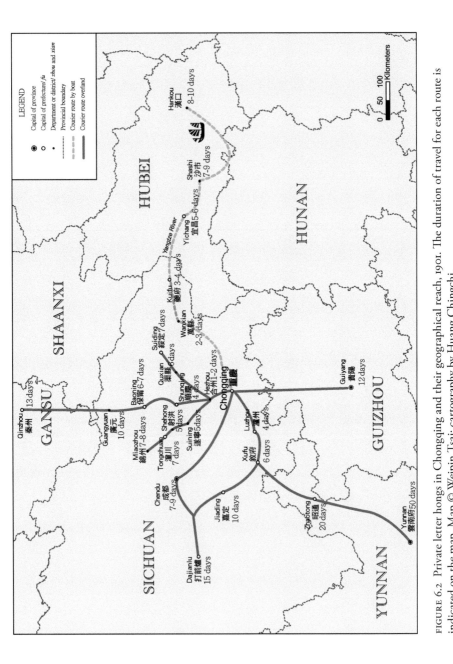

FIGURE 6.2 Private letter hongs in Chongqing and their geographical reach, 1901. The duration of travel for each route is indicated on the map. Map © Weipin Tsai; cartography by Huang Chingchi.

Shanghai, the Huyuchang 胡寓昌 courier could pass on the letter to its partner in Hankou, and the partner's courier would handle the stretch from Hankou to Shanghai. A letter to Xi'an in Shaanxi Province could be delivered to Guangyuan by the hong named Songbochang 松柏長, and from there a collaborator at Guangyuan would deliver the letter to its final destination in Xi'an. In 1901 the IPO only had post offices at Chongqing, Chengdu, Jiading, Baoning and Xufu. The IPO's route between Chongqing and Yichang, a treaty port on the border between Hubei and Sichuan, had only recently been connected overland, while the hong service was available by boat. This put the IPO at a disadvantage. With scarcely five offices in the province, the IPO service was clearly behind that offered by the hongs. Indeed, at this stage, the IPO did not have routes operational to connect Chongqing to Gansu, Guizhou, Yunnan, or Shaanxi.

Watson's report noted that the hongs operated a sophisticated model in terms of rates and charges, which for a letter varied from twenty-four copper cash to 180 copper cash based on distance (see table 6.1); postage could be paid on delivery. If the letter went beyond the range of the hong's own couriers and had to involve another hong to complete the route, the postage would often be split into two parts: the initial amount for local service would be paid to the first hong by the sender, and the second part would be paid by the recipient to the supporting hong. But how affordable were such rates for an ordinary person at that time? In the same report, Watson commented, "All the necessaries of life may be enjoyed in this favoured region of all-round prosperity by him who possessed an annual income of 30,000 cash."[19] This equates to an income of twenty-five hundred cash per month, or around eighty-two cash per day. When Isabella L. Bird traveled from Chongqing to Baoning, she paid twenty-five thousand cash to engage a group of seven men to accompany her (three chair bearers and four luggage porters) for the nineteen-day journey. The price was negotiated with a transport agency, which would certainly have taken a cut. It might be reasonable to assume that each man would receive around 150 cash per day. She also observed that a cotton weaver in Chongqing around 1897 received six hundred cash for six days' work.[20]

19. "Chunkiang, 1892–1901," 1:158.
20. Bishop, *The Yangtze Valley*, 195, 180.

When Watson himself took a trip from Guanxian to Songpan in Sichuan, he paid thirty-two hundred cash per "coolie" for a thirteen-day journey, for a total of 246 cash per day.[21] Although the daily rate for Watson's "coolies" seems relatively high in this context, there may have been specific reasons for the difference in rate.

Charges for parcels ranged from sixty copper cash per catty (approximately twenty-one ounces) within Sichuan to two hundred cash per catty for destinations in other provinces. The hongs also transferred silver and bank drafts. Insurance was available when transmitting valuable items, providing full value in case of loss through neglect by the hong and half value if lost through robbery, though there was no payout if the courier was killed. In short, this was a mature business, well organized, and the Customs commissioner noted that the hongs were believed to be "entirely trustworthy" by local populations.[22]

The Setting of Postage Rates

Of all of the misconceptions about the IPO that circulated during its first decade of operation, the most contentious were those of its perceived high postage rates and its perception as a foreign institution. The issue of the Chinese nature of the IPO was discussed in chapter 5, but the matter of postage rates merits some examination here. One of the hurdles that the IPO had to overcome early in its existence was Chinese people's resistance to using postage stamps, as this was alien to them. Back in 1885, Henry Kopsch had obtained a report from one Mr. Wilkinson, a British postal agent at Ningbo, which explained how the British General Post Office in China had learned from its experience in Hong Kong to permit letters on the Chinese mainland to be transported and delivered without postage stamps affixed. Wilkinson criticized the "inflexibility of Herr [Gustav] Detring's scheme" for its failure to persuade potential customers to switch to using the modernized postal service, and advised Kopsch and the Chinese Maritime Customs Service (CMCS) to accommodate some of the "Chinese ways" of doing business.[23] In response to Wilkinson's

---

21. Watson, "Journey to Sungp'an," 97.
22. "Chunkiang, 1892–1901," 1:170.
23. Henry Kopsch to IG, February 4, 1885, SHAC679 (1) 14907.

report, Kopsch suggested allowing firms to pay on account, leasing post office boxes to merchants, permitting commutation of postage in particular circumstances, and dropping the requirement for prepayment of postage on letters to be delivered within China. As was discussed in chapter 3, Detring did, of course, seek to work collaboratively with private letter hongs, though with disastrous results; but Hart had remained firm on the principle of prepayment.

In their deliberations at that time over the initial pricing of postage stamps, Hart and Detring settled on the unit known as the candarin (see chapter 3), as opposed to use of the Haikwan tael, which was the notional currency used within the CMCS at the time for the calculation of Customs duties, based on a table of exchange rates against the various physical silver currencies in use in different parts of China and Southeast Asia. The silver candarin, which was also a weight-based measurement, being one-tenth of a mace (*qian* 錢), was used as the unit for postage stamps until 1897, when it was changed to "cent" against the Mexican dollar.[24] Although both candarin and cent were called *fen* (分) in Chinese, they had different values, and this has created much confusion in postal history and philatelic discussions.[25]

Back in 1884, Kopsch had advocated adopting the cent for postage stamps. He had also pointed out that, in order to compete with the British General Post Office, it was necessary for the Customs Postal Service to reduce its charges from those in force at the time. Kopsch noted that the British General Post Office had already made its services available in certain large postal markets in China and overseas, at lower rates than the Customs Postal Service; these included treaty ports and routes between Ningbo and Shanghai, in addition to its presence in Cochin China (Vietnam), Hong Kong, Japan, Korea, and the Spanish territory of Manila (present-day Philippines). Kopsch pointed out that for mail between Ningbo and Shanghai, the British General Post Office charged two Mexican cents (twenty-three Ningbo copper cash), while the Customs Postal

24. "Youzheng kaiban zhangcheng" 郵政開辦章程 [The regulations for the inauguration of the post office], enclosure, in "Postal: Enclosing Chinese Version of Regulations and Yamên Memorial," IG Circular 709 (2nd ser.), April 30, 1896, in *Docs. Ill.*, 2:63; J. Mencarini, "Note on the Postage Stamps of China, 1878–1805," in Report (1905), lxvii.

25. *Hongyinhua youpiao*, 2:399–403.

Service charged three candarins (forty-eight Ningbo copper cash). To all treaty ports and to the foreign destinations mentioned, the British General Post Office charged five cents, but the Customs Postal Service charged between three and six candarins.[26] Private letter hongs charged thirty cash to neighboring towns from Ningbo, fifty cash for Ningbo to Shanghai, two hundred cash for Ningbo to Tianjin, and four hundred cash for Ningbo to Beijing.[27]

Prior to the establishment of the IPO, Customs postal stamps were sold with currency exchange conducted at the local Customs House, as this was possible given the small volume of mail. But when planning was being conducted for the national introduction of postal services, new issues came under consideration: the appropriate face value of stamps, arrangements for the handling of payment and currency exchange at local offices including postal agencies, and methods of handling financial accounting in a way that would scale as the service grew. At the beginning of 1897, in order to ensure that the service would be competitive, as well as to better cope with issues of currency exchange at diverse locations across China, the Mexican dollar was chosen to be the denomination for postage stamps and also the effective currency in use in local branches—although the Haikwan tael would remain the unit of account for the service. This decision had a significant impact on the working procedures of the IPO, and Van Aalst was instructed to draw up rules for the IPO's accounting system. His reflections on this issue are insightful. He wrote, "The fluctuations of exchange, the bewildering rates at the various ports, the interminable currency conversions have long been a source of annoyance to Accountants and Auditors alike. The object aimed at in adhering so scrupulously to such a medley of irrational and constantly changing rates, namely, a minutely accurate distribution of expenditure, has been found unattainable and—considering the ever-increasing work of all kinds imposed on the Customs—certainly not worth such an outlay of labour, time, and money as has hitherto been bestowed upon it."[28]

26. Henry Kopsch to IG, December 31, 1885, SHAC 679 (1) 14907.

27. "Ningbo, 1882–1891," in *Decennial Reports 1882–91*, 380.

28. "Postal Accounts," enclosure, in IG Circular 762 / Postal No. 26, January 20, 1897, in *Inspector General's Postal Circulars 1–89*, 85, TMA, W2-2833.

The new rules were that the value of all silver and copper coins received at postal branches or shops operating as postal agencies, in whatever currency was in operation locally, had to be converted to Mexican dollars and cents; official exchange rates for this purpose were published regularly and displayed at local post offices and agency shops. The experience of post office customers, therefore, was of purchasing stamps or other services at a fixed price in Mexican dollars, though the local price could fluctuate depending on the exchange rate. For the purposes of accounting and entry on official forms, however, the Mexican dollar was further converted to Haikwan taels, at the rate of one Haikwan tael to one and a half Mexican dollars.[29]

The formal switch to the institutional use of the Mexican dollar was a meaningful and significant change in modern Chinese history, coming at a time when there was no unified central currency in China. The candarin was fundamentally a unit of weight, and its abandonment in favor of the cent, a unit of currency, was indicative of an important shift. In practical terms, the Mexican dollar was a familiar and trusted store of value, well regarded both by merchants and the general public due to its stable silver quality and its widespread availability. The Mexican dollar had first arrived, via Canton, in the early nineteenth century, and had long been accepted by the CMCS for the payment of tariffs; it was also widely accepted by traditional Chinese banks. Although there were other foreign silver dollars in China, the Mexican dollar, according to a 1910 survey by the Qing central government, was the most widespread, representing approximately one-third of the silver currency in circulation, having been the most popular silver currency for the previous sixty years. Although by the 1880s several provincial governments were minting their own silver coins, these were not in a position to compete with the Mexican dollar due to the coins' limited availability and unstable quality.[30] Even when the Qing government launched a standardized silver coin in 1910, with a dragon emblem on one side and the characters "The Great Qing Silver Coinage" (Da Qing yinbi 大清銀幣) on the other, Francis Aglen, by then the inspector general in charge of both Customs and the

29. "Postal Accounts," 82.

30. Hong, *Zhongguo jinrongshi*, 107–8; Wang Hongbin, *Qingdai jiazhi chidu*, 357–58.

Post, decided to make minimal changes. Despite adding an extra column in official reports to accommodate the new currency, the IPO neither adjusted the values of postage stamps nor changed the monetary denomination in operation.[31] The adoption of the Mexican dollar was a very practical decision, which had the effect of enabling the IPO to both standardize and simplify its operations.

Across China, the currency in use for daily purchases and exchange was copper coin, known as cash *wen* (文), minted locally. Hosea Ballou Morse, in his influential work on modern Chinese history, described the charges of private letter hongs in the late imperial period as "moderate," ranging from "20 cash to 200 cash (2 to 20 cents)." Yet this oversimplifies the situation.[32] Indeed, it is unclear why Morse made such a statement, as it suggests—wrongly—that the conversion between copper cash and silver cents was straightforward and standardized. In practice, copper coins, as received in payment by the private letter hongs, varied widely in their exchange value in different places due to their many different weights and quality; this necessitated the use of tables of market rates for exchange wherever postal business was conducted.[33]

Some caution needs to be adopted when making statements about comparative pricing for different kinds of service. After 1897, postage tariffs were displayed at all IPO branches and postal agencies and were also published in the official *Postal Guide*. Table 6.2 shows the IPO postage rates published between 1897 and 1910. Customers for letter post, parcel post, or money order delivery were required to pay the specified rate in Mexican dollars; this, of course, meant that the local price in copper cash differed according to location. Constructed from numbers provided in the reports of the Customs commissioners at the treaty ports, Table 6.3 demonstrates that a postage stamp cost different amounts of copper cash depending on the location.

31. IG Circular 1701 / Postal No. 244, June 23, 1910, in *Circulars Nos. 135–261*, TMA, 473–74, W2-2838.

32. Morse, *The International Relations*, 3:60.

33. "Dollars and factional parts are no longer to be accepted at face value, but at market rates"; "I.P.O. Revised Tariff," Postal Circular 99, January 30, 1904, in *Postal Secretary's Circulars*, 435, TMA, W2-2833.

Table 6.2. Imperial Post Office domestic letter rates

Letter weight	1897 (coast rate)*	January 1899	April 1902	September 1904	August 1910
Up to ¼ ounce	2 cents	2 cents	—	—	—
Up to ½ ounce, local	4 cents	4 cents	local, ½ cent; domestic, 1 cent	local, 1 cent; domestic, 2 cents**	—
Up to 20 grams (0.7 ounce) ***	—	—	—	—	local, 1 cent; domestic, 3 cents
Up to 1 ounce	8 cents	8 cents	—	—	—

Sources: For postage rates published in 1896: "Chinese Imperial Post," enclosure in "Chinese Imperial Post: Inaugurated by Imperial Decree," IG Circular 706 (2nd ser.), April 9, 1896, in Docs. Ill., 2:46; IG Circular 782 / Postal No. 36, April 24, 1897, in Inspector General's Postal Circulars 1–89, 116, TMA, W2-2833. For rates from 1899 onward: "Tariff of Postage on Mail Matter," enclosure in "Rates of Postage," Postal Circular 13, October 19, 1898, in Postal Secretary's Circulars No. 1–134, 125, TMA, W2-2833. For 1902: "I.P.O. Revised Tariff Notification No.41," Postal Circular 108, July 1, 1904, in Postal Secretary's Circulars No. 1–134, 455, TMA, W2-2833. For 1910: "Domestic Letter Rate and Unit of Weight: Revision of," Postal Circular 241, June 1, 1910, in Circulars Nos. 135–261, 468, TMA, W2-2838. See also Zhongguo youzi kao, 9–10.

* For 1897, only coastal rates were set, as the IPO left private letter hongs to set their own rates for inland services.

** The domestic tariff was made uniform for all places in China.

***From October 1907 onward, following the 1906 Rome Postal Convention, the IPO used 20 grams as the basic unit for international mail, except for Hong Kong, Japan, Macao, and Qingdao. The same rule was applied to domestic mail from August 1910 onward.

Table 6.3. Comparison of exchange and postage rates in copper cash, 1901

	Chefoo	Chongqing	Hankou	Zhenjiang	Ningbo	Wenzhou*	Shantou	Wuzhou	Tianjin
1 Hk.Tl	1,221	1,277	1,326	1,405	1,400	1,415–1,475	—	1,356	1,400
1 Mexican dollar	804	839	868	923	930	930–970	1,020	864	800
1-cent stamp	8.0	8.4	8.7	9.2	9.3	9.3–9.7	10.2	8.6	8.0
2-cent stamp	16.1	16.8	17.4	18.5	18.6	18.6–19.4	20.4	17.3	16.0
4-cent stamp	32.2	33.6	34.7	36.9	37.2	37.2–38.8	40.8	34.6	32.0

*Data for Wenzhou was reported as a range of values.

The decennial reports further demonstrate that IPO rates, by and large, were cheaper than those of the letter hongs. Looking at Tables 6.1–6.3 and comparing IPO rates with those of private letter hongs in Chongqing clearly shows that IPO tariffs for letters were lower. In 1901, for a half-ounce letter from Chongqing to Yichang and Hankou, the hong rate was sixty copper cash, whereas the IPO rate was two cents (equivalent to around 16.8 local copper cash, assuming there was no dramatic difference in the exchange rate between 1901 and 1902). Taking Wenzhou as another example, the private hong rate from this treaty port to Ningbo in 1901 was around seventy local cash; to Shanghai, one hundred cash; and to Tientsin, two hundred cash, whereas the IPO postage rate was less than twenty local copper cash for a letter of one-quarter ounce or under, and less than forty local cash for a letter up to one-half ounce.[34]

The IPO lowered the rates even further in 1902 to attract customers, but this proved to be unsustainable, as income was not sufficient to cover the mail transport by couriers through the districts of the interior, so the rates were adjusted again in 1904. Speaking about the lowering of the tariff, Piry said that "when the low rates and the extensive system of the IPO became known, the public will flow to its counters, and then, and no sooner, will agencies be compelled to submit or break up."[35] Piry's prediction that the hongs would submit quickly was wrong, as they were somehow able to stay in business for the long term.

A Monopoly on Steam Transportation, and the Eight Rules

In addition to competing through postage rates, the IPO also competed with letter hongs through securing monopoly access to steam transportation. Although the IPO was able at this time to connect treaty ports and the majority of provincial capitals, it had limited reach to other inland destinations. Therefore, the adoption of modern forms of transportation was critical. In January 1897 the IPO had made agreements with major foreign steamship companies operating on China's coasts and major rivers to transport mail for the IPO. These agreements included the provision that the steamship companies would not transmit mail for either

34. "Wenchow, 1892–1901," in *Decennial Reports 1892–1901*, 2:79.
35. Report (1905), xxxix.

the private letter hongs or foreign post offices, with the exception of foreign-owned companies transmitting their own national post.[36] The China Merchants' Steam Navigation Company came under this agreement, and in January 1897 it informed the Local Post Office that from the first day of the Chinese New Year, it would only carry mail brought on board by the IPO.[37]

These agreements helped significantly in making the IPO's service more competitive against the native letter hongs, at least for the majority of treaty ports and parts of southern China. If hongs wanted their mail to be carried by these shipping companies, they had to register with the IPO at the places where the IPO had offices. At this time the IPO was only present at treaty ports and in Beijing. Mail handed in by the hongs to the IPO was often referred to as closed mail or clubbed mail. Closed mail would be transported by the steamers together with the IPO mail, and put the hongs at an advantageous position in competition with other hongs that had not registered with the IPO. Although the registered hongs had to pay the IPO for clubbed mail, they were free to set their own postage rates to customers.[38] According to F. E. Woodruff, the Customs commissioner at Wenzhou in 1901, the local hongs at that port were able to increase profit on their overall service because by sending mail through the IPO by steamer, they saved significantly over the costs of using more traditional means of transportation.[39]

The IPO also sought to prohibit all hongs, registered or not, from loading collected mails directly onto vessels, including nonsteamers. Registered hongs had to pay the IPO for costal transportation or mail, and individual bundles could not exceed certain weights and sizes. Most controversially, a penalty was applied to traders, private persons and owners, officers and crews of vessels caught carrying unauthorized letters, papers, and other mail. For traders and private persons, the fine was fifty taels

36. Postal Note 7, January 13, 1897, in *Postal Notes Nos. 1–38*, 8, TMA, W2-2833.
37. China Merchants Steam Navigation Company to the Postmaster of the Local Post Office, Shanghai, January 4, 1897, Shanghai Municipal Archives, U1–5–107.
38. "Enclosure—Chinese Imperial Post," in "Chinese Imperial Post: Inaugurated by Imperial Decree," IG Circular 706 (2nd ser.) / Postal No. 7, April 9, 1896, in *Docs. Ill.*, 2:46, 48.
39. "Wenchow, 1892–1901," in *Decennial Reports 1892–1901*, 2:79.

(Tls.); for owners, officers, and crew, the penalty was Tls. 500.[40] These regulations clearly conflicted with Hart's original instruction that the IPO should avoid disrupting people's livelihoods. Apart from steam launches, the majority of light boats—run either by the letter hongs themselves or by other boat operators—were commonly found in Jiangsu Province and the northern part of Zhejiang Province. This area, covering Hangzhou, Ningbo, and Shanghai, contained a large body of canals, natural waterways, coastal inlets, and small creeks, many of them unnavigable by launches. These water routes supported a high density of population, with a consequent high demand for postal services. The area around the Pearl River Delta in Canton was similar in character.[41]

As result, the new regulations effectively meant that the IPO was launching a war on both letter hongs and the business of water transportation. The water transportation industry had deep roots in Chinese society and had its own guilds. These were under the control of local administrations, and were tied closely with other commercial interests, such as shipping brokers and banking.[42] After the First Sino-Japanese War, the Treaty of Shimonoseki in theory opened up inland waters to foreign steamers, a significant extension of what had been previously permitted under the treaty port system, and this forced the Qing government to relax its inland steamship regulations. China's inland waters were in reality opened to more Chinese steamship operators. The size of Chinese steamship companies, though varied, tended to be small. The majority of steamers were also of smaller sizes, mostly below one hundred tons or even below fifty tons.[43] Nevertheless, in the years following the treaty, there was a steady growth in Chinese steam launch activity accompanying the enlargement of steam networks.[44] In this context, it is no surprise that there was resistance to the IPO's new regulatory regime. This came not just from commercial interests but also from officials; for

40. "Enclosure—Chinese Imperial Post," 2:48–49.

41. Report (1904), v.

42. Teizō, "The Operation of Chinese Junks," 8–10.

43. Zhu Yingui, *Lun Zhaoshangju*, 235–38. It is worth noting that the Regulations for Steam Navigation in Inland Waters (Hua yang lunchuan shi fu Zhongguo nei gang zhangcheng 華洋輪船駛赴中國內港章程) were not ready until 1898; see "Steam Navigation Inland," IG Circular 846 (2nd ser.), September 5, 1898, in *Docs. Ill.*, 2:138–50.

44. Reinhardt, *Navigating Semi-colonialism*, 52–55.

example, the censor of the Southern Yangtze region, Xu Daokun 徐道焜 (1848–?), complained that it was unreasonable to fine individuals for carrying letters for others because it was a widely practiced custom. He was also very concerned over how the rule changes would add extra costs for newspaper publishers and thus potentially interfere with newspaper circulation. The governor-general of Guangdong and Guangxi, Tan Zhonglin 譚鍾麟 (1822–1905), also reported on what he observed locally, commenting, "The Post Office applies many trivial and harsh rules, and people's complaints are already boiling. The new rules of the Post Office will not benefit revenue, but only damage the Government. I am sincerely pleading that this service be withdrawn and closed all together."[45]

In response, Hart drew back. The hongs, he announced, were "virtually to carry on their business as before," although they were still to be encouraged to register with the IPO in order to be able to ship their mail on steamers between the treaty ports. For mail outside treaty ports, Hart instructed postal staff not to interfere with the hongs' operations and what they put in their own bags.[46] He also ordered postal staff, at any location, not to check any passenger's baggage for letters or confiscate any letters from anybody. In addition, he stressed that fines would only be applied to boat owners and their crews, and that none were to be levied on individuals.[47]

This setback demonstrated that the IPO was effectively unable to enforce these regulations completely, even at treaty ports. On his inspection tours, John Patrick Donovan observed the reality of two mail systems existing side by side. When he was in Hangzhou, he noted that there were twenty-one hongs registered with the IPO, but these hongs only oc-

45. Xu Daokun, "Zou chen youzhengju qi suo yi zhangcheng yi dai xin zhi fa" 奏陳郵政局其所議章程一帶信之罰 [Memorial on the post office's policy on laying fines on conveying letters], Guangxu reign year 23, month 2, day 16 (March 18, 1897), database of Ch'ing Palace Memorials and Archives of Grand Council, National Palace Museum, Taiwan, 137382, my translation; Tan Zhonglin, "Zou qing cai youzhengju" 奏請裁郵政局 [Memorial on abolishing the post office], Guangxu reign year 23, month 2, day 2 (March 4, 1897), database of Ch'ing Palace Memorials and Archives of Grand Council, 137544, my translation.

46. IG Circular 776 (2nd ser.) / Postal No. 31, March 30, 1897, in *Inspector General's Postal Circulars 1–89*, 110–11, TMA, W2-2833.

47. IG Circular 779 (2nd ser.) / Postal No. 33, April 9, 1897, in *Inspector General's Postal Circulars 1–89*, 113, TMA, W2-2833.

casionally handed over closed mail—for example, only eighteen bags in the year 1899. No measures were taken by IPO staff to prevent their operation, and most of the letters to nontreaty ports were transmitted by the two largest hongs there. In Ningbo, another treaty port, there were fourteen hongs registered with the IPO, but no efforts of any kind had been made to induce affiliation. As in the case of Hangzhou, letters for nontreaty port locations were predominantly transmitted by hongs, and several large hongs had agents in other cities. Mail smuggling was very common, particularly on the route between Ningbo and Shanghai. In early June 1900 a bundle consisting of thirty-nine letters, under the care of a hong named Ya Hsing 協興, was found in a Chinese steamer. It was the fifth time that the hong had been caught ignoring the regulations, and the head of the steamship was fined fifty taels. This case was exceptional, however, because the task of monitoring compliance was carried out by employees of the CMCS, who received no reward for preventing the smuggling of letters, and few offenders were caught and fined.[48]

After the Boxer Rebellion, the situation began to change. First, in April 1902 the IPO temporarily dropped all transmission fees on hongs' clubbed mail between treaty ports.[49] But the more effective measures came in 1904 when several British shipping companies wanted to stop carrying IPO mail; the IPO swiftly used the opportunity to urge the Ministry of Foreign Affairs to make a new regulation to compel Chinese steamers certified for inland waters traffic to carry IPO mailbags. Under the rule that emerged, the Chinese steam vessels were obliged to carry IPO mail for free, with the exception of heavy loads, under pain of fines or of having their inland waters certificates revoked. Chinese vessels were not allowed to transmit mail for other organizations or as part of their own business, and masters of ships were held responsible for the safety of mailbags.[50] The combined effect of these measures was an increase in clubbed mail received by the IPO from the hongs.

48. John Patrick Donovan, "To the Postal Secretary—Tour of Inspection," June 25, 1900, SHAC, 137 (1) 7603.

49. "I.P.O. Revised Tariff," Postal Circular 57, March 17, 1902, in *Postal Secretary's Circulars No. 1–134*, 327, TMA, W2-2833.

50. IG Circular 1167 / Postal No. 77, July 4, 1904, and enclosure, "Chinese Steamers in Inland Waters and I.P.O. Mails," in *Inspector General's Postal Circulars 1–89*, 242–47, TMA, W2-2833.

The IPO also worked toward securing its position concerning rail transportation. On the whole, the railway companies were willing to collaborate, due to the nature of their Chinese ownership. But alongside their competition with letter hongs, there was an additional area of concern that made it urgent for the IPO to obtain and enforce a monopoly on rail transmission for mail as it related to the activities of foreign postal services that had entered northern China during the Boxer Rebellion and were continuing to provide services after the end of the hostilities.

Prior to 1905 most railway lines under construction were in northern or northeastern China. As was noted in chapter 5, in 1898 the IPO had asked the Zongli Yamen to direct the railway companies to offer some privileges to the IPO in providing space at train stations and traveling passes for mail couriers. Relations continued to develop and, in 1899, at the behest of the Zongli Yamen, the company for the Tianjin-Shanhai Pass Railway agreed to transport mail for free, provided that mail couriers were in uniform.[51] By 1903 several new rail lines had come into operation, with more on the way, and in April of that year the Eight Rules for the Imperial Post Office and Railway Companies (Youzhengju tielu gongsi zhangcheng batiao 郵政局鐵路公司章程八條) were introduced by the Ministry of Foreign Affairs.[52]

The Eight Rules covered the use of facilities on moving trains, rental space for the IPO at railway stations, passes for mail couriers, and arrangements regarding an IPO monopoly on mail transmission by rail. Rule VIII of the regulation stated, "These Rules apply to all places whereto the I.P.O. may extend its operations along the Company's lines. No change can be introduced in them without the sanction of the Wai-wu Pu [Ministry of Foreign Affairs]."[53] This meant that although the IPO might have to negotiate practicalities with railway companies regarding the specific arrangements for new lines, the basic principles were formally established. The Kaifeng-Luoyang Railway, an offshoot of the Beijing-Hankou Railway (which was also known as the Jinghan Railway), was one of the

51. Jules A. Van Aalst to Tianjin postmaster, August 7, 1899, TMA, W2-5.

52. IG Circular 1076 / Postal No. 61, April 16, 1903, in *Inspector General's Postal Circulars 1–89*, 194–96, TMA, W2-2833.

53. Enclosure No. 1, "Rule VIII of the Eight Rules," in IG Circular 1076 / Postal No. 61, 196.

first railway projects to experience the impact of the new rules. In nego-tiations on loans and construction arrangements with the Belgian-led rail-way syndicate, the representatives of the Qing government, led by Sheng Xuanhuai, extracted a commitment to provide cars and facilities to assist the IPO's work, along with a promise that it would not allow the Belgian postal service to gain a foothold along the route.[54] Before the Jinghan Railway opened to the general public in 1905, it was already in use for mail transmission. To take advantage of this, Donovan, then postmaster for Hankou District, ordered the installation of wall-mounted letter boxes at stations along the route, while trains were equipped with a temporary traveling post office for the sorting of correspondence, which was dropped off at stops on the route. This arrangement was later replaced by special railway carriages with dedicated mail rooms.[55]

On the point regarding monopoly use, Rule I declared, "The I.P.O. alone can send mails by trains; any other mail matter brought in by Native or Foreign Agencies or Post Offices, official or private, are to be refused by the Company. As regards military mails, which, under con-tract, the Company is bound to carry, they are to be handed over to the I.P.O. and transported with its mail matter."[56] In theory this rule would target both private letter hongs and foreign post offices, but in reality, some foreign post offices, such as the German and Japanese, did not al-ways abide by the regulations. For example, in 1905, the German postal service insisted on transmitting its mail on the Qingdao-Jinan Railway because the German government had concessions in Shandong and had opened postal branches along the line.[57]

In comparison with steam vessels, it was easier to control mail traffic on trains, but there is no doubt that the rules were flouted and that letter hongs smuggled mail by train. For example, in 1903 it was reported that two private letter hongs at Hankou, one registered and the other nonreg-istered, had been using the Jinghan Railway to transmit mail.[58] Farther

---

54. He, *Jing Han tielu*, 51.
55. Donovan, "Travels and Experiences in China," 1:233.
56. IG Circular 1076 / Postal No. 61, 195.
57. Zhang Yi, *Zhonghua youzhengshi*, 139–41.
58. Théophile A. Piry to Waiwubu, Guangxu reign year 29, month 9, day 21 (No-vember 9, 1903), SHAC, 137 (2) 315. This case referred to the earliest completed stretch of the rail line.

north, some merchants in Jinzhou, Liaoning Province, had their mail sent by two letter hongs in early 1906, but the cargo was confiscated by the IPO at the Shanhai Pass train station. In order to rescue their mail, the Tianjin Chamber of Commerce (Tianjin shangwu zonghui 天津商務總會) wrote to the IPO to request its release.[59]

Thanks to these new regulations compelling steamships and trains to work with the IPO, it was generally successful in extending its reach to inland areas, putting the private letter hongs under pressure. It is not surprising that the hongs attempted, in turn, to protect their interests. A particular bone of contention was the fact that the 1902 postage fee exemption on their clubbed mail was not extended either to steamers beyond the realm of the treaty ports or to the use of railway transportation. In 1904, in a protest fronted by the president of the Shanghai Chamber of Commerce (Shanghai shangwu zonghui 上海商務總會), Yan Xinhou 嚴信厚 (1838–1907), 190 private letter hongs from Shanghai, nearby coastal towns, and the wider Yangtze River region submitted a joint petition to the Ministry of Foreign Affairs to request that just such an exemption should be applied universally across China, regardless of administrative boundary or type of transportation.[60] This request was originally rejected on the ground that the IPO was struggling to turn a profit, as postage rates were set very low. But the hongs eventually won a victory when provincial governors put pressure on the central administration. In October 1906 the IPO was ordered to apply half the full tariff rate, based on gross weight, to all registered hongs' clubbed mail packages on both vessels and trains.[61]

In addition to the issues around fees and access to mechanized transportation methods, the hongs were also concerned about the way the

59. "Zhao lu Tianjin youzhengju dafu Tianjin shangwu zonghui han" 照錄天津郵政局答復天津商務總會函 [Copy of the response of the Tianjin Post Office to the Tianjin Chamber of Commerce], enclosure, in Tianjin postmaster to Niuzhuang postmaster, 1906, TMA, W2-31.

60. "Zhao lu shangwu zonghui Yan dao Xinhou deng yuan bing" 照錄商務總會嚴道信厚等原稟 [Copy of letter from the Chair of Chamber of Commerce Yan Xinhou], 1904, SHAC, 137 (2) 315.

61. IG Circular 1378 / Postal No.149, October 20, 1906, in *Circulars Nos. 135–261*, 42–44, TMA, W2-2838. For the rates prior to 1906, see Postal Circular 57; and "I.P.O. Revised Tariff," Postal Circular 99, 442.

IPO imitated their business methods. Several hongs along the Yangtze River sent a joint petition to the superintendent of trade for the southern ports, the viceroy of Hubei and Hunan, and the Shanghai Chamber of Commerce in 1905 to complain about the IPO's latest extension to its service—that of sending couriers to shops and large houses to collect mail. The hongs were insistent that the IPO should not imitate their ways of doing business, as this added to their concerns about loss of custom.[62] These complaints found no sympathy at the IPO; indeed, Piry felt rather proud that the IPO had provoked such a reaction from the hongs and boasted about their complaints in his annual report. He believed it was correct for the IPO to adopt the "Chinese fashion" by sending collectors to travel around busy city streets to collect mail (fig. 6.3). On collection and on payment of a special fee, letters would be franked immediately and date-stamped. This special fee enabled the letter to be sent as "express delivery," which suited the needs of the Chinese merchants who were Piry's target for this service.[63]

In short, when it came to pushing forward with the IPO's expansion in the period after the Boxer Rebellion, the Qing government brooked no delay in enacting and enforcing new regulations, securing monopolies on rail and steam vessels and favorable terms with emerging ventures. This was complemented by the development by the IPO of a new strategy of cultivating its own postal agencies in order to broaden its reach.

Postal Agencies

For all of the focus on monopolies of transportation, the IPO also tried to secure a breakthrough at the local level in efforts to change postal habits and develop a mass customer base by engaging in head-to-head competition with private letter hongs at the level of city neighborhoods, towns, and even down to the village level. The IPO adopted a method of mapping postal areas by dividing them into sections, with each section

---

62. "Jiang hai neihe ge xinju deng bing" 江海內河各信局等稟 [Petition from the private letter hongs from Shanghai, Yangtze River area and inland rivers], June 13, 1905 [received?], SHAC, 137 (1?) 4278.

63. Report (1905), xliii.

FIGURE 6.3 A postman providing mobile service in suburban areas of Nanjing city, collecting and delivering mail. His right hand holds a bell to attract attention. His left hand holds a banner that reads, "Nanjing Postal Service in suburban areas for mail collection and delivery. Postage stamps for sale." The photograph is undated but is likely to have been taken in the early Republican era. Source: Report (1921). Acknowledgments to Tsai Chia-chi of the Specialist Library of the Chunghwa Postal Museum, Taipei, for providing this image, and to Jamie Carstairs for improving the image quality.

known by a number. As was noted in chapter 5, in 1899 the IPO had planned its expansion around the concept of suboffices. These comprised two types of premises: a full postal branch, at which all critical postal services were available; and shared premises, an existing shop equipped with a letter box, whose owner would undertake simpler postal duties while carrying on with the main business. The latter type took the form of a postal agency (*daiban youzheng fenju* 代辦郵政分局), and was also referred to as a box office.[64] Efforts in recruiting postal agencies really took off after the Boxer Rebellion, and it was through the development of the postal agency network that the IPO was able to rapidly extend its reach for a relatively modest outlay.

The aim of the postal agency plan was to bring owners of local shops under the wing of the IPO and incorporate them into the postal nationalization project. To some extent this had a significant impact on local commerce and demographic hierarchy, as a postal agency inevitably became a new center for information exchange, with its owner assuming the status of gatekeeper for information transmission. While such a shop—whatever its business—would continue with its existing trade, as a postal agency it also acquired another, quite distinctive, identity. Each shop was provided with a wooden signboard to hang up at the front and also given an identification number; each letter box, for which the shop owner retained the key, was also given a unique number. Shops and their proprietors were vetted as to their suitability, and their license could be revoked (see fig. 6.4).[65] Private letter hongs were also welcome to become postal agencies. Each article emanating from a postal agency was marked on the address side with a stamp indicating the city and the postal section. Of the examples in figure 6.5, the one for Canton (far right, on the top line) was closest to the IPO standard sample, but many postal agencies created their own designs, which was allowed provided the agency's registration number and place name were included. Some chops also bore the names of their associated shops, a form of advertisement, such as the two examples on the second row.

Postal agencies acted as the representatives of the IPO, being authorized to perform selected postal duties, including selling postage stamps, postcards, and "Postal Guides," and receiving and registering letters and parcels. Accounts were settled once a month, and the agents were rewarded with a commission of 5 percent of the income from letters and parcels. They were also allowed to keep in the form of commission any excess received over basic conversion rates on the items they sold (such

64. "Box Offices," Postal Circular 27, October 15, 1899, in *Postal Secretary's Circulars No. 1–134*, 194–96,TMA, W2-2833.

65. "Enclosure No. 3, System of Letter-Boxes Adopted in the Argentine Republic," Postal Circular 27, 198.

代辦郵政分局執照

大清郵政局

給發代辦分局執照事照得現在設有郵局處所擬將各該城

鎮劃分若干段每段各立郵政分局一所以便商民人等就近

購買郵票發寄各色信件茲　城（內外）第　段　街

字號鋪東　　情願遵照郵政章程代辦郵政分局事

宜查此人係殷實鋪商並其鋪確在該段合宜之地洵堪准其

代郵政局發售郵票收寄各色信件包裹等類故特頒給執照

以冀商民人等得以推誠相信也須至執照者

郵政局郵政司畫押蓋戳

光緒　年　月　日給

執照第　號

為

FIGURE 6.4 A license for a postal agency. Source: Enclosure No 3, in Postal Circular No. 27, October 15, 1899, in *Postal Secretary's Circulars No. 1–134*, TMA, W2-2833.

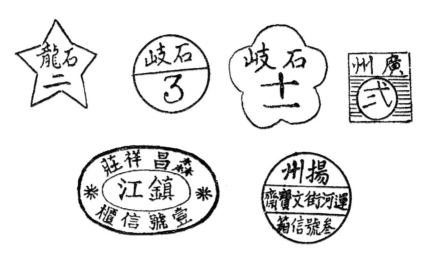

FIGURE 6.5 Various chops used by postal agencies. The top row shows chops from different locations in Canton Province. The stamp on the top right, for No. 2 Postal Agency in Guangzhou, is the one closest to the official model, placing the characters for the location at the top, and the registered number of the postal agency in the middle of the bottom half. The second and third stamps from the right were used by the No. 11 and No. 3 Postal Agencies in Shiqi, respectively. The stamp at top left was used by the No. 2 Postal Agency in Shilong. The bottom row shows two chops from Jiangsu Province. On the right is the mark for the No. 3 Postal Agency in Yangzhou, as indicated at top and bottom. The middle portion reads, "Wenbao stationery store by Canal Street." On the left is a stamp from the No. 1 Postal Agency in Zhenjiang. The name of the shop, "Senchangxiang House," is shown at the top of the oval. Source: Sun Junyi, *Qingdai youchuo zhi*, 167, 214.

as exchange of local copper cash to and from silver currency such as the Mexican dollar).[66]

At the start of the enactment of the postal agency plan, agencies were often set up in places where a full postal branch was yet to be established but where locations had commercial importance, such as market towns and larger villages. As time went on, postal agencies were gradually extended to more inland and rural areas. Due to a shortage of skilled and experienced postal staff, many inland prefectures and important towns

66. "17°. For each ordinary letter, large or small, posted at a Box Office the shopkeeper is entitled to a commission of 2 large cash ($0.002); for ordinary prints, books, samples, etc., 1 cash ($0.001); for each registered article, 5 large cash ($0.005); and for each parcel, 10 cash ($0.010)"; Postal Circular 27, 196.

were still awaiting full postal branches. The demands associated with faster expansion exposed issues around training and quality control of service provision, as a growing problem developed around provision of sufficiently capable managers to provide adequate supervision at the local level. To address this serious problem, from 1907 onward the IPO decided to divide postal agencies into two classes: first-class agencies for medium-size towns, and second-class agencies for smaller or newly opened locations.[67]

Piry's view was that postal agencies were very well suited to their task of localizing and embedding the service into individual communities, as the shops that hosted them were broadly regarded as "solid and reliable establishments, even more so than regular Offices under junior Clerks." Indeed, comparing a young branch office clerk, newly posted and still unknown to the locals, with an existing shop manager who would already be a familiar face in the neighborhood and equipped with local knowledge, it is clear that the latter would typically be in a better position to establish the service within that community. In order to exploit and develop the strengths of these local connections, selected agents began to be paid a salary over and above their regular commission on postage stamps and currency exchange in return for taking on additional responsibilities. These new duties included timely distribution of local mail, promotion and display of service advertisements and new regulations, and engaging in continuing and focused competition with their local rivals, the private letter hongs.[68] These additional responsibilities demonstrate that postal agencies were no longer passive agents carrying out mechanical procedures of the postal business but engaged in a far more proactive process of advocacy and promotion. This in turn gave the shopkeepers themselves a new and elevated social status, as their business shifted focus from everyday commerce to a new role as local representative of the official postal service, part of a rapidly growing national utility.

There was another way in which the IPO took advantage of having a good pool of postal agencies at its disposal. When there was a need to set up a full postal branch, the most experienced agency in the area would

67. "IPO Agencies: Revised System," Postal Circular 160, February 14, 1907, in *Circulars Nos. 135–261*, 71–72, TMA, W2-2838.

68. Postal Circular 160, 71–72.

FIGURE 6.6 The postal agency in Yongchun, Fujian Province, serves as a local information hub. The long signboard placed horizontally above the window, and the one placed vertically next to the man seated to the left of the group, bear the Chinese characters "Postal Agency for the Great Qing Imperial Post Office" (Da Qing youzheng daiban fenju 大清郵政代辦分局). On both vertical frame pillars of the central group of men there are two smaller wooden boards. The one on the left reads, "The postmaster orders—important official bureau" (Ben youzhengsi shi guanju zhongdi 本郵政司示 官局重地); the one on the right reads, "The postmaster orders—noise prohibited" (Ben youzhengsi shi jinzhi xuanhua 本郵政司示 禁止喧譁). These two smaller boards were not part of the official signage for postal agencies. Photographed by John Preston Maxwell, ca. 1904–1907. Source: Historical Photographs of China, University of Bristol; permission by Cadbury Research Library, University of Birmingham.

be considered as priority for promotion.[69] For example, Enping District in Canton had a postal agency open in 1902, run by an apothecary owner. As the area added additional postal agencies, this agency was promoted to a third-class branch, and later moved to a more prominent location after receiving a further promotion to a second-class branch.[70] Also in 1902, Gong District in Henan saw a postal agency open; this soon became very popular among the local gentry. It was promoted to a third-class branch some years later and then to a second-class branch in 1917.[71] Another example can be found in Huanren District of Liaoning. In 1911 a postal agency was set up inside the Red Emperor Guan temple in the district. It was turned into a third-class branch in 1913, and was promoted again to a second-class branch in 1916.[72] The consequence of all this activity was that postal agencies, though in strict hierarchical terms on the lowest rung of the growing postal estate, were nevertheless regarded as a very important asset of the IPO. In Piry's words, "Much depends upon these modest pioneers, who, at the head of their numerous establishments, command the situation at so many points."[73] The postal agencies not only provided postal services but were a symbol of ownership and participation for local Chinese and became increasingly important for recruitment.

Chinese Staff

The IPO's personnel system originated with the CMCS, which in turn had been much influenced by the British civil administration system of the nineteenth century. Before separation from the CMCS in May 1911,

69. "A First Class Agency can be made a Branch or Inland Office, and a Second Class Agency a First Class Agency when results raise their importance to the standard of the higher establishment"; see "Postal Agencies: General Rules," enclosure, in Postal Circular 160, 73.
70. *Minguo Enpingxian zhi, juan* 12:14.
71. *Minguo Gongxian zhi, juan* 7:7.
72. *Minguo Huanrenxian zhi, juan* 11:31–32.
73. "Postal Operations: General Instructions," Postal Circular 164, March 26, 1907, in *Circulars Nos. 135–261*, 103, TMA, W2-2838.

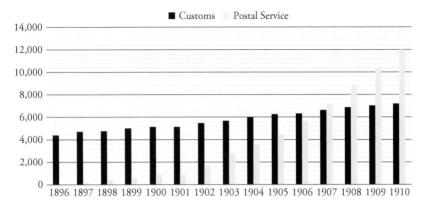

FIGURE 6.7 Staff numbers of the Chinese Maritime Customs Service and the Imperial Post Office, 1896–1910. Source: *Service List.*

IPO staff were on the payroll of the CMCS.[74] The payments to native postal staff were lower than those of the CMCS until changes were made in 1908.[75] Despite this, the IPO cultivated its own personnel, with an emphasis that was clearly different from that of the CMCS, being much closer to the interests and concerns of the general public. The Chinese staff of the IPO rapidly outgrew the number of foreign staff; additionally, the number of IPO staff soon exceeded that of the overall CMCS (see fig. 6.7).

It is instructive to explore the differences between the CMCS and the IPO. The establishment of the CMCS had been a consequence of the Treaty of Nanjing and subsequent treaties, going back to 1842. To distinguish it from China's existing, internally focused, Customs practice, it was usually referred to in Chinese as either new Customs (*xinguan* 新關) or foreign Customs (*yangguan* 洋關), and the inspectorate general was generally regarded by Chinese people as the agent of foreign powers.[76] Although some scholarship, including the present monograph, has provided different perspectives on how the institution developed under Robert Hart, who came to be seen by many of his British contemporaries as too

---

74. Liu Chenghan, "Youzheng renshi zhidu," 59–60; Yanxing [Pan Ansheng], "Youzheng kaoshi zhidu," 75–79.

75. "Revised Natives Ranks and Salaries," Postal Circular 197, August 21, 1908, in *Circulars Nos. 135–261,* 258, TMA, W2-2838.

76. Chen Shiqi, *Zhongguo jindai haiguanshi,* 50–57.

close to China and too conscientious in furthering its interests (even, on occasion, where there was conflict with British ones), it remains the case that the inspectorate general was an organization managed and run by foreigners and supported by a substantial body of Chinese clerks. Catherine Ladds has observed that the structure of the CMCS was a strict hierarchy, with commissioners of Customs at treaty ports taking a role that was in form and practice very similar to that of a "district officer of colonial administrative service."[77] This view was held by many of Hart's Chinese contemporaries, and their criticism of the exclusion of Chinese from the top ranks of the inspectorate general began to appear as early as the 1880s.[78]

This situation in the CMCS did not noticeably change until Francis Aglen's time, following the change in political climate after 1911; but even then movement was slow when it came to promoting Chinese to the indoor staff of the Revenue Department. The Customs College (Shuiwu xuetang 稅務學堂) was established in 1908 in Beijing, with the clear aim of cultivating young talented Chinese for the country's revenue work and providing new native blood for the indoor staff of the CMCS. A year after the inaugural class of the Customs College graduated in 1913, Aglen changed the rules to allow the new graduates to enter the Revenue Department at the level of probationer fourth assistant C and third clerk B or C.[79] Fourth assistant had been the entry level for most foreigners for the indoor staff, and those hired into these roles might expect to have the opportunity to be promoted to commissioner one day.

The IPO was able to shape its approach to organizing its personnel differently (fig. 6.8). There were two particularly distinctive aspects. First, the IPO allowed for greater opportunity for lower-ranking CMCS staff to transfer into management positions, which became necessary as post office expansion proceeded and there was a need for more people in senior roles. Second, in recognition of the fact that the success of the IPO was dependent on persuading ordinary Chinese to use its services, there was a focused effort to recruit and develop native people. This view led the

77. Ladds, *Empire Careers*, 91.
78. Van de Ven, *Breaking with the Past*, 153–56.
79. Chihyun Chang, *Government, Imperialism and Nationalism in China*, 67–68.

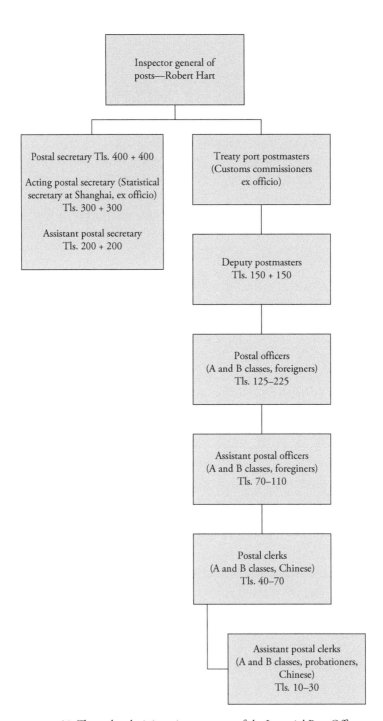

FIGURE 6.8 The early administrative structure of the Imperial Post Office. Although further changes of detail were made to the ranks of the staff, the basic structure in relation to the CMCS was consistent until formal separation in 1911. The diagram presents information from IG Circular 881/Postal No. 46, January 20, 1899, in *Inspector General's Postal Circulars 1–89*, TMA, W2-2833. Monetary unit in the source is "Tls." This should be understood as Hk. Tls.

IPO to develop its own policies in the classification and remuneration of staff, most notably in finding ways to recruit and retain native Chinese.

The IPO's administrative structure demonstrates that overall postal responsibility sat with the inspector general. Reporting to the inspector general was the postal secretary, who was ranked alongside the commissioners of treaty ports; treaty port commissioners in turn acted as postmasters for their respective treaty port areas, providing direct local supervision. What this structure conceals, however, is a shortage of people at all ranks with postal knowledge and experience. As previous chapters have demonstrated, the consequence of this was a steep learning curve for those CMCS commissioners drafted to assist with the postal project—most notably, Detring, Kopsch, Van Aalst, and Piry. In addition to studying the postal regulations of other countries and the rules of the Universal Postal Union, those charged with building and running the new service also spent time visiting foreign post offices to learn about their methods and policies—for example, Henry F. Merrill went to Washington, DC; Donovan, and Van Aalst and Piry went to the General Post Office in London; and Alfred E. Hippisley went to Hong Kong. Yet no amount of study or knowledge exchange could address the largest problem facing the organization: an ongoing shortage of staff.

Prior to the foundation of the IPO in 1897, the number of staff members in each Customs post office was small, and typically a member of the CMCS outdoor staff, such as a tidewaiter, examiner, or watcher, took charge of postal work. This individual, a foreigner, would be supported by one or two additional outdoor staff colleagues and one Chinese staff member during busy periods. The new positions that came with the creation of the IPO meant that these outdoor staff would, if they carried on with postal work, have the potential to be transferred into management-type work. They could be promoted to the rank of postal officer (see fig. 6.7), with the responsibility of running a branch, organizing and managing postal connections between branches, and overseeing the work of postal clerks, including probationers. Some of them might eventually be promoted as postmasters, with overall responsibility for a substantial postal territory.

The *Service List* of 1908 can be used as an example to demonstrate how post office expansion made possible a degree of social mobility among foreign staff that would previously not have been open to them within the CMCS. Close examination demonstrates that, after ten years of operation, more than half of the IPO's district postmasters and deputy postmasters in that year had originally come from relatively low-ranking CMCS outdoor staff. As an example, H. D. Summers, introduced in chapter 5, joined the CMCS in 1891 as a third-class tidewaiter, but by 1906 had been promoted to district postmaster in charge. Indeed, while the Tianjin Customs commissioner was nominally in charge of postal affairs at the treaty port, in practice Summers had primary responsibility for day-to-day running of the service. O. E. M. Bünese, a German who joined the CMCS in 1887 as a third-class tidewaiter, became a deputy postmaster in 1906, stationed in Shanghai. J. L. McDowall, a watcher when he joined the CMCS in 1888, became deputy postmaster in 1906, and then district postmaster in 1908.[80] A similar career path was shared by two other British CMCS employees, J. Tweedie and D. Mullen. Tweedie was a watcher in Canton in 1892, but deputy postmaster in Taiyuan by 1906. Mullen also entered the CMCS as a watcher in Canton in 1888, gradually rose to second-class tidewaiter, and was transferred to Nanjing to open the post office there, as was noted in chapter 4. He had a good career in the IPO and was promoted to deputy postmaster in 1907 in Shenyang, transferring to Xi'an the following year.[81] A. H. Hyland, another British employee, joined the CMCS in 1892 in Canton as a watcher, later transferring to tidewaiter; he was promoted to district postmaster in 1905 for the entire Canton postal district.[82]

Chinese postal clerks were entrusted with critical tasks, such as opening new branches prior to the Boxer Rebellion, and restoring the service after it ended. Hippisley, the officiating postal secretary during Piry's leave in 1908, issued comments in a reflective circular about the IPO that shed light on the overall direction of the organization. He came from an old, landed family in Somerset, England, and was seen at the time as a strong candidate to succeed Hart, favored by elements in the British government. As Hippisley wrote,

> Unlike the Customs, therefore, the Post Office functions chiefly for natives, must develop chiefly in the interior, and must aim at shaping

80. *Service List (1908)*, 181, 178.
81. *Service List (1907)*, 177; *Service List (1908)*, 181.
82. *Service List (1907)*, 176; *Service List (1908)*, 181.

its organisation in such manner as will best suit Chinese ideas and best meet Chinese wants. In order to attain this end, the bulk of the work will have to be conducted—not in a foreign, but—in the Chinese language, and the vast majority of offices of trust in the interior will be held by Chinese, and usually by natives of the province in which those offices are located. The number of foreign employés will always be a comparatively small one; and as their duties will be confined to the supervision of large areas, a reading and speaking knowledge will with them be a *sine quâ non* if they would avoid stagnating in inferior positions in the treaty-port Offices.[83]

The IPO as whole still had difficulty in recruitment, however. Compared with the telegraph and railway sectors, the postal service was significantly behind. For example, after Ding Richang set up the Fuzhou Telegraph School (Fuzhou dianbao xuetang 福州電報學堂) in 1876, other provincial governors followed his lead and opened their own such schools over the following two decades. The Qing government also sent students abroad to learn telegraph techniques in the 1880s.[84] By contrast, there was no formal postal training established until 1910, when postal subjects were combined with telegraph courses in the curriculum of the School of Transportation (Jiaotong chuanxisuo 交通傳習所).[85] Instead, the IPO took a more ad hoc approach by either modifying existing training methods from the CMCS or inventing new ones as they went along. In practice, this style of working—essentially, one of continuous improvisation—was reasonably effective, as evidenced repeatedly in the early days of the postal service from stamp creation, to relay design, to the competition with private letter hongs. This means that instead of having a well-thought-out plan, the postal work was done through constant modification in order to blend imported Western methods with Chinese ways.

Originally the IPO wanted to liaise with local schools, starting with those in Canton and Shanghai, to recruit promising native youths. This

83. Postal Circular 181, January 31, 1908, in *Circulars Nos. 135–261*, 166, TMA, W2-2838. Emphasis in the original.

84. Sun Li, *Wan Qing dianbao*, 74–75.

85. "Ben bu zou kai Jiaotong chuanxisuo dagai qingxing zhe" 本部奏開交通傳習所大概情形摺 [Memorial on reporting the general situation of a newly opened school of transportation by this board], Xuantong reign year 2, month 2, day 28 (April 7, 1910), in *Jiaotong guanbao*, issue 12, 5–6.

method seemed sensible, and would avoid separating families.[86] But it would take years to bear significant fruit, so it was necessary to resort to other methods, one of which was to bring in men from outside. For example, in May 1897, when Hart learned that Aglen, the Customs commissioner at Tianjin at the time, had been unable to recruit enough young men from the local schools to work for the IPO, he said, "I am disappointed such is not the case. I shall order up four from Hong Kong—where I have ten lads waiting." He added, "Many offices complained when I sent them postal clerks (Chinese), saying I ought to let each promote native talent: but I find it's almost the same everywhere—when it comes to the point, native talent is not obtainable."[87]

When Donovan inspected the new post office at Yuyao, near Ningbo, it seems highly likely that he came across one of those four Hong Kong lads. Being attached to a chemist shop, the new post office was very economically furnished. The branch had one assistant postal officer (Portuguese), two assistant postal clerks (Chinese), three assistant postal clerks on probation (Chinese, trained for inland work), one sorter, and six letter carriers. Donovan noted that the assistant postal officer was very "dull" and unable to express himself very well in English. But he was attentive and devoted to work, spoke some French and good Chinese, and was able to read addresses on ordinary Chinese letter covers. By contrast, Donovan was very impressed by an assistant postal clerk, Tye Pao Hua 戴寶華, a native of Hong Kong. According to Donovan, he was bright, intelligent, willing, and healthy, and had studied the postal rules and regulations very well. Another assistant postal clerk Donovan considered to be not as good as Tye, though he was very capable of doing the work assigned to him. Still another, one of the Chinese clerks on probation, was only fifteen years old and knew very little English or even Chinese. For Donovan, this young man certainly ought not to progress up the ranks.[88]

---

86. IG Circular 715 / Postal No. 11, May 28, 1896, in *Inspector General's Postal Circulars 1–89*, 49, TMA, W2-2833.

87. Robert Hart to Francis Aglen, May 12, 1897, SOAS, MS211081.

88. John Patrick Donovan, "Tour of Inspection," June 25, 1900, SHAC, 137 (1) 7603. Tye Pao Hua was one of the few Hong Kong natives to join the system after May 1897 and before 1900, by the time Donovan took his trip; see *Service List (1901)*, 152.

Such a mixture of capable and less capable Chinese clerks in one branch office was commonly seen in other branches, and the established clerks had to supervise those on probation. With the further postal expansion inland, many new branches had no foreign staff and relied instead on Chinese clerks. Chinese postal clerk-in-charge became an important designation; such an individual would be the sole manager of an inland postal branch, without the presence of a foreign postal officer. Candidates for postal clerk had to pass a relatively simple examination in Chinese in the following categories: practical letter writing, simple arithmetic, simple geography, and ordinary office work.[89] The prefect or magistrate would be informed by the district postmaster about the basic personal information of the new postal clerk-in-charge and the date of appointment. Postal clerks-in-charge gradually received recognition as public functionaries, and the local authority came to note that, ideally, changes of personnel should not be too frequent.[90]

Leaving inland post offices entirely in the charge of Chinese staff raised uneasy feelings for the IPO's leadership, and they were particularly concerned by two main issues: honesty and discipline. Hart's comments to James Duncan Campbell summed up the general view shared across those responsible for the IPO's management: "Work requires and Commissioners clamour for more hands: I cannot get our Post offices to train or use Chinese beyond a certain point—they work well, that is, efficiently, but without foreign reliable supervision play tricks in all ranks."[91] Back in 1899, the issue of institutional discipline of both foreign and native staff had been raised, and after studying the postal laws of various countries, Van Aalst decided to use Hong Kong's postal ordinance as a template for regulations intended to ensure the probity of foreign staff. In addition to dismissal, punishment for misconduct by foreign staff included fines and potential imprisonment. For Chinese postal staff, referencing the Qing code, punishments included blows from a heavy bamboo cane and penal

---

89. "Inland Post Offices," enclosure, in "Inland Post Offices," Postal Circular 30, February 20, 1900, in *Postal Secretary's Circulars No. 1–134*, 241, TMA, W2-2833.

90. "Clerks-in-Charge: Appointments of," Postal Circular 112, November 18, 1904, *Postal Secretary's Circulars No. 1–134*, 465, TMA, W2-2833.

91. Robert Hart to James Duncan Campbell, letter 1348, October 23, 1904, in *The IG*, 2:1433.

servitude.[92] Even so, these regulations were clearly not regarded as sufficient to ensure discipline at inland branches, and while it was impossible for the district postmaster to continually check the work of inland post offices, the IPO introduced two additional tools to ensure the maintenance of standards: the assignment of guarantors, and an inspection system.[93]

Guarantors for Chinese Employees

The practice of requiring guarantors was familiar within Chinese society. For example, traditional banks and the pawn trade relied on guarantors to ensure people hired were reliable and trustworthy.[94] In her study on trade practices in Taiwan in the late-nineteenth century, Lin Yuju has identified the emergence of a new class of goods examiners and clerks at native ports as essential to the development of a rapidly growing commercial system. Although these new professionals were contracted to work for local governments, they were not themselves officials. Behind the selection of individuals for these positions, a practice of requiring personal guarantors was adopted, which underpinned confidence in the system by providing checks on candidates' backgrounds as well as a degree of accountability. In the majority of cases, the system ensured that those hired typically came from well-established families with experience in commerce.[95]

Following Chinese custom in this regard, the IPO came up with its own set of rules that included a requirement for guarantors alongside the payment of a sum of money as security, with amounts varying in accordance with the positions.[96] Such rules came to be useful in cases of misconduct. For example, in 1905 a postal clerk in Yuezhou "'slode' with almost

92. "Inland Post Offices," Postal Circular 19, February 20, 1899, in *Postal Secretary's Circulars No. 1–134*, 166–71, TMA, W2-2833.

93. "Inland Post Offices," 241, 250.

94. Wang Yuming, *Ming Qing Huizhou dian shang*, 33–46; Huang Jianhui, *Ming Qing Shanxi shangren*, 369–77.

95. Lin Yuju, *Xiang hai li sheng*, 97.

96. "Securities for Chinese Employés," Postal Circular 144, September 12, 1906, in *Circulars Nos. 135–261*, 26, TMA, W2-2838.

Table 6.4. Guarantor amounts for different Imperial Post Office ranks

Rank	Mexican dollars
Candidate clerks: linguist	400
Candidate clerks: nonlinguist	200
Postal clerks: linguist	1,000
Postal clerks: nonlinguist	500
Clerks in charge of money order offices A: minimum	1,000
Clerks in charge of money order offices B: minimum	750
Writers	Fixed by postmaster
Other employees (sorters, letter carriers, couriers, messengers, etc.)	30
Inland postal agents*	Minimum, 200

* The local postmaster was entrusted to fix a sum for each inland postal agent, which in no case should be less than MX$200.

twenty thousand dollars in his pocket!"[97] Table 6.4 illustrates the amount required when hiring for different ranks. There were additional rules around how security should be handled when individuals were promoted, and around reporting of changes in guarantor arrangements—for example, in case of a change of address, a change of business status, or the death of a guarantor.[98]

Inspecting Clerks

Donovan's tour of inspection in 1900–1901 provides us with a good example of the process of inspecting IPO postal branches and agencies; alongside him, senior Chinese postal clerks were entrusted with a similar task of traveling around the IPO network to conduct inspections. Tours of inspection were typically carried out without any prior warning. When inspections first began, Chinese inspecting clerks were selected from Beijing, but this approach proved inadequate as the IPO's territory expanded.

97. Robert Hart to Francis Aglen, November 7, 1905, SOAS MS211081.
98. "Securities for Chinese Employés," enclosure, in "Securities for Chinese Employés," Postal Circular 144, 28, TMA, W2-2838.

This was not just a question of needing more staff; there were other challenges in using Beijing staff in areas far from the capital, principally relating to lack of local knowledge or of the ability to communicate in local dialects, which limited their effectiveness in the role. Ideally the inspecting clerks should be the eyes and ears of the IPO; however, it seems that, in many cases, they turned up at local post offices but failed to make themselves understood or were unable to understand others. In some cases, after spending several months in a region acquiring local knowledge and learning the dialect, inspecting clerks found themselves transferred to other places, their efforts effectively wasted. Recognizing the benefit that an inspection regime could bring, in 1907 the IPO formally added inspecting clerk to the list of grades for Chinese staff and required that those selected for the role be recruited and trained locally in each postal district.[99]

The combination of the system of guarantors and creation of the role of inspecting clerk was aimed at embedding postal personnel within regional human networks as deeply as possible. Indeed, recruiting people from the locality had always been an IPO priority, though in practice this was difficult to achieve with any consistency. In order to make a post office career attractive to native Chinese, the IPO was also forced to adjust grades and pay scales. The revisions shown in Table 6.5 were introduced in 1902, incorporating additional divisions in grading separating Chinese clerks into linguists and nonlinguists. The intention behind the new scale was to encourage good native employees with language skills to make lasting careers in the IPO and at the same time allow for capable nonlinguist clerks to receive recognition for their work in inland offices. Yet while the revised grades and pay scales theoretically enabled capable men to rise through the ranks, attitudes toward Chinese staff within the IPO's senior management were slow to change and, consequently, promotions and improved remuneration took a very long time to materialize.

According to the new scale, there were five classes of linguist clerk, on comparable pay scales to those for foreign postal officers. But in practice, for years after the introduction of the new pay scale, the highest

---

99. "Inspecting Clerks to be Trained Locally," Postal Circular 165, June 10, 1907, in *Postal Circulars and Instructions, 1906–1911*, 106–7, TMA, W2-2838.

Table 6.5. The revised scale of postal ranks and salaries, 1902

Postmasters	Salary (in Hk.Tls)
Postmaster / deputy postmaster	n/a
Postal officers	
Chief postal officer	225
First to fourth classes	200–125
Assistant postal officers	
Grades A–C	110–80
Probationers	
Postal officer	75
Postal students	50
Auxiliaries	60
Chinese postal clerks—linguists	
Principal postal clerk, grades A–C	250–175
First postal clerk, grades A–D	130–100
Second postal clerk, grades A–B	90–80
Third postal clerk, grades A–B	70–60
Fourth postal clerk, grades A–B	50–40
Candidate postal clerk (probationer), grades A–C	35–25
Student postal clerk, grade C	20
Chinese postal clerks—nonlinguists	
Principal postal clerk	150–130
First to fourth classes, grades A–B	110–20
Candidate postal clerk, grades A–B	15–10

Source: Enclosure 1, "Revised Scale of Postal Ranks and Salaries," in IG Circular 1017 / Postal No. 56, April 4, 1902, in *Inspector General's Postal Circulars 1–89*, 174–84, TMA W2–2833.

positions filled by the most senior Chinese postal staff remained far below the most senior available rank. Even for those on the new grade of inspecting clerk, introduced in 1907 for Chinese staff, the pay was still not as high as assistant postal officer grade A. Tables 6.6 and 6.7 show the career positions of three of the most senior Chinese staff members in 1903, and again in 1908. Chen Yaotang 陳耀棠 (Chan Bǔt-to in the *Service List*), a native of Canton, joined the CMCS in 1896 and was engaged from his arrival on postal work. He was highly praised in 1901 by Van

Table 6.6. The three most senior Chinese postal clerks, 1903

Name	First appointed	Language skills	Station	Rank	Salary (in Hk.Tls.)
Chen Yaotang 陳耀棠	1896	Cantonese, Northern Mandarin, Southern Mandarin	Tengyue (Yunnan)	Third postal clerk B	60
Deng Weifan 鄧維藩	1897	Northern Mandarin	Beijing	Third postal clerk A	70
Deng Weiping 鄧維屏	1897	Northern Mandarin, French	Taiyuan	Third postal clerk B	60

Source: *Service List* (1903), 154.

Table 6.7. The three most senior Chinese postal clerks, 1908

Name	First appointed	Language skills	Station	Rank	Salary (in Hk.Tls.)
Chen Yaotang 陳耀棠	1896	Cantonese, Amoy, Shanghainese, Northern Mandarin, Southern Mandarin, Western Mandarin, English	Hankou	Second postal clerk B	80
Deng Weifan 鄧維藩	1897	Northern Mandarin, English	Beijing	Inspecting clerk	100
Deng Weiping 鄧維屏	1897	Northern Mandarin, French, English	Beijing	Inspecting clerk	90

Source: *Service List* (1908), 189, 193.

Aalst, the postal secretary, for his "quick, neat, accurate, and intelligent" work.[100] After Deng Weifan and Deng Weiping were transferred to roles as inspecting clerks, he became the most senior postal clerk. Although with different job titles, all three men belonged to the linguist clerk grouping. The majority of Chinese postal clerks were nonlinguist clerks—in 1908, around two-thirds. The attrition rate of staff in general caused

---

100. "Postal Secretary's Office Mr. Van Aalst's Memo to Successor 10 October 1901," SHAC, 679 (1) 14908.

difficulties. For example, in 1907, fifty-four linguist clerks were lost to the service, and 199 nonlinguists, through a mixture of resignations and involuntary departures, the latter due either to unsatisfactory performance or to some form of misconduct.[101]

In 1905 Hart wrote a short circular to instruct Customs commissioners at the treaty ports to look out for Chinese people with foreign language skills. Somewhat optimistically, he wrote, "Now that Foreign languages are being taught at so many ports it is becoming easier to find Chinese Clerks locally for both Revenue and Postal Departments . . . educational establishments may be encouraged by work found for their students, and also that Clerks may be locally recruited, when possible, acquainted with the dialect and habits of the place."[102] The reality, however, was not as rosy as Hart anticipated, because while it was true that more language teaching was taking place, Chinese people with foreign language skills were popular in every sphere of activity, and the IPO had to compete with institutions and companies in both the state and private sectors. As Hippisley noted, "Owing to the desire to acquire Western learning now prevailing, the demand for English-speaking Chinese as tutors and professors is, and seems likely to be for some time, so great, and the remuneration offered so liberal, that considerable difficulty is experienced by the I.P.O. in obtaining 'Linguist' clerks who have more than a mere smattering of English."[103]

For all of their differing views, Hart and Hippisley indicate that something profound was happening in Chinese society: a new group of professionals was emerging, in both civil administration and private companies, whose educational and career paths were increasingly divergent from what had gone before. In fact, in 1905, the chief superintendent of the Imperial Chinese Telegraph Administration (Zhongguo dianbao zongju 中國電報總局), F. N. Dresing, wrote to Hart to request that the CMCS and the IPO stop hiring the agency's Chinese men: "For a considerable time past it has been found that many of the Clerks trained and

---

101. Postal Circular 181, January 31, 1908, in *Circulars Nos. 135–261*, 167, TMA, W2-2838.

102. IG Circular 1223 / Postal No.81a, March 4, 1905, in *Inspector General's Postal Circulars 1–89*, 255, TMA, W2-2833.

103. Postal Circular 181, 167.

educated by the Imperial Chinese Telegraph Administration leave our service without permission and are immediately engaged by the Imperial Maritime Customs either as General Office Clerks or as Post Office Clerks."[104] Dresing pointed out that this culture was causing his organization a great inconvenience and also had a very bad disciplinary effect on staff in general, because they were under the impression that even if they were discharged from the Telegraph Administration for negligence of duty or another similar reason, they could be sure of immediate employment in the CMCS or the IPO. Their transferable skills allowed these new Chinese professionals to easily move from one place to another, and the exchange between these three sectors further demonstrated that there was a growing demand for what they could offer.

The wider topic of the development and significance of this new professional class in China from the late nineteenth century onward certainly deserves focused attention, but some useful insights can be gathered just from the early history of the Chinese postal service. Figure 6.9 shows the growth of the IPO workforce between 1897 and 1910. The numbers of foreign postal officers increased very slowly between 1900 and 1906, with little further change in numbers in the last four years.

Acknowledging the important contributions made by the lower-grade employees, sorters, letter carriers, and couriers, Piry adjusted their salaries too. Meanwhile, he deliberately kept promotion to clerkship open to promising workers from these lower ranks.[105] These changes were a direct consequence of internal debates at the most senior level about what kind of institution the IPO should become; the outcome of these discussions was to have significant long-term impact not only on personnel but also on the wider perceptions of the IPO by the general public. The conversation was led by Hippisley and Piry, with little direct involvement from Hart as he had left China for good in April 1908. While Hippisley was officiating postal secretary he addressed the IPO's institutional culture. Tying this together with the question of ensuring appropriate rewards for Chinese staff, he sought to create a more elevated status for

104. Enclosure no. 1, "Chief Superintendent of Imperial Chinese Telegraphs to Inspector General," August 17, 1905, IG Circular 1323 / Postal No. 137, March 24, 1906, in *Circulars Nos. 135–261*, 5, TMA, W2-2838.

105. "Grades and Rates of Pay for Lower Employés," Postal Circular 205, November 18, 1908, in *Circulars Nos. 135–261*, 276–77, TMA, W2-2838.

12,000

10,000

8,000

6,000

4,000

2,000

0

1897 1898 1899 1900 1901 1902 1903 1904 1905 1906 1907 1908 1909 1910

■ Postal officers and above   ■ Chinese postal clerks and writers

Chinese staff (clerks excluded)

FIGURE 6.9 The increase in the Imperial Post Office workforce between 1897 and 1910. Foreign postal officers include postmasters, deputy postmasters, district inspectors, and postal officers, but excludes postal commissioners and those positions within the Inspectorate General. Source: *Service List*, 1897–1910.

the IPO—which, he considered, would follow at least in part from hiring the right people. While appreciative of the hard work of lower-ranked Chinese staff who came almost exclusively from humble backgrounds, and also understanding the benefits of promoting staff from the bottom up, Hippisley believed that senior ranks such as inspecting clerk or nonlinguist clerk responsible for running inland branches should be filled by men "of as high a social standing as possible." He added, "For the duties of the head of an Inland Office bring him into frequent contact with provincial gentry or require him to visit the local Magistrate on business. The bearing and manners which come by birth and breeding are necessary on such occasion; if they are absent, the influence and prestige of the I.P.O. will suffer."[106] Hippisley also believed that, in order to improve the reputation of the institution, the IPO should take more serious and prompt measures to weed out less satisfactory individuals— for example, those who showed a lack of energy or interest during probation, those who demonstrated repeated carelessness in their tasks, or men of any rank who showed the slightest tendency toward dishonesty.

106. Postal Circular 181, 168.

Piry, by contrast, had a different perspective. Instead of supporting the view that clerks with an inferior education should be passed over for promotion or even weeded out, he expressed his gratitude to the existing staff who had brought the postal service to its current level. His stance was that while improvements to salary might eventually enable the IPO to recruit people of higher social standing, he doubted whether highly educated men would really find themselves drawn to what could be seen as a slow-moving, at times quite laborious, career. "The Postal Service has no sinecures to offer," he wrote; "it requires immediate work from each new-comer; and it is a question whether, outside of the business class, where we now recruit most of our men, we would find the born activity and practical sense, together with the readiness for manual operations, which the work generally requires. The young student of classics, bred up for the ordinary official calling in China, hardly comes up to this standard."[107]

Piry was from a working-class French family and had come to China in 1870 at age nineteen.[108] He joined the CMCS in 1874 at the level of fourth assistant B, and also taught French at Tongwen College. Piry translated the *Sacred Edict of the Kangxi Emperor* (*Sheng yu guang xun* 聖諭廣訓) into French, with the title *Le saint édit: Étude de littérature Chinoise*, published by the Statistical Department of the CMCS in 1879. He also translated a seventeenth-century Chinese novel as *Erh-tou-mei, ou, Les pruniers merveilleux: Roman chinois* (*Erh-tou-mei*, or, *The Marvelous Plum Trees: A Chinese Romance*). In 1895, again through the Statistical Department, he published a *Manuel de langue mandarine* (*Manual of the Mandarin Language*), a teaching resource containing Chinese, English, and French.[109] Piry's hobbies included sailing, shooting, and photography.[110]

Piry's attitude toward lower-ranked Chinese postal staff can to some extent be seen as a reaction against the stratified, officer-and-men culture of the CMCS. During his time as postal secretary, he sought to cultivate

107. Postal Circular 197, 261.

108. Thiriez, *Barbarian Lens*, 94.

109. For Piry's careers, see note in "Death of the Emperor Kuang Hsü and of the Empress Dowager: Place Ceremonies in Connection With," IG Circular 1577 (2nd ser.), December 4, 1908, in *Docs. Ill.*, 2:676.

110. Thiriez, *Barbarian Lens*, 94.

a distinctive mode of operation for the IPO. In order to proactively encourage satisfactory performance from lower-ranked staff—that is, the postmen and couriers, the very people who had the most frequent and direct contact with the general public—a reward system for good conduct was introduced. Lower-ranked staff would be rewarded with extra payment, and they would also receive distinctive badges to be worn with their uniforms.[111] Meanwhile, Piry's approach in widely encouraging promotion through the grades stimulated social mobility, and it is clear that the pool of talent available to the service was larger than that originally envisaged, as many individuals from the trades and other walks of life were recruited, when originally it had been anticipated that local school connections would be the main sources of new staff.

To reinforce the social status of the clerk-in-charge of local branches, postmaster grading was created specifically for Chinese staff to run small post offices.[112] The Chinese term for *postmaster* was changed from *fenjuzhang* 分局長 to *youdizhang* 郵遞長 between 1908 and 1911, but for those bearing these ranks in their local communities, the strict administrative terminology was not very important. What was critical, though, was that these terms included the word *zhang* 長, which carries the meaning of "chief" or "manager" within a territory; this indicated a degree of institutional weight and conferred social prestige in the local community. When a clerk-in-charge was transferred to a new place, he would arrive with proper credentials attached to the national postal administration. In cases where postal agencies were upgraded to full postal branches, shopkeepers were often able to enroll as regular staff within the IPO. For example, the Ruixiang shop 瑞祥商號 in the Boxing District of Shandong became a postal agency in 1906. When it was upgraded to a third-class branch in 1911, the shop manager was appointed

---

111. Postal Circular 205, 280. The IPO had uniforms for the winter and summer seasons, and it was required that letter carriers, boatmen, and other employees designated by the commissioners wear uniforms when on duty. The summer uniform was pale blue, while the winter jacket was in a waist-length *magua* style and navy blue. The jackets were fastened at the front with five brass buttons (made in Japan). Uniforms for both seasons bore the Chinese characters for "Great Qing Imperial Post Office." Postal Note 12, February 11, 1897, in *Postal Notes, 1–38*, 14, TMA, W2-2833.

112. Enclosure 2, "List of Titles in the Postal Service," in Postal Circular 181, 176, TMA, W2-2838; "Classification of Staff," enclosure, in Postmaster General's Circular 269, August 28, 1911, in *Circulars Nos. 262–389*, 27, TMA, W2-2840.

subpostmaster. Another example can be found in Guan District, also in Shandong. A postal agency was opened there in 1901 within a local shop, but efforts to build a stable service in the area proved difficult, as the agency changed hands at least three times in a relatively short period before Shen Zicheng 申子誠 became its manager. When the agency was upgraded to a second-class branch in 1919, Shen Zicheng was appointed subpostmaster.[113]

In 1904 the Qing government acknowledged the progress made by the IPO after the Boxer Rebellion, and finally agreed on an official annual grant of Hk.Tls. 720,000. The fund was to come from six Customs stations—Canton, Fuzhou, Hankou, Shanghai, Shantou, and Tianjin— each of which would contribute Hk.Tls. 10,000 monthly. The Customs superintendents at these ports were required to pass the funds on to the Customs commissioners, who would in turn transfer the money to designated accounts of the inspector general at either Hong Kong or Shanghai.[114] Hart was in high spirits over this development. In revealing the plan to Campbell, he noted that the IPO was already generating an income of some Hk.Tls. 330,000, and with the new fund it would have a total of Hk.Tls. 1,050,000 available for expansion and maintenance. But he did not plan to spend it all; Hart wrote, "I shall restrict expenditure to the amount granted, and report and turn over an increasing annual income: this will look more like success, and please our backers. But we must hold on to it as a Customs department—otherwise it will become French and cease to be Chinese and cosmopolitan."[115] Hart saw the approval of the grant as a major recognition on the part of the government, and he believed the full establishment of the post office would take place before he left China.[116]

This recognition from the central government should, in theory, have helped take some financial pressure off Hart, who had recently received a joint petition from many of his own senior commissioners that com-

---

113. *Minguo chongxiu Boxingxian zhi*, juan 10:18. *Minguo Guanxian zhi* juan 2:40–42.

114. IG Circular 1164 (2nd ser.) / Postal No. 76, June 16, 1904, in *Inspector General's Postal Circulars 1–89*, 237, TMA, W2-2833; IG Circular 1169 (2nd ser.) / Postal No. 78, July 18, 1904, in *Inspector General's Postal Circulars 1–89*, 248, TMA, W2-2833.

115. Robert Hart to James Duncan Campbell, letter 1331, June 12, 1904, in *The IG*, 2:1416.

116. Robert Hart to James Duncan Campbell, letter 1332, June 19, 1904, in *The IG*, 2:1418.

FIGURE 6.10 The headquarters of the Chinese Imperial Post Office, Beijing, 1905. The location of the building was very close to the two train stations in Beijing and to the CMCS headquarters. Source: Historical Photographs of China, University of Bristol; permission by Cadbury Research Library, University of Birmingham.

plained about the direction of the CMCS and the impact of postal expansion on it. The petition to the inspector general contained a strongly worded list of complaints, focusing on dissatisfaction over retirement allowances, perceived unfairness in promotions, and what was argued to be the wasteful and unjustified use of Customs funds on the postal service.[117] In private exchanges between Hippisley (who was stationed at Hankou at the time), W. F. Spinney (the Customs commissioner at Jiujiang), and P. von Tanner (the Customs commissioner at Hangzhou), the IPO was regarded as a financial drain rather than as some imminent cash cow.[118]

Unfortunately, the monthly grant fell short from the first month, July 1904, and remained short for the remainder of the decade and beyond. For example, in 1905, only Hk.Tls. 325,000 arrived, which was less than half of what had been promised, as Customs superintendents of the nominated ports found reasons not to remit their full amounts.[119] To manage the shortage, the Board of Revenue instructed the CMCS to continue to fund the IPO by a minimum of Hk.Tls. 300,000 annually.[120] Perhaps to counter this holding back of funding, the central government seemingly felt obliged to help. It gave Hart a mansion, formerly used as the Court of Colonial Affairs (Lifanyuan), to house the IPO (see fig. 6.10).[121]

117. "Memorial to the Inspector General of Chinese Maritime Customs from Certain of the Commissioners of Customs regarding the Causes of Dissatisfaction and Complaint at the Present Time Widespread in the Service, and Suggesting Action for the Removal of the Same," January 1903 [specific date unknown], Alfred E. Hippisley Papers, Bodleian Libraries, University of Oxford, MS. Eng. c. 7294.

118. W. F. Spinney to Alfred E. Hippisley, November 2, 1902, Hippisley Papers; P. von Tanner to Alfred E. Hippisley, December 18, 1902, Hippisley Papers; F. J. Mayers to Alfred E. Hippisley, September 21, 1903, Hippisley Papers.

119. Enclosure 1, "Zongshuiwusi shen cheng Waiwubu" 總稅務司申呈外務部 [Inspector General to Ministry of Foreign Affairs], IG Circular 1326 / Postal No.139, March 28, 1906, in *Circulars Nos. 135–261*, 10, TMA, W2-2838.

120. "Zhailu . . . youzheng jingfei geguan wei neng rushu xieji yi kuan" 摘錄 . . . 郵政經費各關未能如數協濟一款 [Extract regarding postal grant not paid in full by all ports], enclosure, in "Postal Grant: To Be Paid in Full by Ports Concerned," IG Circular 1244 (2nd ser.), April 29, 1905, in *Docs. Ill.*, 2:466–67.

121. Robert Hart to James Duncan Campbell, letter 1388, November 5, 1905, in *The IG*, 2:1486; Robert Hart to James Duncan Campbell, letter 1389, November 12, 1905, in *The IG*, 2:1487; "Zou qianyi gongsuo riqi zhe" 奏遷移公所日期摺 (Memorial on moving the post office headquarters), Guangxu reign year 33, month 3, day 18 (April 30, 1907), in "Zongwu" 總務 (General affairs), in *Youchuanbu zou yi lei bian-xu bian*, 27.

THE OLD IMPERIAL
POST OFFICE, PEKING.

CHAPTER SEVEN

Magnum Opus and the Role of the
Post Office in the Empire's Grand Design

The political trends that dominated the Qing empire's final ten years can be divided loosely into three phases. As noted in chapter 5, between 1901 and 1906 there was a series of internal innovations in central policies within the existing political administrative framework. Reforms introduced in this period included the abolition of the state exam system and the introduction of new models of schooling, as well as land reforms and revised agricultural policies at China's periphery. The second phase began in 1906, when preparations for the introduction of a constitutional monarchy were formally launched. In advance of this, five imperial commissioners had been sent abroad the previous year to learn from other countries' constitutional systems, while setting up a Committee for the Investigation of the Principles of Modern Politics and Government (Kaocha zhengzhi guan 考察政治館). Two important imperial edicts were issued: the first, in September 1906, promised reforms of administrative systems, the legal system, education, the military, and law enforcement; the second, in November, announced new administrative structures at the center of the Qing government, including the creation of eleven ministries.[1] Finally, in August 1908, the government published the "Principles of the Constitution" ("Qinding xianfa dagang" 欽定憲法大綱) and the "Edict on Nine-Year Progressive Preparations for the Introduction of the Constitution" ("Jiunian yubei lixian zhunian tuixing choubei shiyi yu" 九年預備立憲逐年推行籌備事宜諭) with the aim of transitioning to a constitutional monarchy in 1916. In a brief fourteen points, the "Principles of the Constitution" set out the status of the emperor, the rights and privileges of the royal family, the rights and restrictions around the power of government officials and of assemblies both local and national, the situation of the legal system in relation to the power of the emperor, and the obligations and rights of citizens.[2]

Alongside these reforms, tensions between China's peripheral regions and China proper were becoming more evident than in the past, exacerbated by increasing interest in the frontier territories of foreign countries. S. C. M. Paine's analysis of the geopolitical situation in the late nineteenth century notes how Russia had to adjust its position after being defeated by Britain and France in the Crimean War, being pushed away from Afghanistan by Britain, and being beaten by Japan in 1905 over its interests in Korea and Manchuria. Ultimately, in the latter part of this period, Britain, Japan, and Russia arrived at a largely tacit acknowledgment of respective territorial interests. For example, Russia was sympathetic to Britain's interests in new railway construction in the Yangtze River region; in return, the British did not oppose Russia's expansion into Chinese territory north of the Great Wall, while at the same time both also settled on the view that Tibet was to be left to China. Japan, due to its established position in Korea and Manchuria, sought to extend its influence into Inner Mongolia, which was respected by Russia. In response, Japan did not interfere with Russia's interests in Outer Mongolia.[3]

---

1. Zhang Pengyuan, *Lixianpai yu Xinhai geming*, 281–87.

2. Chiba, "Shinmatsu ni okeru kakubu"; Peng Jian, *Qing ji xianzheng bianchaguan*, chap. 2. On the rise of new local elites seeking to accelerate reform see Li Xizhu, *Xinzheng, lixian yu geming*, 214–25.

3. Paine, *The Wars for Asia*, 272–74. See also Lattimore, *Manchuria*, 294–95; and Chang Chi-hsiung, *Wai Menggu zhuquan guishu*, 64.

Change at the Frontiers

As broader geopolitical tensions soared, divisions between Han Chinese, Manchu, and Mongolians were heightened when, as previously noted, Empress Dowager Cixi launched the series of social, economic, and political initiatives known as the New Policies in 1902. The second stage of this initiative, launched in 1906, stressed the importance of equal treatment of Han Chinese and Manchu.[4] This initiative of the Qing court showed that the Manchu rulers were making a conscious response to the rise of nationalism, which they engaged with on two fronts: first, by taking steps to reshape their own discourse on cultural and political identity, through abandoning their long-term policy of resisting assimilation; and, second, by setting out to reconstruct perceptions of the state through constitutional reform, in response to the request from political elites, with the aim of rebuilding state authority.[5]

This major program affected interracial relationships at the frontiers in multiple ways: through the initiation of a land cultivation scheme in Inner Mongolia as well as the legalization of interracial marriage in the territory between Han Chinese and Manchu beginning in 1902; permission for Han Chinese to purchase land in Manchuria as of 1905; the teaching of Chinese in schools in Manchuria as of 1907; and full permission for mixed marriage between Chinese and Mongolians across the empire as of 1910. There were also three further specific objectives for this project to open up Manchuria and Mongolia: to increase revenues for the central government; to address growing concern about aggressive activity on the part of Japan and Russia in Manchuria and Mongolia; and to counter the anti-Manchu discourse circulated by revolutionary groups. While these objectives were interwoven, the Qing government fundamentally hoped that this major land release initiative would lead to a general increase in prosperity, which would in turn enhance the position of the state through further closing the—already diminishing—gap between Han Chinese, Manchu, and Mongolians.

---

4. Li Xizhu, "Qingmo yubei lixian shiqi."
5. Rhoads, *Manchus and Han*, chap. 2.

To facilitate these policy developments at the northern periphery at the same time as accommodating the gradual withdrawal of the military relay courier system, it was essential for the Imperial Post Office (IPO) to develop a presence in these areas. The first critical step was to introduce a postal link between Guihua and Zhangjiakou. While Zhangjiakou was an important center for trade to eastern and middle Mongolia, Guihua, farther to the northwest, performed the same role for western Mongolia and the northwest frontier. These places had received IPO branches in 1903, as discussed in chapter 6. But joining them directly enabled an enormous further improvement in communications throughout a massive area covering Outer Mongolia, across the Great Wall to northern Shanxi Province and northern Zhili Province, and on to Beijing.

Guihua, known today as Hohhot, was an important connecting point to Urga (today's Ulaanbaatar, whose old name in Chinese was Kulun) and Kyakhta in the north, to Uliastai and Kobdo in Outer Mongolia, and to Ürümqi (formerly called Dihua) in Xinjiang.[6] Situated at the northern tip of Shanxi, Guihua had previously received considerable Han migration during the first half of the Qing period. Mongolians in Inner Mongolia already rented out their land to Han migrants, and the Qing court was content to quietly tolerate this. It had become established that incomers from Hebei and Henan would settle in the Rehe area, people from Shandong in the northeast, and people from Shaanxi and Shanxi in the western part of Inner Mongolia.[7] To reflect its growing population size and importance in commerce and as a military station, in 1723 Guihua was given independent prefecture (*ting*) status, with Zhangjiakou following in 1724. This was a device to bring administration in Inner Mongolia closer to the system used in other provinces.[8] When the Qing government introduced its land cultivation scheme in Inner Mongolia in 1902, a headquarters for a General Bureau of Cultivation Affairs (Kenwu zongju 墾務總局) was set up in Guihua. The scheme was to demand that banners open their lands for Han Chinese immigrants, and

---

6. Xu Tan, "Qingdai Shanxi Guihuacheng," 119–29.
7. Lu Minghui, "Qingdai Nei Menggu diqu," 9–11.
8. Gao, *Jinshang yu Ming Qing Shanxi*, 54–55; Xue, "Qingdai Nei Menggu diqu," 60–63.

in return they would receive half of the annual land taxes and land-contract fees.[9]

Zhangjiakou, famous for its horse trade, was known more generally as a regional trading center going back to the Ming dynasty.[10] It was the most important gate town along the line of the Great Wall, on the approach to Mongolia from Beijing. Zhangjiakou was formally opened through the Sino-Russo Treaty of Beijing in 1860, and the Russian Post Office set up offices there in 1870.[11] For the IPO, the Zhangjiakou–Guihua connection would not only share the workload of the military relay courier system for communication with Beijing but also improve merchants' ability to communicate between other inland provinces, such as Gansu, Shaanxi, Sichuan, and their counterparts in Outer Mongolia and along the Russian border. In 1905 a 3,200-*li* (approximately 1,980-kilometer) route connecting Beijing, Nankou, Guihua, and Zhangjiakou was completed.[12] In addition, the Beijing-Zhangjiakou Railway via Nankou was completed in 1909, and it played an important role in the Beijing–Zhangjiakou–Urga postal route.

In short, when the Qing government adjusted its long-term racial and agricultural policies at its northern periphery, these changes could only result in an effective modernization of sovereignty by bringing different ethnic groups closer together. A useful consequence of this activity was that the administration acquired new and coherent transportation and communication networks across the territory. But the activity is also reflective of a fundamental transformation in the mindset of Qing officials,

9. Soni, *Mongolia-China Relations*, 30; Lan, "China's New Administration in Mongolia," 39–58; Taveirne, *Han-Mongol Encounters*, 333–34.

10. Feng Ruofei, *Qingdai queguan*, 35.

11. Russia Additional Treaty of Peking, 1860, in *Zhong wai jiu yuezhang*, 1:440.

12. For the expansion to Datong, Guihua, and Zhangjiakou, see "To the Ministry of Foreign Affairs," Guangxu reign year 29, month 4, day 10 (May 6, 1903), SHAC, 137 (2) 304; "Rehe sheli youju shi" 熱河設立郵局事 [Setting up the post office in Rehe], Guangxu reign year 32, month 4, day 1 (April 24, 1906), ZYJYD 02-02-009-07-006; and "Rehe sheli youju shi" 熱河設立郵局事 [Setting up the post office in Rehe], Guangxu reign year 32, month 4, day 5 (April 28, 1906), ZYJYD 02-02-009-07-008. For the further connection between Guihua, Nankou, and Zhangjiakou, see Report (1905), xxxvii. The Nankou Pass was to the northwest of Beijing; the Nankou train station was completed in 1906 and was one of the stops on the Beijing-Zhangjiakou Railway.

coming to view certain matters that used to be seen as foreign-related affairs as now coming within the province of domestic governance.

Constitutional Change and A New Ministry

Su Quanyou, in his study of the history of the Ministry of Posts and Communications (Youchuanbu 郵傳部), argues that current scholarship has not paid enough attention to the significance of the creation of this ministry. Those relatively few scholars who have examined its activities have either criticized the delay in taking over the postal service from the Chinese Maritime Customs Service (CMCS), attempting to paint the relationship between Robert Hart and the IPO as a product of imperialism; or they have focused on corruption within the newly formed ministry while ignoring its novel administrative approach. For Su, these types of criticism have been based on fixed prejudices, lack of reference to primary sources, and consistent lack of acknowledgment of the fact that the ministry was started from scratch and therefore took time to become established and effective across its broad remit.[13] Yet even if Su's perspective is broadly accepted today, it is still necessary to explore two further questions: Why was the IPO for a considerable period under the management of the Ministry of Posts and Communications in name only? And what was the vision behind the actions of the ministry as it set out the framework of its national communications strategy?

Of the eleven ministries in the Qing government's reorganized central administration in 1906, nearly all were preexisting, though some were given new names and some had only been established in the recent past.[14] The Ministry of Posts and Communications was the only completely new department.[15] It was formed to bring railway, steam transportation, telegraph, and postal services together under one administration.[16] This

13. Su Quanyou, *Qingmo Youchuanbu yanjiu*, 17–22.

14. Chiba, "Shinmatsu gyōsei kōmoku yakuchū (Ichi)," 168.

15. It could be argued that the Ministry of Agriculture, Industry and Commerce (Nong gong shang bu 農工商部) was also new, though it combined the existing Ministry of Works (Gongbu 工部) and Ministry of Commerce (Shangbu 商部).

16. Su Quanyou, *Qingmo Youchuanbu yanjiu*, chap. 1.

marked a significant shift in approach: areas of industrial and economic activity formerly managed by the Ministry of Foreign Affairs were now collectively redesignated as domestic matters in both spirit and operation; in practice, however, this was neither clear cut nor a clean break, as the Ministry of Foreign Affairs remained involved in many aspects.

In this reorganization, the CMCS was nominally downgraded to a bureau under the supervision of a completely new office titled the Bureau of Customs Affairs (Shuiwuchu 稅務處). This bureau was a unique arrangement, drawing its members from the Ministries of Foreign Affairs, Revenue, War, and Civil Appointments (Libu 吏部) and staffed with some experienced or high-performing native Customs clerks. In the public perception at the time, the rationale for the change was to disrupt the intimate relationship between the CMCS and the Ministry of Foreign Affairs.[17] Such a move, without any leak of information prior to the formal announcement, caused deep concerns across foreign legations—and panic in the case of the British legation. Hart learned about this change only a few hours before anyone else. Later he was assured by the government that things remained unchanged with regard to the CMCS itself and that the IPO was still under his care.[18]

Hart chose to stick to a narrative that it was unavoidable that young Chinese would want to have more say in their own affairs, though he admitted to James Duncan Campbell that the change was not a "pleasant winding up of fifty years' service."[19] But after paying his first visit to the new Bureau of Customs Affairs, Hart felt a strong sense of bitterness, as he was received only by two Chinese clerks, and then by the chief of staff. Neither of the two ministers, Tieliang 鐵良 (1863–1938) or Tang Shaoyi 唐紹儀 (1862–1938), was available to see him. His conclusion was, "The

17. Chen Shiqi, *Zhongguo jindai haiguanshi*, 393–95.

18. "Customs Service: Establishment of Shui-wu Ch'u Does Not Affect I.G.'s Relations to Ports; Work to Continue on Old Lines; Circulation of Rumours in Connexion [*sic*] with Deprecated," IG Circular No. 1369 (2nd ser.), September 22, 1906, in *Docs. Ill.*, 2:544; "Customs Service: Notification Embodying Circular No. 1369 and Correspondence Concerning Transfer of Control from Wai-wu Pu to Shui-wu Ch'u Published," IG Circular No. 1381 (2nd ser.), October 30, 1906, in *Docs. Ill.*, 2:548–52.

19. Robert Hart to James Duncan Campbell, letter 1409, May 26, 1906, in *The IG*, 2:1510. See also Chen Shiqi, *Zhongguo jindai haiguanshi*, 389–91; and Van de Ven, *Breaking with the Past*, 153–58.

advent of the *Ch'u* [the Bureau] means the exit of the I.G. [inspector general]."[20]

Following the publication in 1908 of the "Principles of the Constitution" and the nine-year plan, in 1910 the "Frame and Rules of Administration" ("Xingzheng gangmu" 行政綱目) was released, emulating in large measure the Japanese administrative system. This clearly defined five categories of governmental activity: home affairs, foreign affairs, the military, the treasury, and the legal system.[21] Communications and transportation were allocated to home affairs, along with policing, hygiene, education, agriculture, industry, commerce, land regulations, and relationships with non-Han groups at China's peripheral areas. The principal innovation was bringing these sectors into the orbit of internal Chinese policy making and management, with an emphasis on centralization and nationalization and some devolved responsibility to local government. The new reform sought to treat communication-related business as matters relating to the national economy and the general public.[22]

The Qing court acknowledged, however, that changing the central organization would be very complicated and many affairs would have to be managed around a principle of interministerial arrangements, particularly where work involved negotiations with foreigners or the military. Much of what had formerly sat under the jurisdiction of the Ministry of Foreign Affairs was now either allocated to different ministries or had to be coordinated by different departments—requiring extensive intergovernmental consultations before responsibilities could be transferred.[23]

20. Robert Hart to James Duncan Campbell, letter 1417, September 9, 1906, in *The IG*, 2:1517.

21. "Guojia xingzheng shiwu leibie biao diyi" 國家行政事務類別表第一 [The first section on state administrative affairs], in "Xingzheng gangmu" 行政綱目 [Frame and rules of administration], Xuantong reign year 2, lithograph ed., National Palace Museum, Taipei, Gunei 001905.

22. See the sections on the Ministry of Agriculture, Industry and Commerce (Nong gong shang bu 農工商部), the Ministry of Dependencies (Lifanbu 理藩部), the Ministry of Education (Xuebu 學部), the Ministry of the Interior (Minzhengbu 民政部), and the Ministry of Posts and Communications (Youchuanbu 郵傳部), in "Xingzheng gangmu."

23. "Caoding xingzheng gangmu—zai xu" 草定行政綱目—再續 [Draft frame and rules of administration of preparation for constitutionalism—Sequel], *Shenbao*, May 13 and May 14, 1910. See also Chiba, "Shinmatsu gyōsei kōmoku yakuchū (Ni)," 179–80.

One of the challenges facing the new Ministry of Posts and Communications was that in terms of development, management, funding, and regulation, its constituent activities each had quite a different history (see table 7.1). For decades, the mining industry, railways, steamships, and the telegraph had been very much associated with the Self-Strengthening Movement, along with naval and military affairs. In the case of the telegraph, railways, and steamships, these had been generally set up in the form of "government-supervised merchant undertakings" and they were already within the orbit of provincial governors. Centralization in the fields of the telegraph and railways was clearly regarded as more urgent than changes in the postal service, not least because of the high degree of involvement of foreign investment and loans, meaning the effort to bring them under Chinese control would have a far greater impact.[24] So when the Qing government began to push forward with centralized control and regulation of these industries, the Ministry of Posts and Communications had to manage complicated financial matters deeply intertwined with foreign interests. By contrast, the central government decided to continue to leave the IPO essentially untouched, in spite of the fact that there was some pressure expressed within the ministry that the IPO should come over at once.[25]

Consequently, the IPO was allowed to carry on with a high degree of autonomy, much as in the period when it was still attached to the CMCS. In the background, the Ministry of Posts and Communications prepared for the day when it would assume more hands-on control through the creation of appropriate postal regulations and the cultivation of new staff through various educational initiatives. In parallel, the ministry drew up a seven-year plan for developing the IPO, intended to synchronize with the Qing government's schedule of constitutional preparation. The details of the seven-year plan were as follows:

24. "Ben bu zou zun zhang lu dierjie choubei chengji zhe" 本部奏遵章臚第二届籌備成績摺 [Memorial from the Ministry of Posts and Communications on the results made in the second year of the planned preparation], Xuantong reign year 1, month 9, day 22 (November 4, 1909), in *Jiaotong guanbao*, issue 4, 10.

25. According to Robert Bredon, Xu Shichang, the head of the Ministry of Posts and Communications, was particularly keen to take over the Post Office as soon as possible. So Xu designated some men to study the postal archives and accounts. Robert Bredon to Robert Hart, October 9, 1909, SQBH.

Table 7.1. The departmental structure of the Ministry of Posts and Communications

Department	Policy and supervisory responsibilities
Department of Navigation (Chuanzheng si 船政司)	Marine and riverine shipping, construction of docks, improvement of harbors, construction of lighthouses, construction of warehouses, legislation around shipping insurance, other related maritime matters
Department of Land Communications (Luzheng si 路政司)	Control of land communications within the empire and related legislation, collection of funds and arrangement of loans for railway construction, design of routes, purchase of materials, promotion of commercial enterprise *Shared with local administrations:* Promotion of trams / local services
Department of Telegraph (Dianzheng si 電政司)	Control of the telegraph affairs of the empire, erection of land lines, laying of cables *Shared with local administrations:* Construction of telephone and electric lighting systems
Department of Posts and Communications (Youzheng si 郵政司)	Formal responsibility for supervision of the entire postal affairs of the empire, improvement of postal communications, sale of money orders and stamps and transmission of postal parcels (though all these remained under the control of the Chinese Maritime Customs Service until June 1911)

Sources: "Guojia xingzheng shiwu leibie biao diyi" 國家行政事務類別表第一 [The first section on state administrative affairs], in "Xingzheng gangmu" 行政綱目 [Frame and rules of administration], Xuantong reign year 2, lithograph ed., National Palace Museum, Taipei, Gunei 001905; Chiba Masashi, "Shinmatsu gyōsei kōmoku yakuchū (San)." For the translations of the departments, see Brunnert and Hagelstrom, *Present Day Political Organization of China*, 157–58.

In 1910 (Xuantong reign year two):

- Prepare for taking over the IPO through investigating postal expenditure, the postal regulations of other countries, and stamp systems.
- Consult with the Bureau of Customs Affairs on the business related to taking over the IPO.
- Review and enhance postal regulations.
- Expand the School of Transportation (Jiaotong chuanxisuo 交通傳習所) to include postal and telegraph classes.

- Send students to Austria to study postal banking.
- Make plans to abolish the military relay courier system.

In 1911 (Xuantong reign year three):

- Publish new postal regulations, which are to be edited annually and to be formally published and made available.
- Set up postal staff ranking and salary classification. Draw up a program for an entrance exam.
- Review postal districts and formally classify head offices and branches.
- Send representatives to the Universal Postal Union and visit post offices of other countries for study purposes. Purchase franking machines to prevent forgery.
- Standardize postal marks and post-related materials and items.
- Prepare postal banking business; postal savings are particularly urgent.
- Prepare overseas mail steamship service.

In 1912 (Xuantong reign year four):

- Join the Universal Postal Union, and discuss withdrawal of foreign post offices in China with the relevant interests.
- Abolish private letter hongs.
- Expand the sub–post office network at the level of prefecture and county.
- Regulate procedures for undelivered mail.
- Prepare the ground for the establishment of post offices in Mongolia and Tibet.
- Launch overseas mail steamship service.
- Launch postal banking in provinces.

In 1913 (Xuantong reign year five):

- Expand third-class post offices to lower administrative level.
- Launch a free weekly postal newsletter.
- Launch telegraph remittances.

In 1914 (Xuantong reign year six):

- Sign bilateral agreements with countries for mail insurance and remittances.
- Launch postal service in Mongolia and Tibet.
- Set up a machinery station/factory/bureau to produce equipment and supply it to postal branches.

In 1915 (Xuantong reign year seven):

• Launch a postal express at treaty ports.
• Expand fourth-class mail on the outlying traffic routes of the capital through collaboration with reliable shops.
• Expand postal savings and remittances to the second- and third-class post offices in all provinces.

In 1916 (Xuantong reign year eight):

• Issue a special stamp to commemorate the launch of the constitution.
• Promote traveling post office through special express train.
• Expand overseas telegraph remittances and mail insurance to the country members of the Universal Postal Union.[26]

In reality, many items on the seven-year plan were carried out by the IPO in the background, without significant—or in some cases any—involvement from the ministry, though others would have to wait until after the 1911 revolution. One point of concern was the frequency with which the ministry changed hands—in its short life of five years and seven months, there had been twelve different ministers in charge. Chen Bi 陳璧 (1852–1928) was the longest serving, for nineteen months, slightly longer than Xu Shichang 徐世昌 (1855–1939), who served for eighteen months.[27]

Among the achievements of the fledgling administration was cultivating new blood through educational initiatives. Xu Shichang saw a need to develop incomers with management skills and foster a new generation of leaders across the four industries within the ministry's purview. Through expanding the School of Railways (Tielu chuanxisuo 鐵路傳習所) in Beijing, which had only been established in 1909, the larger School of Transportation was opened the following year, with new curriculum content on the postal service and telegraph added, as was noted in chapter 6.[28] This school had two departments: railways, and post

---

26. "Ben bu fen nian chouban youzheng shan dan" 本部分年籌辦郵政繕單 [The list of divided annual plans for developing the post office], Xuantong reign year 2, month 9, day 3 (October 5, 1910), ZYJYD 02-02-009-09-015.

27. Su Quanyou, *Qingmo Youchuanbu yanjiu*, 58–60.

28. "Ben bu zou zun zhang yu chen ci nian choubei shiqing zhe" 本部奏遵章預陳次年籌備實情摺 [Memorial of the Ministry of Posts and Communications on the prepara-

and telegraph, and the first intake of the expanded institution was more than six hundred people. Courses were divided into "advanced class" and "basic class." The former was of two and one-half years' duration, and the latter one and one-half years. Foreign languages, including English, French, and German, were essential elements of the curriculum. The students of telegraphic operations were also required to study postal regulations, while students of the postal service were required to learn about the telegraph, because there was a plan to bring these two departments together in the near future.[29]

Developing suitable regulations was also seen as a priority. Xu Shichang was able to select people from different ministries who had both overseas study experience and foreign languages to take up this task. At the time, British regulations were regarded as best for the marine environment; for railways, the Belgian and French systems were the models; and regulations for postal and telegraphic systems focused on best practices from Austria, Denmark, Japan, and the United States. The ministry also sent students to Austria to study postal banking.[30]

Apart from schools and regulations, Théophile A. Piry was largely left alone to work on postal matters. One of his letters to Hart, who was by then based in London, in early 1909 reveals some interesting aspects of the Ministry of Posts and Communications and the situation of the IPO. He excused himself for not writing as frequently as he believed he should, with the justification that in his view there were not many interesting or unusual things to report. This was partly because he knew no Chinese officials in the ministry (so it was no wonder he had little gossip

tions made for the second year], Xuantong reign year 1, month 12, day 17 (January 27, 1910), in *Jiaotong guanbao*, issue 8, 12–13; "Ben bu zou kaiban Jiaotong chuanxisuo dagai qingxing zhe" 本部奏開辦交通傳習所大概情形摺 [Memorial of the Ministry of Posts and Communications on updating general development of the School of Transportation], Xuantong reign year 2, month 2, day 28 (April 7, 1910), in *Jiaotong guanbao*, issue 12, 5–6. see also Wu Yulun, "Qingmo de tielu jiaoyu," 116–20.

29. "Ben bu zou kaiban Jiaotong chuanxisuo dagai qingxing zhe," 5–6.

30. "Ben bu zou ni ding chuan lu you dian si zheng zhuan lv bing kaiban dagai qingxing zhe" 本部奏擬訂船路郵電四政專律並開辦大概情形摺 [Memorial of the Ministry of Posts and Communications on the preparation for making of specific laws for shipping, railways, the post office, and the telegraph, and general developments of these four departments]. Xuantong reign year 1, month 12, day 17 (January 27, 1910), in *Jiaotong guanbao*, issue 8, 9–11.

to pass on) and partly because things had largely gone very smoothly.[31] Piry did mention, however, that although the noise level had dropped around plans for the ministry to formally take charge of the IPO, he believed these would be revived very soon.

Piry wrote again in September after receiving a long letter from Hart. Hart had told him his health had improved, and he was planning to return to China very shortly. After expressing pleasure at this news, Piry entertained Hart with the latest information. He told him that Yuan Shikai had accepted the role of viceroy of Manchuria, and that Japan was causing trouble again. Regarding the fate of the IPO, Piry wrote,

> We, postal men, are plodding away undisturbed, and success continues to respond, which is a great comfort. Work here, however, is growing out of all proportion. . . . As regards the long-mooted question of separation from the Customs, silence has prevailed this summer, but there are rumors up again—and we feel that when Hsü Shih Ch'ang [Xu Shichang] has taken the matter up it will be settled. Like yourself, seeing how disastrous was to the Hankow Peking Railway the taking over of the control, I would consider as a fatal blow to the P.O. total separation, and I doubt, if the step was taken, whether myself I would have the courage to face the new situation or attempt to carry on the service. At the same time, we cannot go on ignoring so completely. . . . With your authority & influence at hand, a solution would be easily found—and for this reason, a mighty one for the future of your magnum opus, I wish you could appear again on the scene.[32]

Hart did not return to China, and prior to the complications of the Chinese Revolution of 1911 (also the year of Hart's death), the expansion task undertaken in the early years of the twentieth century had already been a mammoth one. Of course, Piry was no Hart, and in any case, the days when foreigners could exert a great amount of influence on the central government had passed. Piry could only work within the boundaries of grand policies that were not decided by himself. One area where his attention was required was in fulfilling the task allocated to postal networks within the central government's evolving conception of national sovereignty.

31. Théophile A. Piry to Robert Hart, February 11, 1909, SQBH.
32. Théophile A. Piry to Robert Hart, September 18, 1909, SQBH.

The Logic of Postal Expansion

In the historiography of China's modernization model, G. William Skinner's study on Chinese regional urbanization between the 1820s and 1893 is often referenced. Excluding Manchuria, Skinner divided China into eight regions: North China, Northwest China, Upper Yangtze, Middle Yangtze, Lower Yangtze, Southeast Coast, Lingnan, and Yungui, and emphasized the importance of self-sufficiency within each region for essential goods, which sat alongside exchange across and between regions for specific products. Together with his "hexagon" model, Skinner offered his views on regional economic activity through the application of a clear hierarchical structure.[33] Although his study examined the period prior to the establishment of China's national post office, Skinner stated that his approach relied heavily on the postal structure of 1915 in compiling data: "The single indicator on which I relied most heavily in developing comparative profiles of economic centrality was the postal status as of 1915."[34] The postal status referred to was the postal hierarchy that assigned service to locations across a region under the designations head office, first-class post office, second-class post office, third-class post office and postal agency. While he qualified the extent to which this could be creditably applied—mainly due to economic development since the end of his chosen study period in 1893 and, in particular, expansion in railway and steamship connections—Skinner observed that particularly in respect to second-class post offices, "the number and configuration of special services [such as express delivery or availability of money orders] turned out to correlate rather closely with other indicators of central functions."[35]

33. G. William Skinner, "Regional Urbanization in Nineteenth-Century China," in Skinner, *The City in Late Imperial China*, 212–15; G. William Skinner, "Cities and the Hierarchy of Local Systems," in Skinner, *The City in Late Imperial China*, 277–79.

34. "Appendix: Criteria and Procedures for Classifying Central Places by Level in the Economic Hierarchy," in Skinner, *The City in Late Imperial China*, 348.

35. Decades later, a similar approach was repeated in the project titled Nineteenth-Century Cities, Yamens, and County-Level Units; see Skinner, Zumou Yue, and Henderson, "ChinaW—Cities, County Seats and Yamen Units (1820–1893)"; see also Wang Zhe and Liu Yayuan, "Jindai Zhongguo youzheng kongjian."

What Skinner observed was that the commercial status of a place was indeed one of the most important factors considered when the postal branch network was being constructed. This point was referenced in chapters 5 and 6 when examining how Deng Weifan and John Patrick Donovan expanded the postal connections. A detailed study of the evolution of the postal administrative hierarchy would provide significant insight into the growth and transformation of townships and trade in modern China. Bringing postal information together with transportation data, population statistics, and other data would require different methods than those that have been employed for this current study, and such an effort is certainly outside its scope. At the scale of this book, however, it has been possible to use analysis of available written documents of the IPO management team to examine the design and construction of postal connections, stage by stage, in the final years of the Qing empire and explore how the IPO's route planning incorporated the following elements: political communications, preexisting centers of administration and trade and their relationships to new ones associated with the rise of the treaty port system, and new methods of transportation.

Postal Districts Reorganized

Looking back at events since the IPO was established, Piry noted in his 1910 annual report that postal expansion had been conducted in two main stages. The first stage, he wrote, had been to focus on the treaty ports, the Yangtze River, and the coast.[36] Even some way through this stage, in 1905, the whole of China—eighteen provinces, plus Manchuria— contained thirty-five postal districts. Most of these postal districts centered on the treaty ports, and they were under the direct supervision of a postmaster who was also the commissioner of Customs, with just a few exceptions: Beijing, Datong in Anhui, and Jinan in Shandong.[37] Figure 7.1 shows the relationship between the treaty ports, provincial capitals, and head offices and sub-head offices of postal districts.[38]

36. Report (1910), 20.
37. "Appendix B: List of Imperial Head and Branch Offices Arranged by Districts," in Report (1905), xlviii–xlix.
38. Information extracted from "Appendix B," xlviii–xlix.

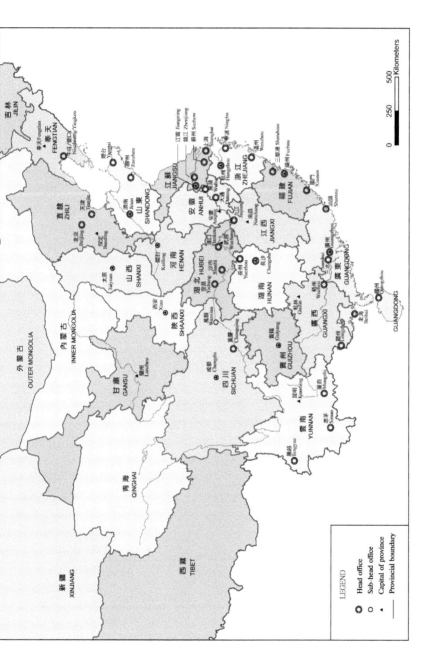

FIGURE 7.1 The distribution of postal head offices and sub-head offices, 1905. Many postal head offices were located at treaty ports, and some inland provincial capitals, such as Anqing, Baoding, Guilin, Nanchang, and Lanzhou, had neither a head office nor a sub-head office in 1905. Map © Weipin Tsai; cartography by Huang Chingchi.

Several provincial capitals—Changsha, Fuzhou, Guangzhou, Hangzhou, and Nanjing—were also treaty ports, and they hosted the head offices of postal districts. Some provincial capitals were equipped with sub-head offices, such as Chengdu, Guiyang, Kaifeng, Taiyuan, and Xi'an, and they could be governed by head offices that were not, however, in the same province. For example, Changsha supervised areas across both Hunan and Jiangxi; the Beijing postal district had jurisdiction over the Kaifeng and Taiyuan subdistricts, while Chongqing postal district had control over some parts of Guizhou, Sichuan, and Yunnan.

Piry's second stage started in 1909, as this was the period of reorganization of postal districts that began with taking over the function of the military relay courier system for inland provinces. Back in 1904, Piry had already concluded there was a need to change the management structure of postal districts to fit the needs of ordinary people in China's interior. He argued that although the existing treaty port-oriented postal district structure had a good rationale as the service evolved, a structure built around the historic provinces and their administrative structures would make more sense from a Chinese point of view.[39] In order to align with the central government's reform programs, it was considered that moving away from the treaty-port-centered postal organization helped to achieve this goal. Important provincial capitals in certain large and populous provinces should become either head offices or sub-head offices of postal districts. In this second stage, the postal service was also brought to China's periphery—notably, to Mongolia, Tibet, and Xinjiang.

In the new hierarchy, there were fourteen postal districts with fifteen head offices and thirty-nine sub-head offices (managing subdistricts). Each head office controlled a postal district, and Jiangsu was equipped with two head offices, Nanjing and Shanghai. Seven out of fifteen head offices were at provincial capitals, while eight out of fifteen head offices were at open ports; among those eight, six—Canton (Guangzhou), Fengtian (Moukden, today Shenyang), Fuzhou, Hangzhou, Jinan, and Nanjing— were also provincial capitals.[40] This alignment certainly reflected the

39. Théophile A. Piry, "General Plan of Development," September 18, 1904, SHAC, 137 (1) 7587; Théophile A. Piry, "Postal Secretary's Report for the Year 1904," February 7, 1905, SHAC, 137 (1) 7587.

40. Report (1910), 21, and its "Appendix B," 25–28. For the definitions of head offices, sub-head offices, branch offices, inland offices, and agencies, see "Enclosure," in "Definition, Classification and Adjustment of Postal Establishments," Postal Circular

progress made on postal route expansion over the previous decade, which had brought provincial capitals into the network, but, just as important, it coordinated with central government's new agenda for crafting information networks throughout the country. The reorganization of postal districts changed the context of postal work significantly from what it had been when the IPO started back in 1896. As Piry put it, "The outcome of this movement is now seen in the re-arrangement of all districts and sub-districts, which are grouped in such a way as to coincide with the geographical and administrative divisions of the Empire."[41]

That said, Piry's "two stages" summary is undoubtedly a simplification. In studying the IPO's postal routes, an important element in the logic behind the design of the network was to consciously move away from an older orientation focused on the political concerns related to the workings of the military relay courier system, bureaucratic hierarchies, and military priorities, and to adopt new approaches based on logistics that would also accommodate present and future needs for rapid transportation and information exchange. This does not mean the IPO did not consider the locations of bureaucratic administrations—after all, it was clear that the IPO would have to replace the military relay courier system, which served communications between the central government and local administrations. But such a concern did not dominate route planning. Creating more contact points on postal routes in order to maximize the usability of services for the greatest number of people became critical. Unlike the military relay courier system, which focused mainly on the principle of fastest possible point-to-point transmission of information using the most direct routes available between regional centers and the imperial capital, the design of postal service routes put the emphasis on optimizing accessibility and overall logistics to increase the overall flow of material. This approach can be seen particularly clearly when we look at the setting up of post offices in hinterland towns on borders between

---

231, December 15, 1909, in *Circulars Nos. 135–261*, 390, TMA, W2-2838. Jinan and Fengtian were started as "self-opened" ports in 1905 and 1907. In the Qing government's view, "self-opened" meant a place opened for trade voluntarily by the Qing administration rather than by coercion though treaty. See "List of Treaty Ports, etc., in Chronological Order," enclosure, in "Résumé of Sir Robert Hart's Work," IG Circular 1535 (2nd ser.), July 17, 1908, in *Docs. Ill.*, 2:647–48;

41. Report (1910), 20.

provinces or the establishment of express delivery points in non-treaty-port cities that featured important commercial neighborhoods.

Postal Route Expansion in Four Stages

While Piry's packed two-stage narrative is certainly one way of looking at it, with the benefit of a more distant perspective, I argue that the expansion of postal routes should in fact be viewed as a more complicated four-stage process. The first, starting with the Custom Service's formalization of postal operations in 1878, was the establishment of point-to-point connections, at first between the northern treaty ports, and then to other ports. The second stage of expansion was to use the treaty ports as main postal hubs, and provincial capitals and major market towns as supporting feeder-hubs, to create true postal networks in their respective regions, progressively moving the service inland from coasts and rivers. Main suboffices were connected to the head offices, with postal agencies connected to suboffices, and so on. Each suboffice had its own local staff and complement of delivery couriers, who would run no farther than from their own station to the next. In a postal district, additional stations were generally only opened after existing ones were well established.[42]

In the third stage, the focus was on developing connections across provinces and postal districts below the treaty port level. Unlike the straightforward point-to-point connections between treaty ports, inter-province connections required more flexibility, and as a consequence featured more complex logistics. The main challenge in establishing interprovince connections was not just about creating point-to-point connections between provincial capitals and the largest markets towns in different provinces but also about establishing meeting points for mail exchange outside of principal high-profile centers. Although old, established trade routes played a part, these were not universally appropriate. New localities had to be explored, and some spots were picked not for their commercial importance but for their strategic location.[43] Through opening more branches in different localities, including using certain

---

42. "Inland Extension," Postal Circular 23, June 26, 1899, in *Postal Secretary's Circulars 1–134*, 178, TMA, W2-2833.

43. Report (1907), 1.

postal agencies even though they were at the bottom of the postal hierarchy, the networks were made to be more flexible in coping with onward transmission, and transregional mail circulation became easier.

"Day-and-Night" Postal Routes in Northern China

Building on the first three stages, the fourth was to construct high-speed postal routes across multiple postal districts by bringing in the "day-and-night" system. Where available, this approach incorporated the most efficient means of transportation in existence at that time, including railway and steamship connections. The system was first introduced in 1905 for the line between Shandong and Zhili, and by 1907 the results were very satisfactory. A standard stage was one hundred *li* (around 62 kilometers) per twelve-hour working day, and by 1907 this was easily achieved in most places. Under the "day-and-night" system the target was to accelerate delivery times on key routes to two hundred *li* (124 kilometers) per twenty-four hours for light mails.[44] In fact, the performance on some lines exceeded this expectation and reached somewhere between two hundred and three hundred *li* (124 to 186 kilometers) per twenty-four hours through the combination of foot couriers, mounted couriers, and other kinds of animal transportation.[45] Although these speeds were not as fast as the military relay courier system, which carried expectations ranging from three hundred *li* per day to six hundred *li* (185 to 372 kilometers) for extremely urgent messages, the two services were fundamentally different in terms of mail volumes, routes, and modes of transportation.[46]

The "day-and-night" system had a great many dependencies on resources not owned by the IPO—not just in its reliance on railway and steamship operations but also its reliance on the cooperation of local governments to expedite passage and, in some places, to provide security. There were more unusual requirements in some areas too. For example,

44. Report (1904), vi; "Fast Day-and-Night Couriers," Postal Circular 162, March 5, 1907, in *Circulars Nos. 135–261*, 100, TMA, W2-2838.

45. For example, it took fifty hours to run the 485-*li* Henanfu–Tongguan route by "day-and-night" courier; fifty-six hours to run the 560-*li* Lamamiao–Xuanhua route; sixteen hours to run the 240-*li* Jilin–Kuanchengzi route; and twenty-six hours to run the 260-*li* Yantai–Laiyang route; Report (1908), 8.

46. Liu Wenpeng, *Qingdai yichuan*, 178–79.

a "day-and-night" service was introduced in 1910 for the 580-*li* (360 kilometer) Lanzhoufu–Liangzhoufu section of the Lanzhoufu–Jiayuguan route in Gansu. This route carried on to Xinjiang. In order to complete this section within fifty-eight hours, couriers with good riding skills, half of them Chinese and half Tibetan, were hired. They were equipped with large Chinese lanterns (fitted inside with small oil lamps) and long swords. Officials along the routes were instructed to give the couriers passage and to open gates for them at any time during the night.[47] In another example, a "day-and-night" service was introduced through Xi'an and Chengdu, which combined the use of the railway and "day-and-night" couriers between Beijing and Shaanxi. This new route was important because it acted as an alternative to the existing route between northern China and Sichuan via Hankou and Chongqing. This Xi'an–Chengdu route, by going through southern Shaanxi, involved an immense amount of difficulty owing to crossings by ferries and the opening of city gates, but it shortened mail transmission time between these two cities, from the previous thirty days by regular means to nine or ten days. Mail from Chengdu to Beijing via Xi'an could be transmitted in fifteen days.[48]

The following example uses northern China as a case study to illustrate how "day-and-night" postal routes were assembled and operated. In her study on the history of railways in China, Elisabeth Köll notes how rail transportation had a direct impact on the price of certain agricultural commodities, such as peanuts, tobacco, cotton, and silk, across wide geographical areas in the 1910s and 1920s. One direct result of this was the growth in opportunities for commercial farming.[49] In his study on the transportation and economics of northern China in the late nineteenth and early twentieth centuries, Xiong Yaping points out that due to a change in the course of the Yellow River in 1855, the Grand Canal became almost redundant in its role of linking the Yellow and Yangtze Rivers, and river transportation throughout the region became fragmented. This change led to the relative rise and fall of a number of cities and towns. Although the arrival of steamships eased some pressure, the combination of water shipping and overland transportation still required

47. Report (1910), 13.
48. Report (1911), 12.
49. Köll, *Railroads and the Transformation of China*, 95–97.

FIGURE 7.2 Unorthodox transportation over city walls. The demands of express delivery services sometimes required unusual measures. At some locations, it could be quicker for a courier to clamber up the city walls (with assistance) rather than wait for the fixed hours of the day when the city gates were open. This photo, estimated as being from the 1910s, was taken in the Henan Postal District. Source: Report (1921). Acknowledgments to Tsai Chia-chi of the Specialist Library of the Chunghwa Postal Museum, Taipei, for providing this image, and to Jamie Carstairs for improving the image quality.

a lot of animal power and manpower to transport goods between producers and ports. Between 1881 and 1937, eight major railways were built in northern China, and this changed the model of transportation in the area. For a long- or middle-distance inland journey, railways became the preferred mode of transport, while water routes and traditional overland routes became supplementary; for shorter inland journeys, while river routes and traditional overland routes remained the main means of transportation, railway stations became commonly used as meeting points.[50]

Postal route design in the first ten years of the IPO's history in northern China reflected this situation. Instead of relying on the Grand Canal, overland relay routes were constructed—as early as 1878, under Gustav Detring's supervision. As time went on, increased availability of rail transportation not only enabled postal route planning to break free from its focus on connections between treaty ports in order to establish interprovincial and interregional connections but also challenged the existing administrative hierarchy in terms of prefecture, subprefecture, department, and district, down to market town and village level. In addition, and also important, the "day-and-night" fast postal route connections sought to complement and utilize the available railway connections.

The GIS map in Figure 7.3 was created to demonstrate how railways played a critical role in constructing "day-and-night" postal routes in northern China. The information on this map was extracted from the postal map album published by the Statistical Department of the CMCS in 1907. For ease of reading, the map, assembled from a mixture of existing and newly collated data, does not include other types of routes and does not show all the stations along the rail lines—only those lines that were used for "day-and-night" postal routes. The map was also made with the intention of emphasizing the important role of lower administrative units at the level of district and below. Districts are shown by the symbol ●, towns and villages as either ▲ or △. From a postal route perspective, the relative importance of individual postal locations does not map neatly to the traditional administrative hierarchy. The symbol ▲ is used to show villages that had postal branches, whereas △ is used for villages with postal agencies. The map exemplifies how the state-making program that

50. Xiong Yaping, *Tielu yu huabei xiangcun*, 32–38, 73–77.

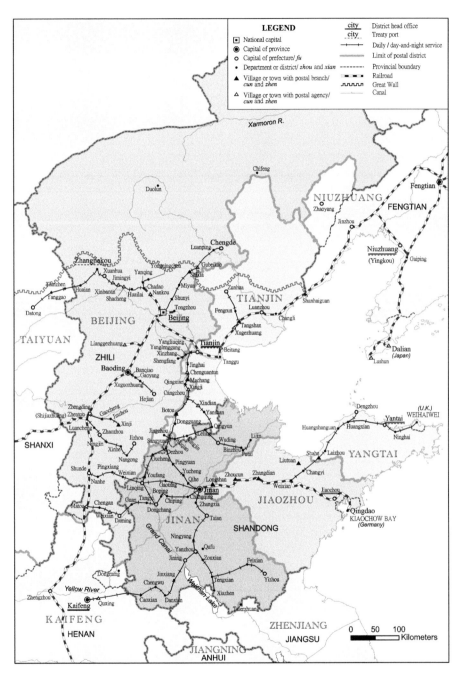

FIGURE 7.3 Railways and "day-and-night" express postal routes in northern China, 1907. Map © Weipin Tsai; cartography by Huang Chingchi.

underpinned the New Policies was supported through the expansion of postal services down to the village level.

Some specific examples shed further light on the critical role played by villages in postal expansion. For example, on the Qingdao-Jinan Railway, villages with significant commercial activity, such as Longshan, Zhangdian, and Zhoucun, had full postal branches. Liutuan, a village under the jurisdiction of Changyi District, was part of the "day-and-night" service on the line between Jinan, Weixian, and Yantai. Liutong was a wealthy location for silk production, and although it was ranked in administrative terms at the village level, it was the financial center of the local district.[51] Another example can be seen on the Beijing–Shanhai Pass Railway, where the important mining villages Tangshan and Xugezhuang were incorporated in the "day-and-night" service.

At this time, Jinan, a "self-opened" port since 1905, was situated at a critical location linking Qingdao and Yantai to the east, Beijing and Tianjin to the north, and Anhui and Jiangsu provinces to the south. Coming at the end point of the west-east Qingdao-Jinan Railway, an overland "day-and-night" connection from Jinan to Shunde Prefecture and the village of Matou in Zhili was the best way to maximize its relative closeness to the north-south Jinghan Railway. Prior to the construction of the railway from Tianjin to Pukou (Nanjing) via Jinan, the effective "day-and-night" service between Tianjin and Jinan, which had a long history dating back to the Customs Postal Service, traveled through multiple districts and villages. Through synchronization of railway timetables and courier activities, at the beginning of 1909 the IPO started to offer an express mail service in order to increase the pressure on native letter hongs. Courier staff chosen to handle express letters were specially trained, and had to follow even stricter protocols than usual. Each express letter had guaranteed delivery dates, and the distributors, who wore uniforms with numbered badges and only delivered express mails, were held responsible if promised dates were not met.[52]

Overall, the IPO's flexibility in the assignment of postal branches and agencies to towns and villages according to the logistical needs of the net-

51. Teng Shougeng, "Liutuan baiyin shichang shimo," 55–56. I wish to thank Wu Qiang for providing me with this source.

52. Enclosure 1, in "'Express Delivery' Service," Postal Circular 220, February 2, 1909, in *Circulars Nos. 135–261*, 331–32, TMA, W2-2838.

work (often driven by the availability of rail or steamship routes), as well as their contemporary significance in population and economic terms rather than according to their traditional hierarchic administrative status, shows that the postal service's creators were well attuned to the practicalities of the market over mere political considerations.

Collaboration with the Military Relay Courier System

As has been noted in previous chapters, voices arguing for abolition of the military relay courier system had been around since the second half of the nineteenth century, and vocal support for the creation of a modern national postal service for the whole country, intended to carry both official and private mail, often included criticism of the old military relay system in its commentary. Comparing the finances of the two systems, it is very clear that the IPO was run far more frugally. By 1910, the IPO employed 11,985 staff, rising to 15,339 in 1911.[53] By contrast, there were more than ten thousand people employed on the military relay courier system in Zhili alone, almost seventy-five hundred in Shandong, around seventy-one hundred in Zhejiang, and around five thousand in Hubei. For a typical main station situated on a major road, the personnel complement might range from seventy to two hundred people; for a smaller station, twenty to thirty.[54]

Piry was scathing on the subject of the military relay courier system: "An old institution, known to work unsatisfactorily, denounced as useless by the two Yangtze Viceroys, the I-Chan [the military relay courier system], is allowed to remain, untouched, extracting heavy subsidies from the State. A large portion of the work this old institution used to do, in fact, is already performed by us, but its name remains on paper though we have practically replaced it for the work."[55]

As result, the IPO's work in transmitting official mail for most provinces allowed it to extend its reach to inland areas very close to the fron-

53. "Youzheng ge qi yuangong renshu" 郵政各期員工人數 [Number of postal staff in different periods], in *Zhongguo youzheng tongji huiji*, 64.

54. "Youzheng-yifu" 郵政-役夫 [Postal service military relay workers], in *Da Qing huidian shili*, juan 690.

55. Théophile A. Piry, "Postal Secretary's Memo: Letter-Hongs at Ports . . . I-Chan (Military Relay System) Subsidies: Practical Considerations Thereon," December 1903, SHAC, 137 (1)7587.

tiers. This provided the IPO with useful learning on how to manage mail over significantly long distances, while at the same time giving local officials the opportunity to become familiar with this relatively new institution; in turn, this led to a steady decrease in local resistance to post office expansion. The existing military relay courier stations and available routes at remote frontiers continued to be important, and were incorporated into the system of the IPO to a much greater extent than in other provinces. Xinjiang, containing the westernmost parts of the overland routes, provides us with a good example to demonstrate cooperation between the IPO and the military relay courier system.

By the end of the Qing dynasty, there were 236 military relay courier stations in Xinjiang, though the telegraph had been introduced in 1893 for urgent communications. The horses of each station numbered between twenty and seventy, depending on the importance of the route and the location of the station. Mules, donkeys, and camels were also used, particularly in the most remote locations. Staff at these locations comprised not just the normal service complement but also translators for the different languages in Xinjiang.[56] In 1909, noting that other provinces were already connected to the new postal service, the governor of Gansu and Xinjiang reported on long-term problems with the military relay courier system in the wider region and urged a change to the new postal service—not just for official mail but also to provide a service for the general public.[57] In preparation for the introduction of the IPO to Xinjiang, a local, temporary arrangement was made for the IPO and the military relay courier system to work together. Mail was to be collected by the staff of the military relay courier system from the post office at Jiayuguan, on the corridor of western Gansu, for onward transmission and delivery to Xinjiang, the expense to be borne by senders and addressees.[58] A postal connection between Beijing and Dihua (today Ürümqi) was therefore established. This connection of 6,600 *li* (4085 kilometers) was soon converted to a "day-and-night" service across Xinjiang, Gansu, and Henan, with a transit time to Beijing of thirty-three days.[59]

56. *Xinjiang tongzhi: Youdianzhi*, 78.
57. Liankui 聯奎 to the Emperor, Xuantong reign year 2, month 2, day 2 (March 12, 1910), in *ZJYS*, 211; Report (1909), 2.
58. Report (1908), 4.
59. Report (1910), 1.

In 1910 this postal link was pushed farther north to Tarbagatai (Tacheng), an important military town on the border between Outer Mongolia, Russia, and Xinjiang. Tarbagatai was nominated as the mail exchange location between the Russian Post Office and the IPO in the Dihua postal district. The Tarbagatai–Dihua route was 1,630 *li* (1,010 kilometers) in length, and took four days and eighteen hours to complete.[60] This route later became part of a grander scheme connecting Mongolia, Xinjiang, and northern China, which will be discussed in chapter 9. In Tarbagatai, mail to Europe was taken by the Russian Post Office, to connect at Omsk with the Trans-Siberian Railway. The postal service in Xinjiang saw successful development over a short period, and in 1910 was upgraded from its former status under Lanzhou to become an individual postal district. In 1911, despite the political upheavals of that year, the mail growth rate in Xinjiang outperformed that of many other areas, and in that year the Post Office completely replaced the military relay courier system in Xinjiang. Items handled in Xinjiang by the Post Office rose from 214,000 in 1910 to 787,000 in 1911; registered articles alone increased to 230,000, and of these nearly 120,000 were official dispatches.[61]

Through aligning postal districts with the provinces of the Qing empire, the IPO moved further to shake off its treaty port heritage and made itself ever more Chinese. Besides this top-level reorganization by redefining postal districts, the IPO also incorporated lower-level administrative units to bring districts and villages into the important "day-and-night" and express services. Despite the declining political realities of the last ten years of the Qing dynasty, the IPO helped the central government in shaping its resurgent discourse for a unified nation under a monarchy through the construction of postal networks across the entire country. It was in this rather unusual climate that the IPO, by projecting a particular, somewhat desirable, image of state-associated modernity, also started to change the urban landscape. Two GIS postal maps (see figs. 7.4 and 7.5) illustrate the expansion of postal networks between 1903 and 1911. The IPO, which represented the sovereignty of the Qing empire, reached all corners of the frontiers prior to the Chinese Revolution of 1911.

---

60. Report (1910), 12.
61. Report (1911), 6.

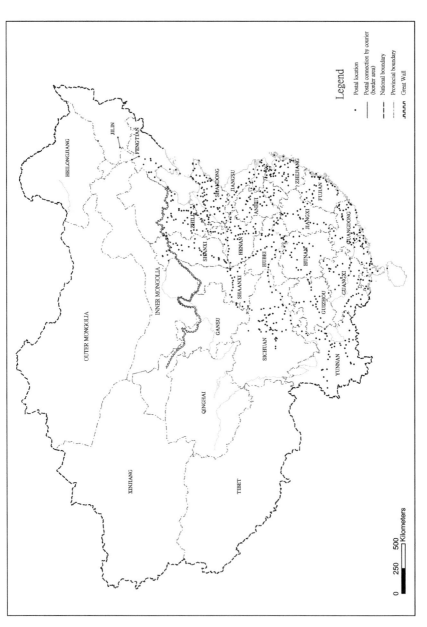

FIGURE 7.4 Postal branch density, 1903. Information extracted from *China—Postal Working Map* (*Da Qing youzheng gongshu beiyong yutu* 大清郵政公署備用輿圖). Map © Weipin Tsai; cartography by Huang Chingchi.

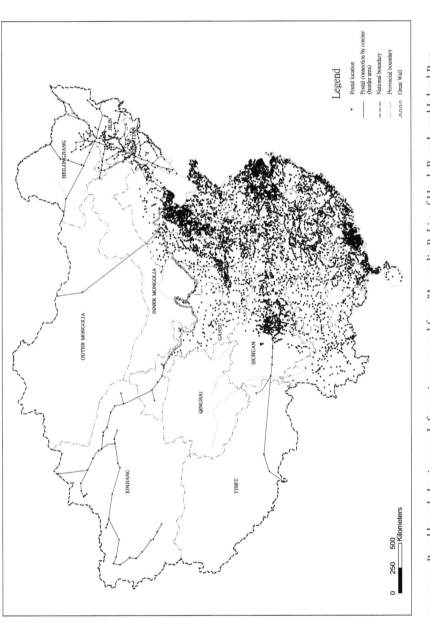

FIGURE 75   Postal branch density, 1911. Information extracted from "Appendix B: List of Head, Branch, and Inland Post Offices Arranged under Districts," in Report (1911). Map © Weipin Tsai; cartography by Huang Chingchi.

Postal Street Presence and the
New Urban Landscape

One unmissable addition to the street furniture of towns and cities was the letter pillar box. For some years, the IPO had set up pillar boxes in cities. The version shown in figure 7.6 represents the one used in Shanghai.[62] The design of the earliest pillar boxes did not reflect any Chinese characteristics. They were built for economy, and were used mainly by foreign residents.

Referencing the designs of letter boxes of other countries, and particularly Argentina, in 1906, the IPO finalized a new design. The cylindrical letter box itself was made of sheet iron, closed at the top by an iron cap that functioned as a lid, and was fixed at the bottom with an iron band. The box, one foot six inches in height and one foot in diameter, was supported by a wooden fluted body three feet in height. Where necessary, the wooden body could be replaced by an iron one, to protect it from white ants. The design of the pillar box had a deep connection to institutional traditions. Since Horatio Nelson Lay's time as inspector general in 1862, the CMCS's colors had been green and yellow, originally represented on institutional flags in the form of a green background with a yellow diagonal cross. From 1873 onward, this design was changed to a bright yellow triangular flag, with an imperial blue dragon and one red pearl.[63] Piry sought to bring imperial and Customs traditions together. He applied the Customs' functional green to the box and pillar, highlighted with imperial yellow, while on the top of the box there were two embossed yellow dragons set around a single red pearl—resembling a royal pattern related to the emperor. Within the circle made by the shape of the two dragons, characters bearing the name "Great Qing Post Office" (Da Qing youzheng 大清郵政), were carved and picked out in the same yellow (see fig. 7.7).

---

62. Francis A. Aglen to E. A. Hewett, January 26, 1901, Shanghai Municipal Archives, U1-2-230. Aglen was the Customs commissioner at Shanghai at the time, while Hewett was the chairman of the Shanghai Municipal Council.

63. IG Circular 5 (1st ser.), April 30, 1873, in *Inspector General's Circulars*, 436; "Enclosure No. 4," in IG Circular 48 (1st ser.), December 31, 1875, in *Inspector General's Circulars*, 667. See also Foster Hall, *The Chinese Maritime Customs*, 38.

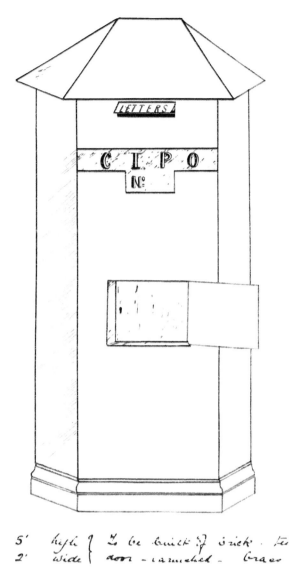

5' [high] To be built of brick · for
2' wide   door - enameled - brass

FIGURE 7.6 A sketch of a letter pillar box, 1901. The pillar box was designed to be five feet high, two feet wide, and one foot six inches deep. The main material was brick. The top was made of brass plate, and the door was made of teak wood. The slot with "Letters" was enameled metal, and "CIPO" (for Chinese Imperial Post Office) was carved in stone. Source: Francis A. Aglen to E. A. Hewett, January 26, 1901, Shanghai Municipal Archives, U1-2-230. Acknowledgment to Chang Tzu-Ning for improving the image quality.

MODEL OF I.P.O. LETTER PILLAR-BOX.

DRAWING A.

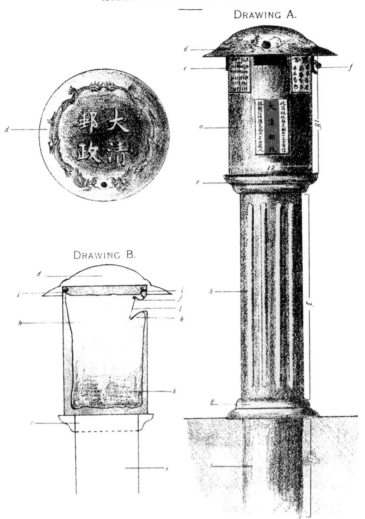

DRAWING B.

FIGURE 7.7 A drawing, originally in color, of an Imperial Post Office letter pillar box, 1906. On the front of the box there is a note, which was deliberately put in the design of the traditional Chinese letter cover (see fig. 9.3 in chapter 9). On a letter cover, the red central area was the customary place for the recipient's name; the white area to the right of this was for the recipient's address, with the sender's name placed on the left. On the front of the pillar box, the red area has four Chinese characters for the Great Qing Post Office. On the right is written that the pillar box only accepts ordinary mail with sufficient postage applied, while on the left there is a note that registered mail should be handed in at a post office and not placed in the box. Source: Postal Circular 156, December 26, 1906, in *Circulars Nos. 135–261*, TMA, W2-2838.

Moving on to the central front of the letter box, "Great Qing Post Office" appeared again on a red plate, along with smaller text in Chinese which read, "This letter box is only for ordinary letters with affixed postage stamps; registered letters should not be inserted but taken to the post office" (ci tong zhi shou tie zu youpiao zhi pingchangxin guahao xinjian xu jiao ju nei bu ke tou ru 此筒祇收貼足郵票之平常信 掛號信件須交局內 不可投入). Only Chinese characters were permitted on the letter box, with an exception for those placed in the foreign settlements. There was an instruction that the supporting pillar should be well cemented two feet into the ground and that the box itself should be "planted well in view at convenient places in streets, on roads, or by the entrance of buildings."[64] Although representations of dragons were already used on stamps both by the Local Post Office of the Shanghai Municipal Council and the IPO, such a combination, of two dragons in imperial yellow on such a large artifact on public display in streets across China, was unprecedented.

In addition to the introduction of the pillar box, newly built post offices also attracted attention from the general public. When Li Gui (see chapter 4) was in Washington, DC, in 1876, he recorded street scenes, bridges, traffic, gardens, and other aspects of modern city landscapes. He was impressed by buildings associated with the US government, as well as embassies, hospitals, and the US Mint. Having an interest in mail services, he also recorded what he encountered of the US postal system. Li noted that female staff outnumbered male, and that post offices, present in cities, towns, and villages, were sometimes crafted with white stone into four-story buildings. The post offices chose busy locations, and placed letter boxes outside their premises. A US letter box, approximately twelve inches high and eight inches wide, had a slim gap in its lid, and people could insert letters into the box at any time; mail was collected every half hour.[65] Li's observation shows the US Post Office Department had established a presence in the living space of the general public and that postal artifacts, including buildings and letter boxes, had become blended into the visual landscape.

64. "I.P.O. Letter Pillar-Boxes," Postal Circular 156, December 26, 1906, in *Circulars Nos. 135–261*, 59, TMA, W2-2838.

65. Li Gui, *Huanyou diqiu xinlu*, 65.

This development was soon to be observed across Chinese towns and cities as the IPO became part of daily life. Location was clearly important. One of many things that remained unchanged even after the Second Opium War was the fact that Customs Houses at treaty ports were located outside city walls. After 1896, post offices no longer had to remain attached to the Customs Houses, or stay within foreign settlements; instead they could be set up in the heart of the city, ideally attached to the local *yamen* hall or a popular temple, or on a busy commercial street. Unfortunately, such ideal locations were not always obtained. As Alfred E. Hippisley, the officiating postal secretary, pointed out, post offices were often opened "in tumble-down premises or in back streets and suburbs away from the busy quarters of the town."[66] He understood that it was possible to save money in this way, but he considered this a false economy that did not always help the IPO gain public recognition. Hippisley felt so strongly about this point that he stated in his 1907 annual report: "Such action was a mistake in a country where native merchants attach so much importance to 'face,' i.e. the effect of appearance, that they are willing to spend hundreds of dollars on carved and gilded shop-fronts. And the consequence has been that the very existence of the Post Office has often remained unknown to those who should resort to it most."[67]

Large and prominent postal buildings therefore carried much weight in projecting an air of trustworthiness and respectability. In 1900 Hart had already designed a layout for a large post office, and his plan set out an ideal that set the standard for future developments. Hart's design laid out the function of each department, and where it should be located, taking into account the spatial relationships between postal staff and the customers. The design was meant to provide the general public with a feeling of welcome, with the lobby treated as an open space, and information provided as clearly as possible, so that customers would not be put off by fear of seeming ignorant of how to use the service. The accessibility of postage stamps and letter boxes was critical; this would allow the customers to cultivate a sense of privacy for their own correspondence without a need to involve any other person—something of a modern notion in itself. We can see an example in the photographs of the Fuzhou Post Office (see figs. 7.8 and 7.9), where the architecture projects a sense

66. Postal Circular 181, January 31, 1908, in *Circulars Nos. 135–261*, 171, TMA, W2-2838.
67. Report (1907), 12.

FIGURE 7.8 Fuzhou Post Office interior, ca. 1906; photo taken by G. F. Montgomery, Customs commissioner at Fuzhou. Source: Stanley Bell, *Hart of Lisburn*. Acknowledgment to Jamie Carstairs for improving the image quality.

FIGURE 7.9 Fuzhou Post Office exterior, ca. 1906. Source: Harvard University, Edward Bangs Drew Collection, Harvard-Yenching Library, EBD00.107.

of propriety. Inside the building there was a long and spacious lobby with white walls, a high ceiling, and a wooden floor. Different departments were neatly arranged with windows, following Hart's instruction, bearing in Chinese and English the names of their respective functions. The building was furnished with an impressive main entrance in something akin to French colonial style, coordinated with the design of the lobby, while a large dark signboard in Chinese and English hung from the center.

No doubt the opening of such a grand space intended for the use of ordinary people would have caused a sensation, and the same surely applies to the headquarters building in Shanghai (see fig. 7.10). In both we see a similar logic: a modern service, housed in large-scale spaces reflecting modern, Western-style architectural practice, in turn projecting a modernized image of the state. But how was this shift perceived by the general public? While some individuals might have been receptive to the space, it is easy to see how others might feel intimidated. The photograph of the entrance to the Fuzhou Post Office supports this concern. In front of the entrance, we see a group of seven postal staff: the three in long gowns are postal clerks, while the other four in uniform are postmen. These postmen acted as the mobile advertisements for the postal service, as their jackets bore the legend "Great Qing" on one side, and "Post Office" on the other. But behind this group we see signs displayed on each side of the entrance saying: "Important place for the postal service; noise prohibited" (*youzheng zhongdi jinzhi xuanhua* 郵政重地 禁止喧嘩). Although not specifically marking out the post office as a restricted place, the wording intentionally presented an authoritative message that those with curiosity but without immediate business should keep away.

The emphasis on the post office as an important space where people should keep noise to a minimum was not only seen in larger post offices but also at local postal agencies. Referring back to figure 6.6, in chapter 6, which shows a postal agency in Yongchun, we can see two small signboards reminding people how to behave around the premises. It is interesting to note that these smaller signboards were not official ones provided by the district postmaster. Rather, the local postal agency wanted to imitate the ambience of a large post office.

One curious journalist in Nanjing carried out an experiment, posting a letter to himself to find out whether the delivery was as efficient as claimed by the IPO. The delivery turned out to be slow, and when he

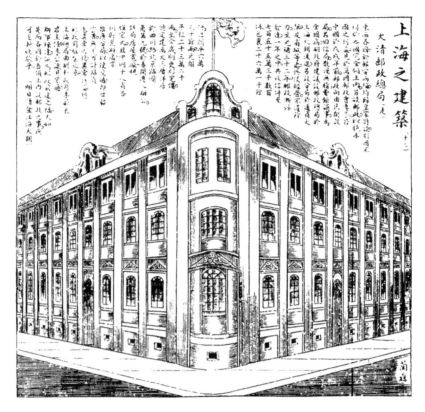

FIGURE 7.10   A line drawing of the headquarters of the Shanghai Postal District.
Source: *Daily Pictorial* (*Tuhua ribao* 圖畫日報), issue 12, Xuantong reign year 1, month 7,
day 12 (August 27, 1909).

made an inquiry, he reported that he was shouted at by the local postal
staff and that he observed that customers in general were treated with
contempt: the staff rolled their eyes at the people with good clothing, but
also scolded those who appeared to come from the country.[68] Similar
treatment was experienced by Zhang Gang (1860–1942), a member of the
local gentry in Wenzhou. Curious about the IPO building in town, Zhang
and two friends decided to drop by one morning in 1902 before a leisurely
visit to several temples. Rather than receiving a warm welcome, they were

68. "Xin youzhengsi zhi zhengjian" 新郵政司之政見 [The policies of the new postal
commissioner], 1910, in *Jiangning shiye zazhi*, issue 6, 81–82.

rebuked by a guard for entering despite having no business to conduct, so the group had to retreat.[69]

The ten years of growth and development after the Boxer Rebellion was a golden period for the IPO. The service was extended to interior provincial counties and reached as far as Outer Mongolia, Tibet, and Xinjiang. The main impact of the New Policies on the IPO was not the immediate end of its affiliation with the CMCS but the incorporation of the IPO within the central government's overall framework for national communications and transportation. The IPO also made postal agreements with Britain, France, Germany, Japan, Russia, the United States, and other countries, despite the fact that it had not yet formally joined the Universal Postal Union. This external and internal expansion overlapped with the Qing empire's New Policies, as the Qing government sought to centralize the management of transportation and communications infrastructure through unified control of railways, the telegraph, steamship services, and the post. This was a significant move in modern Chinese history, because until then there had been no unified approach, as each of these had been managed as "foreign," rather than domestic, concerns. In bringing them together with a domestic focus, the Qing government reframed its approach to communications to incorporate the needs of the general public for the first time in Chinese history. Such a revolutionary change implies an important degree of strategic thinking within the New Policies reforms, as they laid the foundation of a modern administrative structure, later adopted by the Yuan Shikai government and maintained during the Warlord Era, even in the face of constant change at the top organizational levels.

Paradoxically, it can be argued that, for all of the shift in strategic intent, the IPO thrived precisely because it was left alone and continued to operate based on its own logic, while the central government focused on more pressing financial issues relating to railways, the telegraph, and steamships. As postal service expanded, the IPO became a widely visible symbol of a changing China, albeit somewhat uneven in execution, ranging from humble postal agencies and smaller branches in villages and on backstreets to large, newly designed modern buildings in the hearts of

69. Zhang Gang, *Zhang Gang riji,* diary entry, Guangxu reign year 28, month 3, day 15 (April 22, 1902), vol. 2, 767.

thriving cities. This unevenness, it appears, carried through to the experience of IPO customers: for all of its modern, Western-influenced approach, the IPO retained for some a familiar, if somewhat intimidating, air of bureaucracy.

This chapter concludes with a series of charts (figs. 7.11–7.14) and tables (tables 7.2–7.3) that show the growth in Post Office services during this golden decade. They are presented without commentary.

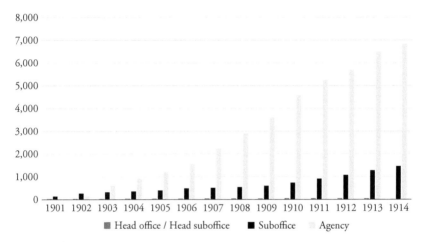

FIGURE 7.11 Growth in the network of Post Office branches and agencies, to 1914. Source: Information extracted from Jiaotongbu youzheng zongju, *Zhongguo youzheng tongji huiji.*

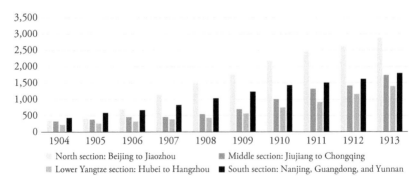

FIGURE 7.12 Growth in the postal branch network, by region, to 1913. Source: Information extracted from Reports (1906–1913).

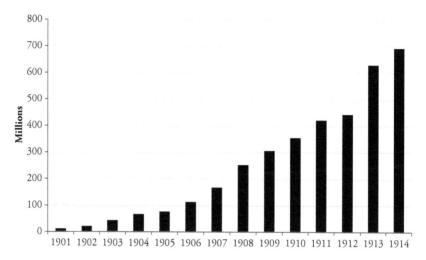

FIGURE 7.13 Letters carried, Chinese postal network, to 1914. Source: Information extracted from Jiaotongbu youzheng zongju, *Zhongguo youzheng tongji huiji*.

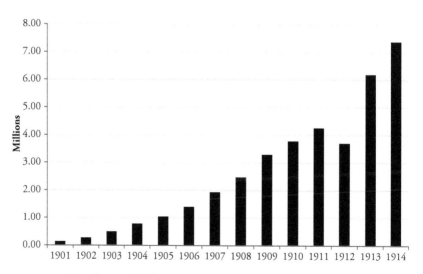

FIGURE 7.14 Parcels carried, Chinese postal network, to 1914. Source: Information extracted from Jiaotongbu youzheng zongju, *Zhongguo youzheng tongji huiji*.

Table 7.2. Mail and population density across Chinese provinces, 1907

Province	Population*	Population per square kilometer	Number of articles dispatched	Number of articles dispatched per 1,000 people
Anhui	23,672,000	167	1,245,000	53
Fujian	22,870,000	190	1,381,000	61
Gansu	10,386,000	32	365,000	19
Guangdong	31,865,000	123	5,469,000	172
Guangxi	5,142,000	25	16,000	3
Guizhou	7,650,000	44	38,000	5
Henan	25,318,000	144	2,463,000	97
Hubei	35,280,000	191	2,097,000	59
Hunan	22,169,000	102	728,000	33
Jiangsu	23,980,000	239	19,247,000	807
Jiangxi	26,532,000	147	707,000	27
Manchuria	8,500,000	9	2,185,000	257*
Shaanxi	8,450,000	43	365,000	19
Shandong	38,248,000	264	1,924,000	50
Shanxi	12,200,000	58	762,000	62
Sichuan	48,725,000	121	641,000	13
Yunnan	12,722,000	33	256,000	20
Zhejiang	11,580,000	120	1,810,000	156
Zhili	20,930,000	69	9,307,000	445

Source: "Report on the Working of the Imperial Post Office, 1907." In *Returns of Trade and Trade Reports, 1907*. Shanghai: Statistical Department of the Inspectorate General of Customs, 1908.

* Incorrectly given as 27 in source data; the correct number is 257.

Table 7.3. Mail and population density, sample of countries, 1909

Country	Area in square kilometers	Number of inhabitants	Number of square kilometers covered by each post office	Number of inhabitants covered by each post office	Total number of post offices	Total number of post office personnel	Total number of pieces of mail	Articles posted per head during the year—corrected figures*
Argentina	2,950,520	6,190,300	1,380	2,895	1,238	2,292	593,388,597	95.9
Austria	900,005	26,150,708	34	2,964	8,821	30,026	1,517,815,970	58.0
China**	4,319,212	418,500,000	1,153	98,285	4,258	11,682	306,820,600	0.7
Denmark	40,384	2,605,268	39	2,520	1,119	5,171	155,881,561	59.8
Egypt	560,000	11,189,978	437	8,749	1,307	1,534	65,600,000	5.9
France	536,408	39,252,245	43	3,205	12,667	55,661	3,163,240,469	80.6
Germany	540,777	60,641,278	13	1,514	40,046	172,162	5,883,751,610	97.0
Great Britain	314,609	44,198,372	13	1,873	23,600	106,833	5,082,070,130	115.0
India	4,522,488	294,361,056	261	17,017	17,298	2,325	808,198,030	2.7
Indochina	820,000	20,500,000	3,037	75,926	270	1,284	15,117,944	0.7
Japan	454,789	52,253,917	66	7,656	6,825	33,710	1,409,441,708	27.0
New Zealand	269,917	919,108	130	445	2,064	54,164	141,357,284	153.8
Russia	22,434,392	140,000,000	1,660	10,365	13,507	26,506	1,114,875,023	8.0
United States	9,592,137	77,177,372	153	1,232	632,659	14,2921	12,668,017,077	164.1

*The calculation given for articles posted per head in China and Indochina were incorrect in the published data in English, though calculations were correct in the Chinese version of the document; corrected figures are shown here.

**Mongolia, Tibet, and Xinjiang excluded.

THE OLD IMPERIAL
POST OFFICE, PEKING.

CHAPTER EIGHT

The Year 1911

Separation, Revolution, and Disconnection

The year 1911 was, of course, a momentous time for every part of the Chinese bureaucracy, but for China's postal service, major change came early. In May the Imperial Post Office (IPO) formally separated from the Chinese Maritime Customs Service (CMCS), not just in name but also in structure and alignment with the central government. In September, Robert Hart passed away during a family holiday near Marlow, Buckinghamshire, and in so doing managed to avoid seeing the demise of the Qing dynasty he had served for nearly all of his adult life. In October, the Wuchang Uprising began and revolution rolled in. There were natural disasters, too, including plague in Manchuria and Shandong and the worst flood in sixty years in the wider Yangtze River area, which caused devastating famine and saw hundreds of thousands of refugees quartered around the walls of Nanjing. In Sichuan and Yunnan, rail services were out of operation for several months due to civil disturbances. Military operations in many provinces were conducted in a climate of anarchy, riot, and piracy, while there was confusion over the future of

China's administration as the machinery of government tried to adjust to the developing situation.

Chapter 7 examined how the IPO was impacted by the Qing government's New Policies reform. As part of what would be its last reorganization, the government moved to recategorize areas of activity that had formerly been treated as foreign-related business—specifically, railways, steamships, the telegraph, and the post office—as internal affairs. In accordance with shifts in frontier policies, the government was looking for a solution to problems caused by the decline of the military relay courier system while at the same time maintaining coherent information networks to help manage its presence in peripheral areas. This need was met through the progressive expansion of the IPO to more remote inland areas and ultimately to China's frontiers, consolidating Qing rule and enabling better observation of local officials operating in these areas.

Although the Qing government reduced funding for the military relay courier system in many provinces during the first decade of the twentieth century, spending was maintained for peripheral areas. The already complex political situation at the frontiers suffered a further twist after the New Policies were introduced, as political developments in Outer Mongolia and Tibet began to pose an increasing threat to the sovereignty of the Qing empire. In the midst of the uncertainty, the IPO performed the delicate task of underpinning an increasingly fragile Chinese state by extending its presence to the outermost reaches. For the Qing government, as for the later republic, the post office became a means to assert national sovereignty in the face of instability and an increasingly fragmented political reality at China's frontiers. Against the backdrop of the fast-moving political situation after the Chinese Revolution of 1911, this chapter and chapter 9 address how the postal service reflected the sovereignty of the new China in both its actual assertion and the discourse surrounding it.

Separation

In November 1909, the vice president of the Ministry of Posts and Communications, Wang Daxie 汪大燮 (1860–1929), had held a meeting with Robert Bredon (1846–1918) to discuss the matter of the ministry's taking over of the postal service. Bredon, who was Hart's brother-in-law, became acting inspector general after Hart left. He was Hart's favored successor, and at the time was in a race with Francis A. Aglen and Alfred E. Hippisley to become inspector general.[1] After the meeting, Bredon sent Wang a memorandum which had first been sent almost a year earlier to the Bureau of Customs Affairs, which had become the supervisory body of the CMCS in 1906. Bredon's memorandum was long and insightful, particularly on the matter of institutional relationships between the Bureau of Customs Affairs, the CMCS, the IPO, and the Ministry of Posts and Communications, but it boiled down to a plea for the continuance of the effective freedom of operation that the IPO had until that point enjoyed. Recalling the provincial governors' previous attempt at breaking up the service, Bredon strongly advised that the central government should make it very clear that, after the administrative changes, the IPO would still be a centralized body under the sole supervision of the Ministry of Posts and Communications: "The definite fixing of the relations of the Imperial Post Office and the Provinces will have to be laid down, and the sooner the better. It should be clearly understood that Provincial officials had no right of control in postal matters. . . . Of course it is understood that support and assistance will continue to be afforded by local officials wherever needed for protection of post-offices, couriers and mails, etc., and for the repression of abuses or punishment of offenders, and that of necessity their legal jurisdiction over the men employed continues to exist as at present."[2]

Bredon, as a close assistant to Hart, knew very well that one of the main reasons for the IPO's successful progress was its having been left alone "without friction with Chinese officials and without questions with foreign Governments."[3] He expressed very strongly that the takeover should mean taking over the whole existing team: native staff, foreign staff, and Théophile A. Piry, the postal secretary. In Bredon's view, Piry should be given the same "freeness of hand" to manage staff and operations as he had previously enjoyed.

1. Van de Ven, *Breaking with the Past*, 159–62.
2. Robert Bredon, "Memorandum," November 1909, SHAC, 679 (6) 1296.
3. Bredon, "Memorandum," November 1909.

Bredon was also careful to note the financial debt to the CMCS that had been built up by the IPO over the previous thirteen years, in large measure due to absence of monetary support from the central government despite an arrangement that had been made in 1904 that included instructions to six provinces to contribute to the postal budget. From the eventual arrangements for the transfer, it is clear that what Bredon suggested in this memorandum was taken very seriously. The whole postal team, both native and foreign, was taken on by the ministry, including Piry. Choosing to disregard public criticism that the IPO remained to some extent foreign controlled, the central government made a judgment to avoid unnecessary change, maintaining the integrity of what by any measure had been a successful organization. Keeping Piry also had the consequence of avoiding conflict with French interests. Nevertheless, in order to bring the organization under necessary control, a new position, director general of posts, was created. Li Jingfang 李經方 (1855–1934), a son of Li Hongzhang and vice president of the Ministry of Posts and Communications at the time, became the first director general of posts.[4]

Aglen was appointed as officiating inspector general in April 1910, and it was he who conducted most of the discussions with the Bureau of Customs Affairs and the Ministry of Posts and Communications over the transfer. When the separation came, Aglen marked the moment in the final joint inspector general's and postal circular on May 30, 1911:

> An important stage in postal development and progress has now been reached, and this Circular, the last that will appear in the Customs series bearing a postal number, is to inform you that I am to-day handing over charge of the Imperial Chinese Posts to Mr. T. Piry, appointed by Imperial Decree Postmaster General under the Ministry of Posts and Communications. . . .
>
> I cannot conclude this Circular without expressing, in the name of the Inspector General, Sir Robert Hart, the thanks which are due to all those members of the Customs Service, past and present, who have borne the burden and heat of the day and whose efforts have contributed so much to the success that has been achieved. The position won has not been attained without sacrifices in which all have taken a

---

4. Postmaster General's Circular 262, May 31, 1911, in *Circulars Nos. 262–389*, 1, TMA, W2-2839.

share, many receiving no other reward than the consciousness of work well done. The Service, in bidding farewell and wishing all prosperity to the Administration which has sprung from it, will, I feel sure, continue to take the friendliest interest in, and always work in the closest harmony with, the Imperial Post Office.[5]

This farewell note described the close relationship between the two institutions, and, in a rather melancholy fashion, promised to continue the relationship in the future. For Aglen, this may indeed have been a heartfelt moment, as he would have recalled the disagreement between himself and close colleagues over a joint petition concerning postal funding and its impact on senior CMCS staff remuneration back in 1902–3 (briefly recounted in chapter 6). At the time, Aglen had told Hippisley that, although he understood his colleagues' reasoning on the issue, he disagreed with those who had chosen to attack Hart over it. In 1902 he wrote, "It is represented as a strong protest against the IG's [inspector general's] administration . . . and . . . any such movement is badly timed, and seeing how much the IG has done and is doing for the service, a proof of ingratitude towards Sir Robert and a blow directed against him at time when he is old and hampered by all kinds of difficulties."[6] In the end Aglen signed the petition himself, but he seemed to regret having done so. In the absence of a satisfactory response from Hart, Frederick J. Mayers, the deputy commissioner of Tianjin Customs, was furious. He wrote that Hart was out of touch and that Aglen had not only failed to understand the feelings of the service but also suffered from "a blind faith in the I.G. and thinks the latter has done all the service could possibly expect. In other words, being an entirely selfish man, and having nothing to complain of himself, he does not see that others may have good cause to be dissatisfied."[7]

5. IG Circular 1802 / Postal No.261, May 30, 1911, in *Circulars Nos. 135–261*, 633–34, TMA, W2-2838.

6. Francis A. Aglen to Alfred E. Hippisley, January 5, 1903, Alfred E. Hippisley Papers, Bodleian Libraries, University of Oxford, MS. Eng. c. 7294. Aglen dated the letter 1902, but this is highly likely to be a mistake; Hippisley penciled the arrival date on the top of the letter as January 5, 1903.

7. Frederick J. Mayers to Alfred E. Hippisley, September 21, 1903, Hippisley Papers.

The day after Aglen's final postal circular was released, Piry issued his own first circular under the new official title of postmaster general. He assured his staff, both Chinese and foreign, that their conditions and prospects of employment remained the same as under the CMCS and that nothing should worry them. He described the postal service as Hart's "magnum opus" and wrote: "The change means no departure from existing principles and policy, and is but the natural result of progress in the national institutions of China among which the Imperial Post Office has now taken rank."[8]

Ten years into his stewardship of the IPO, Piry was pleased with the IPO's independence from the CMCS. He told those with whom he came into contact that he had got everything he asked for. According to Bredon, Piry expressed his joy "in quite a childlike way," believing that "the I.P.O is now on the same footing as the I.M.C. [Imperial Maritime Customs], and he on the same as I.G!" Bredon added, "He signed himself 'Postmaster General'—a free translation I think of his Chinese title which I understand is 'Tsung pan' [總辦, literally, general manager]."[9]

Yet behind this harmonious facade lay some furious bickering, both over the debt the CMCS regarded as owed by the IPO, and at a personal level over Piry's pension. Seemingly unable to leave Hart alone in London on what was officially a period of sick leave, Piry wrote to complain about Aglen and to seek Hart's intervention on both counts. On the matter of his pension, Piry wrote that he had been treated badly by Aglen, as the latter had refused to pay an amount totaling 43,000 Haikwan taels (Hk.Tls.) in pension and deferred leave to which he considered himself entitled after so many years of duty. He had never anticipated that his honorable and hardworking career would end thus; he had been shocked when his pension request was denied, and he felt he was being "thrown out of the Service faring little better than a dog." Piry appealed to Hart: "Where are you, my poor old chief, to right an awful wrong & warm my heart again?"[10] Piry also brought the case to Li Jingfang, and the argument soon got out of hand, turning publicly ugly when Aglen refused to

8. Théophile A. Piry, "Postmaster General's Circular 262."
9. Robert Bredon to Robert Hart, June 4, 1911, SQBH.
10. Théophile A. Piry to Robert Hart, June 13, 1911, SQBH.

attend Piry's farewell party, which had been organized at the CMCS headquarters in Beijing and to which the entire headquarters staff had been invited. In the end, the party was canceled.[11]

Alongside Piry's pension dispute was a disagreement over accounting arrangements for the six treaty-port postal grants. This issue dated back to 1904, when the Qing government had agreed to fund the IPO out of contributions from six treaty ports. Yet, as was discussed in chapter 6, the Customs superintendents of the six treaty ports did not make their full contributions at any point, with the consequence being that the IPO had been running a substantial deficit, the gap being funded by the CMCS. By spring 1910, the IPO owed the CMCS Hk.Tls. 1,780,000, and the figure was even higher by 1911.[12] As part of the transfer from the CMCS to the Ministry of Posts and Communications, it was agreed in principle that the ministry would take over this debt and pay it back to the CMCS, but arrangements for this were not formalized prior to reorganization. The issue became a live one in June, when Piry asked Aglen to wire him the six treaty-port postal grants from the latest season, totaling Hk.Tls. 119,302.71.[13] Aglen refused to transfer the funds unless Piry agreed to treat the amount as new debt, to be added to the existing outstanding total.[14] Piry did not consider the funds from the six treaty ports to be part of the indebtedness to the CMCS, and in reply to Aglen he wrote, "I desire to state officially that the lack of these funds may cause serious embarrassment to the I.P.O. and that, considering the relations hitherto existing between Customs and Posts, I am unable to see on what grounds they are withheld."[15] In his letter, Piry wrote to Hart that he believed Aglen "clutches too hard any money he can get" in order to make himself popular among his staff by increasing their salaries and pensions.[16] Piry added that although the ministry was prepared to manage

11. Francis A. Aglen to Théophile A. Piry, June 10, 1911, SQBH; Théophile A. Piry to Robert Hart, June 12 and June 23, 1911, SQBH.

12. Enclosure 1, Shuiwuchu to Acting IG, in IG Circular 1802 / Postal No. 261, May 30, 1911, 638–39.

13. Théophile A. Piry to Francis A. Aglen, June 17, 1911, SQBH.

14. Francis A. Aglen to Théophile A. Piry, June 20, 1911, SQBH.

15. Théophile A. Piry to Francis A. Aglen, July 5, 1911, SQBH.

16. Théophile A. Piry to Robert Hart, July 11, 1911, SQBH.

the dispute, if the IPO did not get all the funding to which he believed it was entitled, he would refuse to sign his name on the final account settlements.

Although Piry lost the battle over his own pension and deferred leave payment, he did have some success in the fight over postal funds. The central government's decision was to grant the disputed Hk.Tls. 119,302.71 to the IPO, and on this occasion it was to be counted toward the overall debt. In the future, however, the funds of the six provinces were to be sent to the postmaster general's account directly, without going through the CMCS.[17] Having said that, it seems likely that the Ministry of Posts and Communications had no intention of adopting the IPO's debt and paying off the CMCS. By the time the accounts were finally settled in late August, the IPO owed the CMCS a total of Hk.Tls. 1,845,117.46, including outstanding bills to the CMCS's Statistical Department.[18] It was agreed at this point that the IPO should pay back the amount in five years, with interest; but it transpired that this did not happen, as the postal service did not make sufficient surplus for it to be possible. Consequently, the IPO continued to receive loans from the CMCS, and occasionally from the Bank of Communications (Jiaotong yinhang 交通銀行).[19] It was not until 1919 that the Post Office (Youzheng ju 郵政局, the re-branded organization and successor of the IPO as of 1912) made the first repayment to the CMCS. The final installment was paid at the end of December 1925.[20]

17. Postmaster General's Circular 267, August 2, 1911, in *Circulars Nos. 262–389*, 21, TMA, W2-2839.

18. "Youchuanbu zha zhun Youzheng zongju zongban yu zong shuiwusi zhuo ding hu ren zhi youzheng qian haiguan kuanxiang qingdan" 郵傳部扎准郵政總局總辦與總稅務司酌定互認之郵政欠海關款項清單 [Ministry of Posts and Communications approval of the arrears list of the Post Office to the Customs Service, as agreed by postmaster general and inspector general of the Customs], in *Jiaotongshi youzheng bian*, 2:886–87.

19. "Youzheng zongju xiang Jiaotong yinhang jiekuan hetong" 郵政總局向交通銀行借款合同 [Loan contract between Directorate General of Posts and Bank of Communications], in *Jiaotongshi youzheng bian*, 2:901–6.

20. "Youzheng ji qian haiguan dian kuan tan huan benxi banfabiao" 郵政積欠海關墊款攤還本息辦法表 [Post Office loan payment schedule to Customs Service, capital and interest], in *Jiaotongshi youzheng bian*, 2:892–901.

Revolution

As an arm of the state, the IPO had a long-standing role in Qing government efforts to suppress seditious material. As early as 1903 it was enacting instructions to seize prohibited newspapers, based on lists of titles provided by the government. The IPO treated the named publications as "unmailable matter." These were either returned to the senders at branch windows or set aside if found in letter boxes and then destroyed on a monthly basis. No special searches were to be carried out on sealed mail or parcels, however.[21] The pressure on the IPO from the central government increased as time went on, and postal staff were soon being asked to liaise with local officials to identify suspicious items of mail. These were to be recognized by their uniform appearance and by their arrival in quantity from abroad, often addressed to particular officials or students. In order to retain institutional integrity, postal staff were ordered not to open mail at any point but to refer content to postmasters (who were generally foreigners) at the treaty ports where mail entered China; the postmasters were instructed to bring it to the attention of local officials.[22]

As the Qing government sought to tighten the security net, additional legal provisions were introduced between 1908 and 1910. In 1908 the first Chinese press laws (*baolü* 報律) were introduced, intended to tighten controls on both domestic and foreign newspapers. Domestic newspapers were now required to register with their respective local authorities or they would be refused transportation by the IPO. Foreign newspapers containing matter contravening the press laws were to be confiscated and destroyed; the IPO worked together with the CMCS on these matters.[23] In 1910 the Regulations Governing the Detention and/or Surrender of Chinese Correspondence for the Judicial Investigation of Criminal Cases brought in even firmer policing and judicial mechanisms to manage "antisocial" content within the scope of the criminal law. Postal

21. Postal Note 25, October 7, 1903, in *Postal Notes, Nos. 1–38*, 35, TMA, W2-2833.

22. IG Circular 1579 / Postal Circular 212, December 5, 1908, in *Circulars Nos. 135–261*, 299, TMA, W2-2838.

23. IG Circular 1584 / Postal Circular 215, December 21, 1908, in *Circulars Nos. 135–261*, 303, TMA, W2-2838.

branches, from head offices to postal agencies, were required not only to confiscate problematic items but also to keep written records of their actions.[24]

In the wave of trouble in 1911 associated with the Railway Protection Movement, Sichuan was the first province to be badly affected, beginning in July. Beginning on September 7, Chengdu fell into horror due to a brutal crackdown ordered by acting governor-general Zhao Erfeng 趙爾豐 (1845–1911). The massacre "triggered an open rebellion throughout the entirety of Sichuan."[25] On October 12, W. W. Ritchie, postmaster in charge in Chengdu, reported on the situation in his area. He recorded that local postal business had been affected by the presence of rebels on the streets, and shops had little or no business. Ritchie wrote again the next day that he had learned of serious violence in the city between the Qing troops and rebels. Around three thousand rebels had been killed and forty boats captured. Communications, meanwhile, had become very difficult, and no news from any direction could be trusted. When a messenger sent by the postal branch at Guanxian, about fifty *li* (approximately thirty-one kilometers) northwest of Chengdu, arrived, he explained that he had been searched by the troops, but a letter on thin paper sewn into the band of his sleeve went undetected. The message noted that the post office at Guanxian was struggling. The rebels were occupying the county, and the post office was short of funds. News about other post offices also slowly came through; on September 27, a courier was dispatched from Rongxian, about 120 *li* (approximately seventy-four kilometers) south of Chengdu, for Jiading. The surrounding villages had already been attacked by rebels, and he had to place the mail in a temple and flee. The situation did not permit anyone to be sent to recover the bags. Ritchie learned that other post offices near Chongqing had also encountered problems: postal

24. "Yashu yin xingshi qing kouliu renfan youjian zhangcheng" 衙署因刑事請扣留人犯郵件章程 [Regulations governing the detention and/or surrender of Chinse correspondence for the judicial investigation of criminal cases], enclosure, in "Detention and/or Surrender of Chinese Criminal Correspondence: Regulations," Postal Circular 251, October 3, 1910, in *Circulars Nos. 135–261*, 518–21, TMA, W2-2838. See also "Memo of Instructions on Lists and Reports of Special Data," enclosure, in "Lists and Reports of Special Data," Postal Circular 232, January 11, 1910, in *Circulars Nos. 135–261*, 397, TMA, W2-2838.

25. Xiaowei Zheng, *The Politics of Rights*, 197, and chap. 7.

clerks had been attacked by the rebels, while many roads had been damaged. On October 15, Ritchie recorded similar situations in other places and noted that more mail services had been suspended. In Chengdu, on the order of Zhao Erfeng, troops at each city gate stopped the postal couriers, opened mail, and read letters. Although Ritchie wrote to the governor-general to protest, Zhao saw nothing wrong in it.[26]

John Patrick Donovan was stationed in Jinan at the time, and he recorded what he saw in the city and the surrounding places in Shandong that October. He noted that the situation was changing rapidly, that all sorts of rumors were rife, and that Yuan Shikai had been recalled once again from his retirement by the Qing government to manage the situation. Many post offices in the province were looted, and many postal routes ceased operating. Qing officials demanded a takeover of the postal headquarters at Jinan, as they wanted to step up censorship on the propaganda of the revolutionaries. Piry instructed Donovan to come to a temporary arrangement with the officials if possible. In the end Donovan agreed to examine any letters that looked suspicious for as long as he was still able to manage postal affairs.[27]

Compared with Shandong, post offices suffered even greater trials in the Yangtze River area, as a consequence of more severe fighting between Qing troops and the revolutionaries. In Hankou, twenty-seven postal branches out of thirty-two were destroyed, and postal staff moved to four boats moored in the river.[28] Jinan's experience of looting and route closures was also seen in the Yangtze River area, but some larger post offices managed to secure agreements to continue services, either with local officials or with the revolutionaries, as it was considered that keeping the postal service running would benefit all parties. The main principle to be observed by post offices during this time was to "remain friendly with all."[29] This meant keeping good relationships with officials, as well as the general public, and putting any political distinctions aside. Piry recom-

26. W. W. Ritchie to Théophile A. Piry, October 12, October 13, and October 15, 1911, SHAC, 137 (1) 7606.

27. John P. Donovan, "Travels and Experiences in China," 1:350–51.

28. Report (1911), 12.

29. Théophile A. Piry to J. Hinrichs, November 25, 1911, Zhejiang Provincial Archives, L090-4-104.

mended that postmasters claim strict political neutrality if they were able to, noting, "Should a request be made to you to abandon neutrality, you should diplomatically point out that the IPO is a national institution, non-political, established and working only for the benefit of China and its people . . . a public convenience, helpful alike to all parties and harmful to none and should therefore enjoy general support and protection."[30]

Although the larger post offices were in the hands of the revolutionaries in Hankou (see fig. 8.1), Nanjing, and Ningbo, mail services were eventually allowed to operate with some censorship applied.[31] Donovan was transferred to Nanjing in early 1912. He immediately visited the local republican authority there, and made the acquaintance of General Huang Xing 黃興 (1874–1916), who had just been elected president of the Provisional Government of the Republic of China. Donovan also toured inland postal branches and noted that many of them had come under attack. He reported that the damage was not as bad as he had anticipated, however, due to the coldness of the weather and the courage of the Chinese staff.[32]

J. Hinrichs, the postmaster at Ningbo, also recorded the situation in his area. Hinrichs, a German, had only been transferred to Ningbo in June 1911.[33] He said that the day after the revolutionary party had occupied Ningbo, he had quietly covered up the "Great Qing" (Da Qing 大清) characters on the signboards and replaced them with the characters for the city's name, Ningbo (寧波). He instructed other postal branches to also insert their local place-names on signage. He also reported that the Great Qing Bank (Da Qing yinhang 大清銀行) in the town had closed down, the manager having embezzled $20,000. The Post Office had more than $400 deposited with the bank, while the CMCS had almost double that amount.[34] Meanwhile, postal clerks in inland offices were worried and uneasy. Jonathan W. Innocent, the Ningbo customs commissioner

30. Théophile A. Piry to J. Hinrichs, November 6, 1911, Zhejiang Provincial Archives, L090-4-104.

31. J. Hinrichs to Théophile A. Piry, s/o/no. 17, November 15, 1911, SHAC, 137(1) 4090. For the situation in Nanjing, see Donovan, "Travels and Experiences in China," 1:353–57.

32. Donovan, "Travels and Experiences in China," 1:354.

33. Ningboshi youdianju, *Ningboshi youdian zhi*, 36.

34. J. Hinrichs to Théophile A. Piry, s/o/no. 18, November 15, 1911, SHAC, 137 (1) 4090.

FIGURE 8.1 The Customs House, Post Office, and barricades in Hankou during the Chinese Revolution of 1911. Both the Customs House, on the left, and the Post Office, on the right, with the sign reading "Great Qing Imperial Post Office" (Da Qing youzheng zongju 大清郵政總局) on the wall, were occupied by the revolutionary army in 1911. Source: Image courtesy of Joanna Dunn, Philippa Lamb, and Historical Photographs of China, University of Bristol.

and district postmaster, from time to time reassured them, telling them not to be afraid and that they should keep calm and continue with their work as usual.[35]

The momentary power vacuum provoked a variety of responses from the private letter hongs. Those in Hangzhou, Ningbo, and Shanghai came together to use the opportunity to push for an amendment of the rules in their favor, ceasing to hand in their mailbags to the Post Office and writing to the provisional Ningbo martial government pressuring for change. In their letter, they argued that now that the country was returned to the "Great Han nation," they did not see why they should continue to obey the rules made by the previous tyrannical Manchu government. They said that instead of reentering the "tiger's mouth" (meaning returning to the restrictions imposed on them by the IPO), they were determined to save their industry by taking charge of their own mail deliveries.[36] In other places—notably, Anqing and Zhenjiang—private letter hongs issued statements using such terms as *republic* (*gonghe* 共和) and *liberty* (*ziyou* 自由), claiming they should have freedom to transmit mail without the existing restrictions.[37] Ultimately these efforts were short-lived and unsuccessful, as they were not supported by the provisional governments nor taken up by the Republican leadership.[38]

Services in other provinces were also affected by riots and fighting. A postmaster in Xi'an was wounded, while Guangdong and Henan reported that money order services had been interrupted and parcels lost. With communications broken, the chiefs of postal districts had to make their own decisions on how to cope with the situation. To lessen the risks

35. J. Hinrichs to Théophile A. Piry, s/o/no. 23, November 30, 1911, SHAC, 137 (1) 4090.

36. "Ningbo jun zhengfu waijiao jian jiaotong buzhang zhi han youzhengju" 寧波軍政府外交兼交通部長致函郵政局 [Minister of foreign affairs and communications of the Ningbo military government to post office], enclosure, in J. Hinrichs to Théophile A. Piry, December 23, 1911, SHAC, 137 (1) 4090.

37. "Ge sheng xin ye lianhe hui bing" 各省信業聯合會禀 [Joint petition by private letter hongs of various provinces], 1912 [?], SHAC, 137 (2) 315.

38. "Ningbo jun zhengfu waijiao jian jiaotong buzhang zhi han youzhengju," December 23, 1911. See also Postmaster General's Circular 286, April 11, 1912, in *Circulars Nos. 262–389*, 87–88, TMA, W2-2839. For how private letter hongs tried to break away from the control of the IPO in 1911, see Harris, "The Post Office and State Formation," 149–51.

of total loss, some Chinese postal clerks divided postal funds and postage stamps among themselves, burying them underground.[39]

As 1912 progressed, the situation was gradually brought under control, even if only temporarily. In the words of John Jordan, the British minister to China at the time, neither Yuan Shikai nor the revolutionaries had "much stomach to fight." Both Sun Yat-sen (1866–1925) and Yuan Shikai were competing for support from foreign countries. For the British, it was very important to restore order as soon as possible so that the CMCS operation of securing funding for loan repayments and indemnities would not be affected too much. As the leader favored by both the British government and the main international syndicates who had investments in China, Yuan Shikai was able to put pressure on the revolutionaries and held talks in Beijing.[40] He was elected as the provisional president on February 14. Pointing out that moving the capital south would leave the north vulnerable to both internal uprising and aggression from Japan and Russia, Yuan persuaded the Nanjing delegation to agree to his remaining in Beijing.[41]

For Yuan Shikai in the aftermath of the revolution, perhaps the most difficult challenge was to unify the country, as local generals had taken charge in their own territories.[42] Compared with this fragmented situation, reorganization of the central government in Beijing was relatively easy: thanks to the extensive reforms enacted toward the end of Qing rule, the bureaucratic structure of central government was already in good shape under the New Policies and with preparations for a constitutional monarchy. In December 1911, Yuan Shikai had instructed the provisional government in Beijing that the administration should maintain its existing structure.[43] This principle was adopted by the entire Beiyang government between 1912 and 1927. The old Ministry of Posts and Communications was given a new name: Ministry of Communications (Jiaotongbu 交通部), but its staff continued to work in the same

39. Report (1911), 2–3.
40. Van de Ven, *Breaking with the Past*, 163, 164–67.
41. Jerome Chen, *Yuan Shih-Kai*, 106–7.
42. Jerome Chen, *Yuan Shih-Kai*, 110–11.
43. "Linshi gonghe zhengfu Yuan bugao neiwai daxiao wenwu guanya" 臨時共和政府袁布告內 外大小文武官銜 [Provisional republican government Yuan notice to civil and military offices at all levels], December 26, 1911, in *Linshi gongbao*, 11.

buildings.[44] Shi Zhaoji 施肇基 (1877–1958, known also as Alfred Sao-ke Sze), the new head, was a familiar face as he had joined the old ministry back in 1906, and most of the subsequent directors shared a similar background. In February 1912, Piry was able to issue announcements on how to move the postal service forward under the new political regime. He minimized the change as much as possible, and most routine practice remained the same.[45]

In order to cope with the uncertainty caused by the disunited north and south, and to avoid waste, the existing postage stamps continued to be used with temporary surcharge marks printed on top. The first surcharge mark introduced consisted of the four characters *lin shi zhong li* 臨時中立, meaning "provisional neutrality."[46] Sun Yat-sen was not pleased by the wording of this mark, as it did not spell out the name of the new country, so a second surcharge mark was added vertically; this had four characters, *Zhong hua min guo* 中華民國, meaning "Chinese Republic" (see fig. 8.2).[47] Sun Yat-sen was still displeased by the combination of the two surcharge marks as he felt the first mark, "provisional neutrality," represented something of an assault on the newly established republic. He wrote to Yuan Shikai about this, and the stamps with the "provisional neutrality" characters were withdrawn, with all the stamps remaining in use bearing only the vertically stamped characters for the Chinese Republic. Newly designed replacement postage stamps, printed by the company Waterlow in London, did not arrive until May 1913 and were gradually released to postal districts; the old stamps with the surcharge mark remained in use until exhausted.[48]

---

44. "Jiaotongbu tongxing ge bu yuan deng chu ben bu ji zai jiu Youchuanbu ban-gong wen" 交通部通行各部院等處本部即在舊郵傳部辦公文 [The Ministry of Communications informs all departments and offices that the ministry still operates on the site of the old Ministry of Posts and Communications], April 23, 1912, in *Linshi gongbao*, 343. See also Postmaster's Circular 297, December 3, 1912, in *Circulars Nos. 262–389*, 108, TMA, W2-2839.

45. "Memorandum of Instructions," enclosure, in Postmaster's Circular 280, February 16, 1912, in *Circulars Nos. 262–389*, 75, TMA, W2-2839.

46. Report (1911), 3–4.

47. Postmaster's Circular 284, March 23, 1912, in *Circulars Nos. 262–389*, 80, TMA, W2-2839.

48. Postmaster's Circular 282, February 22, 1912, in *Circulars Nos. 262–389*, 77, TMA, W2-2839; Postmaster's Circular 315, May 31, 1913, in *Circulars Nos. 262–389*, 230,

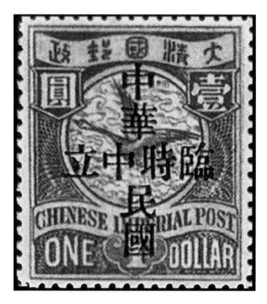

FIGURE 8.2 An over-printed postage stamp temporarily used after the Chinese Revolution of 1911. On this one-dollar IPO stamp, the original red Chinese characters on the top horizontally read as "Da Qing guo you zheng," meaning "the Post Office of the Great Qing." The crossed surcharge added on reads vertically "Zhong hua min guo" (the Republic of China), and horizontally "Lin shi zhong li" (provisional neutrality). Source: Jiaotongbu youzheng zongju, *Zhongguo youpiao mulu* 中國郵票目錄: 12.

Reflecting on the events of 1911, the "Report on the Working of the Chinese Post Office" of 1911 summarized the situation: "The Post Office . . . stood its ground, and, to the advantage of the Service and public alike, all parties shortly realised the inexpediency of interference, and the Post Office preserved inviolate its independence. The centuries-old Imperial dragon standard gave place to the five-barred flag of the Republic of China; but the Post Office, as before, went on."[49]

TMA, W2-2839; Yanxing [Pan Ansheng], *Zhonghua youzheng fazhan shi*, 395; *Hongyinhua youpiao*, 2:379.

49. Report (1911), 1–2.

This was not the whole story, however, as the Post Office was now attached to a new weak central government, and this had an impact on the postal service. One of the main challenges facing the republican administration was to demonstrate that it could bring together the Chinese nation and dutifully meet its financial commitments as set out in existing treaties with foreign countries. In his first speech to the Provisional Senate (Canyiyuan 參議院) in Beijing, Yuan Shikai claimed he had the support of the "five races" of the country, as well as friendly foreign countries, and that his government would have the ability to accumulate sufficient funds to pay outstanding indemnities and loans.[50] But although no one wanted to cast doubt openly on the financial situation, it appeared unlikely that Yuan would be able to quickly assert control over the whole country, particularly in those places where he did not have loyal troops stationed. Meanwhile, neither Britain nor Russia was willing to recognize the new republic unless Yuan compromised over territories they considered to be in their sphere of interest—respectively, Outer Mongolia and Tibet.[51]

This evolving situation seriously challenged the presence of the Post Office in Outer Mongolia and Tibet. Histories, local and geopolitical tensions, and indeed eventual outcomes were different between these two territories; but when examined together, their stories illuminate the role of the Post Office within China's notion of sovereignty. They also reveal something extraordinary about the realities of postal expansion at the furthest extremes of distance, inhospitable terrain, and sparsity of population.

Disconnection: Tibet

According to the Seven Year Plan published in 1910, the Post Office was not originally due to arrive in Tibet until 1914, but this was very soon followed by a requirement to accelerate the timetable. For the Post

50. Yuan Shikai, "Zai Canyiyuan kai yuan li shang yanshuo ci" 在參議院開院禮上演説詞 [Speech at the inauguration of the provisional senate], April 29, 1912, in *Yuan Shikai quanji*, 19:752–53.

51. Jerome Chen, *Yuan Shih-k'ai*, 140–43.

Office, however, the method of expansion to Tibet was rather different from any previously employed. In normal circumstances, postal routes over distance were expanded point-to-point from existing postal locations, each new main point typically becoming its own local hub as well as a base for the next point-to-point expansion. A normal expectation would have been that existing routes from Sichuan would be extended to Lhasa, and on to other Tibetan destinations. But this was not the case in Tibet, where postal routes were instead constructed by working backward from a very small, obscure CMCS post named Yadong. Situated at the border between Sikkim and Tibet, the Yadong Customs House was established in 1894. Working back from Yadong, the stretch of the route connecting to Tibet and Sichuan, and hence to the rest of China, was completed in 1911, though it was only in operation for a few months. The way this route was constructed, and then so soon disconnected, reflected not only the weakness of Beijing's rule over Tibet (whether Qing or republican) but also the unique geopolitics in the area.

Political Background and Yadong

The Yadong Customs Station's coming into being was a consequence of the Sikkim-Tibet Convention of 1890 and subsequent agreements signed in 1893. Between its opening and its withdrawal in 1914, this Customs station never collected a single tariff payment. The establishment of Yadong as a trading post illustrates the complex interweaving of interests in the region between Britain, Qing China, India, and Tibet. Britain had for years sought trade between Sikkim and Tibet, particularly for the "fledgling Indian tea industry," but the opening up of the tea trade was resisted by both Tibetan authorities and Qing officials, particularly those in Sichuan, which was a large supplier of teas consumed in Tibet.[52]

In the earlier part of the nineteenth century, Sikkim paid tribute to Tibet, while China was Tibet's suzerain. In 1888 the British Army occupied Sikkim and it became a British protectorate. Their troops were defeated, and the Tibetan authorities asked Beijing to intervene. When the Zongli Yamen turned to Robert Hart for advice, he recommended his

52. Booz, "Fear of Indian Tea," 279.

brother, James, to lead negotiations on China's behalf. James had joined the CMCS in 1867. When Robert was considering taking up the post of British minister to China in 1885, James was regarded as his ideal successor as inspector general, both by Robert Hart himself and by the British legation.[53] James Hart's Sikkim mission was originally expected to be a short assignment, but he ended up staying in Darjeeling, in the north of Sikkim, for five years. Most of the time he stayed in an establishment called the Woodlands Hotel, where he was able to conveniently access telegraph facilities.[54] From the inspector general's perspective, the most important task was to maintain peace between Britain and China, and to prevent further military conflict between British India and China.[55] Hart noted that Beijing did not necessarily seek to challenge Britain's position in instituting a protectorate over Sikkim, but he instructed James that what must be avoided was any wording that would cause Beijing embarrassment or loss of face.[56]

Location of the proposed trading post was a significant issue during the lengthy negotiations. The British preferred Pagri (also recorded as Pharijong or Phagri), but this was rejected by Lhasa, so when the convention was signed in 1890, the trading post location was yet to be decided.[57] Pagri was an important town both militarily and for trade, and was the northern gateway to the Chumbi Valley, which, with its mild climate, was the most habitable place in the border area between Bhutan, Sikkim, and Tibet.[58] Tibetan officials strongly rejected the idea of Pagri, as a tariff station had already been set up there, and they refused to let

53. Chen Shiqi, *Zhongguo jindai haiguanshi*, 307.

54. James Hart to IG, April 21, 1889, in *Xizang Yadongguan dangan*, 1:23.

55. Robert Hart to James Duncan Campbell, letter 707, July 7, 1889, in *The IG*, 1:752; Robert Hart to James Duncan Campbell, letter 731, December 22, 1889, in *The IG*, 1:775.

56. IG to James Hart, telegram 19, May 9, 1889, in *Xizang Yadongguan dangan*, 1:28.

57. Article IV of the Sikkim-Tibet Convention states, "The question of providing increased facilities for trade across the Sikkim-Tibet frontier will hereafter be discussed with a view to a mutually satisfactory arrangement by the High Contracting Powers"; Sikkim-Tibet Convention, 1890, signed in Calcutta on March 17, 1890, and ratified in London on August 17, 1890, in *Zhong wai jiu yuezhang*, 3:1183.

58. Lü Qiuwen, *Zhong Ying Xizang jiaoshe*, 38; Macdonald, *Twenty Years in Tibet*, 50–52.

the CMCS take it over.[59] In 1889, Yadong was suggested by Shengtai 升泰, the *amban*, or Qing imperial resident (*banshi dachen* 辦事大臣), based in Lhasa, but no agreement was reached at that stage. Around ten *li* (around 6.2 kilometers) east of Yadong was Renjingang (Rinchinggong, 仁進岡), a more substantial town where Chinese officials and Tibetan troops were stationed. From Renjingang it was possible to travel a further 160 *li* (around ninety-nine kilometers) north to reach Pagri. The idea of Yadong was included in a proposal in May 1891, and its selection was a compromise agreed upon toward the end of negotiations.[60] Although Yadong was close to the border with Sikkim, it was a small village with very poor facilities. Available flat ground was limited, and its climate was more severe than that of Pagri. To James Hart's eyes, it was a deserted place.[61]

Originally, Robert Hart did not anticipate that the Qing government would want to have a Customs station in this location. Both Britain and its administration in India wanted to trade tea, but neither China nor Tibet agreed, as they both wanted to maintain the existing tea trade from Sichuan. The gradual realization that a Customs station had become a possibility was a surprise to Hart. He was doubtful as to how realistic it would be to open trade between India and Tibet, in part because of the difficult location, but also because of the ongoing prohibition on Indian tea.[62] But he then saw that the primary motivation for the Zongli Yamen wanting to set up a Customs station in Yadong was not the collection of tariffs but the guarding of sovereignty, as well as to encourage Tibet to open up (see fig. 8.3).[63] In a letter to James Duncan Campbell, he wrote, "It is amusing to have in my time planted the Customs at Hongkong (England), Macao (Portugal), Mengtszu (Yunnan), Lungchow

59. Robert Hart to James Duncan Campbell, letter 801, June 19, 1891, in *The IG*, 2:848.

60. Lü Qiuwen, *Zhong Ying Xizang jiaoshe*, 29; James Hart to IG, telegram 113, May 11, 1891, in *Xizang Yadongguan dangan*, 1:163.

61. James Hart to IG, telegram 26, July 9, 1889, in *Xizang Yadongguan dangan*, 1:40.

62. Robert Hart to James Duncan Campbell, letter 779, November 23, 1890, in *The IG*, 1:822; Robert Hart to James Duncan Campbell, letter 786, January 27, 1891, in *The IG*, 2:832; Robert Hart to James Duncan Campbell, letter 851, August 7, 1891, in *The IG*, 2: 897.

63. IG to James Hart, telegram 139, July 23, 1891, in *Xizang Yadongguan dangan*, 1:176; IG to James Hart, telegram 146, October 20, 1891, in *Xizang Yadongguan dangan*, 1:184.

FIGURE 8.3 The Chinese Customs House in Yadong, late nineteenth century. The Customs House was outside the village, and Chinese and Tibetan officials lived there. Customs staff were not allowed to enter the village to purchase food supplies without permission. Source: Annie R. Taylor, *Pioneering in Tibet*. Acknowledgment to Jamie Carstairs for improving the image quality.

(Kwangsi), Chungking (Szechuan), Seoul, etc. (Corea) and now Yatung (Tibet)! We have helped to keep China quiet and the dynasty on its legs, and I hope this is something: for otherwise I don't see much in return for all the work done and thought expended on it."[64]

Trading efforts with Tibet consistently came to nothing, and the British began to run out of patience. Not without warning, as the situation had been difficult for some time, in 1903 Francis Younghusband (1863–1942) marched troops into the Chumbi Valley; his expedition reached Lhasa in 1904. In his memoir, Younghusband noted how little effort was made by Qing officials to engage with Tibetan communities, in particular taking little trouble to learn the Tibetan language. In his view, the Qing officials were more concerned with how soon they might be able to

64. Robert Hart to James Duncan Campbell, letter 915, January 8, 1894, in *The IG*, 2:957.

return to their own civilized country.[65] Imperial failures over Tibet are also documented by Chinese sources. Taking Ding Baozhen 丁寶楨, Sichuan governor between 1876 and 1886, as an example, historian Feng Mingzhu stresses how high-ranking officials at the frontier not only failed to deliver the policies of the central government but also worsened the trust between Beijing and Lhasa. Youtai 有泰, the *amban* from 1902 to 1906, refused to bring the Qing military to engage with Younghusband's troops at both Jiangzi (Gyantse) and Lhasa, deliberately forcing the Dalai Lama the 13th to come to the negotiating table, something he had been resisting for a lengthy period.[66] W. Randall McDonnell Parr, the Customs commissioner at Yadong who was on a special mission to assist Youtai at the time, witnessed how Younghusband's troops brutally killed many Tibetans between Tuna and Guru using artillery, machine guns, rifles, and kukris. The heaps of dead bodies showed this was not a war but a massacre.[67]

The Convention between Great Britain and Tibet was signed in September 1904 without the signature of any Qing official. In the treaty, Gartok (present-day Garyarsa), Jiangzi, and Yadong were nominated as trade marts, and British troops would continue to be stationed at Chumbi until these were set up and associated indemnities paid off by Tibet.[68] In order to secure its sovereignty and have British troops withdraw from Chumbi sooner, the Qing government began a series of negotiations with the British. In 1906 Britain agreed to let the Qing government pay off the indemnities for Tibet within three years, and in January 1908 the British government ordered its troops to leave Chumbi after receiving the final payment.[69] As a result of this development, the Agreement between Great Britain, China and Tibet Amending Trade Regulations of 1893 was signed in April 1908 in Calcutta.

For Britain this new agreement meant the further opening up of Tibet, and it made the British presence in the area more secure, particu-

65. Younghusband, *India and Tibet*, 322.

66. Feng Mingzhu, *Zhong Ying Xizang jiaoshe yu Chuan Zang*, 104–15, 128–31.

67. W. Randall McDonnell Parr to Robert Hart, April 15, 1904, in *Xizang Yadongguan dangan*, 2:940.

68. Ying Zang tiaoyue 英藏條約 [Convention between Great Britain and Tibet (1904)], Appendix 3, Articles II and VII, in Feng Mingzhu, *Zhong Ying Xizang jiaoshe yu Chuan Zang*, 410–11.

69. Lü Qiuwen, *Zhong Ying Xizang jiaoshe*, 105–7.

larly after Britain's special interest in Tibet was recognized by Russia in 1907.[70] For the Qing government, the withdrawal of British troops gave the opportunity for Tibet to be incorporated into the New Policies and reorganizations to be carried out at other peripheries. To achieve this, the central government made sure it had the right people to implement the policies, and Zhang Yintang 張蔭棠 (1864–1937) was appointed as a new assistant imperial resident. He was eager to put in place a program of reform, similar to what had been done in Mongolia and Manchuria.[71] In the new 1908 agreement, both telegraph lines and postal service were addressed, and this had direct impact on the postal arrangements and on the issue of sovereignty in the period immediately following.

While Article VI of the agreement focused on the telegraph, Article VIII was on postal matters:

> The British Trade Agents at the various trade marts now or hereafter to be established in Tibet may make arrangements for the carriage and transmission of their posts to and from the frontier of India. The couriers employed in conveying these posts shall receive all possible assistance from the local authorities whose districts they traverse and shall be accorded the same protection as the persons employed in carrying the despatches of the Tibetan Authorities. When efficient arrangements have been made by China in Tibet for a postal service, the question of the abolition of the Trade Agents' couriers will be taken into consideration by Great Britain and China.[72]

When the British troops entered Tibet, they brought their field post offices with them. The field post offices were part of the British-run Indian Post Office, and acted as suboffices at the frontiers, while base post offices were equal to head offices.[73] After the withdrawal of British troops from Chumbi, the field post offices did not leave Tibet, as the IPO was yet to be established in the area.[74] Against this background, Bredon, now

70. Younghusband, *India and Tibet*, 378.

71. Feng Mingzhu, *Zhong Ying Xizang jiaoshe yu Chuan Zang*, 177–82.

72. "Appendix VI: Agreement between Great Britain, China and Tibet Amending Trade Regulations in Tibet, of 5 December 1893. Signed at Calcutta, 20 April 1908," in Lamb, *The McMahon Line*, 1:262.

73. Virk, *Postal History*, 9.

74. Zhang Yutang to IG (Robert Bredon), January 28, 1909, in *Xizang Yadongguan dangan*, 2:1059; Zhang Yutang to IG (Robert Bredon), November 18, 1909, in *Xizang*

acting inspector general, was ordered to introduce post offices to Tibet. Zhang Yutang 張玉堂, the first native Chinese to hold the position of Customs commissioner for the CMCS, began the initial investigation and preparations at Yadong.[75] It should be noticed that prior to the arrival of the British field post offices, the Tibetan relay system was a highly profitable business for the staff and messengers associated with the department of the Qing imperial resident, due to the latter's control of relay station resources. Relay system staff could also be bribed to carry private mail.[76]

Postal Connections between Tibet and Western Sichuan

In order to manage challenging conditions in this unknown territory, Piry decided to send Deng Weiping there to set up post offices. Deng Weiping, no doubt one of the most experienced inspecting clerks, had also recently passed the English test, after having previously learned French.[77] He arrived at Yadong in December 1909 and started his tour to Jiangzi and Lhasa in February of the following year. For Deng, the most essential work included talking to local officials in these places and training up courier teams, which constituted at least twenty Han Chinese soldiers and a hundred Tibetan soldiers.[78] In addition, Piry also sent twenty trunks of postal stationery from the CMCS Statistical Department in Shanghai, and a junior Chinese postal clerk was transferred from Canton to assist Deng.[79] Wang Chug Tsering 王曲策忍, a Tibetan who had joined the Yadong Customs station in 1894 and spoke Hindi, Nepalese, and Tibetan, was also assigned to learn about the provision of postal services.[80]

Yadongguan dangan, 2:1098. The field post offices did not leave Tibet until the outbreak of the First World War in 1914; see Virk, *Postal History*, 37.

75. Zhang Yutang to IG (Robert Bredon), May 26, 1908, in *Xizang Yadongguan dangan*, 2:1035.

76. Maurer, "The Tibetan Governmental Transport," 7–10.

77. Zhang Yutang to IG (Robert Bredon), December 31, 1909, in *Xizang Yadongguan dangan*, 2:1105. For Deng Weiping's qualification, see *Service List (1909)*, 194.

78. Wang Chug Tsering to IG (Aglen), June 15, 1910, in *Xizang Yadongguan dangan*, 2:1135.

79. Zhang Yutang to IG (Robert Bredon), December 31, 1909, in *Xizang Yadongguan dangan*, 2:1105–6. Théophile A. Piry to Zhang Yutang, January 18, 1910, in *Xizang Yadongguan dangan*, 2:1110.

80. For Wang Chug Tsering's background, see *Service List (1905)*, 80.

As mentioned earlier, the customary and indeed most direct way to connect new postal routes in Tibet to the rest of the IPO's network would have been to extend through the border with Sichuan via Chengdu, then on to Lhasa and other important connections; but this seemingly logical approach was not feasible in this case. First, the IPO had to start from Yadong and build a postal route to Lhasa. Second, while military relay stations were in place between Chengdu and Lhasa, given the political tensions after 1908 at the border of Sichuan and Tibet, it was not possible for these to be adopted by the IPO in a straightforward manner. Instead, the IPO routes had to be constructed using a mix of approaches, partly by creating new connections, and partly—after Deng Weiping's arrival—incorporating some of the military relay stations.

According to Annie Taylor (1855–1922), a member of the Tibet Pioneer Christian Mission and also a somewhat unfriendly neighbor to successive Customs commissioners at Yadong, there were three highways from China's borders to Lhasa. The first one was from Chengdu to Yazhou to Dajianlu (present-day Kangding) to Litang to Batang to Chamdo (present-day Changdu) and then to the border with Tibet.[81] This route had been used by the official military relay system from the time of the reign of Emperor Kangxi. The second route, called the Tea Road, was from Dajianlu to Naqu (Nag-chu-ka) to connect with Lhasa. The third was from Xining, at the southeast corner of Gansu, to Naqu, and on to Lhasa.[82] This was a famous caravan route, and Naqu was one of the main gateways for Lhasa; foreigners had to wait there until they got permission to enter Lhasa.[83] Of the three routes, the official one was the shortest, and had many rest houses along the route, but it was also the most mountainous. The Xining caravan route was the longest, but least mountainous. Horses, mules, and yaks were the most typical forms of transportation on all of these routes.[84]

With these options in mind, the one used by the IPO in 1910–11 was the first, starting from Chengdu. But before examining how the postal

---

81. Taylor, *Pioneering in Tibet*, 37; "Yizhan lucheng" 驛站路程 [Postal routes of the military relay courier system], in *Jue zhi quan lan*, 40–41.

82. Taylor, *Pioneering in Tibet*, 37–38.

83. Charles Alfred Bell, *The People of Tibet*, 122–24.

84. Taylor, *Pioneering in Tibet*, 39.

connection was constructed between Chengdu and Yadong via Lhasa, it is worth exploring the early work of the IPO in Chengdu. Compared with other provinces, the growth of IPO mail volumes in Sichuan was slow despite its large population and generally prosperous economy, the main reason being the prevalence of traditional customs and continuing use of private letter hongs, which were well-rooted in the province.[85] Yang Shaoquan 楊少荃 (Yang Shao-Chien, 1862–1943), who came from a Christian family in Hubei and who joined the IPO in 1900, provided a firsthand account of the situation in Chengdu and the surrounding areas. Yang spoke English, Northern Mandarin, Southern Mandarin, and Western Mandarin and was rapidly promoted to inspecting clerk in 1904. Even given his fast-track promotion, Yang did not feel this was a career for him, as the limitations imposed by the organization were too heavy. In his view, this type of job was well suited to younger men because he saw that a postal career provided good training in character building, requiring development of important characteristics such as honesty, punctuality, efficiency, and cleanliness. But after several years of running between far-flung places to open post offices, the work became for him "rather mechanical, with little opportunity for personal initiative."[86] He left the postal service in 1906 and worked with a Quaker missionary, Rev. Robert John Davidson, in education. Yang joined the West China Border Research Society in 1930, and was its vice president and then president between 1934 and 1936.[87]

When Yang Shaoquan arrived in Chengdu with his wife and son in late 1901, he saw that the only newspapers were those arriving occasionally from Shanghai. There were only a few schools, and some of those were founded by missionaries. As usual, the first task was to find a place to rent for the post office. He tried locations near two temples, but nothing was suitable. He also tried commercial streets, but his efforts were in vain as the IPO did not want to pay a deposit. Through a new acquaintance, Yang finally secured a small house from which to open the first post office in Chengdu (see fig. 8.4). The next challenge was to find people

85. Report (1906), 67.

86. Yang, "The Beginning of the Chinese Post Office in Szechwan," 11.

87. For Yang Shaoquan's background, see *Service List (1902)*, 159. See also Zhou Shurong, *Faxian bianjiang*, 65.

FIGURE 8.4 Chengdu's first post office, filmed in 1902. On the right is an assistant postal officer named Newman, sent to Chengdu in the spring of 1902 to establish the use of letter boxes. The dark-colored boxes in front are letter boxes; signboards carrying the Chinese characters for "postal letter box" (*youzheng xingui* 郵政信櫃) are laid on the ground on both sides. Both sets of items were IPO property, to be placed under the care of postal agencies. Were the engagement to cease, the items were to be returned to the IPO. Source: Shaoquan Yang, "The Beginning of the Chinese Post Office in Szechwan."

to employ. Again he had limited luck, but he eventually managed to recruit two people, one for indoor clerical work, and one postman. Mail was sent to Chongqing twice a week.[88] He noted that the locals customarily used private letter hongs coming from Chongqing (referred to as *dabang* 大幫), and had never heard of the IPO.

88. Yang, "The Beginning of the Chinese Post Office in Szechwan," 7–9. Yang recorded that him and his family departed Chongqing for Chengdu in October 1901.

In 1902 Yang Shaoquan focused on adding a postal connection with Gansu, and on developing further extensions to the west of Chengdu. He observed that people were very conservative outside Chengdu. He traveled to Yazhou and set up a postal connection to link with Chengdu. From Yazhou, he headed to Dajianlu, and found the journey extremely difficult because of bad roads and cold weather. He and his companion were unable to buy rice along the trip, and had to carry their own. By the end of 1902, the IPO had its very own Chengdu–Yazhou–Dajianlu route, which became a vital link years later when Deng Weiping sought to connect Lhasa with Chengdu.[89] Figure 8.5 shows that, by 1907, the postal route at the Sichuan border had not advanced further from Dajianlu since 1902.

To connect Chengdu with Lhasa, the route between Dajianlu, Batang, and Chamdo had to be in place, but a series of upheavals between 1902 and 1906 prevented further extensions. Given the increasingly fragile political situation in Tibet, the Qing government sought to strengthen its control over Tibetan inhabitants at the Sichuan-Tibet borders. From 1902 onward it made attempts to replace the centuries-old native chieftain system with a centrally appointed official. Despite strong resistance from local populations, Zhao Erfeng led a military campaign that brought new rules and a new administrative structure to Batang in 1906 and to Chamdo in 1909.[90] Zhao, then the border commissioner of the provinces of Sichuan and Yunnan (Chuan Dian bianwu dachen 川滇邊務大臣), was promoted to assistant imperial resident to Tibet in March 1908 while still retaining his original position. He enlarged his military force, which caused great concern among the Tibetans. The new administrative arrangement once again demonstrated the Qing government's determination to exercise control over its peripheral areas in the New Policies era. What followed Zhao's successful military campaign were land reforms, mining, and other industries, as well as new educational institutions.[91] As a consequence, official postal services became an urgent requirement across the large border area.

89. Yang, "The Beginning of the Chinese Post Office in Szechwan," 10.

90. Feng Mingzhu, *Zhong Ying Xizang jiaoshe yu Chuan Zang*, 128–31, 186–91, 215–16; Younghusband, *India and Tibet*, 372–75.

91. Xiuyu Wang, *China's Last Imperial Frontier*, 161–62, 220–25.

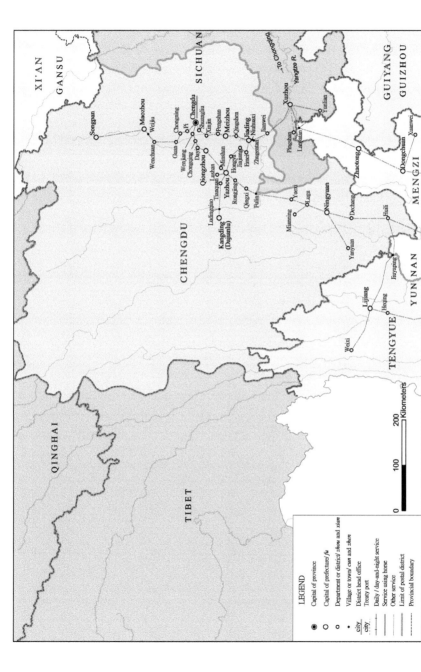

FIGURE 8.5 A postal map of eastern Tibet and western Sichuan, 1907: routes between Chengdu and Dajianlu in western Sichuan province in 1907. The postal routes had not been extended west from Dajianlu since 1902. Map © Weipin Tsai; cartography by Huang Chingchi.

With the support of the imperial resident Lianyu 聯豫, Qing military troops entered Lhasa in February 1910.[92] By May the postal route between Yadong and Lhasa was up and running.[93] (See fig. 8.6.) This was a period of wider disturbance, and by the time the service was initiated, the Thirteenth Dalai Lama had already fled from Lhasa and settled in Darjeeling. By the end of 1910, the IPO had established branches in Yadong, Jiangzi, Shigatse, Pagri, and Lhasaand, and 23,600 articles had been handled by the service. The IPO's mounted couriers collaborated with military relay personnel, and on average traveled 200 *li* (approx. 124 kilometers) per day. The Yadong–Lhasa line was about 1,300 *li* (approx. 805 kilometers) in length, and it took the couriers six days to complete this stretch; it only took one day for the Jiangzi–Shigatse segment.[94] Although Gartok was also a trade mart, it was on the far western side of Tibet and out of the way from the Chumbi Valley, Jiangzi, Lhasa, and Yadong. A decision was taken to leave Gartok out of current planning, as the field post office there already provided service to connect with Siliguri.[95]

The Lhasa–Chambo line to eastern Tibet was connected later in 1910, while the Dajianlu–Batang line in western Sichuan was completed in early 1911. To fully join up the service at the borders, the 1,200-*li* (approx. 743 kilometers) Chambo–Batang line was also completed soon afterward. This meant that a Beijing–Lhasa postal route, estimated at fifty to fifty-five days, was now joined up without any gaps: Beijing to Chengdu, fifteen or sixteen days; Chengdu to Dajianlu, five to seven days; Dajianlu to Batang, nine days; and Batang to Chamdo to Lhasa, twenty days.[96] Such a lengthy transit time could be considered impractical, however, as the Indian routes via Calcutta by sea could connect Beijing and Lhasa in forty to forty-five days.[97] For important communications, the telegraph

92. Younghusband, *India and Tibet*, 390.

93. Zhang Yutang, "Annual Trade Report for Yadong Port for Xuantong 2nd year (1910)," February 25, 1911, in *Xizang Yadongguan dangan*, 2:1163.

94. Report (1910), 11, 16.

95. Zhang Yutang to IG, January 28, 1909, in *Xizang Yadongguan dangan*, 2:1059.

96. This estimated figure was given in Report (1910), 1. For the breakdown figures for different stretches, see Report (1911), 12–13. For the travel time for the Chengdu–Dajianlu line, see Liu Yuan, Ye Yushun, and Ah Wang Dan Zeng, *Zhongguo Xizang youzheng youpiaoshi*, 26–27.

97. Report (1910), 1.

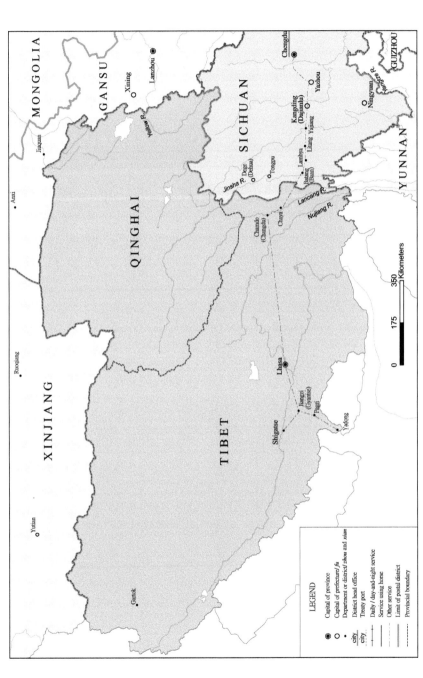

FIGURE 8.6 A postal map of Tibet, 1911, showing connections between Yadong, Lhasa, and Chengdu. Map © Weipin Tsai; cartography by Huang Chingchi.

was an option: in 1899, telegrams took five to seven days to reach Beijing from Yadong (including personal delivery from Rhenock to Yadong) when weather permitted.[98] In 1911 Tibet became a distinct postal district, and the post office in Lhasa even provided a money order service.[99] Deng Weiping was appointed postmaster in Lhasa, the first Chinese postmaster for an entire postal district. In 1911 the numbers of articles dealt with in this district rose to fifty thousand.[100] But with the winds of revolution blowing into Sichuan in October of that year, postal arrangements were soon affected.

On November 27, 1911, Customs commissioner Zhang Yutang reported on chaos caused by Chinese soldiers who were swarming into Tibet from Sichuan. Rather than being ordered there or indeed driven by any political motivation, the soldiers were acting out of desperation, having gone unpaid for months. They looted Lhasa and Jiangzi; Lianyu was captured, and one of his Chinese assistants was killed. Believing Zhang Yutang would have a substantial amount of money in his possession because of his position, some of these soldiers planned to attack the Customs House and murder him on November 20. Fortunately, Zhang received a tip-off late the night before. Having been awakened from sleep, Zhang and his two staff equipped themselves with weapons. They packed up the telegraph code notebook, cash, and some valuables, and abandoned the Customs House. In the dark they jumped on horses and fled to the Chumbi Valley to seek refuge within the British Trade Agency, arriving there before dawn.[101] Shortly afterward, Deng Weiping also retreated from Lhasa and joined Zhang. On December 1, under the protection of several junior British officers, they managed to cross the border and enter Darjeeling in disguise.[102]

In June 1912 Yuan Shikai sent troops to the border and planned to advance on Tibet. Aware at this time that Yuan Shikai's government was

98. P. H. S. Montgomery to IG, March 6, 1899, in *Xizang Yadongguan dangan*, 2:656.

99. "Appendix B: List of Head, Branch, and Inland Post Offices Arranged under Districts," in Report (1910), 26.

100. Report (1910), 11.

101. Zhang Yutang to IG (Aglen), November 27, 1911, in *Xizang Yadongguan dangan*, 2:1186–87. See also Macdonald, *Twenty Years in Tibet*, 79.

102. Wang Chug Tsering to IG, December 5, 1911, in *Xizang Yadongguan dangan*, 2:1188.

also being pressured by Russians over the situation in Mongolia and Xinjiang, London also exploited Yuan Shikai's desire to receive recognition from Britain. The *Times* had a good description of the strategy employed by Westminster to put pressure on Yuan Shikai: "The Chinese Republic has been plainly warned that it will not be recognized by the British Government until it undertakes to respect the autonomy of Tibet, in accordance with well-understood treaty obligations."[103] John Jordan also threatened that a further military campaign might risk British willingness to provide further loans. Jordan's action had the necessary effect, and the campaign ended soon afterward.[104]

In the eyes of many old China hands from Britain, Yuan Shikai was a strongman. As J. O. P. Bland, an influential British journalist who had previously worked for the CMCS, described him, "Yuan, as President, proved himself a past-master in all the arts of mandarin intrigue: expert in opportunism, prudent in counsel, of many devices; a very Ulysses for stratagem, unwavering in the execution of his plans."[105] Yet even a man like Yuan had, sometimes, to pull back. Chinese troops completely withdrew from Tibet in November 1912, and in the meantime, negotiations between Britain and China had been progressing. Yuan Shikai wanted to bring Tibet into the Chinese republic under a claim of sovereignty; however, Britain insisted China only had suzerainty, and further insisted that no Chinese officials should be reinstated. Between this time and the end of the talks leading up to the Simla Convention in 1914, these disagreements of principle, as well as a related dispute over border boundaries, were still not settled.[106]

Wang Chug Tsering replaced Zhang Yutang as Customs commissioner, and stayed behind until Yadong Customs was closed down in 1914. In order to find a way for the Post Office to reconnect with Tibet, Piry proposed a mailbags exchange in Tibet, but the British government declined in May 1912.[107] In the same month Lhasa opened its own post

103. "The Problems of China and Tibet," *Times* (London), September 5, 1912.

104. Lamb, *The McMahon Line*, 2:433–36. See also Feng Mingzhu, *Zhong Ying Xizang jiaoshe yu Chuan Zang*, 270.

105. Bland, *China, Japan and Korea*, 34.

106. Lamb, *The McMahon Line*, 528–29.

107. British Minister John N. Jordan to Ministry of Foreign Affairs, "Yin Zang jiaohuan youdai shi gui youzheng zongban suo ni banfa weineng yun ren you" 印藏交換

offices.[108] The Chinese Post Office in Yadong was never reopened, since no Chinese postal routes extended beyond Chamdo.

For Deng Weiping, the assignment to set up postal routes in Tibet was his final mission as inspecting clerk. A native of Wanping in Zhili, he and his brother Deng Weifan had opened many post offices in northern China. In 1910 there were forty-eight inspecting clerks on the *Service List*, and most of them were assigned to a geographical area near where they came from.[109] Although Deng Weiping became the first Chinese postmaster for the entire Tibetan postal district, his career went relatively quiet after his transfer back to Zhili. He was appointed postmaster for the First Class Post Office of Baoding, the most important station in the province after Beijing, but despite his excellent record and well-recognized merits, he mysteriously was not one of the first Chinese staff promoted to acting deputy commissioner in 1914. Two of his contemporaries, Liu Shufan 劉書蕃 and Chen Yaotang, were the first to gain such a rank. Given Deng's reputation, his direct line manager, W. Henne, was much puzzled by his failure to be promoted, and made an appeal to Henri Picard-Destelan, the chief secretary. Picard-Destelan, a Frenchman, was in charge during Piry's trip to Madrid to attend the Seventh Postal Union Congress. The congress was postponed due to the outbreak of the First World War, but Piry had already left China by this time.

In his letter, Henne wrote,

> I note with regret that the name of Mr. Teng Wei-ping, First Class Postmaster at Paodingfu, is not included in the list of promotions. . . . Being in this District only a comparatively short time, and relying upon the fact that Mr. Teng's merits and qualifications are better known at the Directorate General than to me, I did not think it necessary and advisable to ask specially for his promotion, taking it for granted that, if his colleagues of the same rank would be advanced, he would not be overlooked. He used to be the second on the list and has now been jumped by Mr. Chan Bŭt-to [Chen Yaotang], and while I

郵袋事貴郵政總辦所擬辦法未能允認由 [Chinese postmaster general's proposal on exchange of mailbags between India and Tibet cannot be accepted by His Majesty's government], May 11, 1912, ZYJSD 02-02-010-02-007.

108. Liu Yuan, Ye Yushun, and Ah Wang Dan Zeng, *Zhongguo Xizang youzheng youpiaoshi*, 59–62.

109. *Service List (1910)*, 197–99.

do not think that Mr. Teng will grudge Messrs. Liu Shu-fan and Chan Bŭt-to their appointment as Acting Deputy Commissioners . . . he certainly must feel hurt that he has not been, like the others, promoted in his substantive rank.[110]

With no further information currently available to us, this remains a mystery. Deng was finally promoted to deputy commissioner in 1917, and he was transferred to Beijing in 1922. He was still serving at the same rank in 1929 at the Beijing headquarters.[111] By contrast, Liu Shufan had a more successful career trajectory. Liu, a Fujian native, joined the IPO in 1898. He took the same route as Deng in promotion to inspecting clerk, and learned both English and French.[112] He was promoted to commissioner in 1920, in charge of the Shaanxi Postal District.[113] After the establishment of the Nanjing government in 1927, he was appointed head of the postal service for the new regime.[114]

110. W. Henne to Henri Picard-Destelan, June 22, 1914. Théophile Piry Collection, Special Collections, Queen's University of Belfast, MS19.

111. *Postal Service List for 1922*, 10. *Guomin zhengfu Jiaotongbu Youzheng zhiyuanlu*, 180.

112. *Service List (1910)*, 197. Liu Shufan's English name on the *Service List* was Lau Chu Huang.

113. Chen Yaotang and Liu Shufan were the first two Chinese promoted to the commissioner rank after the establishment of the Post Office. On their promotion in 1920, Chen oversaw the Gansu postal district, while Liu was in charge of Shaanxi. See *Postal Service List for 1922*, 10.

114. *Postal Service List for 1922*, 10; *Guomin zhengfu Jiaotongbu Youzheng zhiyuanlu*, 2.

THE OLD IMPERIAL
POST OFFICE, PEKING.

CHAPTER NINE

Myths, Legends, and the World's Longest Overland Postal Route

As time went on, the Qing government increasingly came to consider the presence of the Post Office an important symbol and projection of the state, particularly in peripheral areas where Qing sovereignty was challenged. This was certainly the case in Tibet, albeit the postal presence there turned out to be short-lived. These challenges intensified as China moved into the republican era. The republic's new leaders faced additional challenges in their search for a sovereign identity. Questions of China's sovereignty focused not only on how to express "five races under one nation" and maintain the country's territorial integrity but also on how to gain satisfactory recognition from international powers. Tang Chi-hua's research outlined the effort made by the Beiyang government in acquiring a sense of self-determination in the following three aspects: the revision of existing treaties, equal recognition in international discourse, and asserting sovereignty in Mongolia.[1] Building on this scholarship, this

---

1. Tang, *Bei "feichu bupingdeng tiaoyue,"* chaps. 2, 3, 6.

chapter will demonstrate that in all these aspects the Post Office played a significant part.

The Chinese Post Office finally joined the Universal Postal Union in 1914. While the change was highly symbolic for China, it was little noticed elsewhere, as the world's attention had shifted to Europe in the run-up to the First World War. Geopolitical tensions in Asia remained, however, and throughout the first decade of the young republic, three major issues dominated China's agenda internationally: Tibetan independence, Outer Mongolian autonomy, and Japan's Twenty-One Demands. Against this broader background, and amid increasing calls (particularly after 1918) for the abolition of unequal treaties, the Post Office had an important role in the process of building a modern nation. It is also important to note that the particular concerns of this period drove the discourse associated with early attempts at capturing the history of the Post Office. The founding narrative of any significant institution carries substantial weight, bearing a lasting influence that should not be underestimated, and stories or even myths associated with that narrative can be persistent, even when conflicting details emerge. The nationalistic perspective that emerged in this period not only fit well with the politics of the time but also had a long-lasting impact on institutional discourse after 1949 in both mainland China and Taiwan. This chapter therefore takes time to reflect on early attempts to record and interpret major events in the Post Office's creation and development, as well as the actions and motivations of those doing the recording and interpreting.

The Four-Circular Discourse, Nationalism, and Foreign Direction

The *four-circular discourse*, a term coined for this chapter, refers to four important circulars issued by Robert Hart, Francis A. Aglen, and Théophile A. Piry (see appendixes 1–4). These four documents are Hart's IG Circular 706 / Postal No. 7 (1896) and IG Circular 709 / Postal No. 9 (1896); Aglen's IG Circular 1802 / Postal No. 261 (1911); and Piry's Postmaster General's Circular 262 (1911), all of which have been examined individually in previous chapters. The first two circulars are generally regarded as the foundation of the institutional history of the Chinese postal service. In IG Circular 706, Hart referenced his conversation with Prince Gong and Wenxiang during his first visit to Beijing in 1861 as the embryonic beginning of the postal enterprise. In IG Circular 709, Hart set out the basic narrative around the part played by the Chinese Maritime Customs Service (CMCS) in initiating and doing the groundwork for the postal enterprise, referencing the work in providing service between the treaty ports, going back thirty years. He acknowledged the contributions of Gustav Detring, Henry Kopsch, and Li Gui; but, equally, he made sure history did not forget what he regarded as the negligence of Thomas F. Wade, acting in tacit agreement with Li Hongzhang, during the talks for the Chefoo Convention back in 1876. As was noted in chapter 3, it is possible that Hart did not have the full picture as to Li and Wade's motivations in excluding the postal proposal from the Chefoo Convention; but it is certainly Hart's perception that has become accepted as historic fact. What is also worth noting is that, in these two circulars, potential conflict with private letter hongs was at the center of Hart's concerns, while other potentially contentious issues such as Universal Postal Union membership or competition from foreign post offices were not raised. This reflects what Hart considered to be the main area of danger for the fledgling service, and also his previously expressed view that the issue of foreign post offices in China was "political rather than postal."[2]

The discourse arising from these two circulars was supported by Aglen's heartfelt farewell peroration, "in the name of the Inspector General, Sir Robert Hart," in his final postal memorandum as the Imperial Post Office (IPO) moved out of the orbit of the CMCS. Though Aglen was fully aware of the complaints of many senior foreign Customs staff who blamed expenditure on the postal service for overstretching the resources of the CMCS, it was important to maintain the facade of harmony and fellow feeling. Yet, for Aglen, while the Post Office was a glorious chapter in the CMCS's good work, it nevertheless belonged to the past. Behind his melancholy words, which should no doubt be read as a straightforward expression of feeling, he also made clear his ongoing concern about the CMCS's postal loans rendered to the Post Office.

2. Robert Hart to Francis A. Aglen, January 13, 1897, SOAS, MS211081.

Piry, on the other hand, had somewhat different motives when setting forth his version of history. In his first circular issued after the separation of the Post Office from the CMCS, he not only reinforced Aglen's fraternal tone but went further in framing the postal service as Hart's "magnum opus." Alongside this, he celebrated the Post Office's independent status within the country's national institutions: a more coherent structure under the Ministry of Posts and Communications, further expansion to come, and future career opportunities for postal staff. Piry saw himself as Hart's successor in taking the Post Office—an institution that by this time already had more staff and stations than the CMCS—forward. While the reorganization of central government had downgraded the status of the CMCS, it had raised the position of the Post Office. Yet for all their respective writers' different motivations, and despite the disputes between Aglen and Piry that became quite heated during the period of formal separation, these four circulars share a common perspective, which is to demonstrate a spirit of loyalty toward the Qing government and to rally round the idea that the Post Office project was intended to bring benefit to China and its people. Indeed, Aglen's quotation of Hart's words from fifteen years earlier admirably sums up this message, noting that their shared motive was to support "the Imperial Post functioning widely and fully appreciated, the people finding in it and its developments an everyday convenience and the Government a useful servant."[3]

But neither Hart, nor Aglen, nor Piry, was to have the last word, and a series of events soon transpired that would lead to a wholly different perspective. While the Post Office as an organization had enjoyed a relatively smooth transition to the new republic, the institutional discourse was about to change significantly. In the new climate of Chinese nationalism, tension arose between Piry and his Chinese staff. This tension formally kicked off the process of Chinese postal staff formulating their own version of institutional history.

It started with a petition. In May 1912, the *Asia Daily* (*Ya xi ya ribao* 亞細亞日報) used a large space to publish a long petition to the Provisional Senate on a single issue: China should take back its "postal privilege"

---

3. IG Circular 1802 / Postal Circular 261, May 30, 1911, in *Circulars Nos. 135–261*, 633–34, TMA, W2-2838.

(*youquan* 郵權). The petition was jointly written by three men: Feng Nong 馮農, Huo Shulin 霍澍霖, and Liu Mian 劉勉. It caused a sensation in political circles in Beijing and forced responses from the French embassy, the Ministry of Communications, and the Ministry of Foreign Affairs. The three men were all engaged in postal matters, though in unconventional ways. Feng Nong, the group's leader, scored the highest on the examination given to fourteen students selected out of hundreds of applicants to study postal banking in Austria, and it was there that he met his petition coauthors in the early summer of 1910. Huo Shulin, a young diplomatic apprentice in the Chinese Embassy in Austria, had been assigned to join the group to study postal banking; Liu Mian, already a student in France, had been instructed to move to Austria for the same reason.[4]

The petition focused on four aspects. It criticized Piry for disobeying the director general of Posts; for interfering with the business of the School of Transportation; for ignoring and even insulting students returning from Austria; and for nepotism, favoritism, and unfair treatment of Chinese staff in regard to salary and promotion. The authors observed that, although they understood the historical background of the Post Office and why the institution had required foreigners to set it up, this situation had now changed. The petition requested the Chinese government to consider the following steps: it should make it very clear to the French government that it should not interfere with China's Post Office; capable Chinese staff should be promoted; foreign staff should have their contracts amended, providing for equal pay with Chinese staff; and Piry should be removed from his role as postmaster general and reduced to the level of senior consultant, which would also mean the removal of his power in all personnel arrangements.[5]

On seeing the petition, the French ambassador, Pierre de Margerie, wrote to Lu Zhengxiang, the Minister of Foreign Affairs, to express the French government's concern over the matter. Margerie complained that

4. Feng Nong, "Qianqi shouhui youquan yundong," 7. There were another six Chinese, already in Europe at the time, who joined the group, making twenty students in total studying postal banking in Austria that year; Zhang Yi, *Zhonghua youzhengshi*, 324.

5. Feng Nong, Liu Mian, and Huo Shulin, "Shang canyiyuan shouhui youquan qingyuanshu."

someone in the Chinese government had leaked important documents to Feng and a foreign newspaper journalist. He demanded reassurance from the republican government that it would respect the 1898 agreement that management of the Post Office would remain in French hands.[6] Whether intended primarily as a personal attack on Piry, or more generally on the French government, the petition certainly fully embraced the discourse of national sovereignty and the vision of "young China." But behind the political ideology lay a series of unpleasant personal exchanges between Piry and the students who had returned from Austria, as well as poor management of the Directorate General.

In a short memoir written in 1948, Feng set out in detail how the group's feelings toward Piry, and their vision for the future of the Post Office, had turned into a very personal struggle. He recalled how, in the winter of 1911, he and his colleagues completed their courses and short-term apprenticeships in local post offices in Austria. After a farewell party, they each departed in different directions; some went to Britain, Germany, or Switzerland, but others went back to China, by train via Siberia; Feng was in the latter group. During the journey they learned of the outbreak of the Chinese Revolution of 1911, and the news that the revolutionary army had taken Nanjing. This aroused their excitement, but on reporting to the Directorate General in Beijing, they realized that, despite the completion of their studies, there was no immediate future for them, as the Directorate was not able to give them positions.[7]

The group drew the conclusion that the Directorate General had failed to assert its supervisory position over Piry. Due to constant changes in its leadership, the Directorate was lacking in direction but full of speculation.[8] Their resentment took a personal turn when the first formal meeting did not work out well. Assembled in a room in the Directorate quarters, the returned students were expecting to finally meet the minister, but he did not attend. Instead a section chief and several other individuals turned up carrying papers and pens. Among this group was Piry. On realizing that Piry planned to conduct an oral examination of the

6. Pierre de Margerie to Lu Zhengxiang, July 2, 1912, ZYJYD, 03-02-023-04-001.
7. Feng Nong, "Qianqi shouhui youquan yundong."
8. For details on the frequency of leadership change, see Yanxing [Pan Ansheng], *Zhonghua youzheng fazhanshi*, 408–9.

group, Feng protested. He explained that they had previously passed such an examination before they were sent to Austria, so there was no need for a further one. According to Feng, Piry's attitude on hearing this statement was arrogant and contemptuous. Feng's response was to say that the group's members were happy to show their grades in order to prove their qualifications, but if a further examination was really necessary, then it should be at ministry level rather than the level of Piry's office. After saying this, Feng and his colleagues stormed out of the room.

Unable to take a job relating to postal services, Feng turned to journalism and planned his revenge on Piry. In order to make a strong case, he needed inside information on the operation of the Post Office, and made contact with a Chinese postal clerk named Chen within the Directorate General who found a way to transcribe some relevant documents related to the matters raised in the petition. In the end, the petition did not bring down Piry, and the postal clerk was dismissed.

This was not the only case being made against Piry around this time. Another petition came his way from his own office, authored by his three assistant postal secretaries, Oliver H. Hulme, H. V. Poullain, and Arthur Walter Stursberg. Hulme and Stursberg were British and had joined the IPO in 1906; Poullain was French, joining in 1909.[9] This trio's main accusation against Piry repeated one of the Chinese group's earlier complaints: favoritism. Their complaint concerned Jean Paul Friedrich Jokl (also known as Pabst Jokl), an Austrian who was regarded as one of a group of "first rate" and "promising" young men recruited by the CMCS in Europe in late 1904.[10] Tall and handsome, Jokl was fluent in English, French, and German and was also an excellent violinist. He soon became a regular guest in Madame Piry's drawing room, in the fine house on Legation Street, next door to the Belgian Legation. Jokl's repertoire included Johannes Brahms's *Hungarian Dances*, and Piry's eldest daughter, Jeanne, often accompanied him on the piano. There was some gossip that "'Papa' had him in mind as a future son-in-law."[11]

---

9. *Service List (1910)*, 188, 195.

10. James Duncan Campbell to Robert Hart, Z/1451, November 11, 1904 [?], in Hart and Campbell, *Archives of China's Imperial Maritime Customs*, 3:851; *Service List (1905)*, 21.

11. Stursberg, *No Foreign Bones in China*, 118.

Jokl moved from the CMCS to the Post Office in 1912 as Piry's private secretary, at a salary of 200 Haikwan taels (Hk.Tls.) per month. This move was regarded as an injustice by the three assistant postal secretaries, as they considered that Jokl, lacking any prior experience in the postal service, should not be promoted over them. The final straw came when Jokl's salary was increased twice, shortly after his arrival, to Hk.Tls. 300. The joint letter asked Piry to consider applying similar treatment to other members of his team. Instead of a proper response from Piry, the letter was returned to the members of the group with a note: "Let each man write his own letter. T.P." The immediate result of this exchange was that Hulme was posted to Kunming, Poullain to Nanjing, and Stursberg to Qingdao.[12]

It is highly likely that Feng was not aware of this episode. Finding that their own campaign had been unsuccessful in bringing about change within the postal service, Feng and his friends decided to form the Chinese Nationwide Postal Association (Zhonghua quanguo youzheng xiehui 中華全國郵政協會) in Beijing in the summer of 1912. With the support of several prominent political figures, including Liang Shiyi 梁士詒 and Zhu Qiqian 朱啓鈐, who belonged to a clique closely associated with individuals inside the Ministry of Communications, this association was the first organization for Chinese postal staff.[13] They went on to shape an anti-Piry movement to complement their broader campaign for a nationalist assertion of "postal privilege."

Piry did take some measures to address the dissatisfaction of his Chinese staff. A new grade, Chinese accountant, was created to accommodate Chinese employees of outstanding merit, to be introduced in all postal districts. There were multiple ranks, starting with probationary accountant, Hk.Tls. 70–90 per month, rising to a maximum of Hk.Tls. 250 for a first accountant and Hk.Tls. 350 for a chief accountant. Although the annual leave benefits were not on an equal footing with foreign accountant grades, the rank and pay scale elements were applied equally across Chinese and foreign staff. Recruits returning from the postal banking study program in Austria would enter at the probationer level, while the remainder of those on higher grades would be recruited from the ranks

---

12. Stursberg, *No Foreign Bones in China*, 118–19.
13. Feng Nong, "Qianqi shouhui youquan yundong," 8.

of distinguished inspecting clerks. This was an unprecedented move by the Post Office, designed as it was with the clear goal of treating senior Chinese and foreign staff on an essentially equal basis. As Piry put it, "The principal point for District Postmasters to note is that, as regards position, functions, and authority, Chinese Accountants rank with foreign Accountants of the same grade, precedence being always regulated by seniority in that grade."[14]

But this measure alone was not sufficient to extinguish anti-Piry sentiment, as the Postal Association planned to mobilize postal staff across the whole country to hold a strike with the aim of forcing Piry to resign. It attracted more than a thousand members in a short time, and had support from some senior staff in the Ministry of Communications. Feng was the association's secretary, and an experienced postal clerk named Liu acted as liaison officer. Several of the Austrian group were also members of the association and took on administrative responsibilities for the campaign.

To suppress what he described as an "uprising," Piry issued a circular to assert his authority: "A notice calling upon the Chinese staff for the supply of reports and documents regarding Postal affairs, and signed by certain people that have no connection whatever with the Service, is being published and circulated in the name of a so-called Postal Association. . . . References are made in this notice to previous charges against the Post Office and its foreign staff, based on utterly erroneous and unfounded criticisms, which, although they attracted a certain amount of attention in the metropolitan press last year, have left the Service unaffected."[15]

Piry instructed postmasters to apply discipline and ban all postal employees from discussing, either verbally or in writing, service matters, or from disclosing any documents. Anyone committed to this course was to be either immediately suspended or discharged. Piry also dismissed the

---

14. Postmaster General's Circular 292, August 17, 1912, in *Circulars Nos. 262–389*, 97–98, TMA, W2-2839.

15. Postmaster General's Circular 313, May 20, 1913, in *Circulars Nos. 262–389*, 226, TMA, W2-2839. Zhang Yi, *Zhonghua youzhengshi*, 325, mistakenly has this as Postmaster General's Circular 20. This could be a consequence of quoting Feng Nong, "Qianqi shouhui youquan yundong."

liaison officer, Liu, and arranged for some Chinese staff considered loyal to join the association in order to affect the morale of the group. He also asked his foreign subordinates to write to the press to put his view forward, emphasizing that the Post Office was already a Chinese institution and its staff were public servants. It was wrong, he deemed, for the postal staff to participate in subversive political activities against existing authority. He also successfully prevented Feng's article, written in German, from being published. Feng in turn described the actions taken by Piry as the "devil's clutches." In the end, Piry managed to dissipate the momentum of the campaign by offering those who had studied in Austria automatic entry to the Post Office without taking any additional exams. Feng himself was "persuaded" to join a department within the Ministry of the Communications and later the Preparation Committee for Postal Banking of the Ministry of Communications (Jiaotongbu choubei chujin weiyuanhui 交通部籌備儲金委員會) and, as a consequence, the Postal Association soon died away.[16]

Thirty-five years later, setting out his version of postal history after the end of the Second Sino-Japanese War, Feng expressed regret for failing to keep on fighting and allowing the Postal Association to close. He thought if he had stayed on in the association, China would have been able to claim its "full postal privilege" earlier. But in spite of his regrets, and despite the fact that in Feng, Huo, and Liu's 1912 petition the term "unequal treaty" was still not much used because it had not yet become popular at that time, their actions have come to be regarded as the first significant action on this topic, and the petition shaped the discourse on postal privilege within postal historiography from the 1920s onward.

On April 24, 1922, more than four hundred Chinese postal workers unexpectedly went on strike due to the raise of the guarantor fee from sixty to one hundred Mexican dollars.[17] In addition to demanding the fee raise be dropped, they also asked for a pay raise and shorter working hours. Two days later, more than eight hundred postal workers and staff went on strike, and the Shanghai Postal Union (Shanghai youwu gonghui

16. Feng Nong, "Qianqi shouhui youquan yundong," 8, 9.
17. For a discussion of guarantors, see chapter 6. For the amended fee see "Instruction No. 251, Additions and Amendments to Instructions: No. 56," 15 December 1921, *Postal Circulars and Instructions*, vol. V, 1919–1922, 228.

上海郵務工會) was informally set up.[18] The organization was formally established in 1924. Soon after, postal workers in other large cities also formed professional groups.[19] By this time, Piry had already long departed, having passed away in 1918, a year after he took sick leave and subsequent retirement. Against this background and that of the Northern Expedition of the Kuomintang, senior Chinese postal staff also set up the Shanghai Postal Staff Association (Shanghai youwu tongren xiejinhui 上海郵務同仁協進會) in 1927. Initially, information relating to the establishment of the association was kept secret from senior foreign staff.[20] Several postal strikes were conducted during these years. Apart from adopting the (by then) fashionable terminology "unequal treaty" (bupingdeng tiaoyue 不平等條約) the main discourse of the new postal associations was still very much based on the one presented in the 1912 petition, but with a new target: Henri Picard-Destelan, another Frenchman and Piry's former deputy, who took over running the Post Office from Piry.

In this new political climate, in 1926 Xie Bin published an influential book on the history of communications, *The History of the Postal Service, Telecommunications and Air Transportation in China* (*Zhongguo youdian hangkongshi* 中國郵電航空史), which is regarded even today as one of the most important works on the subject.[21] Xie Bin, from Hengyang in Hunan, gained a scholarship after 1911 to study in the United States and then in Japan.[22] Being an active Kuomintang member and official based in Canton, he had excellent access to original documents. In his introduction to the book, Xie criticized the contemporary Chinese administration, and specifically the Beiyang government, for failing to turn the tide after Piry's departure and continuing to allow Picard-Destelan to control the Post Office.[23]

18. "Youchai bagong ji xiang 郵差罷工紀詳 [Detailed record on postmen's strike]," *Shenbao*, April 26, 1922; "Youchai bagong zuo yi jiejue 郵差罷工昨已解決 [Postmen's strike was resolved yesterday]," *Shenbao*, April 27, 1922.

19. *Wushinian lai Zhonghua Minguo yougong*, 1–12.

20. Liu Chenghan, *Cong you tan wang*, 1:146–47.

21. Xie Bin, *Zhongguo youdian hangkongshi*.

22. Huang Jue 黃覺, "Zhongguo youdian hangkongshi xu" 中國郵電航空史序 [Foreword to the history of the postal service, telecommunications, and air transportation in China], in Xie Bin, *Zhongguo youdian hangkongshi*.

23. Xie Bin, *Zhongguo youdian hangkongshi*, 2–3.

The next prominent book on this topic was Lou Zuyi's *The History of the Development of the Chinese Postal Courier Service* (*Zhongguo youyi fadashi* 中國郵驛發達史), published in 1940. Lou Zuyi, of Zhejiang origin, joined the Post Office after graduating from Hangchow University (Zhijiang daxue 之江大學). He was transferred to Shanghai in 1928, and later moved to the postal headquarters in Nanjing. Between 1928 and 1930 he was a regular contributor for the Shanghai-based journal *Postal Voice* (*You sheng* 郵聲).[24] Lou was very sympathetic toward postal strikes, and he and several other postal officers, including Liu Chenghan 劉承漢 (1901–92), wrote for various forums supporting calls for postal reform in the early 1930s.[25] But in his own book Lou chose to avoid making specific attacks on the French government or on senior postal staff of French nationality. Instead he highlighted the issue of foreign post offices in China, and the Chinese government's efforts to force them out, particularly after China had become a full member of the Universal Postal Union.

In a later article, published in 1948, Lou changed tack and elected to name those he considered culpable. In this article, titled "The History of How Our Country Took Back Postal Privilege" ("Woguo shouhui youquan de jingguo" 我國收回郵權的經過), he traced how the French government had forced the Qing government to place French nationals in managerial positions in the Post Office and how French imperialism continued to exercise power over the Chinese government even after 1911. Lou recycled Feng Nong's list of grievances in the 1912 petition and named Piry as a major player in supporting French imperialism and preventing Chinese staff, including those returned from Austria, from accessing their rights. He also recalled a popular saying in the Postal Service when Piscard-Destelan was in the office—"Co-D.G's [Co-Director General] decision is final"—and asserted that Piscard-Destelan was regarded as the "Postal Emperor."[26]

It is worth noting that both Feng's short memoir and Lou's article were published in an organizational journal titled *Modern Postal Service* (*Xiandai youzheng* 現代郵政), which first came out in August 1947 (see fig. 9.1). It is also known that an internal postal service journal with

24. Zhizhi, "Zhuming youzheng shixuejia Lou Zuyi," 62–63.
25. Shen Yunlong, *Liu Chenghan xiansheng fangwen*, 102–4.
26. Lou, "Woguo shouhui youquan," 3.

FIGURE 9.1 The cover of the first issue of the institutional journal *Modern Postal Service* (*Xiandai youzheng* 現代郵政), August 1947. A motorcycle in the foreground is accompanied by other forms of postal transportation. Acknowledgments to Tsai Chia-chi of the Specialist Library of the Chunghwa Postal Museum, Taipei, for providing this image, and to Chang Tzu-Ning for improving the image quality.

the same name was in existence from April 1939 with Feng as editor, though it appears to have ceased publication in 1941.

Another interesting aspect is that while the articles discussed so far, including the 1912 petition, took a hostile view toward the French, there was generally a softer tone concerning Robert Hart and the role of Britain in China's postal history. In the discourse around the impact of unequal treaties in relation to the postal issues, the role of postal staff of British nationality was not a major target, despite the fact that they constituted the largest group among foreign employees. This divide in the construction of the institutional history of the Chinese Post Office can also be detected in the works of three senior retired postal officers in Taiwan: Liu Chenghan, Pan Ansheng, and Zhang Yi. In addition to a book on postal history that covered foreign countries, Pan published many articles on Hart. Making the most of his access to a rich supply of institutional materials, Pan's descriptions of Hart were often laced with humor, sometimes bordering on satire. Though he criticized Hart for nepotism, for delaying China's membership in the Universal Postal Union, and his protection of British interests, Pan could not help but praise Hart as an "immortal character" in modern Chinese postal history. Pan thought it was remarkable for a foreign employee of the Qing government to have acted so loyally and consistently over his long career, in the midst of foreign imperialism.[27] Holding the view that in the historical circumstances it was unavoidable that the Qing government should employ foreigners in the initiation of the postal service, Liu considered that it was not productive to fix postal history within a discourse of imperialism without considering the contributions made by foreign staff in the historical context.[28] Echoing Liu, Zhang—who joined the Post Office in 1936 in Jiujiang immediately after his university education and retired in 1983 in Taipei—acknowledged issues relating to postal privilege and foreign postal staff, writing, "The foreign staff also made their contributions to the postal service of our country, and some of the stories are even worthy of commemoration."[29]

---

27. Yanxing [Pan Ansheng], *Hede shiliao*, 1, 159, my translation.
28. Liu Chenghan, *Cong you tan wang*, 1:149–50.
29. Zhang Yi, *Zhonghua youzhengshi*, 330–31, my translation.

Indeed, a rare Chinese voice acknowledging the contribution of foreign staff was heard in 1949. Alongside writing by Feng and Lou attacking foreign postal staff, an article by Li Xiyong 李希庸 published in the same institutional journal presented a different perspective. Titled "To the Cherished Memory of Mr. Poletti" ("Huainian Balidi xiansheng" 懷念巴立地先生), Li's article stressed that for him, the issue at stake was the system of using foreigners within the service rather than animosity toward individual foreign staff. Reporting his sadness about the recent death of Frank Poletti, who had passed away alone in a hospital in Shanghai, he wrote that from the bottom of his heart he wanted to pay tribute to this member of the foreign postal staff who had devoted forty years to the Chinese postal service. Li recalled that he had known about the existence of Poletti at Shenyang before the Northeast China Incident in 1931. At that time Li was a low-ranking mail sorter, while Poletti was already postmaster for the whole of Liaoning Province. Liu wrote that, like most of his Chinese colleagues, he had despised Poletti because the latter lived in a luxurious home with a large garden, had a private driver, and enjoyed a salary that was apparently forty to fifty times higher than the pay of a sorter.[30]

Frank Poletti, from Milan, had joined the IPO in Shanghai in 1906 at the age of nineteen.[31] Li said his view about Poletti completely changed during the Northeast China Incident. He saw that while most public servants had abandoned their offices and fled, the Post Office was the only official body that remained in operation. Poletti managed the situation with strenuous efforts to make sure staff were paid and contingent postal routes created. By an unlikely chance, Li was one of two Chinese staff members called in to minute the conversation between Poletti and some Japanese military officers who represented the Manchukuo in taking over the Post Office. Li witnessed Poletti, speaking in standard and clear Mandarin, asking the Japanese to treat fairly any Chinese postal staff who voluntarily chose to stay. As for himself, Poletti declined to stay and work for the Manchukuo, stating, "I am an official of the Chinese Gov-

30. Li Xiyong, "Huainian Balidi xiansheng," 21–22.

31. "Memo. of Service, Chinese Maritime Customs Service [of Poletti]" and "Memo. of Service, Chinese Post Office [of Poletti]," Specialist Library of Chunghwa Postal Museum (Zhonghua youzheng bowuguan zhuanye tushushi 中華郵政博物館專業圖書室), Taipei.

ernment, and I only take orders from the Chinese Government."[32] Poletti was warned that the Japanese planned to assassinate him, and he made this intelligence known to foreign legations and an Italian member of the Lytton Commission, which was formed under the supervision of the League of Nations and was sent to China to investigate the Mukden Incident in 1932.[33] Poletti arranged for important documents and for any movable property of the Post Office to be sent away in secret. While preparing for the withdrawal, he was in constant receipt of medical attention and needed an intravenous drip to keep him going. He was among the last of the group to leave.[34]

The fact that Poletti's conduct during the Northeast China Incident was affectionately recalled by his Chinese subordinate years later suggests that the range of available perspectives on postal history is wider than some might suggest, even just from a Chinese point of view.[35] Nevertheless, the dominant perspective, certainly among Chinese historians, is the one arising from the legacy of the Opium Wars and struggles against unequal treaties.

This is not to say that other perspectives disappeared from view. Foreign staff within the CMCS were also engaged in the compilation of postal history—notably, Hosea Ballou Morse and Stanley F. Wright (1873–1953). For the most part taking as their starting point the discourse of the four circulars previously discussed, the narratives of these foreign employees of the Chinese government reflect their own need to find meaning and purpose from being engaged in a collective enterprise, with the responsibility of stewarding hybrid institutions for the benefit of a country that was not their own but to which they were sworn to serve. A good example, focused on vision, progress, and achievement, was manifested by Hugh Kirkhope in his efforts to provide an institutional narrative to celebrate the Post Office's first twenty-five years in 1921.[36]

32. Li Xiyong, "Huainian Balidi xiansheng," 21, my translation.

33. "Riben jue duo dongbei youzheng" 日本攫奪東北郵政 [Japanese snatched postal service in northeast China], August 1932, Academia Historica (Guoshiguan 國史館), Taipei, 020-991200-0252.

34. Zhang Yi, *Zhonghua youzhengshi*, 394.

35. Liu Chenghan, *Cong you tan wang*, 279–83; Zhang Yi, *Zhonghua youzhengshi*, 310; Yanxing [Pan Ansheng], *Zhonghua youzheng fazhanshi*, 426–27.

36. Hsueh, "Waiji youyuan Zhongwen yiming," 97. The same article was also collected in *Docs. Ill.*, 7:276–94.

Kirkhope, a British citizen, joined the Post Office in August 1911—in the period between its separation from the CMCS and the 1911 revolution—and was promoted to acting deputy commissioner in 1921.[37] Around this time the majority of commissioners were still, by far, foreigners.[38] In a document titled "Historical Survey" that traveled through postal history from ancient China to the contemporary era, Kirkhope ended the narrative on a high note, taking the Post Office's condition as a culmination of what had gone before: "It is impossible to conceive to what extent the course of the country's history during the past decade would have varied had not the National Post existed in such a state of development. It is safe to say, however, that the time of the nation's greatest need was the Administration's supreme opportunity, and it was not neglected. The unifying influence of the National Post is undeniable." Kirkhope concluded with a whimsical touch, quoting the eighteenth-century English poet William Cowper while at the same time giving a nod to republican ideals of a united China and the Post Office's role in making this a reality:

> To the work of the Chinese Postal Service there is a side which is extremely romantic; the illustrations included in this Report must be left to depict it. But when the last-stage courier on the long line—the longest in the world (4,400 miles)—which connects Peking and Kalgan [Zhangjiakou] with Tihwa [Ürümqi] in Chinese Turkestan, arrives—
>
> > ". . . the herald of a noisy world,
> > News of all nations lumbering at his back."
>
> perchance it may occur to the dwellers in that far-off, isolated community to regard him as an outward and visible sign of the happiest method of "peaceful penetration."[39]

---

37. *Postal Service List for 1922*, 4.

38. According to the *Postal Service List for 1922*, 1–4, 10–11, there were thirty-one foreign commissioners and acting commissioners, thirty foreign deputy & acting deputy commissioners; three Chinese commissioners and acting commissioners, and nineteen Chinese deputy & acting deputy commissioners.

39. Hugh Kirkhope, "Historical Survey," in Report (1921), 12. The phrase "peaceful penetration" was a reference to an infantry tactic used in the First World War by British and allied troops to advance their position through trench raiding.

Kirkhope's "Historical Survey" should in theory have been approved by the director general of Posts, Liou Fou-tcheng 劉符誠, before being printed. The piece presented a romanticized version of postal history, which sought to align the service ever closer with the experience and concerns of the country and the people. The opening of the longest overland postal route in the world was certainly an appropriate achievement with which to celebrate the twenty-five-year history of the Post Office.

This romantic vision had a significant impact on the ethos of the institution. Although it only occupied a few lines in the whole essay, it packed in a lot in its articulation of shared history between the institution and China. But the story of the creation of this "longest postal route" is in itself an illuminating tale. To do Kirkhope's grand narrative justice, we need to look in detail at the critical challenges in the construction of the route.

The Longest Postal Route

As was the case in Tibet, the driving force behind the creation of routes to China's far north and west was a mixture of geopolitics, the consequences of the Qing government's New Policies, and urgency of postal expansion as a means of projecting sovereignty. Each of these elements continued into the republican era. The making of the longest route required three main components: the connection between Beijing and Ürümqi; the connection between Beijing, Zhangjiakou, and Kulun (also known as Urga, and today as Ulaanbaatar); and the connection between Kulun and Ürümqi via Uliastai and Chenghuasi.

Chapters 6 and 7 addressed the extension of postal routes to Zhangjiakou (1903) and some parts of Xinjiang, including the provincial capital Ürümqi (1909). But this longest postal route had also to connect Beijing with Kulun and finally join up with Ürümqi through the huge territory of Outer Mongolia. Most of the physical effort in joining up these sections falls into the period between 1910 and 1918. But political tensions related to postal activity in these regions were much older.

Russian Postal Services in China after the Second Opium War

Mongolia in the late Qing period was divided into Inner and Outer Mongolia, both considered part of the Qing empire. The name Outer Mongolia referred to the areas beyond the Gobi Desert, including the regions of Khalkha, Kobdo (Hovd in the postal system, and as it appears in fig. 9.2), Altai (overlapping with Chenghuasi; Chenghwasze in the postal spelling), and Tannu-Urianghai. Each region contained several entities—known as banners—not directly administered by the Qing government. The government appointed representatives to oversee their affairs, and there were other government-appointed figures including a regional military governor of Uliasutai; an imperial agent, or *amban*, at Kulun; an assistant military governor and an imperial agent at Kobdo; and an imperial agent at Altai, who resided at Chenghuasi.[40]

When Aleksei Matveevich Pozdneev (1850–1920), a historian of modern Mongolia, made his second expedition to the region in 1892–93, he recorded the routes, weather conditions, and geographical features that had to be considered for the journey. He also recorded the places and temples visited, the lifestyle and customs of banners, and the characteristics of the people he encountered. In addition to this catalog of local color and customs, Pozdneev's travelogue also provides a detailed account of contemporary transportation methods and routes, as well as information about the Russian mail service in Mongolia and on to Beijing and Tianjin. Many of the routes he traveled overlapped with the longest postal route discussed here, and his insightful observations provide a wonderful contemporary background for this period in postal history. The information collected by Pozdneev and, more generally, by the Russian mail service would provide valuable intelligence for Russia, resembling what Mark Bell did in Xinjiang and China proper in the 1880s for the British government.[41]

Pozdneev also witnessed the style in which the military relay courier system transmitted official correspondence. For example, on his way to Kulun, he saw a Chinese messenger coming from the residence hall of

40. Brunnert and Hagelstrom, *Present Day Political Organization of China*, 442, 452–54.

41. Hevia, *The Imperial Security State*, 89–90.

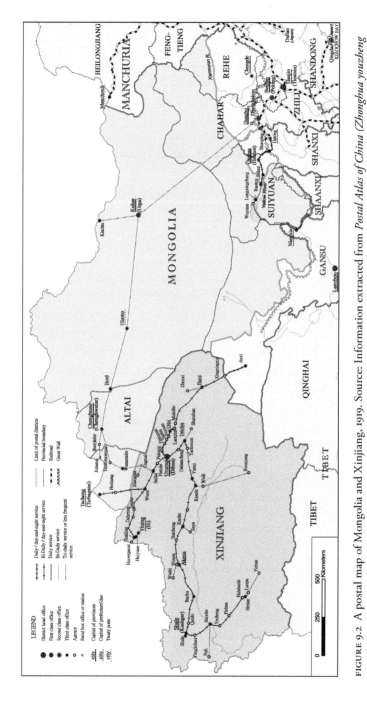

FIGURE 9.2. A postal map of Mongolia and Xinjiang, 1919. Source: Information extracted from *Postal Atlas of China* (*Zhonghua youzheng yutu* 中華郵政輿圖). Map © Weipin Tsai; cartography by Huang Chingchi.

the Uliasutai imperial agent, carrying a package. This Han Chinese was supported by three Mongolian drivers, and behind this cart there was another group, comprising the Chinese messenger's servant (also a Chinese) and two guides. So in total, in order to deliver a single package, it required two Chinese, five Mongolian drivers, and ten horses.[42]

Across this remote area, only a few towns boasted Han Chinese merchants and Qing officials. When staying in Kulun, for example, Pozdneev observed the imbalance in wealth distribution and commercial status between the Chinese and Mongolians. He noticed that, while Mongolian shops were simple or even shabby, the Chinese shops were adorned with exotic products that were tastefully displayed: "Here let me say only that never in the shops of the Urga [Kulun] merchants does one see such outward trimmings, such carving, such fine designs, and such bright colours on the door and windows as one finds on the buildings which house the Peking shops. Their signs, which are also always artistic and clever, are invariably in two languages, Chinese and Mongolian. In Chinese, however, which the Mongols cannot read, there are only the three characters denoting the name, while in Mongolian the specialties of the shops are described in somewhat more detail."[43]

A Chinese shop was normally divided into two or three small rooms and typically sold all sorts of Chinese products and a few manufactured products from Europe. As Lai Hui-min has noted in her research on a long history of trade dating back to the reign of Emperor Qianlong, the trading activities demonstrated constant exchanges among China, Mongolia, Russia, and parts of Europe.[44] Most of the Chinese shops were owned by merchants from either Beijing or Shanxi; some Chinese merchants owned more than one shop with different names across town, because by so doing they might achieve more sales.[45] A similar commercial model, involving traders from Shanxi and Zhili, could also be found in Xinjiang. Their networks, which connected Mongolia, Xinjiang, and the North China Plain or even Tibet through Sichuan, involved move-

42. Pozdneev, *Mongolia and the Mongols*, 122.
43. Pozdneev, *Mongolia and the Mongols*, 66.
44. Lai, *Man daren de hebao*.
45. Pozdneev, *Mongolia and the Mongols*, 67–68; Lai Hui-min, *Man daren de hebao*, 252.

ments of commodities and exchange of apprenticeships in multiple languages.[46]

Between the signing of the Kyakhta Boundary Treaty in 1727 and the Sino-Russian Treaty of Beijing in 1860, several towns were opened for trade to Russia in Outer Mongolia and Xinjiang—specifically, Ili, Kashgar, Kulun, Kyakhta, Tarbagatai, and Zhangjiakou.[47] Zhangjiakou was the most important gate town on the line of the Great Wall on the approach to Mongolia, as well as the most important stop between Beijing and Kulun. Kulun, where the imperial agent resided, was a location of both political and military importance. The imperial agent at Kulun oversaw affairs relating to the Mongolian tribes, and was also in control of Kyakhta and trade with Russia.[48] Despite its small size, Kyakhta was divided into two parts: a Russian quarter and a Chinese area, which was called the trade town (*maimaicheng* 買賣城). The status of Kyakhta was further reinforced by the Sino-Russian Treaty of Tianjin in 1858, in which it was agreed that one of the two permitted routes for Russian diplomats traveling to Beijing was to be that via Kyakhta (the other was through open coastal ports). The restrictions on Russian trade in general were gradually loosened in this period; in the Kyakhta Boundary Treaty, it had been agreed that officially accredited Russian merchants could enter Beijing once every three years to conduct business, but that the group should not exceed two hundred people. In fact, the group was always in excess of two hundred and, en route to Beijing, it would stop at Kulun and Zhangjiakou.

In her work on postal communications in the late nineteenth century, Ying-wan Cheng notes that the Qing government was extremely cautious in its dealings with Russia and explains why Russia did not gain the same rights as Great Britain regarding postal services in either the bilateral Sino-Russian part of the Treaty of Tianjin in 1858 or the Sino-Russian Additional Treaty of Peking, 1860.[49] Rather than allowing Russian diplomats

46. Millward, *Beyond the Pass*, chap. 5.
47. Kyakhta Boundary Treaty/Treaty of Frontier (1727), Article IV, in *Zhong wai jiu yuezhang*, 1:33; Sino-Russian Additional Treaty of Peking, 1860, Articles V–VII, in *Zhong wai jiu yuezhang*, 1:440–41; Fletcher, "Sino-Russian Relations," 318–32; Feng Ruofei, *Qingdai queguan*, 44–45.
48. Lai, *Man daren de hebao*, 142–44; Mayers, *The Chinese Government*, 93.
49. Ying-wan Cheng, *Postal Communication in China*, 59–61.

to arrange their own mail couriers, in Article XI of the Sino-Russian Treaty of Tianjin it was agreed that official correspondence of the two nations between Beijing and Kyakhta should be delivered by the military relay courier system on the basis of equally shared costs, with all mail journeys to be completed within a half month. Parcels were to be delivered four times a year on equally shared costs by both countries.[50]

This arrangement was improved in the Russian Additional Treaty of Beijing and, more important, both Russian merchants and officials were permitted to hire people to deliver messages *after* reporting to appropriate Qing officials in the region.[51] The provisions of the Treaty of Beijing differed from those of the Sino-British Treaty of Tianjin, where the text allowed the British representatives to send and receive correspondence at seaports through transmission arranged by themselves without the requirement for prior permission from local governors. In 1863 the Russian Merchants' Post was set up by the Russian Merchants' Guild to transmit its correspondence, providing free transmission for its members between Tianjin, Beijing, and Kyakhta through Zhangjiakou and Kulun. Those who were not members of the guild were able to use the service by paying the appropriate fees.[52] From Kyakhta to Kulun the mail was carried either by Russian merchants with caravans or by their agents. From Kulun to Zhangjiakou, crossing the Gobi Desert, Mongolian banner armies were contracted for the job. From Zhangjiakou onward, it was often the case that Chinese letter hongs were hired to complete the transmission.[53] The offices of the Russian Merchants' Guild in Beijing, Kulun, Kyakhta, Tianjin, and Zhangjiakou also acted as collection points. Kobdo and Uliasutai were included in the service.[54]

Although in receipt of financial support from the Russian government, the Russian Merchants' Post was far from reliable, and mail often

50. Sino-Russian Treaty of Tianjin, Article XI, in *Zhong wai jiu yuezhang*, 1:268.

51. Sino-Russian Additional Treaty of Peking, 1860, Article XII, in *Zhong wai jiu yuezhang*, 1:445–46.

52. Pozdneev, *Mongolia and the Mongols*, 400; Hellrigl, *The Postal History of Mongolia*, 32.

53. Ying-wan Cheng, *Postal Communication in China*, 59–60. See also Hellrigl, *The Postal History of Mongolia*, 33. Hellrigl provides a slightly different view on the length of time the Russian Merchants' Post lasted.

54. Li Songping, *Ke you wai shi*, 110.

spent much longer in transit than expected.[55] Indeed, its unsatisfactory nature provided Charles Mitchell Grant, an Englishman, with the opportunity to set up a rival service. Grant's service, which ran for almost five years beginning in 1867, managed to reduce the journey time between Kyakhta and Tianjin from sixteen or seventeen days to eleven or twelve days. Although Grant's postal service was more expensive and only operated between March and November, it was very successful. His firm also transmitted telegrams four to six times per month between Kyakhta and Tianjin.[56]

In the meantime, the Russian government tried to improve the mail service between China and Mongolia in response to repeated complaints from merchants over lost business. For example, some tea orders placed by Russian merchants from Irkutsk, near Kyakhta, did not reach Hankou for more than three months.[57] In March 1870 the Russian Imperial Post finally took over the Russian Merchants' Post and engaged private Mongolian firms to manage the mail service. Russian post offices were subsequently established in Beijing, Kulun, Kyakhta, Tianjin, and Zhangjiakou.[58] Pozdneev observed that, for the distance between Kyakhta and Zhangjiakou, the service was shared by two local contractors. He was appalled by the work ethic of the Mongolians employed, as they would use transport subsidized by the Russian government for their own business use and "considered this as their legal right." When challenged, the Mongolians responded by saying "the camels are ours, we can carry everything on them that we need."[59] The punctuality of the service did not appear to be a factor in their thinking, either.

In addition to Mongolian riders, the Russian Imperial Post also hired private letter hongs to work for them between Mongolia and China proper.[60] The engagement of hongs with the Russian Imperial Post went on for a lengthy period and could prove hazardous. For example, in 1891, a

55. Pozdneev, *Mongolia and the Mongols*, 401.
56. Hellrigl, *The Postal History of Mongolia*, 34; Pozdneev, *Mongolia and the Mongols*, 401. See also Casey, *The Russian Post Offices in the Chinese Empire*, 14–17.
57. Pozdneev, *Mongolia and the Mongols*, 402.
58. Li Songping, *Ke you wai shi*, 110; Zhang Yi, *Zhonghua youzhengshi*, 123; Pozdneev, *Mongolia and the Mongols*, 402.
59. Pozdneev, *Mongolia and the Mongols*, 403.
60. Wang Menghsiao, "Qingdai zhi minxinju," 13.

Chinese man contracted to work for the Russian Imperial Post was robbed somewhere near Zhangjiakou by four Chakhar Mongolian riders in the daytime.[61] He was bitten and fell from his horse, and the mailbag was seized, along with two horses. Another robbery case in 1894 was even more serious; a contracted private letter hong, Xiguangyu 西光裕, was asked to deliver an official check for Tls. 40,000 from Zhangjiakou to Beijing, and the check was lost. Li Jinhai, a Xiguangyu employee, was mobbed by five men at around seven or eight o'clock in the evening. The robbers took the mailbag away after firing a gun, but without hurting Li.[62] In yet another case, some Russian letters together with banknotes worth more than Tls. 10,000 were taken by robbers in the Zhangjiakou area. This was being handled by a Chinese letter hong, Zhongtonghe 中同和. The hong had sent a messenger on a donkey on this mission, and he was attacked by a group of eight men in the evening.[63]

The options open to ordinary Chinese people and merchants were to use private letter hongs, or the services of commercial firms who traveled between Mongolia and China proper. Shanxi merchants formed the largest commercial bloc in the north, and many of them had branches in varied cities in other provinces. Through their large networks, many Shanxi traditional banks (*piaohao* 票號) also ran courier services. When this kind of service was not available, sometimes traditional banks and shops would collectively hire someone to run mails for them.[64]

In summary, prior to the establishment of the Chinese Post Office, the Russian Imperial Post had already made its appearance in the treaty ports in northern China, Mongolia, and Xinjiang. Although it might not be entirely accurate to describe the mail service in the second half of the

61. A. P. Cassini to Zongli Yamen, "E ren fu Zhangjiakou di xin bei jie . . ." 俄人赴張家口遞信被劫 . . . [Messenger of Russian Post to Zhangjiakou was robbed . . .], October 23, 1891, ZYJYD, 01-17-038-01-001.

62. A. P. Cassini to Zongli Yamen, "E guo song xin ju fu you Zhangjiakou fu Jing zai Yulin difang bei jie . . ." 俄國送信局夫由張家口赴京在榆林地方被劫 . . . [Messenger delivering Russian mail robbed at Yulin on his way to Beijing . . .], March 31, 1894, ZYJYD, 01-17-038-03-001.

63. Zongli Yamen to Li Hongzhang, "E songxinren zai Wanquanxian difang bei qiang . . ." 俄送信人在萬全縣地方被搶 . . . [Messenger for Russian mail robbed in Wanquan County . . .], April 4, 1896. ZYJYD, 01-17-038-05-001.

64. Wang Menghsiao, "Qingdai zhi minxinju," 16; Peng Yingtian, *Minxinjü fazhansh*, 77–78; *Shanxi piaohao shiliao*, 841–46.

nineteenth century as totally satisfactory to every party, the joint franchised mail service model between the Russian Imperial Post, Mongolian couriers, and Chinese private letter hongs functioned for several decades.

The 1909 Kulun Incident and the Chinese Post Office

After Russia's defeat by Japan in 1905, geopolitical conflict in North Asia reached a new level as Russia had to withdraw from Manchuria. As part of the so-called Great Game, Russia was also concerned it might only be a question of time before Japan moved into Outer Mongolia with Britain's approval. In addition, by 1907 the Qing government was seeking to push its New Policies agenda from Inner Mongolia into Outer Mongolia, which raised huge concerns in the region, giving a boost to Mongolian independence movements. Although there had already been a noticeable degree of interaction between Han Chinese and Mongolians in interracial marriage, commercial activity, and land rental, new moves by the central government to open up Outer Mongolia faced strong resistance, as the locals believed their autonomy would be badly affected by such innovations.

Sando 三多 (1876–1941) was appointed as the imperial agent in Kulun in 1909; his previous post was as deputy lieutenant general of Guihua, a place that was seen as having successfully adopted the Qing government's land reform initiative. When he arrived in Kulun in November, Sando was eager to apply a more aggressive approach in moving things forward. Echoing what other officials did at the borders of Sichuan and Tibet, he set up several administrative departments in Outer Mongolia to align with the central government's New Policies.[65] The relationship between Beijing and Outer Mongolia deteriorated.

The Ministry of Posts and Communications had originally planned to introduce the postal service to Kulun by 1912 but had to speed up its schedule as Qing sovereignty increasingly came under challenge. In October 1908 the Qing officials in Kulun notified Beijing that Russia had increased its military strength in Kyakhta to more than three thousand

---

65. Ewing, "Ch'ing Policies in Outer Mongolia," 153; Soni, *Mongolia-China Relations*, 30–31.

men.[66] In May 1909 around one hundred Russian soldiers entered Kulun under the instruction of Russian consul Yakov Shishmarev (1833–1915).
The Qing government regarded this action as an affront and demanded
the soldiers be removed, with promises that they would not return. Consul Shishmarev denied it was Russia's intention to challenge Qing sovereignty, and claimed that the troops were present only to protect the mail
between Kulun and Kyakhta.[67] To Qing officials it appeared out of pro-
portion to call in military force for the protection of mail; there had been
incidents of lost mail in the past without such a reaction. It also seemed
to be an unusual act on Shishmarev's part, as he had a reputation for being friendly and helpful toward both Qing officials and Mongols. He had
been the consul in Kulun for more than forty years, and when Shishmarev
retired, Sando recommended him to the Qing Emperor for a state hon-
or.[68] The suspicion was that using protection of the mail as justification
for troop movements might be a cover-up for something else, though quite
what remained a mystery.

The Qing court believed that the way to prevent such incidents oc-
curring again was to have China's sovereign postal service connect Inner
and Outer Mongolia, regardless of expense. To implement this, a Chinese postal inspector, Wang Zhaolin 王肇琳, was sent to Kulun.[69] Wang
was from Zhili, and had joined the Post Office in 1901.[70] He recruited a
team of locals, some of whom also had previous courier experience, and
a weekly service was introduced for the Kulun to Zhangjiakou route on
January 14, 1910. There were 2,000 *li* (approximately 1,240 kilometers)
between Kulun and Zhangjiakou following the telegraph line. The route
incorporated nine changes of horses, and the journey took seven to nine

---

66. Yanzhi 延祉, "... Zou chen Kulun qingxing ..." ...　奏陳庫倫情形 ... [...
Report on the situation in Kulun ...], Xuantong reign year 1, month 3, day 13 (May 2,
1909), ZYJYD, 03-46-001-01-008.

67. I. J. Korostovetz to Ministry of Foreign Affairs, "Kulun E bin bai ming xi yin huan
ban bing baohu wanglai youjian ..." 庫倫俄兵百名係因換班並保護往來郵件 ... [One hundred Russian soldiers entering Kulun for changing shift and protecting mail ...], Xuantong reign year 1, month 3, day 26 (May 15, 1909), ZYJYD, 03-46-001-01-013.

68. Feng Jianyong, *Xinhai geming yu jindai Zhongguo*, 56–57.

69. Ministry of Foreign Affairs to Bureau of Customs Affairs, "Zhang Ku shiban
youzheng shi" 張庫試辦郵政事 [Zhangjiakou and Kulun have postal trial], February 16,
1910, ZYJYD, 02-02-009-09-001.

70. *Service List (1907)*, 184.

days. The postal business in Kulun did better than expected, thanks to its flourishing Chinese community, and government correspondence from and to Kulun was now transmitted by the Post Office rather than by the military relay couriers. To reflect the importance of Kulun and to satisfy demand, a postal money order service was also introduced.[71] To guarantee the safety of mail, the military lieutenant governor of Chakhar, residing at Zhangjiakou, was requested to form alliances with the tribal leaders along the route to ensure the security of the relay.[72]

The service was soon extended to Kyakhta using contracted Mongolian mounted couriers. The distance between Kyakhta and Kulun on the high roads was 860 *li* (532 kilometers), and the journey took almost two days to complete. Strategically, the Zhangjiakou–Kulun–Kyakhta route now also linked to railways at both ends connecting to Beijing (Kyakhta connected with the Siberian train to Harbin and on to Beijing). From Kulun through Kyakhta to Beijing via Siberia would take twelve to thirteen days, whereas it would take seven to nine days from Kulun to Zhangjiakou, with the final leg to Beijing by train adding an additional day.[73]

The couriers brought together by Wang Zhaolin soon proved to be very difficult to maintain, however, due to a shortage of horses and riders. Only a few months after the inauguration of the Kulun to Kyakhta and Kulun to Zhangjiakou lines, the Post Office had to involve military relay couriers for transmission (see fig. 9.3).[74] When Henry George Charles Perry-Ayscough, a postal officer of British nationality, traveled through many of these locations in Outer Mongolia on his way back to Europe in 1912, he shed some light on reality. He noted that instead of having formal stages lined up between Zhangjiakou and Kulun, his colleagues "farm out the carrying of their letters across the desert to a

71. Report (1910), 11.

72. Bureau of Customs Affairs to Ministry of Foreign Affairs, "Kulun an she youju shi" 庫倫安設郵局事 [Post Office set up in Kulun], March 16, 1910, ZYJYD, 02-02-009-09-003.

73. Report (1910), 11–12. Although the Trans-Siberian Railway did not go through Kyakhta directly, it went through Ulan-Ude (Udinsk), around 190 kilometers to the northeast. Regular transportation was set up between these two places, and it was convenient for mail from Kulun to be transmitted to Ulan-Ude; Report (1910), 4.

74. Report (1910), 11–12.

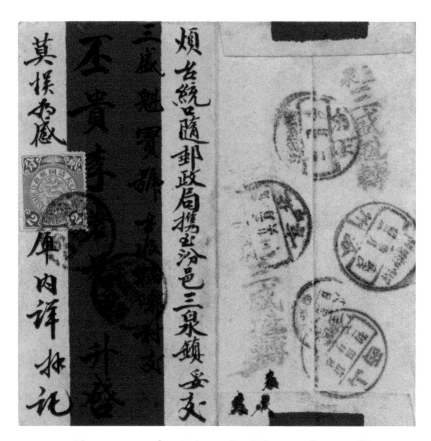

FIGURE 9.3 A letter cover sent from Kulun to Guo Village near the town of Sanquan in Fenzhou, Shanxi Province, posted in late April 1910. The letter cover instructs the hybrid mail couriers involved, covering areas from Kulun to Shanxi Province via Zhangjiakou and Beijing. There were three mail systems engaged: the military relay courier system, the IPO, and a private shop which was either a letter hong itself or a commercial shop with a messenger service. On the front cover (left) is a two-cent postage stamp and the recipient's name, which is in the largest font size and almost in the center of the red banner. To right of the recipient's name are the delivery instructions: "Please trouble the military courier (taitongkou 台統口) followed by the Post Office to deliver the mail to Sanquan Town in Fenzhou, and safely hand it to the honorable shop Sanshengkui 三盛魁 . . . to bring to Guo Village." On the back cover (right), beside the round IPO postage chops, there are two repeated red chops which read, "Sanquan Sanshengkui [letter hong] transmits." The sender put his location, Kulun, on the left-hand side next to the recipient's name. The seven IPO postage chops all together show that the letter was transmitted through Zhangjiakou, Beijing, Fenzhou, and Sanquan town. The chop stamped in Zhangjiakou is dated Gengxu year, third month, twenty-fourth day (May 3, 1910), and the chop stamped in Sanquan town is dated Gengxu year, fourth month, second day (May 10, 1910). This means that the transmittal from Zhangjiakou to Sanquan took seven days. It normally took seven to nine days from Kulun to Zhangjiakou; therefore it is likely that the letter started its journey from Kulun between April 24 and April 26, 1910. Source: Tsai Ming-feng, *Da Qing youzheng*.

Mongolian, who knows mouth by mouth where to find Mongolian encampments, and rides for these to change horses."[75]

As tensions rose, Russia set up three new consulates in Outer Mongolia for strategic reasons: in Uliasutai in 1909, and in Kobdo and Chenghuasi in early 1911. Russian consulates in Kulun and other locations were required to monitor movements of all parties, and acted as secret information channels between the region and St. Petersburg.[76] This discreet collaboration finally brought a Mongolian delegation, approved by the eighth Jebtsundamba Khutuktu, to St. Petersburg in late July and August 1911, the journey of which Qing officials were kept in ignorance.[77] The Russian Imperial Post opened in Uliasutai in October 1911, and Mongolians were contracted to transport mail between Uliasutai and Kulun. When asked whether they would also agree to transport mail for the Chinese Post Office, the Mongolians refused. In the end, plans to further expand the Uliasutai–Kulun routes were postponed because of the instability in the region.[78]

Mongolia's independence was declared in December 1911, and the government of the eighth Jebtsundamba Khutuktu, now elevated to the title Bogd Khan, was formed in Kulun. According to Lu Lüren 路履仁, who was the Chinese postal clerk in Kulun, all of the Qing officials were expelled apart from those who worked in the Post Office and the telegraph agency.[79] The Zhangjiakou–Kulun–Kyakhta route became the first casualty of the situation and was halted.[80] Although it was soon resumed, it was difficult to maintain its original design, and parcel delivery and remittances ceased.

75. Perry-Ayscough and Otter-Barry, *With the Russians in Mongolia*, 65.

76. Sizova, "The Political Role of the Russian Consulates," 10–17.

77. Ewing, "Revolution on the Chinese Frontier," 111–12.

78. Théophile A. Piry to Minister of Communications, June 15, 1912, SHAC, YZ (2) 638; "Report to the Director General of Posts," November 17, 1912, SHAC, YZ (2) 638. See also Ministry of Communications to Ministry of Foreign Affairs, "Wai Meng youzheng shi you" 外蒙郵政事由 [Postal matters in Outer Mongolia], September 26, 1914, ZYJYD, 03-32-164-01-083.

79. Lu Lüren, "Wai Menggu jianwen," 65–68. I wish to thank Lai Hui-min for providing me with this source.

80. Report (1911), 12.

Trilateral Talks and the Final Stretch from Kulun to Ürümqi

Regional-level wars did not end after 1912, as not all Mongolians shared a single view. In Inner Mongolia, different banners and tribes had divergent opinions on the Qing empire, and this resulted in a rather confusing situation. Some banners had clearly signed up for an independent Mongolia, some were leaning toward supporting the Qing government to form a constitutional monarchy, and some were talking to both the Bogd Khan and the new republican governments.[81] Yuan Shikai continued to send troops north to work with banners who were sympathetic to his government. Russia and the Bogd Khan government signed an agreement in October 1912, but Russia also continued talks with the republican government, without involving Mongolia, and they reached an agreement in April 1913. In the agreement, Mongolia would acquire autonomy and self-government under Chinese sovereignty. The Bogd Khan government was unhappy over Russia's intervention, and it decided to talk directly to China and Japan. Trilateral negotiations—involving China, Mongolia, and Russia—began in September 1914 in Kyakhta and continued until June 1915.

The process of the trilateral negotiations was divided into two main areas of discussion. The first focused on issues of sovereignty, and the second on more practical issues, such as tariffs and the functioning of railways, the telegraph, postal services, criminal jurisdiction, and so on. The outcome on sovereignty was reached early, by the beginning of November, and stayed within the provisions of two previous agreements from 1912 and 1913.[82] Having achieved a less than satisfactory result over Tibet, and having only recently become a member of the Universal Postal Union, China saw the Post Office as the most significant matter impacting on sovereignty—though agreement proved to be very hard to reach. According to the memoir of Chen Lu 陳籙 (1877–1939), who was one of the representatives at the negotiations, the discussions over postal and tele-

---

81. Tachibana, "The 1911 Revolution and 'Mongolia.'" See also Bulag, "Independence as Restoration," 1–16; and Nakami, "A Protest against the Concept of the 'Middle Kingdom.'"

82. Chang Chi-hsiung, *Wai Menggu zhuquan guishu*, 234–37, 261.

graph matters were very tense and ended in acrimony in December 1914.[83] While China stressed its postal privilege and ownership of the telegraph, Mongolia and Russia argued that the issues involved were industrial or commercial matters and should therefore be considered as part of the domestic affairs of Mongolia, since under the treaty it would function as an autonomous entity. Under the terms of agreement between Mongolia and Russia in 1912, Russia had already gained the right to build railways in Mongolia, and China decided not to challenge this. What remained to be discussed were postal and telegraphy matters.[84]

There were already telegraph connections between Kyakhta and Zhangjiakou. Russia and Mongolia wanted China to recognize Mongolia's postal privilege; in return, Chinese postal facilities in Kulun and Kyakhta would be retained.[85] In April 1915 Russia put pressure on China to give up its telegraphy facilities in Outer Mongolia, but China insisted on ownership or, at the very least, that Mongolia should be required to purchase the facilities.[86] In May 1915 the Beijing government had received an ultimatum from Japan over its Twenty-One Demands. Following this development, Russia threatened to withdraw from agreeing to retain Chinese postal branches in Kulun and Kyakhta and also from allowing Chinese officials and the Chinese Post Office to use the facilities of the military courier relay stations in Outer Mongolia should China refuse to give up the telegraph lines.[87] The Bogd Khan government also ordered the

83. Chen Lu, *Zhi shi biji*, 17–22.

84. Bi Guifang 畢桂芳 and Chen Lu to Ministry of Foreign Affairs, "Guanyu tielu youdian shi E reng jian bu rangbu" 關於鐵路郵電事俄仍堅不讓步 [Russia did not give way on railway, post office and telegraph], December 24, 1914, ZYJYD, 03-32-173-02-041. By this time, both Bi and Chen thought that China could really only keep the Post Office.

85. Bi Guifang and Chen Lu to Ministry of Foreign Affairs, "E yun bao cun wo Ku Qia yuanyou youju" 俄允保存我庫恰原有郵局 [Russia allowing us to keep the original post offices in Kulun and Kyakhta], January 3, 1915 [according to the time/date on the telegram transcription], ZYJYD, 03-32-173-02-035.

86. "Wai Meng dianbao shi" 外蒙古電報事 [Telegram on Outer Mongolia matter], May 13, 1915, ZYJYD, 03-32-165-03-048.

87. Chen Lu, *Zhi shi biji*, 34–36; Alexander Miller to the Ministry of Foreign Affairs, "Yuxian jinggao quxiao Zhongguo zhu Ku dayuan deyong Menggu youzheng taizhang you" 預先警告取消中國駐庫大員得用蒙古郵政台站條文由 [Advance warning on ending usage of military courier relay stations in Mongolia for the Chinese staff stationed at Kulun], May 15, 1915, ZYJYD, 03-32-176-01-004.

Chinese Post Office in Kyakhta to close, and this raised tensions further.[88] The Chinese Post Office in Kulun had already been closed for some time, and the situation did not improve until the conference in Kyakhta reached agreement. Until that point, Chinese merchants had to use Russian post offices for remittances, and this created much inconvenience.[89]

A twenty-two-article tripartite agreement was signed on June 7, 1915. Article 18 stated that Chinese postal facilities in Kulun and Kyakhta would be retained; Article 19 stated that buildings and offices for Chinese officials and security guards in Kobdo, Kulun, and Uliasutai belonged to China; Article 20 allowed Chinese officials to use the military courier relay stations when necessary.[90] These three points provided legal cover and secured facilities on the ground for the Chinese Post Office to run and indeed to resume its expansion after the end of negotiations. The Zhangjiakou–Kulun–Kyakhta line was running again, and the plans for linking the Uliasutai–Kulun routes were once again explored (see fig. 9.4).

In 1914 there were nine Russian post offices registered in China and Mongolia, and by the end of the First World War the number had increased to eighteen.[91] Table 9.1 shows the presence of foreign post offices in China in 1915. It is noticeable that the numbers of foreign post offices—and particularly those of the Japanese and Russian postal services—had grown in the previous ten years. The revenue of the Chinese Post Office grew too; and from 1915 onward the organization started to make a surplus: around $302,592 in 1915, $937,403 in 1916, and $1,422,000 in 1917 (in Mexican dollars).[92]

The tables were turned after Russia's own revolution at the end of 1917, when Russia sought to withdraw its station in Uliasutai. The costs for the

88. Bi Guifang and Chen Lu to Ministry of Foreign Affairs, "Guanyu youzheng shi mishi dui yuanyi ershier tongyi bugenggai . . ." 關於郵政事密使對原議二十二同意不更改 . . . [Secret agent agreed not to change the original clause 22 as previously discussed . . .], May 16, 1915, ZYJYD, 03-32-173-02-080.

89. Inspectorate General of Posts to Ministry of Communications, June 8, 1915, SHAC, YZ (2) 638; Beijing Commerce Association (Jingshi shangwu zonghui 京師商務 總會) to Ministry of Foreign Affairs, ". . . Kulun youju dui yu shangren suo ji chao kuan . . ." . . . 庫倫郵局對於商人所寄鈔款 . . . [. . . On merchants using the (Russian) post office in Kulun to transfer money . . .], April 12, 1915, ZYJYD, 03-02-040-01-008.

90. Chang Chi-hsiung, *Wai Menggu zhuquan guishu*, 265.

91. Zhang Yi, *Zhonghua youzhengshi*, 126.

92. Report (1917), 9.

FIGURE 9.4 Postal service for heavy mail between Zhangjiakou and Kulun, run by Mongolian couriers assisted by camels. The wording "Chinese Post Office" (Zhonghua youzheng 中華郵政) can be seen on the mailbox carried by the second camel from the left. Source: Report (1921). Acknowledgments to Tsai Chia-chi of the Specialist Library of the Chunghwa Postal Museum, Taipei, for providing this image, and to Jamie Carstairs for improving the image quality.

Table 9.1. Foreign countries' post office locations across China, 1915

Country	Postal locations
France	Beihai, Beijing, Chongqing, Fuzhou, Guangzhou, Hankou, Mengzi, Ningbo, Qiongzhou, Shanghai, Tianjin, Xiamen, Yunnanfu (Kunming)
Germany	Beijing, Fuzhou, Guangzhou, Hankou, Jinan, Nanjing, Shanghai, Shantou, Tianjin, Weixian, Xiamen, Yantai, Yichang, Zhenjiang,
Japan	Andong, Beijing, Changchun, Changsha, Dadonggou, Fengtian, Fuzhou, Guangzhou, Hangzhou, Hankou, Harbin, Jilin, Jinan, Jiujiang, Liaoyang, Nanjing, Niuzhuang, Qinhuangdao, Shanghai, Shanhaiguan, Shantou, Shashi, Suzhou, Tanggu, Tianjin, Tielinxian, Xiamen, Wuhu, Yantai, Yichang, Zhenjiang
Russia	Ang'angxi, Beijing, Chenghuasi, Dihua, Hailar, Hankou, Harbin, Kuanchengzi (Changchun), Kulun, Kyakhta, Shanghai, Shufuxian, Tacheng, Tianjin, Yantai, Yiningxian, Zhangjiakou
United Kingdom	Fuzhou, Guangzhou, Hankou, Ningbo, Qiongzhou, Shanghai, Shantou, Shufuxian, Tianjin, Xiamen, Yantai
United States	Shanghai

Source: "A List of Foreign Post Offices in China" 在中國之外國郵局清單. SHAC, YZ (2) 322.

Russian Post Office to maintain the postal service in this area were much higher than its income, and in 1917 Russia decided to withdraw.[93] This withdrawal provoked the Chinese to reflect on their communication networks and strategic arrangements across northern China, Outer Mongolia, and Xinjiang, particularly in relation to information security. As regards the telegraph, the station at Uliasutai belonged to Russia, and China also lost its telegraph station at Kulun. It was reasoned that if China could seize this opportunity to establish post office facilities in Kobdo and Uliasutai, then it would be able to rebuild its information networks, including setting up telegraph stations to connect to Gansu and Xinjiang.[94]

93. Inspectorate General of Posts to Ministry of Communications, December 21, 1917, in *TYS*, 3:313–14; Ministry of Communications to Ministry of Foreign Affairs, ". . . Wuliyasutai difang Eguo youjian jun song jiao Zhongguo youju banli . . ." . . . 烏里雅蘇台地方俄國郵件均送交中國郵局辦理 . . . [. . . Russian mail in Uliasutai area all managed by Chinese Post Office . . .], May 31, 1918, ZYJYD, 03-02-036-01-001.

94. Ministry of Communications to Inspectorate General of Posts, February 8, 1918, in *TYS*, 3:317–21.

In a broader context, the timing for asserting postal privilege in Outer Mongolia coincided with developments in global politics. An important turning point around the discourse of sovereignty arrived when China formally joined the First World War in 1917 and announced that it was breaking away from its formal relationship with Germany. For young China, this step was very significant, as it was regarded as "China's first independent participation in world politics."[95] Despite anticipated financial losses, an Kulun–Uliasutai route was inaugurated in early April 1918.[96]

In November of that same year the route was further expanded from Uliasutai to connect to Kobdo in the west, and from there farther west to Chenghuasi, which already had an existing connection with Ürümqi. In this design, the two largest cities in Outer Mongolia and Xinjiang—Kulun and Ürümqi—were now connected. Altogether, at 10,125 *li* (approximately 6,230 kilometers), the Ürümqi–Chenghuasi–Kobdo–Uliasutai–Kulun–Zhangjiakou route was the longest overland postal route in the world at the time.[97] This line complemented the Ürümqi–Jiayuguan–Lanzhou–Xi'an–Beijing line, at 6,600 *li* (4,085 kilometers).

Hugh Kirkhope's colorful, somewhat romanticized version of the Post Office's twenty-five-year institutional history presented an uplifting narrative that combined the leadership of the Qing court and the subsequent republican government with the individual efforts of postal staff, both Chinese and foreign. In many ways, his listing of the creation of the "longest postal route" as one of the Post Office's finest achievements, in the face of huge distances and multiple practical obstacles, is justified. No doubt for the employees of the Chinese Post Office, the operation of this postal route was marked as a glorious achievement both for the Chinese

---

95. Reinsch, *An American Diplomat in China*, 253. See also Guoqi Xu, *China and the Great War*, 164–67.

96. A. H. Hyland to Inspectorate General of Posts, April 5, 1918, in *TYS*, 3:314.

97. The Dihua–Chenghuasi route was 1,900 *li* (approximately 1,180 kilometers), the Chenghuasi–Kobdo–Uliastai–Kulun route was 5,525 *li* (approximately 3,420 kilometers), and the Kulun–Zhangjiakou route was 2,700 *li* (approximately 1,670 kilometers); see "Zhonghua minguo qinian youzheng shiwu zonglun, shangbian" 中華民國七年郵政事務總論 [Report on the working of the Chinese Post Office, 1918 (part one)], in Zhang Zhihe and Hu Zhongyuan, *Zhongguo youzheng shiwu zonglun*, 1:485. The same whole line was counted as 10,075 *li* (approximately 6,240 kilometers) in 1921; see Report (1921), 50.

modernization project and for Chinese nationalism. Unfortunately, what Kirkhope might not have anticipated when he wrote his "Historical Survey" was that Chinese postal services in Outer Mongolia would once again be interrupted at the end of 1921, after Mongolia formally claimed independence.

The hybrid nature of the Post Office clearly had a significant impact on the actual management of postal operations, as well as the making of institutional history. While the *four-circular discourse* dominated postal history prior to 1911, the Chinese perspectives came to the fore when there was a progressive shift to an overtly patriotic tone in the available historical sources. The story of the making of the longest overland postal route in 1921 reflected the intention of senior postal officials, both Chinese and foreign, to highlight the important role played by the Post Office in the state-building project of the young republic. Instead of focusing on the divergence between foreign and Chinese staff, the senior management team was more eager to celebrate achievement in the name of the republic than to examine the internal politics. But although its aims are transparent to us, the history presented nevertheless provides readers with an opportunity to review the great sweep of modern Chinese history in multiple dimensions.

EPILOGUE

During one of my trips to China for this project in the early 2010s, I was fortunate to be shown around the four-story General Post Office Building in Shanghai. The building is situated by the Suzhou Creek, not far from busy Nanjing Road. It was completed in 1924. Unlike most historical buildings in Shanghai today, which are used for all kinds of activity unrelated to their original purposes, a postal branch was still attached to the building, and some space was in use for a postal museum. Indeed, before that visit, I had posted items from that post office on a number of occasions, using my visits as an excuse to enter, soak up the atmosphere, and let imagination take me back in time. On this occasion, entering the building from an obscure side door, my guide and I climbed up a stone staircase and entered a large room. The room had a high ceiling and was floored with what must surely have been the original large-patterned tiles. The room housed some items of furniture, among them several chunky wooden desks that certainly had the appearance of something from history. The largest was very imposing, designed to be used by two clerks sitting opposite each other. Both sides of the desk were equipped with drawers, and its top was large enough to be used as an enormous, flat platform, spacious enough to accommodate a wall-size map, or to become the locus of a group discussion. I was told that the desks belonged to the "old post office" before 1949.

In its earliest days, the status of the Chinese Post Office was ambivalent; it never appeared at the high table with the Bureau of Railways (Tiedaobu 鐵道部) and the Chinese Maritime Customs Service (CMCS), because of its lowly revenue income and, initially at least, its limited reach. Its success arose in largely unglamorous fashion out of the myriad reforms undertaken in the closing period of the Qing dynasty. Yet along with its visible but seemingly mundane role of collecting and delivering mail, it carried the flag for two important missions: the construction of a unified national communications network across China's enormous land mass for use by the general public for the first time in Chinese history, and the projection of national sovereignty. This book has explored how this came about, with the project given official sanction to proceed (but without direction from the central government in any significant form) and driven by a small group of people within the CMCS on an extremely tight budget. Indeed, the Post Office is exceptional by its very nature, not just in being the largest, most far-reaching institution established in the late Qing era but also because of its unequivocal success at such a crisis-ridden time.

The approach of this book has been largely chronological, the result of much thought as to the best way to proceed. When planning out the structure, a part thematic, part chronological approach was originally considered, and some experimental structuring conducted along those lines. In the end, I rejected this as a way forward, concluding that although a thematic approach could potentially provide a good path in engaging with theories and frameworks, it carried with it an unavoidable downside in the loss of the narrative approach (which I eventually adopted). I found the impact of events, together with the relationships and indeed the rivalries of the key figures involved in the creation of the Post Office, critically important in reflecting the complex sociopolitical context of the late Qing period. I have sought in this monograph to bring the human stories to the foreground while at the same time attempting to contribute to the wider scholarship on the history of Chinese modernization in relation to concepts of sovereignty and the development of communications.

In this light, I have used stories to illuminate the modernization process: in this telling, Robert Hart; Qing government officials of both high and low rank; postal staff both senior and junior, Chinese and foreign; and Chinese communities all played their respective parts, and their voices are all heard within the narrative. In so doing, I have attempted to show how the relationships between key figures—for example, Robert Hart, Li Hongzhang, Prince Gong, Wenxiang, Thomas F. Wade, Weng Tonghe, Zhang Zhidong—proved to be the critical factor in the success or failure of various postal initiatives at different times. These individuals' paths intertwined over several decades, and their relationships continually evolved. Their respective rise and fall in power and position was what ultimately decided when and how China's first national postal service was established. Another example is the career of Deng Weiping, a Chinese postal clerk who took part in the expansion of postal routes in northern China after the Boxer Rebellion. Ten years later he was sent to Tibet as a postmaster, though this position only lasted a few months and ended after the Chinese Revolution of 1911. The trajectory of Deng's career was embedded within the ebb and flow of the external political situation and the growth of the institution. His stories also provide space and depth through which to reflect on the elements of historical contingency so important in shaping the Post Office in this Chinese context.

Aside from the narrative approaches described, I was much stimulated in the writing of the book by the valuable work of philatelists. Their methods in bringing artifacts together with literature are scientific, inspirational, and challenging, while their attention to detail is admirable. Without artifacts, modern postal history would only be half presented. Many cases discussed in the book have had to use either artifacts or images to prove or challenge theories abstracted from incomplete or ambiguous written records. Postal systems were designed to be used by people, and by engaging with the practical realities of franking chops, postage stamps, and letter covers, the dry lists of rules and regulations issued at the headquarters in Beijing become live and real.

Inevitably, due to limitations of space, some themes could not be addressed in detail. Among them is the field of postal maps. In 1903 the

Post Office released a wall-size map titled "China—Postal Working Map," intended for internal use only. This single sheet was followed in 1907 by a much larger project, the *China—Postal Album* (*Da Qing youzheng yutu* 大清郵政輿圖), a book twenty inches tall by twelve and a half inches wide, which, when opened and the sheets unfolded, boasted maps nearly double these dimensions. It contained twenty-one maps, each corresponding to one of the Chinese provinces. This was an important in-house creation of the Post Office and the Statistical Department of the CMCS. Two updated wall-size national maps were produced in 1917 and 1920, while the second, third, and then fourth editions of the *China—Postal Album* were released in 1919, 1933, and 1936, respectively. During the Beiyang government period and the Nanjing government era, these postal maps had important roles to play. For the officials the maps provided useful, practical information, while for the general public those maps were both educational and a source of national pride: an expression of imagined national space. As was noted in chapter 7, the rich information embedded in the postal maps, particularly in relation to the hierarchy of the postal branches as well as the main transportation and telegraph routes, would require a team to fully explore and examine questions relating to urbanization, communication, and trade. Those maps helped me clarify ideas, allowing me to visualize how the postal routes were unfolded and expanded, and showed how villages, towns, and cities were brought together within the growing postal network. Each dot on a map is meaningful.

My aim with this book has been to provide a broad narrative context to the origins of the Post Office in China. Much work remains to be done in fully assimilating the place and significance of the institution in China's early twentieth-century transformation. Where depth is lacking, I offer both my apologies and my encouragement to other scholars to take up the baton.

APPENDIX ONE

IG Circular 706 /
Postal No. 7, Hart, 1896

Circular 706.
Postal No. 7.
Inspectorate General of Customs
Peking, 9th April 1896

SIR,

An Edict assenting to the Yamên's proposal to introduce a Government postal system was issued on the 20th March and communicated to me officially a few days later. This postal idea, as you know, has long occupied the attention of the Chinese authorities—the suggestion to establish an Imperial Post on Western lines having been made by myself so far back as June 1861, when I first came to Peking; but differences of opinion at the capital and in the provinces, and changes from time to time not only in the occupants of the official posts most concerned, but in the earlier and later views of those officials themselves, have combined to discourage effort and delay action till now. Government has, however, at last taken the matter seriously, and the Decree just received creates an Imperial Post for all China and confides its management to myself. Notwithstanding the fact that the sanction is both definitive and Imperial, a very modest beginning will still be made, and the system will be both introduced quietly and developed slowly; but while procedure will be so planned as to avoid friction in respect of whatever might hurt deserving people's livelihoods by unnecessary interference with existing institutions or embarrass and occasion difficulties for officials and governments, it is confidently expected that some future day will see the Imperial Post functioning widely and fully appreciated, the people finding in it and its developments an everyday convenience and the Government a useful servant and, in this populous, industrious and letter-loving country, a perennial source of revenue. I append an English version of the regulations laid before the Emperor in the Yamên's Memorial—necessarily brief to invite perusal, and yet presenting a sufficiently comprehensive scheme to warrant sanction; they are but the outline, so to speak, of a programme yet to be filled in, and they and this Circular will of course be supplemented by detailed rules and followed up by fuller explanations and instructions later on.

I am, etc.,

(signed) ROBERT HART
Inspector General
To
The Commissioners of Customs

APPENDIX TWO

IG Circular 709 /
Postal No. 9, Hart, 1896

Circular 709.
Postal No. 9.
Inspectorate General of Customs
Peking, 30th April 1896

SIR,
1—In continuation of my Circulars Nos. 706 and 707:
Postal:
I now append the Chinese version of the regulations issued in Circular No. 706 and the Memorial in which the Yamên submitted them to the Emperor.

2—Private postal establishments have existed and prospered and official couriers have functioned usefully in this country for centuries, and therefore the postal idea is neither new nor original; but the comparison of their procedure and its results with the successful working of national Post Offices by other Governments has naturally convinced every inquirer how much better the public are served by the latter and what an important addition to the revenues of the State must follow the introduction and full development of Western postal methods. A very proper desire on the part of Chinese officials not to engage in a business competition with the people in every city and province who make a livelihood out of carrying letters, etc., and an equally proper unwillingness to assume responsibilities toward other powers until able to fulfil them, have united to embitter discussion and postpone decision; and although inaugurated with the full support of the Government, the Imperial Post cannot be expected to answer even moderate expectations, whether as a public convenience or as a revenue-yielding measure, so long as those adjuncts are wanting which make success possible elsewhere, namely good roads with reliable communication. During the three dozen years it has been maturing, many Yamên Ministers, several Viceroys and Governors, some representatives abroad, and various Customs officials have had occasion to handle the project, and it has more than once been on the point of inception, more especially in the year 1876, when both a national post and Government mint on Western lines were excluded by a conspiracy of silence, so to speak, from the Chefoo Convention. This long delay has naturally made room for other complications and embarrassments, but some compensation may perhaps be found in the thought that the offspring of Native appreciation will be a healthier national growth and more generally welcome than the issue of a distasteful negotiation. We have now done with the past and its discouraging uncertainties, and if we are beginning a future for which various difficulties are in store, time and tide are in our favour, and we need fear neither failure nor disaster, but, on the contrary, look for stability and growth, with patience for support and prudence for guide.

3—Before concluding this circular it is only fitting that I should mention the names of two Commissioners, Mr. KOPSCH and Mr. DETRING, and place it on record that what there has been of success in the working of the experiment the Customs have kept alive the last 30 years is mainly due to courier arrangements and office details initiated or superintended by the latter, and that to the former, for inquiries made when deputed to travel on postal business some years ago and for reports, suggestions and Chinese versions of various postal rules and regulations, the Imperial Post of the future will be largely indebted. Nor should I omit to add the name and acknowledge the services of a very helpful auxiliary, the Ningpo Office Writer Mr. LI KUEI, now occupying a territorial post which does him much honour in Chehkiang. To all three recognition and thanks are due for the good work they have done.

I am, etc.,

(signed) ROBERT HART
Inspector General
To
The Commissioners of Customs

APPENDIX THREE

IG Circular 1802 /
Postal No. 261, Aglen, 1911

Circular 1802
Postal No. 261
Peking, 30th May 1911

SIR,

1—An important stage in postal development and progress has now been reached and this Circular, the last that will appear in the Customs series bearing a postal number, is to inform you that I am to-day handing over charge of the Imperial Chinese Posts to Mr. T. PIRY, appointed by Imperial Decree Postmaster General under the Ministry of Posts and Communications.

To those who have studied postal affairs in recent years, the step now taken will come as no surprise. Ever since the establishment, in 1906, of the Yu-ch'uan Pu, it has been evident that, sooner or later, the Postal Administration would be brought under the direct control of the proper Board, and that its continuance as a department of the Imperial Maritime Customs was only a question of time. By deferring the act of separation until the ripe fruit was ready to drop from the parent tree, the Chinese Government has shown its wisdom and the confidence it has reposed in its Customs advisers.

While step by step the paths of Customs and Posts have been gradually diverging, orderly preparations have been quietly made to meet the situation of to-day, and the result has been that the Customs Service is now in a position to hand over a Postal Administration in all respects adopted to the requirements of the East and yet embodying many of the most important features of Western practice. It will, I feel convinced, be a matter of very general regret that circumstances have made it impossible for the Inspector General to present in person to the Chinese Government the Service he created and nursed with such unremitting care through all the difficult and trying years of infancy. But it must give him the greatest satisfaction to feel that the words he used 15 years ago, when notifying to the Service the receipt of an Imperial Decree establishing the Imperial Chinese Post, have been more than justified and that the day has come which sees "the Imperial Post functioning widely and fully appreciated, the people finding in it and its developments an everyday convenience and the Government a useful servant."

2—The enclosed correspondence with the Shui-wu Ch'u will acquaint you with the more immediate steps which have led to separation and the arrangements sanctioned by the Yu-Ch'uan Pu, whereby the Postal Staff, foreign and Chinese, is assured of continued and useful employment under regulations regarding pay, promotion, leave, and retiring allowances which have been laid down by the Inspector General and which are to continue in force.

The Board's Memorial appended to the correspondence enclosed expresses in terms complimentary to the Customs Service the Chinese Government's appreciation of postal work performed and progress made, and pays a well-earned tribute to the Postal Secretary, Mr PIRY, for his share in the administration. The Memorial also lays down the policy to be pursued in the future, and places on record the debt incurred by the Postal Administration to the Imperial Maritime Customs. You will see that the Postmaster General (總辦) will be subordinate to a Director General (局長), who will occupy a position in the Ministry analogous to that of an Under Secretary of State, and that for the present the holder of this office will be His Excellency Li CHING-FANG (李經方). The instructions received direct from the Yu-Ch'uan Pu in regard to the changes now made will be communicated to the Postal Staff by the Postmaster General.

3—I cannot conclude this Circular without expressing, in the name of the Inspector General, Sir ROBERT HART, the thanks which are due to all those members of the Customs Service, past and present, who have borne the burden and heat of the day and whose efforts have contributed so much to the success that has been achieved. The position won has not been attained without sacrifices in which all have taken a share, many receiving no other reward than the consciousness of work well done. The Service, in bidding farewell and wishing all prosperity to the Administration which has sprung from it, will, I feel sure, continue to take the friendliest interest in, and always work in the closest harmony with, the Imperial Post Office.

I am, etc.,

F. A. AGLEN,
Officiating Inspector General, ad interim.

APPENDIX FOUR

Postal Circular 262, Piry, 1911

Postal Circular 262
Peking, 31st May 1911

SIR,

1—A memorial recommending the transfer of the Postal Service from the control of the Shui-wu Ch'u, under the Inspector General, to that of the Ministry of Posts and Communications, emanating from His Excellency SHÊNG *Kung-pao,* President of that Board, and supported by his Cabinet Ministers, was submitted to the Throne on the 26th May, and received the Imperial sanction the same day. In consequence, on the 28th May (the 1st day of the 5th moon), the date fixed by the Imperial Decree, the act of separation of the Posts from the Customs was virtually accomplished, and effectively completed on the 30th May, on which day I notified by telegram all heads of districts and sub-districts in the following words:—

> "Under Imperial Decree, the Postal Service is placed under the control of Ministry of Posts and Communications, myself being appointed Postmaster General to continue management of establishments and Staff, both Chinese and foreign; conditions and prospects of employment as under Customs regime assured. Notify Staff.
> —PIRY, *Postmaster General."*

2—The central Administration of the Postal Service as a State institution is constituted at Peking as follows:—

> Minister of Posts and Communications: His Excellency SHÊNG *Kung-pao.*

Acting Vice-President of the Ministry of Posts and Communications and
Director General of Posts: His Excellency Li CHING-FANG.
Postmaster General: T. PIRY.

Certain modifications will be found necessary in the titles employed in the Postal Service, in order to bring them into line with
those used in other Departments of the Ministry; these modifications
will, however, imply no change of functions, status or pay, and will be
notified later on. Meanwhile, it is to be noted that the name of the
office hitherto styled Inspectorate General of Posts is changed to that
of Directorate General of Posts.

The routine of the Service will be carried on exactly as hitherto,
and all despatches, letters, memoranda, etc., will continue to be addressed directly to me, the Postmaster General, as the responsible head
of the executive Department of the Directorate General of Posts.

3—In his parting Circular No. 261 (Postal), notifying the Customs
and Postal Staffs that he has handed over the Imperial Post Office to
me, Mr Aglen, the Inspector General, sums up the close relationship
of the Customs and the Posts in the past and outlines, in comforting
words, the situation for the future. The change means no departure
from existing principles and policy, and is but the natural result of
progress in the national institutions of China, among which the Imperial Post Office has now taken rank. The transfer had to come sooner
or later, and now that all arrangements are made, the Staff, both Chinese and foreign, are to be complimented on the conditions obtained
regarding their prospects. From the beginning of the negotiations,
His Excellency SHÊNG *Kung-pao* instructed me to allay, by appropriate assurances, any misapprehension that might exist among the Staff,
Chinese or foreign, about their career in the Postal Service, and to
notify all that as regards continuity of employment, conditions of
service, pay and retiring allowances, existing rules and precedents
would remain in force, in a manner similar to those that prevail in the
Imperial Maritime Customs. Official despatches confirming this clear
understanding have since been received, based on which my telegram
of the 30th was despatched. Copies of the Chinese correspondence and
an English version of the Memorial and the Imperial Decree will be
found enclosed with this Circular. It is therefore expected that everyone in the Service, Chinese and foreign, will dismiss apprehension and
continue with tranquility in their duties, remembering, however, that
they are members of one great central Administration, for the prosperity

of which every effort must be put forward. Under the full patronage of the State, the Postal Service now enters upon a new career, and, with such a vast and promising country to develop, has every prospect of becoming one of the greatest postal organisations in the world. To continue to work with this end in view, I rely, as in the past, on the loyal and continuous devotion of all members of the Staff.

4—I cannot close this Circular without paying, in the name of all the Postal Staff, now about to be severed from its original base, a just tribute of admiration and gratitude to the founder and creator of the Postal Service, Sir ROBERT HART, Bart, G.C.M.G, now on furlough. From the beginning, the plan of development he so ably conceived has been faithfully followed and has brought postal enterprise to its present high standard. This plan, it is hoped, notwithstanding changes necessary to meet the requirements of the State, will be persevered with and bring the founder's *magnum opus* to a successful completion.

To our former colleagues of the Customs Service, too, who during the 14 years of close relationship have always tendered cheerfully and loyally their services to the Postal Department, with no other reward than the satisfaction of a duty well done, our fullest and heartiest thanks are due. I have confidence that the same amiable relations which have always prevailed between the two Services will continue; and I wish to impress on all members of the Postal Staff the extent of their indebtedness to the parent Service, the Imperial Maritime Customs.

I am, etc.,

T. Piry,
Postmaster General.

Bibliography

Abbreviations for Archival Materials and Short References Used in the Footnotes

Docs. Ill.: Wright, Stanley F., ed. *Documents Illustrative of the Origin, Development, and Activities of the Chinese Customs Service.* 7 vols. Shanghai: Statistical Department of the Inspectorate General, 1937–40.

Hart Journals 1854–1863: Bruner, Katherine F., John K. Fairbank, and Richard J. Smith, eds. *Entering China's Service: Robert Hart's Journals, 1854–1863.* Cambridge, MA: Harvard University Asia Center, 1986.

Hart Journals 1863–1866: Smith, Richard J., John K. Fairbank, and Katherine F. Bruner, eds. *Robert Hart and China's Early Modernization: His Journals, 1863–1866.* Cambridge, MA: Harvard University Asia Center, 1991.

MS Chinese 3: H. B. Morse Letters, 1886–1907. Houghton Library, Harvard University.

MS Chinese 4: Sir Robert Hart Papers, 1865–1919. Houghton Library, Harvard University.

MS Chinese 5: Henry Ferdinand Merrill correspondence with Sir Robert Hart, Robert Bredon, Sir Francis Aglen, and others. Houghton Library, Harvard University.

Postal Service List: *Postal Service List for 1922.* Shanghai: Supply Department of the Directorate General of Posts, 1923.

QXWTK: Liu Jinzao 劉錦藻, ed. *Qingchao xu wenxian tongkao* 清朝續文獻通考 [Encyclopedia of the historical records of the Qing dynasty]. 400 *juan.* Shanghai: Shangwu yinshuguan, 1936.

Report (1904): "Report on the Working of the Imperial Post Office, 1904." In *Returns of Trade and Trade Reports, 1904.* Shanghai: Statistical Department of the Inspectorate General of Customs, 1905.

Report (1905): "Report on the Working of the Imperial Post Office, 1905." In *Returns of Trade and Trade Reports, 1905.* Shanghai: Statistical Department of the Inspectorate General of Customs, 1906.

Report (1906): "Report on the Working of the Imperial Post Office, 1906." In *Returns of Trade and Trade Reports, 1906*. Shanghai: Statistical Department of the Inspectorate General of Customs, 1907.

Report (1907): "Report on the Working of the Imperial Post Office, 1907." In *Returns of Trade and Trade Reports, 1907*. Shanghai: Statistical Department of the Inspectorate General of Customs, 1908.

Report (1908): "Report on the Working of the Imperial Post Office, 1908." In *Returns of Trade and Trade Reports, 1908*. Shanghai: Statistical Department of the Inspectorate General of Customs, 1909.

Report (1909): "Report on the Working of the Imperial Post Office, 1909." In *Returns of Trade and Trade Reports, 1909*. Shanghai: Statistical Department of the Inspectorate General of Customs, 1910.

Report (1910): "Report on the Working of the Imperial Post Office, 1910." In *Returns of Trade and Trade Reports, 1910*. Shanghai: Statistical Department of the Inspectorate General of Customs, 1911.

Report (1911): *Report on the Working of the Chinese Post Office, 1911*. Shanghai: Supply Department of the Directorate General of Posts, 1912.

Report (1917): *Report on the Working of the Chinese Post Office, 1917*. Shanghai: Supply Department of the Directorate General of Posts, 1918.

Report (1921): *Report on the Chinese Post Office: For the Tenth Year of Chung-Hua Min-Kuo (1921) with Which Is Incorporated an Historical Survey of the Quarter-Century (1896–1921)*. Shanghai: Supply Department of the Directorate General of the Posts, 1922.

Service List: The *Service List* of the Chinese Maritime Customs Service was an internal annual publication printed by the Shanghai-based Statistical Department of the Inspectorate General of Customs from 1875 onward. Between 1897 and 1910, the personnel list of the Postal Department was included. Harvard University and the library at the School of Oriental and African Studies Archives, University of London.

SHAC: Second Historical Archives of China (Zhongguo dier lishi danganguan 中國第二歷史檔案館), Nanjing, China.

SOAS MS211081: Hart, Robert. Copies of Correspondence of Sir Robert Hart to Sir Francis Aglen. School of Oriental and African Studies Archives, University of London.

SQBH: Sir Robert Hart Collection, Special Collections, Queen's University of Belfast, MS15.

The IG: Fairbank, John King, Katherine Frost Bruner, and Elizabeth MacLeod Matheson, eds. *The I. G. in Peking: Letters of Robert Hart, Chinese Maritime Customs, 1868–1907*. 2 vols. Cambridge, MA: Belknap Press of Harvard University Press, 1975.

TMA: Tianjin Municipal Archives (Tianjinshi danganguan 天津市檔案館), Tianjin, China.

TYS: Qiu Runxi 仇潤喜, Li Guangyu 李光燏, et al., eds. *Tianjin youzheng shiliao* 天津郵政史料. 5 *ji* (6 vols. total, 2 vols. for the 2nd *ji.*). Beijing: Beijing hangkong hangtian daxue chubanshe, 1988–93.

WRJ: Weng Tonghe 翁同龢. *Weng Tonghe riji* 翁同龢日記 [Weng Tonghe diary]. Edited by Yijie Chen 陳義杰. 6 vols. Beijing: Zhonghua shuju, 1989.

WRJPY: Weng Tonghe 翁同龢. *Weng Tonghe riji pai yin ben* 翁同龢日記排印本 [A typeset edition of the diary of Weng Tonghe, with index]. Edited by Zhongfu Zhao 趙中孚. 6 vols. Taipei: Chengwen chubanshe, 1970.

YWSM: Wenqing 文慶, Jia Zhen 賈楨, and Baoyun, eds. *Chouban yiwu shimo* 籌辦夷務始末 [The complete account of managing barbarian affairs]. Photolithograph of the original edition. Beijing: Palace Museum, 1929–31.

ZJYS: *Zhongguo jindai youzheng shiliao* 中國近代郵政史料 [The historical materials of the modern Chinese postal service]. Beijing: Quanguo tushuguan wenxian suowei fuzhi zhongxin, 2005.

ZYJYD: Zhongyang yanjiuyuan Jindaishi yanjiusuo danganguan 中央研究院近代史研究所檔案館 [Archives, Institute of Modern History, Academia Sinica]. Taipei.

Other Sources

Baark, Erik. *Lightning Wires: The Telegraph and China's Technological Modernization, 1860–1890*. Westport, CT: Greenwood, 1997.

Bai Shouyi 白壽彝. *Zhongguo jiaotongshi* 中國交通史 [History of Chinese transportation]. Beijing: Tuanjie chubanshe, 2007.

Bayly, C. A. *Empire and Information: Intelligence Gathering and Social Communication in India 1780–1870*. Cambridge: Cambridge University Press, 1996.

Bell, Charles Alfred. *The People of Tibet*. Delhi: Motilal Banarsidass, reprint, 1994.

Bell, Stanley. *Hart of Lisburn*. Lisburn, UK: Lisburn Historical Press, 1985.

Benton, Gregor, and Hong Liu. *Dear China: Emigrant Letters and Remittances, 1820–1980*. Berkeley: University of California Press, 2018.

Bickers, Robert. "Infrastructural Globalization: Lighting the China Coast, 1860s–1930s." *Historical Journal* 56, no. 5 (2013): 431–58.

———. "Throwing Light on Natural Laws: Meteorology on the China Coast, 1869–1912." In *Treaty Ports in Modern China: Law, Land and Power*, edited by Robert Bickers and Isabella Jackson, 180–201. Abington, UK: Routledge, 2016.

Bishop, Mrs. J. F. (Isabella L. Bird). *The Yangtze Valley and Beyond: An Account of Journeys in China, Chiefly in the Province of Sze Chuan and among the Man-tze of the Somo Territory*. London: John Murray, 1899.

Bland, John Otway Percy. *China, Japan and Korea*. London: Heinemann, 1921.

Booz, Patrick. "Fear of Indian Tea and the Failure of British India to Break the Chinese Tea Monopoly in Tibet." In *Buddhist Himalaya: Tibet and the Himalaya*, edited by Alex McKay and Anna Balikci-Denjongpa, vol. 1, 277–90. Gangtok, India: Namgyal Institute of Tibetology, 2011.

Brunnert, H. S., and V. V. Hagelstrom. *Present Day Political Organization of China*. Taipei: Cheng Wen, 1971.

Bulag, Uradyn E. "Independence as Restoration: Chinese and Mongolian Declarations of Independence and the 1911 Revolutions." *Asia-Pacific Journal: Japan Focus* 10, no. 52 (2012): article 3. http://japanfocus.org/-Uradyn_E_-Bulag/3872/article.html.

Burger, Werner. *Ch'ing Cash*. 2 vols. Hong Kong: University Museum and Art Gallery, University of Hong Kong, 2016.

Campbell, Robert Ronald. *James Duncan Campbell: A Memoir by His Son.* Cambridge, MA: Harvard University Asia Center, 1970.

Campbell-Smith, Duncan. *Masters of the Post: The Authorized History of the Royal Mail.* London: Allen Lane, 2011.

Cao Qian 曹潛. *Zhonghua youzhengshi Taiwan bian* 中華郵政史臺灣編 [The history of the Chinese postal service, Taiwan volume]. Taipei: Jiaotongbu youzheng zongju, 1981.

Casey, Raymond. *The Russian Post Offices in the Chinese Empire (Part II).* Geneva: Feldman Galleries, 2012. http://www.davidfeldman.com/wp-content/uploads/2014/01/176_Russia_web.pdf.

Chang Chi-hsiung 張啓雄. *Wai Menggu zhuquan guishu jiaoshe 1911–1916* 外蒙主權歸屬交涉 1911–1916 [Disputes and negotiations over Outer Mongolia's national identity, unification or independence, and sovereignty, 1911–1916]. Taipei: Institute of Modern History, Academia Sinica, 2012.

Chang, Chihyun. *Government, Imperialism and Nationalism in China: The Maritime Customs Service and Its Chinese Staff.* Abingdon, UK: Routledge, 2013.

Chang Ken-Ming 張肯銘. "Cong renshi dao rentong: Wan Qing Zhongguo chaoye dui Deguo junshi nengli de renzhi, 1861–1890" 從認識到認同：晚清中國朝野對德國軍事能力的認知, 1861–1890 [From acquaintance to approval: The understanding of German military capacity among Chinese government and society in the late Qing period]. MA thesis, National Taiwan Normal University, 2011.

Chen, Hailian. "Technology for Re-engineering the Qing Empire: The Concept of 'Arts' and the Emergence of Modern Technical Education in China, 1840–1895." *ICON: Journal of the International Committee for the History of Technology* 26, no. 1 (2021): 10–43.

Chen Hsi-yuan 陳熙遠. "Changjiang tu shang de xiansuo: ziran dili yu renwen jingguan de lishi bianqian" 長江圖上的線索：自然地理與人文景觀的歷史變遷 [Unraveling political and cultural geography: Historical clues on a tattered map of the Yangtze River]. *Zhongyang yanjiuyuan Lishi yuyan suo jikan* 中央研究院歷史語言研究所集刊 [Bulletin of the Institute of History and Philology] 85, no. 2 (2014): 269–358.

Chen, Jerome. *Yuan Shih-k'ai.* Stanford, CA: Stanford University Press, 1972.

Chen Ling-chieh 陳令杰. "Qingmo haiguan yu Da Qing youzheng de jianli" 清末海關與大清郵政的建立 1878–1911 [Chinese Maritime Customs Service and the establishment of the Chinese Imperial Post in late Qing, 1878–1911]. MA thesis, National Tsing Hua University, 2012.

Chen Lu 陳錄. *Zhi shi biji* 止室筆記 [Notes from the study called Zhi shi]. *Jindai Zhongguo shiliao congkan* 近代中國史料叢刊 [Collectanea of modern Chinese history], compiled by Shen Yunlong 沈雲龍. Taipei: Wenhai chubanshe, 1968.

Chen Shiqi 陳詩啓. *Zhongguo jindai haiguanshi* 中國近代海關史 [The history of modern Chinese Customs Service]. Beijing: Renmin chubanshe, 2002.

Chen Tse-chuan 陳志川. "Haiguan shouci dalong youpiao sheji huituzhe zhi kaozheng" 海關首次大龍郵票設計繪圖者之考證 [Verification on the designer of Customs' first large dragon postage stamps], *Guocui youkan* 國粹郵刊 [Cathay philatelic journal], no. 1, first published in Shanghai, March 1, 1942; reprint version (Taibei: 1982): 1.

Chen Yue 陳悅. "Shen Baozhen, Li Hongzhang jiao yi dui Zhongguo jindai haifang jianshe zhi yingxiang" 沈葆楨、李鴻章交誼對中國近代海防建設之影響 [Impact of the friendship between Shen Baozhen and Li Hongzhang on China's modern coastal defenses]. In *Jindai Zhongguo haifangshi xinlun* 近代中國海防史新論 [New study on modern Chinese costal defenses], edited by Jinsheng Mai 麥勁生, 4–34. Hong Kong: Sanlian shudian, 2017.

Cheng, Ying-wan. *Postal Communication in China and Its Modernization, 1860–1896.* Cambridge, MA: Harvard University Asia Center, 1970.

Chiba Masashi 千葉正史. "Shinmatsu gyōsei kōmoku yakuchū (Ichi)" 清末行政綱目訳註 (一) [A copy of the scheme of administrative reform by the late Qing government, with Japanese translation (part 1)]. *Tōyō daigaku bungakubu kiyō–shigakuka hen* 東洋大學文學部紀要–史學科篇 [Bulletin of Toyo University, Department of History, Faculty of Literature] 37 (2011): 165–86.

———. "Shinmatsu gyōsei kōmoku yakuchū (Ni)" 清末行政綱目訳註 (二) [A copy of the scheme of administrative reform by the late Qing government with Japanese translation (part 2)]. *Tōyō daigaku bungakubu kiyō–shigakuka hen* 東洋大學文學部紀要–史學科篇 [Bulletin of Toyo University, Department of History, Faculty of Literature] 38 (2012): 177–212.

———. "Shinmatsu gyōsei kōmoku yakuchū (San)" 清末行政綱目訳註 (三) [A copy of the scheme of administrative reform by the late Qing government with Japanese translation (part 3)]. *Tōyō daigaku bungakubu kiyō–shigakuka hen* 東洋大學文學部紀要–史學科篇 [Bulletin of Toyo University, Department of History, Faculty of Literature] 39 (2013): 123–82.

———. "Shinmatsu ni okeru kakubu ritsuan chūbi rikken kyūkanen keikaku" 清末における各部立案籌備立憲九ヶ年計畫 [Nine-year plan of each ministry's preparation for the constitution during the late Qing period]. *Toyō daigaku bungakubu kiyō–shigaku ka hen* 東洋大學文學部紀要–史學科篇 [Bulletin of Toyo University, Department of History, Faculty of Literature], 42 (2016): 93–124.

Ch'u, T'ung-tsu. *Local Government in China under the Ch'ing.* Stanford, CA: Stanford University Press, 1962.

Cohen, Paul A. *Discovering History in China: American Historical Writing on the Recent Chinese Past.* New York: Columbia University Press, 1984.

Copy of Prince Kung's Answer to Sir Frederick Bruce's Memorandum Relative to the Affairs of China. London: Harrison and Sons, 1864.

Cordier, Henri. "Thomas Francis Wade." *T'oung Pao* 6, no. 4 (1895): 407–12.

Correspondence Relative to the Earl of Elgin's Special Missions to China and Japan, 1857–1859. London: Harrison and Sons, 1859.

Correspondence respecting Affairs in China. 1859–60. London: Harrison and Sons, 1861.

Correspondence respecting the Attack on the Indian Expedition to Western China, and the Murder of Mr. Margary. London: Harrison and Sons, 1876.

Correspondence respecting the Revision of the Treaty of Tien-tsin. London: Harrison and Sons, 1871.

Da Qing huidian shili 大清會典事例 [Supplementary cases to the collected statutes of the Qing dynasty]. Compiled by Kun Gang 崑岡 et al. Guangxu reign, 1899, 1220 *juan*.

Da Qing youzheng gongshu beiyong yutu 大清郵政公署備用輿圖 [China—Postal Working Map], prepared by the Inspectorate General of Customs and Post. Shanghai: Oriental Press, 1903.

Da Qing youzheng yutu 大清郵政輿圖 [China—Postal Album]. Shanghai: Statistical Department of the Inspectorate General of Customs, 1907.

Decennial Reports on the Trade, Navigation, Industries, etc., of the Ports Open to Foreign Commerce in China and Corea, and on the Condition and Development of the Treaty Port Provinces, 1882–91. Shanghai: Statistical Department of the Inspectorate General of Customs, 1893.

Decennial Reports on the Trade, Navigation, Industries, etc., of the Ports Open to Foreign Commerce in China, and on the Condition and Development of the Treaty Port Provinces, 1892–1901. 2 vols. Shanghai: Statistical Department of the Inspectorate General of Customs, 1904.

Donovan, John Patrick. "Travels and Experiences in China," unpublished manuscript. 2 vols. CWML MSS208, School of Oriental and African Studies Archives, University of London.

———. *Yesterday and To-day in China.* London: Drane's, 1923.

Drew, Edward. "Sir Robert Hart and His Life Work in China." *Journal of Race Development* 4, no. 1 (1913): 1–33.

Ewing, Thomas E. "Ch'ing Policies in Outer Mongolia 1900–1911." *Modern Asian Studies* 14, no. 1 (1980): 145–57.

———. "Revolution on the Chinese Frontier: Outer Mongolia in 1911." *Journal of Asian History* 12, no. 2 (1978): 101–19.

Fan Baichuan 樊百川. *Qingji de yangwu xinzheng* 清季的洋務新政 [The new policies toward foreign affairs during the Qing dynasty]. 2 vols. Shanghai: Shanghai shudian chubanshe, 2009.

Favereau, Marie. *The Horde: How the Mongols Changed the World.* Cambridge, MA: Harvard University Press, 2021.

Fei Xiaotong 費孝通. "Jiceng xingzheng de jianghua" 基層行政的僵化 [On the rigidity of the lowest level of bureaucracy]. In *Fei Xiaotong wenji* 費孝通文集 [Collected works of Fei Xiaotong], vol. 4. Beijing: Qunyan chubanshe, 1999.

Feng Jianyong 馮建勇. *Xinhai geming yu jindai Zhongguo bianjiang zhengzhi bianqian yanjiu* 辛亥革命與近代中國邊疆政治變遷研究 [A study on the Xinhai revolution and the transformation of frontier politics in modern China]. Harbin: Heilongjiang jiaoyu chubanshe, 2012.

Feng Mingzhu 馮明珠. *Zhong Ying Xizang jiaoshe yu Chuan Zang bian qing* 中英西藏交涉 與川藏邊情 [Sino-British negotiations over the Tibet matter and the situation at the Tibet-Sichuan border]. Beijing: Zhongguo zangxue shubanshe, 2007.

Feng Nong 馮農. "Qianqi shouhui youquan yundong zhi huiyi" 前期收回郵權運動之回憶 [Memoir on the early period of the movement for taking back the postal privilege]. *Xiandai youzheng* 現代郵政 [Modern postal service] 2, no. 5 (1948): 7–9.

Feng Nong, Liu Mian, and Huo Shulin. "Shang canyiyuan shouhui youquan qingyuanshu" 上參議院收回郵權請願書 [A petition to the provisional senate regarding taking back postal privilege]. *Yaxiya ribao* 亞細亞日報 [Asiatic daily news], May 1912.

Feng Ruofei 豐若非. *Qingdai queguan yu bei lu maoyi: Yi Shahukou Zhangjiakou he Guihuacheng wei zhongxin* 清代榷關與北路貿易：以殺虎口張家口和歸化城為中心 [Native customs and commerce in northern trade routes in the Qing dynasty: The case study of Shahukou, Zhangjiakou, and Guihua]. Beijing: Zhongguo shehui kexue chubanshe, 2014.

Feng Xianliang 馮賢亮. *Ming Qing Jiangnan de zhou xian xingzheng yu defang shehui yanjiu* 明清江南的州縣行政與地方社會研究 [A study on the district magistrates and local society of Jiangnan during the Ming and Qing dynasties]. Shanghai: Shanghai guji chubanshe, 2015.

Fletcher, Joseph. "Sino-Russian Relations, 1800–62." In *Late Ch'ing 1800–1911, Part 1*, edited by John K. Fairbank, 318–32. Vol. 10 of *The Cambridge History of China*. Cambridge: Cambridge University Press, 1978.

Foster Hall, B. E. *The Chinese Maritime Customs: An International Service, 1854–1950*. Bristol, UK: University of Bristol, 2015.

Further Correspondence respecting Affairs in China (Expedition up the Yang-Tze-kiang). London: Harrison and Sons, 1861.

Gao Chunping 高春平. *Jinshang yu Ming Qing Shanxi cheng zhen hua yanjiu* 晉商與明清山西城鎮化研究 [A study on the Shanxi merchants and urbanization in Shanxi Province]. Taiyuan: San Jin chubanshe, 2013.

Giles, Herbert A. *Chinese Sketches*. London: Trübner, 1876.

Guo Songtao 郭嵩燾. *Guo Songtao xiansheng nianpu* 郭嵩燾先生年譜 [Personal chronology of Mr. Guo Songtao]. Edited by Yin Zhongrong 尹仲容 and Lu Baoqian 陸寶千. 2 vols. Taipei: Institute of Modern History, Academia Sinica, 1971.

Guomin zhengfu Jiaotongbu Youzheng zhiyuanlu 國民政府交通部郵政職員錄 [Postal service list of the nationalist government's Ministry of Communications]. 18th ed. Shanghai: Jiaotongbu Youzheng zongju gongyingchu, 1929.

Guozhong 國忠. "Lue tan Guizhou jindai youzheng yunshu" 略談貴州近代郵政運輸 [A brief discussion on modern postal transportation in Guizhou]. In *Zhongguo geji zhengxie wenshi ziliao-youdian shiliao* 中國各級政協文史資料-郵電史料 [Historical materials on posts and telegraph of all levels of the Chinese People's Political Consultative Committee], vol. 3, edited by Beijingshi Youzheng guanliju wenshi zhongxin 北京市郵政管理文史中心 et al. Beijing: Beijing Yanshan chubanshe, 1995.

Halsey, Stephen R. *Quest for Power: European Imperialism and the Making of Chinese Statecraft*. Cambridge, MA: Harvard University Press, 2015.

Harris, Lane J. "Overseas Chinese Remittance Firms, the Limits of State Sovereignty, and Transnational Capitalism in East and Southeast Asia, 1850s–1930s." *Journal of Asian Studies* 74, no. 1 (2015): 129–51.

———. "The Post Office and State Formation in Modern China, 1896–1949." PhD diss., University of Illinois at Urbana-Champaign, 2012.

Harrison, Henrietta. *The Man Awakened from Dreams: One Man's Life in a North China Village, 1857–1942*. Stanford, CA: Stanford University Press, 2005.

———. *The Missionary's Curse and Other Tales from a Chinese Catholic Village*. Berkeley: University of California Press, 2013.

———. "Village Politics and National Politics: The Boxer Movement in Central Shanxi." In *The Boxers, China, and the World*, edited by Robert Bickers and Rolf Gerhard Tiedemann, 1–16. Lanham, MD: Rowman and Littlefield, 2007.

Hart, Robert. *"These from the Land of Sinim": Essays on the Chinese Question*. London: Chapman and Hall, 1901.

Hart, Robert, and James Duncan Campbell. *Archives of China's Imperial Maritime Customs: Confidential Correspondence between Robert Hart and James Duncan Campbell 1874–1907.* Edited by Chen Xiafei and Han Rongfang. 4 vols. Beijing: Foreign Languages Press, 1990–94.

He Hanwei 何漢威. *Jing Han tielu chuqi shi lue* 京漢鐵路初期史畧 [Brief account of the early history of Jinghan Railway]. Hong Kong: Zhongwen daxue chubanshe, 1979.

Hellrigl, Wolfgang C. *The Postal History of Mongolia, 1841–1941: The History of the Russian and Chinese Post Offices in Mongolia, and the Postage Stamps and Postal History of Independent Mongolia.* London: Royal Philatelic Society, 2011.

Herman, John E. "Empire in the Southwest: Early Qing Reforms to the Native Chieftain System." *Journal of Asian Studies* 56, no. 1 (1997): 47–74.

Hevia, James L. *English Lessons: The Pedagogy of Imperialism in Nineteenth-Century China.* Durham, NC: Duke University Press, 2003.

———. "An Imperial Nomad and the Great Game: Thomas Francis Wade in China." *Late Imperial China* 16, no. 2 (1995): 1–22.

———. *The Imperial Security State: British Colonial Knowledge and Empire-Building in Asia.* Cambridge: Cambridge University Press.

Hippisley, Alfred E. Collection of Alfred E. Hippisley. Bodleian Libraries, Oxford University.

Ho Huei-ching 何輝慶. "1888 nian xiao long jia gai 'Taiwan youpiao' beihou de gushi" 1888 年小龍加蓋 "臺灣郵票" 背後的故事 [The story behind the 1888 Taiwan stamp overprint on small dragon issue]. *Yazhou youxuejia* 亞洲郵學家 [Asian philatelist] 5 (2015): 55–65.

Hong Jiaguan 洪葭管. *Zhongguo jinrongshi* 中國金融史 [The banking history of China]. Chengdu: Xinan caijing daxue chubanshe, 1998.

Hongyinhua youpiao 紅印花郵票 [The revenue surcharges, China 1897]. Edited by Jiaotongbu youzheng zongju 交通部郵政總局. 2 vols. Taipei: Jiaotongbu youzheng zongju, 1987.

Horowitz, Richard S. "Politics, Power and the Chinese Maritime Customs: The Qing Restoration and the Ascent of Robert Hart." *Modern Asian Studies* 40, no. 3 (2006): 549–81.

Hou Jie 侯傑 and Qin Fang 秦方. "Haizhan yu paotai—yi dierci yapian zhanzheng shiqi sanci Dagu haizhan wei zhongxin" 海戰與炮臺—以第二次鴉片戰爭時期三次大沽海戰爲中心 [A study of three sea battles near Dagu during the Second Opium War]. In *Jindai Zhongguo haifangshi xinlun* 近代中國海防史新論 [New study on modern Chinese costal defenses], edited by Jinsheng Mai 麥勁生, 278–98. Hong Kong: Sanlian shudian, 2017.

Howland, Douglas. "An Alternative Mode of International Order: The International Administrative Union in the Nineteenth Century." *Review of International Studies* 41, no. 1 (2015): 161–83.

———. "Japan and the Universal Postal Union: An Alternative Internationalism in the 19th Century." *Social Science Japan Journal* 17, no. 1 (2014): 23–39.

———. "Telegraph Technology and Administrative Internationalism in the 19th Century." In *Concepts from International Relations and Other Disciplines,* edited by Maximilian Mayer, Mariana Carpes, and Ruth Knoblich, 183–99. Vol. 1 of *The Global Politics of Science and Technology*. Heidelberg: Springer, 2014.

Hsiao, Kung-chuan. *Rural China: Imperial Control in the Nineteenth Century*. Seattle: University of Washington Press, 1967.

Hsiao Kung-chuan 蕭公權. *Weng Tonghe yu wuxu weixin* 翁同龢與戊戌維新 [Weng Tonghe and the wuxu reform]. Taipei: Lianjing chuban shiye gufen youxian gongsi, 1983.

Hsueh Ping-wen 薛聘文. "Waiji youyuan Zhongwen yiming kao" 外籍郵員中文譯名考 [Chinese names of the foreign staff in the postal service]. In *Youzheng ziliao* 郵政資料 [Postal service research], vol. 5, 87–107. Taipei: Jiaotongbu youzheng zongju youzheng bowuguan bianyin, 1971.

Hu Yufen 胡燏棻. "Bianfa ziqiang shu" 變法自強疏 [Memorandum on reform and self-strengthening]. In *Zhongguo jindaishi ziliao congkan wuxu bianfa 2* 中國近代史資料叢刊戊戌變法2 [Materials on modern Chinese history series wuxu reform 2], edited by Zhongguoshi xuehui 中國史學會, 277–901. Shanghai: Shanghai renmin chubanshe, 1957.

"Hua yang shuxinguan zhaoshang rugu zhangcheng" 華洋書信館招商入股章程 [Regulations for share purchasing of the Chinese-Foreign Postal Agency]. In *Chuqi youzheng* 初期郵政 [The early period of the postal service]. N.p., n.d.: Reprint of 1878 regulations. Kuo Ting-yee Library, Institute of Modern History, Academia Sinica.

Huang Jianhui 黃鑒暉. *Ming Qing Shanxi shangren* 明清山西商人 [Shanxi merchants in the Ming and Qing dynasties]. Taiyuan: Ming Qing Shanxi jingji chubanshe, 2002.

Huang Jun 黃濬. *Hua sui ren sheng an zhi yi* 花隨人聖盦摭憶 [Reminiscences of the Huasui rensheng studio]. Reprint. Hong Kong: Longmen shudian, 1965.

Huangchao zhanggu hui bian. Wai bian 皇朝掌故彙編外編 [Collected historical records of the imperial dynasty, foreign affairs]. Edited by Zhang Shouyong 張壽鏞. *Jindai Zhongguo shiliao congkan* 近代中國史料叢刊 [Collectanea of modern Chinese history], compiled by Shen Yunlong 沈雲龍. Taipei: Wenhai chubanshe, 1986.

Hunter, Janet. "A Study of the Career of Maejima Hisoka 1835–1919." PhD diss., University of Oxford, 1976.

Inspector General's Circulars, First Series, 1861–1875. Shanghai: Statistical Department of Inspectorate General, 1879.

Jia Shucun 賈熟村. "Li Hongzhang yu Guo Songtao de youyi" 李鴻章與郭嵩燾的友誼 [On the friendship between Li Hongzhang and Guo Sontao]. *Anhui shixue* 安徽史學 [Historiography Anhui] 1 (2002): 20–25.

Jiaotong guanbao 交通官報 [Gazette of transportations]. *Jindai Zhongguo shiliao congkan* 近代中國史料叢刊 [Collectanea of modern Chinese history], compiled by Shen Yunlong 沈雲龍. Taipei: Wenhai chubanshe, 1987.

Jiaotongshi youzheng bian 交通史郵政編 [Transportation history, postal service]. Edited by Jiaotong tiedaobu jiaotongshi bianzuan weiyuanhui 交通鐵道部交通史編纂委員會. 4 vols. Shanghai: Jiaotong tiedaobu, 1930.

Jin haiguan mi dang jie yi 津海關秘檔解譯 [Selection of archival materials of the Tianjin Maritime Customs Service]. Edited by Tianjinshi danganguan and Tianjin haiguan. Beijing: Zhongguo haiguan chubanshe, 2006.

Jue zhi quan lan 爵秩全覽 [Guides to ranks and emoluments], ed. Guangxu Ronglutang, 1904. *Jindai Zhongguo shiliao congkan* 近代中國史料叢刊 [Collectanea of modern Chinese history], compiled by Shen Yunlong 沈雲龍. Taipei: Wenhai chubanshe, 1967.

John, Richard R. *Spreading the News: The American Postal System from Franklin to Morse.* Cambridge, MA: Harvard University Press, 1995.

King, Paul. *In the Chinese Customs Service: A Personal Record of Forty-Seven Years.* London: T. Fisher Unwin, 1924.

Knollys, Henry. *Incidents in the China War of 1860, Compiled from the Private Journals of General Sir Hope Grant.* Edinburgh: W. Blackwood, 1875.

Koffsky, Peter L. *The Consul General's Shanghai Postal Agency, 1867–1907.* Washington, DC: Smithsonian Institution Press, 1972.

Köll, Elisabeth. *Railroads and the Transformation of China.* Cambridge, MA: Harvard University Press, 2019.

Kopsch, H. *Brevities on Eastern Bimetallism.* Shanghai: Eastern Bimetallic League / North China Herald Office, 1896.

Kwan Sze Pui Uganda 關詩珮. "Fanyi zhengzhi ji Hanxue zhishi de shengchan: Wei tuo ma yu Yingguo waijiaobu de Zhongguo xuesheng yiyuan jihua (1843–1870)" 翻譯政治及漢學知識的生產：威妥瑪與英國外交部的中國學生譯員計畫 (1843–1870) [The politics of translation and the production of Sinology: Sir Thomas Francis Wade and the student interpreter program (1843–1870)]. *Zhongyanyuan Jindaishi yanjiusuo jikan* 中研院近代史研究所集刊 [Bulletin of the Institute of Modern History Academia Sinica], 81 (2013): 1–52.

Ladds, Catherine. *Empire Careers: Working for the Chinese Customs Service, 1854–1949.* Manchester, UK: Manchester University Press, 2013.

Lai Hui-min 賴惠敏. *Man daren de hebao: Qingdai Keerke Menggu de yamen yu shanghao* 滿大人的荷包：清代喀爾喀蒙古的衙門與商號 [Manchu officials' purse: The governmental offices and firms of Khalkha Mongols]. Beijing: Zhonghua shuju, 2020.

Lamb, Alastair. *The McMahon Line: A Study in the Relations between India, China and Tibet, 1904 to 1914.* 2 vols. London: Routledge and Kegan Paul, 1966.

Lan Mei-hua. "China's New Administration in Mongolia." In *Mongolia in the Twentieth Century: Landlocked Cosmopolitan*, edited by Stephen Kotkin and Bruce A. Elleman, 39–58. Armonk, NY: M. E. Sharpe, 1999.

Lattimore, Owen. "Chinese Turkistan." In *Studies in Frontier History: Collected Papers, 1928–1958*, 183–99. London: Oxford University Press, 1962.

———. *Manchuria: Cradle of Conflict.* New York: Macmillan, 1932.

Lavelle, Peter B. *The Profits of Nature: Colonial Development and the Quest for Resources in Nineteenth-Century China.* New York: Columbia University Press, 2020.

Leibo, Steven A. "Not So Calm an Administration: The Anglo-French Occupation of Canton, 1858–1861." *Journal of the Hong Kong Branch of the Royal Asiatic Society* 28 (1988): 16–33.

Li Ciming 李慈銘. "Yuemantang riji—zhailu" 越縵堂日記—摘錄 [Diary from the Study of Outstanding Frugality—Extract]. In *Dierci yapian zhanzheng* 第二次鴉片戰爭 [The Second Opium War], vol. 2, edited by Qi Sihe 齊思和 and Zhongguo shixuehui 中國史學會, 115–32. Shanghai: Shanghai renmin chubanshe, 1978.

Li Gui 李圭. *Huanyou diqiu xinlu* 環游地球新錄 [New records of travels around the world]. Edited by Zhong Shuhe 鍾叔河. Changsha: Hunan renmin chubanshe, 1980.

———. "Li Gui de huanyou diqiu xinlu" 李圭的環游地球新錄 [Li Gui's new records of travels around the world], edited by Zhong Shuhe 鍾叔河. In *Wang Tao Manyou suilu / Li Gui Huanyou diqiu xinlu / Li Shuchang Xiyang zazhi / Xu Jianyin Ouyou zalu* 王韜：漫游隨錄 / 李圭：環游地球新錄 / 黎庶昌 西洋雜志 / 徐建寅 歐游雜錄 [Wang Tao's random jottings from wanderings / Li Gui's new records of travels around the world / Li Shuchang's miscellaneous notes on the West / Xu Jianyin's miscellaneous notes on a trip to Europe], edited by Zhong Shuhe 鍾叔河 187–354. Changsha: Yuelu shushe, 1985.

Li Hongzhang 李鴻章. *Li Wenzhonggong quan shu* 李文忠公全集 [Collected writings of Li Hongzhang]. Edited by Rulun Wu 吳汝綸. *Jindai Zhongguo shiliao congkan* 近代中國史料叢刊 [Collectanea of modern Chinese history], compiled by Shen Yunlong 沈雲龍. Taipei: Wenhai chubanshe, 1980.

———. "Xu" 序 [Preface]. In *Wang Tao Manyou suilu / Li Gui Huanyou diqiu xinlu / Li Shuchang Xiyang zazhi / Xu Jianyin Ouyou zalu* 王韜：漫游隨錄 / 李圭：環游地球新錄 / 黎庶昌 西洋雜志 / 徐建寅 歐游雜錄 [Wang Tao's random jottings from wanderings / Li Gui's new records of travels around the world / Li Shuchang's miscellaneous notes on the West / Xu Jianyin's miscellaneous notes on a trip to Europe], edited by Zhong Shuhe 鍾叔河. Changsha: Yuelu shushe, 1985.

Li Songping 李頌平. *Ke you wai shi* 客郵外史 [Tale of foreign postal services in China]. Hong Kong: Baoan youpiao she, 1966.

Li Ta-chia 李達嘉. "Cong yi shang dao zhong shang: sixiang yu zhengce de kaocha" 從抑商到重商：思想與政策的考察 [From restraint to encouragement of commerce: An investigation into ideas and policies]. *Zhongyanyuan Jindaishi yanjiusuo jikan* 中研院近代史研究所集刊 [Bulletin of the Institute of Modern History, Academia Sinica] 82 (2013): 1–53.

Li Xiyong 李希庸. "Huainian Balidi xiansheng" 懷念巴立地先生 [To the cherished memory of Mr. Poletti]. *Xiandai youzheng* 現代郵政 [Modern postal service] 4, no. 4 (1949): 21–22.

Li Xizhu 李細珠. *Difang dufu yu Qingmo xinzheng—Wan Qing quanli geju zai yanjiu* 地方督撫與清末新政—晚清權力格局再研究 [Local governors and new policy reforms—Further study on the power structure in late Qing]. Beijing: Shehui kexue wenxian chubanshe, 2012.

———. "Qingmo yubei lixian shiqi de ping manhan zhenyu sixiang yu manhe zhengce de xinbianhua—yi Guangxu sanshisannian zhi manhan wenti zouyi wei zhongxin de tantao" 清末預備立憲時期的平滿漢畛域思想與滿漢政策的新變化—以光緒三十三年之滿漢問題奏議爲中心的探討 [The problem of Manchu-Han integration in the process of preparing constitutionalism and the new policies]. *Minzu yanjiu* 民族研究 [Eth-nonational studies] 3 (2011): 35–50.

———. *Wan Qing baoshou sixiang de yuanxing: Woren yanjiu* 晚清保守思想的原型：倭仁研究 [The prototype of late Qing conservative thought: A study of Woren]. Beijing: Shehui kexue wenxian chubanshe, 2000.

———. "Woren jiaoyou shulue" 倭仁交遊述略 [A brief account on Woren's circle of friends]. *Jindai Zhongguo* 近代中國 [Modern China] 9 (1999): 96–116.

———. *Xinzheng, lixian yu geming: Qingmo minchu zhengzhi zhuanxing yanjiu* 新政, 立憲與革命: 清末民初政治轉型研究 [New policies, constitutional establishment and revolution: A study of political transformation during the late Qing and early republican era]. Beijing: Beijing Shifan daxue chubanshe, 2016.

Lin Yuju 林玉茹. "Tongxun yu maoyi—Shijiu shiji mo Taiwan he Ningbo jiao shangren de xunxi chuandi" 通訊與貿易——十九世紀末臺灣和寧波郊商人的訊息傳遞 [Communication and trade—The information transmission between jiao merchants of Ningbo and Taiwan at the end of the nineteenth century]. *Taida lishi xuebao* 臺大歷史學報 [Historical inquiry] 58 (2016): 157–93.

———. *Xiang hai li sheng: Qingdai Taiwan de gangkou, renqun yu shehui* 向海立生: 清代台灣的港口, 人群與社會 [Coastal lives: Port cities, communities, and society in Qing-era Taiwan]. Taipei: Lianjing chubanshe, 2023.

Linshi gongbao 臨時公報 [Provisional government gazette]. Edited by Luo Jialun 羅家倫 et al. / Zhonghua minguo shiliao congbian 中華民國史料叢編. Reprint. Taipei: Zhongguo guomindang zhongyang weiyuanhui dangshi shiliao bianzuan weiyuanhui, 1968.

Liu Chenghan 劉承漢. *Cong you tan wang* 從郵談往 [Postal service memoir], 4 vols. Taipei: Guangwen shuju, 1969.

———. "Youzheng renshi zhidu zhi fagui hua" 郵政人事制度之法規化 [The legalization of the postal personnel regulation]. In *Youzheng ziliao* 郵政資料 [Postal service research], vol. 2, 59–72. Taipei: Jiaotongbu youzheng zongju youzheng bowuguan bianyin, 1968.

Liu, Lydia He. *The Clash of Empires: The Invention of China in Modern World Making.* Cambridge, MA: Harvard University Press, 2004.

Liu Wenpeng 劉文鵬. *Qingdai yichuan ji qi yu jiangyu xingcheng guanxi zhi yanjiu* 清代驛傳及其與疆域形成關係之研究 [A study of the military postal service of the Qing dynasty and its relationship to the formation of frontiers]. Beijing: Zhongguo renmin daxue chubanshe, 2004.

Liu Yuan 劉原, Ye Yushun 葉于順, and Ah Wang Dan Zeng 阿旺丹增. *Zhongguo Xizang youzheng youpiaoshi* 中國西藏郵政郵票史 [Postage stamps and the postal history of Tibet]. Lhasa, Tibet: Xizang renmin chubanshe, 2009.

Liu Zhenhua 劉振華. "Li Fengbao, Xu Jianyin zhuchi goumai tiejiajian kao lun" 李鳳苞、徐建寅主持購買鐵甲艦考論 [On the purchase of the ironclad warship organized by Li Fengbao and Xu Jianyin]. *Junshi lishi yanjiu* 軍事歷史研究 (Military historical research) 1 (2009): 81–88.

Lou Zuyi 樓祖詒. "Woguo shouhui youquan de jingguo" 我國收回郵權的經過 [The history of how our country took back postal privilege]. *Xiandai youzheng* 現代郵政 [Modern postal service] 2, no. 4 (1948): 2–13.

———. *Zhongguo youyi fadashi* 中國郵驛發達史 [The history of the development of the Chinese postal courier service]. Shanghai: Zhonghua shuju, 1940.

Lovell, Julia. *The Opium War: Drugs, Dreams and the Making of China.* Basingstoke, UK: Picador, 2011.

Lu Lüren 路履仁. "Wai Menggu jianwen ji lue" 外蒙古見聞記略 [What I saw and heard in Outer Mongolia]. In *Wenshi ziliao xuanji* 文史資料選集 [Selected works of literature and history sources], edited by Zhongguo renmin zhengzhi xieshanghuiyi quanguo weiyuanhui wenshi ziliao yanjiu weiyuanhui, 22 *juan*, 63 *ji*, 65–82. Beijing: Zhong-guo wenshi chubanshe, 2000.

Lu Minghui 盧明輝. "Qingdai Nei Menggu diqu kengzhi nongye fazhan yu tudi guanxi de shanbian qian xi" 清代內蒙古地區墾殖農業發展與土地關係的嬗變淺析 [A simple analysis of the evolution of relationships between the development of agricultural rec-lamation and land in Inner Mongolia in the Qing dynasty]. In *Nei Menggu kenwu yanjiu* 內蒙古墾務研究 [Research in Inner Mongol cultivation], edited by Haiyuan Liu 劉海源, vol. 1, 8–25. Hohhot: Nei Menggu renmin chubanshe, 1990.

Lü Qiuwen 呂秋文. *Zhong Ying Xizang jiaoshe shimo* 中英西藏交涉始末 [Negotiations between China and Britain on the Tibet question]. Taipei: Chengwen chubanshe, 1999.

Lü Shih-Chiang 呂實強. *Ting Jih-Chang yu ziqiang yundong* 丁日昌與自強運動 [Ting Jih-Chang and China's self-strengthening]. Taipei: Zhongyang yanjiuyuan Jindaishi yanjiusuo, 1987.

Lu, Yilu 鹿憶鹿. *Yiyu, yiren, yishou: Shanhaijing zai Mingdai* 異域‧異人‧異獸：山海經在明代 [Foreign lands, barbarians and strange animals: the classics of mountains and seas in Ming dynasty: the Classics of Mountains and Seas in Ming dynasty]. Taipei: Xiuwei jingdian chubanshe, 2021.

Lunchuan zhaoshangju 輪船招商局. Edited by Chen Xulu 陳旭麓 and Gu Tinglong 顧廷龍 et al. Shanghai: Shanghai renmin chubanshe, 2002.

Luo Gang 羅剛. *Liu gong Mingchuan nianpu chugao* 劉公銘傳年譜初稿 [The first draft of Liu Mingchuan's biography]. 2 vols. Taipei: Zhengzhong shuju, 1983.

Macdonald, David. *Twenty Years in Tibet*. New Delhi: Gyan, 2008.

Maclachlan, Patricia L. *The People's Post Office: The History and Politics of the Japanese Postal System, 1871–2010*. Cambridge, MA: Harvard University Asia Center, 2012.

Mao Haijian 茅海建. *Tianchao de bengkui: Yapian zhanzheng zai yanjiu* 天朝的崩潰：鴉片戰爭再研究 [The collapse of the celestial empire: A new study of the Opium War]. Beijing: Sanlian shudian, 2005.

———. *Cong jiawu dao wuxu: Kang Youwei "woshi" jianzhu* 從甲午到戊戌：康有為《我史》鑒注 [From jiawu to wuxu: An annotated edition of Kang Youwei's "My History"]. Beijing: Sanlian shudian, 2009.

———. *Jindai de chidu* 近代的尺度：兩次鴉片戰爭軍事與外交 [Military and diplomacy in the two Opium Wars: Military and diplomacy in the two Opium Wars]. Shanghai: Shanghai sanlian shudian, 1998.

———. *Kuming tianzi* 苦命天子 [The ill-fated emperor]. Beijing: Shenghuo, dushu, xinzhisanlian shudian, 2013.

———. *Tianchao de bengkui—Yapian zhanzheng zaiyanjiu* 天朝的崩潰—鴉片戰爭再研究 [The collapse of the celestial dynasty—New study of the Opium Wars]. 16th ed. Beijing: Shenghuo, dushu, xinzhisanlian shudian, 2014.

———. *Wuxu bianfa de lingmian: "Zhang Zhidong dangan" yuedu biji* 戊戌變法的另面："張之洞檔案"閱讀筆記 [Another perspective on the wuxu reform: A study note on Zhang Zhidong's archival materials]. Shanghai: Shanghai guji chubanshe, 2014.

———. *Wuxu bianfa shishi kao er ji* 戊戌變法史事考二集 [Examination of historical facts of the Wuxu reform, part 2]. Beijing: Shenghuo dushu xinzhi sanlian chuban-she, 2011.

Martin, W. A. P. *A Cycle of Cathay.* New York: Fleming H. Revell, 1897.

Maurer, Petra. "The Tibetan Governmental Transport and Postal System: Horse Services and Other Taxes from the 13th to the 20th Centuries." *Buddhism, Law and Society* 5 (2019–20): 1–58.

Mayers, William Frederick. *The Chinese Government: A Manual of Chinese Titles, Categorically Arranged and Explained, with an Appendix.* Shanghai: American Presbyterian Mission Press, 1878.

Melius, Louis. *The American Postal Service: History of the Postal Service from the Earliest Times.* Alpha Editions, 2019.

Migliavacca, Giorgio, and Tarcisio Bottani. *Simone Tasso e le poste di Milano nel Rinascimento* [Simon Taxis and the posts of the state of Milan during the Renaissance]. Bergamo: Corponove, 2008.

Millward, James A. *Beyond the Pass: Economy, Ethnicity, and Empire in Qing Central Asia, 1759–1864.* Stanford, CA: Stanford University Press, 1998.

Minguo chongxiu Boxingxian zhi 民國重修博興縣志 [Boxing County gazetteer, republican revised edition]. Edited by Zhang Qibing 張其丙 et al. Jinan: Jinan wenyazhai yinshuaju, 1936.

Minguo Enpingxian zhi 民國恩平縣志 [Enping County gazetteer, republican edition]. Edited by Yu Picheng 余丕承, Gui Zhan 桂站, et al. Jiangmen: Shengtang guanghua shuju, 1934.

Minguo Gongxian zhi 民國鞏縣志 [Gong County gazetteer, republican edition]. Edited by Yang Baodong 楊保東, Wang Guozhang 王國璋, Liu Qinglian 劉蓮青, Zhang Zhongyou 張仲友. Kaifeng: Jingchuan tushu, 1937.

Minguo Guanxian zhi 民國冠縣志 [Guan County gazetteer, republican edition]. Edited by Hou Guanglu 侯光陸, Chen Xiyong 陳熙雍, et al. Liaocheng: N.p., block-printed edition, 1934.

Minguo Huanrenxian zhi 民國桓仁縣志 [Huanren County gazetteer, republican edition]. Edited by Hou Xijue 侯錫爵, Luo Mingshu 羅明述, et al. Benxi: N.p., stereotype edition, 1937.

Morse, Hosea Ballou. *The International Relations of the Chinese Empire.* 3 vols. London: Longmans, Green, 1910–18.

Mosca, Matthew W. *From Frontier Policy to Foreign Policy: The Question of India and the Transformation of Geopolitics in Qing China.* Stanford, CA: Stanford University Press, 2013.

———. "The Qing State and Its Awareness of Eurasian Interconnections, 1789–1806." *Eighteenth-Century Studies* 47, no. 2 (2014): 103–16.

Nakami, Tatsuo. "A Protest against the Concept of the 'Middle Kingdom': The Mongols and the 1911 Revolution." In *The 1911 Revolution in China: Interpretive Essays,* edited by Shinkichi Etō and Harold Z. Schiffrin, 129–49. Tokyo: University of Tokyo Press, 1984.

Ningboshi youdian zhi 寧波市郵電志 [History of the postal service and telegraph of Ningbo city]. Edited by Ningboshiyoudianju 寧波市郵電局. Shanghai: Shanghai shehui kexue yuan chubanshe, 1999.

"Obituary: Sir Rutherford Alcock, K.C.B., D.C.L." *Geographical Journal* 10, no. 6 (1897): 642–45. http://www.jstor.org/stable/1774914.

The Origin and Organisation of the Chinese Customs Service. Shanghai: Statistical Department of the Inspectorate General of Customs, 1922.

Osterhammel, Jürgen. *The Transformation of the World: A Global History of the Nineteenth Century*. Translated by Patrick Camiller. Princeton, NJ: Princeton University Press, 2014.

Otte, Thomas G. *The Foreign Office Mind: The Making of British Foreign Policy, 1865–1914*. Cambridge: Cambridge University Press, 2011.

Padget, Peter I. *The Postal Markings of China*. London: China Philatelic Society of London, 1978.

Paine, S. C. M. *The Wars for Asia, 1911–1949*. New York: Cambridge University Press, 2012.

Papers Relating to the Rebellion in China and Trade in the Yang-Tze-Kiang River. London: Harrison and Sons, 1862.

Patterson, Wayne. *William Nelson Lovatt in Late Qing China: War, Maritime Customs, and Treaty Ports, 1860–1904*. Lanham, MD: Lexington Books, 2020.

Paullin, Charles Oscar. *Diplomatic Negotiations of American Naval Officers, 1778–1883*. Baltimore: Johns Hopkins Press, 1912.

Peng Jian 彭劍. *Qing ji xianzheng bianchaguan yanjiu* 清季憲政編查館研究 [A study on the constitutional affairs editors of the Qing dynasty]. Beijing: Beijing daxue chubanshe, 2011.

Peng Yingtian 彭瀛添. *Minxinju fazhanshi: Zhongguo de minjian tongxun shiye* 民信局發展史: 中國的民間通訊事業 [Development of native letter hongs: The communication business in Chinese society]. Taipei: Zhongguo wenhua daxue chubanbu, 1992.

Perry-Ayscough, H. G. C., and R. B. Otter-Barry. *With the Russians in Mongolia*. London: John Lane / Bodley Head, 1914.

Postal Circulars and Instructions, vol. V, 1919–1922. Published for the Use of the Postal Service by Order of the Co-Director General. Shanghai: Supply Department of the Directorate General of Posts.

Pozdneev, A. M. *Mongolia and the Mongols*. Edited by John R. Krueger. Translated by John Roger Shaw and Dale Plank. Bloomington: Indiana University, 1971.

Qingji waijiao shiliao 清季外交史料 [Sources on the history of foreign relations during the Qing period]. Compiled by Wang Yanwei 王彥威 and Wang Liang 王亮. 269 *juan*. Reprint, 10 volumes, edited by Li Yumin, Liu Limin, and Li Chuanbin. Changsha: Hunan shifan daxue chubanshe, 2015.

Qingji Zhong Ri Han guanxi shiliao 清季中日韓關係史料 [Historical materials on the relationship between China, Japan, and Korea in the late Qing period]. Edited by Guo Tingyi 郭廷以 and Yushu Li 李毓澍. 10 vols. Taipei: Institute of modern history, Academia Sinica, 1972.

Qingmo Taiwan haiguan linian ziliao, 1867–1895 清末台灣海關歷年資料 [Maritime Customs Annual Returns and Reports of Taiwan, 1867–1895]. Edited by Huang Fusan (黃富三) and Lin Man-Houng (林滿紅). 2 vols. Taipei: Zhongyang yanjiuyuan Taiwanshi yanjiusuo choubeichu chuban, 1997.

Qingmo Tianjin haiguan youzheng dangan xuanbian 清末天津海關郵政檔案選編 [Selected postal archives at Tianjin customs of the late Qing dynasty]. Translated by Xu Heping 許和平 and Zhang Junyuan 張俊桓. Edited by Tianjinshi danganguan

天津市檔案館 and Zhongguo jiyou chubanshe 中國集郵出版社. Beijing: Zhongguo ji-you chubanshe, 1988.

Qingshigao 清史稿 [Draft history of the Qing dynasty]. Compiled by Zhao Erxun et al. 529 *juan*. Beijing: Qingshiguan, 1928.

Rasmussen, O. D. *Tientsin: An Illustrated Outline History.* Tianjin: Tientsin, 1925.

Rawski, Evelyn Sakakida. *Early Modern China and Northeast Asia: Cross-border Perspectives.* Cambridge: Cambridge University Press, 2015.

Reinhardt, Anne. *Navigating Semi-colonialism: Shipping, Sovereignty, and Nation-Building in China, 1860–1937.* Cambridge, MA: Harvard University Asia Center, 2018.

Reinsch, Paul S. *An American Diplomat in China.* Garden City, NY: Doubleday, Page, 1922.

Reisz, Emma. "An Issue of Authority: Robert Hart, Gustav Detring and the Large Dragon Stamp." *Jiyou Bolan* 集郵博覽 [Philatelic panorama] 371 (2018): 150–70.

Ren Zhiyong 任智勇. "1850 nian qian hou Qing zhengfu de caizheng kunju yu ying-dui" 1850 年前後清政府的財政困局與應對 [The Qing government's fiscal quagmire and its response around 1850]. *Lishi yanjiu* 歷史研究 (Historical research) 2 (2019): 68–88.

Rennie, David Field. *Peking and the Pekingese during the First Year of the British Embassy at Peking.* 2 vols. London: John Murray, 1865.

Rhoads, Edward J. M. *Manchus and Han: Ethnic Relations and Political Power in Late Qing and Early Republican China, 1861–1928.* Seattle: University of Washington Press, 2000.

Seal, A. E., trans. "Translation from Kohl's Handbook—China," *Collectors' Club Philatelist* 8, no. 1 (1929): 23–34.

Segal, Zef. "Communication and State Construction: The Postal Service in German States, 1815–1866." *Journal of Interdisciplinary History* 44, no. 4 (2014): 453–73.

Shanxi piaohao shiliao 山西票號史料 [Historical materials on Shanxi remittance banks]. Edited by Huang Jianhui 黃鑒輝 and Zhongguo Renmin yinhang Shanxisheng fen-hang 中國人民銀行山西省分行. Taiyuan: Shanxi jingji chubanshe, 2002.

Shen Xuefeng 申學鋒. *Wan Qing caizheng zhichu zhengce yanjiu* 晚清財政支出政策研究 [Research on fiscal expenditure policy in the late Qing dynasty]. Beijing: Zhongguo renmin daxue chubanshe, 2006.

Shen Yunlong 沈雲龍. *Liu Chenghan xiansheng fangwen jilu* 劉承漢先生訪問記錄 [Reminiscences of Mr. Liu Ch'eng-han]. Edited by Lin Quan 林泉. Taipei: Institute of Modern History, Academia Sinica, 1997.

Sizova, Alexandra. "The Political Role of the Russian Consulates in Mongolia in the Mongolian National Liberation Movement in the Early 20th Century." Research Paper WP BRP 119/HUM/2016, Higher School of Economics, Moscow, 2016. https://papers.ssrn.com/sol3/papers.cfm?abstract_id=2727103.

Skinner, G. William, ed. *The City in Late Imperial China.* Stanford, CA: Stanford University Press, 1977.

Skinner, George William, Zumou Yue, and Mark Henderson. *ChinaW—Cities, County Seats and Yamen Units (1820–1893).* Database, 2008. Harvard Dataverse, https://dataverse.harvard.edu/dataset.xhtml?persistentId=doi:10.7910/DVN/JCT5NE.

Smith, Richard J. "Li Hung-chang's Use of Foreign Military Talent: The Formative Period, 1862–1874." In *Li Hung-Chang and China's Early Modernization*, edited by Samuel C. Chu and Kwang Ching Liu, 119–42. Armonk, NY: M. E. Sharpe, 1994.

Soni, Sharad Kumar. *Mongolia-China Relations: Modern and Contemporary Times*. New Delhi: Pentagon Press, 2006.

Ssu-ma Ch'ien. "Ssu-ma Hsiang-ju Memoir." In *The Memoirs of Han China, Part III*, edited by William H. Nienhauser Jr. and translated by Chiu Ming Chan, Hans van Ess, William H. Nienhauser Jr., Thomas D. Noel, Marc Nürnberger, Jakob Pöllath, Andreas Siegl, and Lianlian Wu. Vol. 10 of *The Grand Scribe's Records*. Bloomington: Indiana University Press, 2019.

Stursberg, Peter. *No Foreign Bones in China: Memoirs of Imperialism and Its Ending*. Edmonton: University of Alberta Press, 2002.

Su Mei-fang 蘇梅芳. "Li Hongzhang ziqiang sixiang zhi yanjiu" 李鴻章自強思想之研究——援滬至天津教案時期 (1862–1870) 的自強之道 [Li Hongzhang's thought on self-strengthening during his time in Shanghai and the Tianjin massacre period (1862–1870)]. *Chengda lishi xuebao* 成大歷史學報 [Bulletin of the History Department, National Ch'eng Kung University] 17 (1991): 147–213.

Su Quanyou 蘇全有. *Qingmo Youchuanbu yanjiu* 清末郵傳部研究 [A study on the Ministry of Posts and Communications]. Beijing: Zhonghua shuju, 2005.

Su Ran 蘇冉, trans. *Yuandong guoji guanxishi, 1840–1949* 遠東國際關係史 1840–1949 [History of international relations in the Far East, 1840–1949]. Original *Международные отношения на Дальнем Востоке, 1840–1949*, edited by E. M. Zhukov and Institut vostokovedeniiă (Akademiiă nauk SSSR). Beijing: Shijie zhishi chubanshe, 1951.

Sun Junyi 孫君毅. *Qingdai youchuo zhi* 清代郵戳志 [Collection of postage franking and mail marks of the Qing dynasty]. Beijing: Zhongguo jiyou chubanshe, 1984.

Sun Li 孫藜. *Wan Qing dianbao ji qi chuanbo guannian, 1860–1911* 晚清電報及其傳播觀念, 1860–1911 [Telegraphy and ideas of communications in the late Qing, 1860–1911]. Shanghai: Shanghai Shudian chubanshe, 2007.

Tachibana, Makoto. "The 1911 Revolution and 'Mongolia': Independence, Constitutional Monarchy, or Republic." *Journal of Contemporary China Studies* 3, no. 1 (2014): 69–90.

Taiwanshi 台灣史 [Taiwan history]. Edited by Taiwansheng wenxian weiyuanhui 台灣省文獻委員會. Taipei: Zhongwen tushu gufen youxian gongsi, 1990.

Tang Chi-hua 唐啓華. *Bei "feichu bupingdeng tia yue" zhe bi de beiyang xiuyue shi 1912–1928* 被 "廢除不平等條約" 遮蔽的北洋修約史, 1912–1928 [Treaty revision campaign of the Beiyang government, 1912–1928]. Beijing: Shehui kexue wenxian chubanshe, 2010.

Taveirne, Patrick. *Han-Mongol Encounters and Missionary Endeavors: A History of Scheut in Ordos (Hetao) 1874–1911*. Leuven, Belgium: Leuven University Press, 2004.

Taylor, Annie R. *Pioneering in Tibet*. London: Morgan and Scott, 1895.

Teizō, Koizumi. "The Operation of Chinese Junks." In *Transport in Transition: The Evolution of Traditional Shipping in China*, translated by Andrew Watson, 1–13. Ann Arbor: University of Michigan Center for Chinese Studies, 1972.

Teng Shougeng 滕守耕. "Liutuan baiyin shichang shimo" 柳疃白銀市場始末 [History of the silver market in Liutuan]. In *Changyi wenshi ziliao* 昌邑文史資料 [Historical materials of Changyi], vol. 4, edited by Shandongsheng Changyixian weiyuanhui wenshi ziliao yanjiu weiyuanhui, 55–61. Changyi: Changyixian weisheng xitong yin-shuachang, 1989.

Teng, Ssu-yü, and John K. Fairbank. *China's Response to the West: A Documentary Survey, 1839–1923.* Cambridge, MA: Harvard University Press, 1954.

Thiriez, Regine. *Barbarian Lens: Western Photographers of the Qianlong Emperor's European Palaces.* London: Routledge, 2019.

Tianjin haiguan dangan 天津海關檔案 [Archival materials of the Tianjin Maritime Customs Service]. Edited by Tianjinshi danganguan 天津市檔案館. 30 vols. Tianjin: Tianjin guji chubanshe, 2013.

Tianjin jianshi 天津簡史 [An abridged history of Tianjin]. Edited by Tianjin shehui kexueyuan lishi yanjiusuo tianjin jianshi bianxiezu 天津社會科學院歷史研究所《天津簡史》編寫組. Tianjin: Tianjin renmin chubanshe, 1987.

Tsai Chen-feng 蔡振豐. *Wan Qing waiwubu zhi yanjiu* 晚清外務部之研究 [A study of the Ministry of Foreign Affairs in the late Qing period]. Taipei: Zhizhi xueshu chubanshe, 2014.

Tsai Ming-feng 蔡明峰. *Da Qing youzheng: Bantu tuozhan moshi zhi yanjiu* 大清郵政: 版圖拓展模式之研究 [The Great Qing Postal Service: A study on its expansion]. Taipei: Panlong youpiao gongsi, 2007.

———. *Ru shi wo ji: Qingdai youchuo yange yu yanjiu, youlu tantao* 如是我集: 清代郵戳沿革與研究、郵路探討 [A study on the evolution of postal franking and postal routes of the Qing dynasty]. Taipei: Panlong youpiao gongsi, 2011.

Tsai, Weipin. "Breaking the Ice: The Establishment of Overland Winter Postal Routes in the Late Qing China." *Modern Asian Studies* 47, no. 6 (2013): 1749–81.

———. "The First Casualty: Truth, Lies and Commercial Opportunism in Chinese Newspapers during the First Sino-Japanese War." *Journal of the Royal Asiatic Society* 24, no. 1 (2014): 145–63.

———. "The Inspector General's Last Prize: Chinese Native Customs 1901–1931." *Journal of Imperial and Commonwealth History* 36, no. 2 (2008): 243–58.

———. "Yi Chongqing he Chengdu lai kan Da Qing youzhengju he minxinju zai Qing mo de gong sheng" 以重慶和成都來看大清郵政局和民信局在清末的共生 [Coexistence of the Imperial Post Office and private letter hongs]. *Youshi yanjiu* 郵史研究 (Postal history research) 37 (2020): 34–47.

Universal Postal Union. *Convention of Paris.* London: George Edward Eyre and William Spottiswoode, 1879.

Van Aalst, J. A. *Chinese Music.* Beijing: The French Bookstore, 1939.

Van de Ven, Hans J. *Breaking with the Past: The Maritime Customs Service and the Global Origins of Modernity in China.* New York: Columbia University Press, 2014.

Vér, Márton. "The Postal System of the Mongol Empire in Northeastern Turkestan." PhD diss., University of Szeged, 2016.

Virk, Daljit Singh. *Postal History of Indian Military Campaigns: Sikkim–Tibet, 1903–1908.* New Delhi: Philatelic Congress of India, 1989.

Von Gumpach, Johannes. *The Burlingame Mission: A Political Disclosure, Supported by Official Documents.* London: Forgotten Books, 2018.

Wade, Geoff. "The 'Native Office' (土司) System: A Chinese Mechanism for Southern Territorial Expansion over Two Millennia." In *Asian Expansions: The Historical Experiences of Polity Expansion in Asia*, edited by Geoff Wade, 69–91. Abingdon, UK: Routledge, 2017.

Wang Hongbin 王宏斌. *Qingdai jiazhi chidu: Huobi bijia yanjiu* 清代價值尺度: 貨幣比價研究 [Measures of value in the Qing dynasty: A study on the parity rate of various currencies]. Beijing: Shenghuo, dushu, xinzhi sanlian shudian, 2015.

Wang Kaixi 王開璽. "Xinyou zhengbian yu zhengtong huangquan sixiang—Cixi zhengbian chenggong yuanyin zai tantao" 辛酉政變與正統皇權思想—慈禧政變成功原因再探討 [The Xinyou coup d'état and orthodox thinking on imperial power—A further inquiry into the reasons for the success of Cixi's coup]. *Qingshi yanjiu* 清史研究 (Studies in Qing history) 4 (2002): 49–56.

Wang Menghsiao 王孟瀟. "Qingdai moye zhi wenbaoju" 清代末葉之文報局 [The wenbao bureau in the late Qing period]. In *Youzheng ziliao* 郵政資料 (Postal service research), vol. 2, 1–6. Taipei: Jiaotongbu youzheng zongju youzheng bowuguan bianyin, 1968.

———. "Qingdai zhi minxinju" 清代之民信局 [Private letter hongs in the Qing dynasty]. In *Youzheng ziliao* 郵政資料 [Postal service research], vol. 2, 7–24. Taipei: Jiaotongbu youzheng zongju youzheng bowuguan bianyin, 1968.

Wang Qingcheng 王慶成. "Wan Qing Huabei cunluo" 晚清華北村落 [The villages in north China in the late Qing period]. *Xiandaishi yanjiu* 現代史研究 [Modern Chinese history studies] 3 (2002): 1–40.

Wang Tao 王韜. *Manyou suilu, Fusang youji* 漫游隨錄‧扶桑游記 [Random jottings from wanderings, and travelogue to Japan]. Changsha: Hunan renmin chubanshe, 1982.

Wang Weijiang 王維江. *"Qingliu" yanjiu* "清流" 研究 [A study of the "pure stream"]. Shanghai: Shanghai shiji chubanshe, 2009.

Wang Xiuyu. *China's Last Imperial Frontier: Late Qing Expansion in Sichuan's Tibetan Borderlands*. Lanham, MD: Lexington Books, 2011.

Wang Yuming 王裕明. *Ming Qing Huizhou dian shang yanjiu* 明清徽州典商研究 [Research on Huizhou pawnbroker in the Ming and Qing dynasties]. Beijing: Renmin chubanshe, 2012.

Wang Zhe 王哲 and Liu Yayuan 劉雅媛. "Jindai Zhongguo youzheng kongjian yanjiu—Ji yu duo banben youzheng yutu de fenxi" 近代中國郵政空間研究—基於多版本郵政輿圖的分析 [The historical analysis of the modern China postal space with the modern China postal atlas]. *Zhongguo jingjishi yanjiu* 中國經濟史研究 [Research on Chinese economic history] 2 (2019): 63–81.

Watson, W. C. Haines. "Journey to Sungp'an." *Journal of the China Branch of the Royal Asiatic Society* 36 (1905): 51–102.

Watt, John Robertson. *The District Magistrate in Late Imperial China*. New York: Columbia University Press, 1972.

Wei Hsiu-mei 魏秀梅. *Qingdai zhi huibi zhidu* 清代之回避制度 [The system of avoidance during the Qing dynasty]. Taipei: Zhongyang yanjiu yuan jindaishi yanjiusuo, 1992.

———. "Wenxiang zai Qingdai houqi zhengju zhong de zhongyaoxing" 文祥在清代後期政局中的重要性 [The importance of Wenxiang in the political situation of the late Qing dynasty]. *Taiwan Shida lishi xuebao* 臺灣師大歷史學報 [Bulletin of historical research] 32 (2004): 121–46.

Wenxiang 文祥. "Ziding nianpu shang" 自訂年譜上 [Personal chronology, part one], *Wen Wenzhong gong (Xiang) shi lue* 文文忠公(祥)事略 [Biography of Wenxiang]. Edited by Hong Liangpin 洪良品 and Jindai Zhongguo shiliao congkan 近代中國史料叢刊 [Modern China historical materials series]. Taipei: Wenhai chubanshe, 1968.

Wright, Mary Clabaugh. *The Last Stand of Chinese Conservatism: The T'ung-Chih Restoration, 1862–1874*. Stanford, CA: Stanford University Press, 1957.

Wright, Stanley F. *China's Struggle for Tariff Autonomy: 1843–1938*. Taipei: Cheng-wen, 1966.

———. *Hart and the Chinese Customs*. Belfast: William Mullan and Sons, 1950.

Wu Fuhuan 吳福環. *Qingji Zongli Yamen yanjiu* 清季總理衙門研究 [A study of the Zongli Yamen in the late Qing period]. Taipei: Wenjin chubanshe, 1995.

Wu Han 吳晗. *Huangquan yu shenquan* 皇權與紳權 [On the power of emperors and the power of gentries]. Shanghai: Guancha she, 1948.

Wu, Shellen Xiao. *Empires of Coal: Fueling China's Entry into the Modern World Order, 1860–1920*. Stanford, CA: Stanford University Press, 2015.

Wu Xiangxiang 吳相湘. *Wan Qing gongting shi ji* 晚清宮廷實紀 [A true record of the imperial court in the late Qing period]. Taipei: Zhengzhong shuju, 1952.

Wu Yulun 吳玉倫. "Qingmo de tielu jiaoyu he tielu xuetang" 清末的鐵路教育和鐵路學堂 [Railway schools and education in the late Qing period]. *Shanxi shida xuebao* 山西師大學報 [Journal of Shanxi Teachers University] 1 (2005): 116–20.

Wushinian lai Zhonghua Minguo yougong yundong 五十年來中華民國郵工運動 [The postal workers' movement of the Republic of China in the past fifty years]. Edited by Zhonghua Minguo youwu gonghui quanguo lianhehui 中華民國郵務公會全國聯合會. Taipei: Zhonghua Minguo youwu gonghui quanguo lianhehui, 1980.

Xia Dongyuan 夏東元. "Lun Sheng Xuanhuai" 論盛宣懷 [On Sheng Xuanhuai]. *Shehui kexue zhanxian* 社會科學戰綫 [Social Science Front bimonthly] 4 (1981): 57–71.

Xie Bin 謝彬. *Zhongguo youdian hangkongshi* 中國郵電航空史 [The history of the postal service, telecommunications, and air transportation in China]. Shanghai: Zhonghua shuju, 1928.

Xie Shicheng 謝世誠. *Li Hongzhang ping zhuan* 李鴻章評傳 [A critical biography of Li Hongzhang]. Nanjing: Nanjing daxue chubanshe, 2006.

Xinjiang tongzhi: Youdianzhi 新疆通志：郵電志 [Xinjiang gazette: Postal and telegraph], vol. 51. Edited by Xinjiang Weiwu'er zizhiqu difangzhi bianzuan weiyuanhui 新疆維吾爾自治區地方誌編纂委員會. Ürümqi: Xinjiang renmin chubanshe, 1998.

Xiong Yaping 熊亞平. *Tielu yu huabei xiangcun shehui bianqian, 1880–1937* 鐵路與華北鄉村社會變遷, 1880–1937 [Railways and social transformation in rural villages of northern China, 1880–1937]. Beijing: Beijing renmin chubanshe, 2011.

Xizang Yadongguan dangan xuanbian 西藏亞東關檔案選編 [A selection of the archival materials of Yadong Customs House in Tibet]. Edited by Zhongguo dier lishi danganguan 中國第二歷史檔案館 and Zhongguo zangxue yanjiu zhongxin 中國藏學研究中心. Translated into Chinese. 2 vols. Beijing: Zhongguo zangxue chubanshe, 1996.

Xu, Guoqi. *China and the Great War: China's Pursuit of a New National Identity and Internationalization*. Cambridge: Cambridge University Press, 2005.

Xu Jianguo 徐建國. *Cong xingsheng dao shuaibai: Jindai Zhongguo minxinju, 1866–1934* 從興盛到衰敗：近代中國民信局, 1866–1934 [From prosperity to decline: Private letter hongs in modern China, 1866–1934]. Beijing: Zhongguo shehui kexue chubanshe, 2017.

Xu Tan 許檀. "Qingdai Shanxi Guihuacheng de shangye" 清代山西歸化城的商業 [The commerce of Shanxi Guihua in the Qing dynasty]. *Wen shi zhe* 文史哲 [Journal of literature, history and philosophy] 4 (2009): 119–29.

Xue Zhiping 薛智平. "Qingdai Nei Menggu diqu she zhi shu ping" 清代內蒙古地區設治述評 [Analysis of governance and management in Inner Mongolia during the Qing dynasty]. In *Nei Menggu kenwu yanjiu* 內蒙古墾務研究 [Research in Inner Mongol cultivation], edited by Haiyuan Liu 劉海源, vol. 1, 57–80. Hohhot: Nei Menggu renmin chubanshe, 1990.

Yabuuchi Yoshihiko 藪内吉彦 and Keisuke Tahara 田原啓祐. *Nihon yūbin hattatsushi, tsuketari Tōkaidō Ishibe-eki no yūbin sōgyō shiryō* 日本郵便発達史, 付東海道石部駅の郵便創業史料 [History of Japanese post offices: Founding and development of the Japan postal service in the Meiji era]. Tokyo: Akashi shoten, 2000.

Yang, Shaoquan. "The Beginning of the Chinese Post Office in Szechwan," *West China Missionary News* 34, no. 10 (1932): 7–11.

Yanxing 晏星 [Pan Ansheng 潘安生]. *Hede shiliao* 赫德史料 [Histories related to Robert Hart]. Taipei: Jiaotongbu youzheng zongju youzheng bowuguan, 1969.

———. "Youzheng kaoshi zhidu zhi xingcheng" 郵政考試制度之形成 [Formation of the postal staff examination system]. In *Youzheng ziliao* 郵政資料 [Postal service research], vol. 2, 73–108. Taipei: Jiaotongbu youzheng zongju youzheng bowuguan bianyin, 1968.

———. *Zhonghua youzheng fazhanshi* 中華郵政發展史 [The developing history of the Chinese postal service]. Taipei: Taiwan shangwu yinshuguan, 1994.

Youchuanbu zou yi lei bian-xu bian 郵傳部奏議類編-續編 [The collection of memorials from the Ministry of Posts and Communications]. *Jindai Zhongguo shiliao congkan* 近代中國史料叢刊 [Collectanea of modern Chinese history], compiled by Shen Yunlong 沈雲龍. Taipei: Wenhai chubanshe, 1967.

Younghusband, Francis Edward. *India and Tibet*. London: John Murray, 1910.

Youzhan xuancui 郵展選粹 [Prize selection from the Rocpex, Taipei '81]. Edited by Jiaotongbu youzheng zongju 交通部郵政總局. Taipei: Jiaotongbu youzheng zongju bianyin, 1982.

Yuan Shikai. *Yuan Shikai quanji* 袁世凱全集 [Complete collection of Yuan Shikai]. Edited by Luo Baoshan 駱寶善 and Liu Lusheng 劉路生. 36 vols. Henan: Henan daxue chubanshe, 2013.

Yuan Zhen 原貞. "Liangci yapian zhanzheng qijian Zhong Ying jiaoshezhong kouyizhe de zhutixing he nengdongxing (1840–1842, 1856–1860)" 兩次鴉片戰爭期間中英交涉中口譯者的主體性和能動性 (1840–1842, 1856–1860) [Subjectivity and motivation of interpreters in Sino-British negotiations during the two Opium Wars (1840–1842, 1856–1860)]. MPhil thesis, Lingnan University, 2017

Zhang Deyi 張德彝. *Hanghai shuqi* [Record of curiosities from an ocean voyage]. Edited by Zhong Shuhe 鍾叔河. Changsha: Xinhua shudian, 1981.

Zhang Deze 張德澤. *Qingdai guojia jiguan kaolue* 清代國家機關考略 [A study on the state bureaucracy of the Qing dynasty]. Beijing: Xueyuan chubanshe, 2001.

Zhang Gang 張棡. *Zhang Gang riji* 張棡日記 [Diary of Zhang Gang]. Edited by Wenzhou tushuguan 溫州圖書館. 10 vols. Beijing: Zhonghua shuju, 2019.

Zhang Guoji 張國驥. *Qing Jiaqing Daoguang shiqi zhengzhi weiji yanjiu* 清嘉慶、道光時期政治危機研究 [Research on the political crises during the reigns of Jiaqing and Daoguang in Qing dynasty]. Changsha: Yuelu shushe, 2011.

Zhang Hairong 張海榮. "Jiawu zhan hou Qing zhengfu de shizheng gaige, 1895–1899 nian" 甲午戰後清政府的實政改革，1895–1899 年 [Political reform of the Qing government after the Sino-Japanese War, 1895–1899]. PhD diss., Beijing University, 2013.

Zhang Pengyuan 張朋園. *Lixianpai yu Xinhai geming* 立憲派與辛亥革命 [The constitutional faction and the Xinhai revolution]. Taipei: Zhongyang yanjiuyuan Jindaishi yanjiusuo, 1983.

Zhang Yi 張翊. *Zhonghua youzhengshi* 中華郵政史 [History of the Chinese Postal Service]. Taipei: Dongda tushu gongsi, 1996.

Zhang Zhidong 張之洞. *Zhang Zhidong quanji* 張之洞全集 [Complete works of Zhang Zhidong]. 12 vols. Edited by Yuan Shuyi 苑書義, Sun Huafeng 孫華峰, and Li Bingxin 李秉新. Shijiazhuang: Hebei renmin chubanshe, 1998.

Zhang Zhiyong 張志勇. "Hede yu Zhong Ying Dian'an jiaoshe" 赫德與中英滇案交涉 [Hart and the Sino-British negotiations after the Yunnan incident]. In *Zhongguo shehui kexueyuan Jindaishi yanjiusuo qingnian xueshu luntan* 中國社會科學院近代史研究所青年學術論壇 [Youth Academic Forum of the Institute of Modern History, Chinese Academy of Social Sciences], edited by Zhongguo shehui kexueyuan Jindaishi yanjiusuo, 88–109. Beijing: Shehui kexue wenxian chubanshe, 2007.

Zheng, Xiaowei. *The Politics of Rights and the 1911 Revolution in China*. Stanford, CA: Stanford University Press, 2018.

Zhizhi 執之. "Zhuming youzheng shixuejia Lou Zuyi–shang" 著名郵政史學家樓祖詒–上 [Eminent postal history scholar Lou Zuyi, part 1]. *Zhongguo youzheng* 中國郵政 [Chinese postal service] 2 (2012): 62–63.

Zhonghua youzheng yutu 中華郵政與圖 [Postal Atlas of China]. Beijing: Jiaotongbu youzheng zongju [Ministry of Communication, the Directorate General of Posts], 1919.

Zhong Shuhe 鍾叔河. "Lun Guo Songtao" 論郭嵩燾, *Lishi yanjiu* 歷史研究 [Historical research] 2 (1984): 117–40.

———. "Li Gui de huanyou diqiu xinlu" 李圭的環游地球新錄 [Li Gui's new records of travels around the world]. *Wang Tao Manyou suilu / Li Gui Huanyou diqiu xinlu / Li Shuchang Xiyang zazhi / / Xu Jianyin Ouyou zalu* 王韜：漫游隨錄／ 李圭：環游地球新錄／ 黎庶昌 西洋雜志／ 徐建寅 歐游雜錄 [A collected volume of Wang Tao's Random jottings from wanderings, Li Gui's New records of travels around the world, Li Shuchang's Miscellaneous notes on the west and Xu Jianyin's Miscellaneous notes on the trip to Europe]. Edited by Chen Shangfan, Zhong Shuhe, Ren Guangliang, and Yu Yueheng. Changsha: Yuelu shushe, 1985.

———. *Zouxiang shijie: Jindai Zhongguo zhishi fenzi kaocha xifang de lishi* 走向世界：近代中國知識份子考查西方的歷史 [Going global: History of the modern Chinese intellectuals who studied the West]. Beijing: Zhongghua shuju, 1985.

Zhong wai jiu yuezhang daquan 中外舊約章大全 [Complete collections of old treaties between China and foreign countries]. Edited by Haiguan zongshu Zhong wai jiu yue zhang daquan bianzuan weiyuanhui 海關總署中外舊約章大全委員會. 3 vols. Beijing: Zhongguo haiguan chubanshe, 2004.

Zhongguo haiguan yu Yihetuan yundong 中國海關與義和團運動 [The Chinese Maritime Customs Service and the Boxer Uprising]. Edited by Zhongguo jindai jingjishi ziliao congkan bianji weiyuanhui 中國近代經濟史資料叢刊編輯委員會. Beijing: Zhonghua shuju, 1983.

Zhongguo haiguan yu youzheng 中國海關與郵政 [The Chinese Maritime Customs Service and the Postal Service]. Beijing: Zhonghua shuju, 1983.

Zhongguo Qingdai youzheng tuji 中國清代郵政圖集 [Picture album of China's Qing dynasty postal service]. Edited by Beijingshi youzheng guanliju wenshi zhongxin 北京市郵政管理局文史中心. Beijing: Renmin you dian chubanshe, 1996.

Zhongguo youzheng shiwu zonglun 中國郵政事物總論 [A complete collection of the reports on the working of the Chinese Post Office]. Edited by Zhang Zhihe 張志和 and Hu Zhongyuan 胡仲元. 3 vols. Beijing: Beijing Yanshan chubanshe, 1995.

Zhongguo youzi kao 中國郵資考 [A study on postage rates in China]. Edited by Liu Chenghan 劉承漢, Hsueh Ping-wen 薛聘文, Lu Taiyu 盧太育, and Wang Shiying 王士英. Taipei: Jiaotongbu Youzheng zongju, 1957.

Zhongguo youpiao mulu 中國郵票目錄 [Postage stamp catalog, Republic of China, 1878–1996]. Edited by Jiaotongbu Youzheng zongju. Taipei: Jiaotongbu Youzheng zongju, 1996.

Zhongguo youzheng tongji huiji 中國郵政統計彙輯 [Collected statistics of the Chinese Post Office]. Edited by Jiaotongbu youzhengzongju 交通部郵政總局. Taipei: Jiaotongbu Youzheng zongju, 1956.

Zhou Shurong 周蜀蓉. *Faxian bianjiang: Huaxi bianjiang yanjiu xuehui yanjiu* 發現邊疆：華西邊疆研究學會研究 [Discovering frontiers: A study on the West China Border Research Society]. Beijing: Zhonghua shuju, 2018.

Zhou, Yongming. *Historicizing Online Politics: Telegraphy, the Internet, and Political Participation in China.* Stanford, CA: Stanford University Press, 2006.

Zhou Zhichu 周志初. *Wan Qing caizheng jingji yanjiu* 晚清財政經濟研究 [A study of the finance and economics of the late Qing]. Jinan: Qilu shushe, 2002.

Zhu Marlon 朱瑪瓏. "Waijiao qingbao yu gangji baoye: Yi 1874 nian Taiwan shijian Ri Zhong liang guo lunchuan yun bing xiaoxi wei li" 外交情報與港際報業：以 1874 年臺灣事件日、中兩國輪船運兵消息爲例 [Diplomatic intelligence and interport journalism: The news of Japanese and Chinese troop steamers during the Formosa Incident of 1874]. *Zhongyanyuan Jindaishi yanjiusuo jikan* 中研院近代史研究所集刊 [Bulletin of the Institute of Modern History, Academia Sinica] 93 (2016): 1–39.

Zhu Yingui 朱蔭貴. *Lun Zhaoshangju* 論招商局 [The exposition of China merchants]. Beijing: Shehui kexue wenxian chubanshe, 2012.

Zhuang Jifa 莊吉發. *Qingchao zouzhe zhidu* 清朝奏摺制度 [The memorial system of the Qing dynasty]. Beijing: Gugong chubanshe, 2016.

Index

private letter hongs (*minxinju*)
(*continued*)
"coast postal hongs" (*lunchuan xinju*),
171; coexistence with other postal systems, 122, 137; Customs commissioners'
reports on, 207; Customs Postal Service
and, 115; Dachang postage rates and,
108; geographical reach of, *210*; Hart's
postal circulars and, 338; as impediment
to creation of national post office, 9;
inland, 171; IPO competition with, 151,
155–58, *159*, 224–26, 239; as postal agencies, 228; Russian Imperial Post and,
359–60, 361; survey of hongs at treaty
ports (1882–91), *152–54*; Taiwan Post
Office and, 129, 131; volume of mail
carried by, 132; Wenbao bureaux and,
124
provincial governors (*xunfu*), 8, 24, 62;
attitude toward foreigners, 206; Hart
and IPO criticized by, 17; postal expansion and, 179; reforms after Boxer
Rebellion and, 193; Taiwan crisis (1874)
and, 120; Wenbao bureaux and, 122
Prussia, postal service in, 5

Qianlong Emperor period, 67, 356
Qihe, postal branch in, 111, 112, 113,171,
172, 176,189
Qing dynasty/government, 206, 220, 252,
339; ancestral worship rites, 32; anti-
Westernization clique in, 70; CMCS
revenue for, 50; final set of reforms,
193–94, 255–56; foreign affairs, 39;
funding of IPO and, 306; information
system for postal permits, 8–9; Korea
and, 127; Kulun Incident (1909) and,
361–62, 365; military relay courier system, 8; modernization project of, 2,
120; persuaded to institute national
post office, 10; relations with Russia,
357; split between Beijing and
Chengde, 40; Tibet and relations with
British India, 320–24; upheavals of
nineteenth century and, 19–20

Qing officials, 15, 136; differing perspectives among, 16; Han Chinese, 14, 31;
Manchus, 14, 23, 31; postal expansion
and local officials/gentry, 177–84, 186;
reluctance about implementing
change, 55
Qiongzhou, treaty port of, *154*
Qiu, Lansun, 118

Railway Protection Movement, 309
railways, 4, 5, 74, 83, 267, 295; Beijing-
Hankou (Jinghan) Railway, 187, 202,
223, 224, 268; Beijing-Shanghai Pass
Railway, 280; Beijing-Zhangjiakou
Railway, 259; Bureau of Railways
(Tiedaobu), 374; "day-and-night" system and, 275, 278, *279*; Eight Rules and,
223–26; geopolitics and, 256; Hart's
vision of progress and, 64; impact on
agricultural economics, 276; Indochina-
Yunnan Railway, 163; interrupted by
civil disturbances, 300; Kaifeng-
Luoyang Railway, 223; Li, Hongzhang's
growing support for, 95; New Policies
reforms and, 301; postal services combined with, 167–68; as preferred mode
of transport, 278; Qingdao-Jinan Railway, 224, 280; resistance to, 73; School
of Railways (Tielu chuanxisuo), 266;
Self-Strengthening Movement and, 263;
Tianjin-Shanghai Pass Railway, 223;
traditional relay methods combined
with, 123; Trans-Siberian Railway, 283,
363n73
Record of Foreign Lands (Yiyuzhi), 48
Red Emperor Guan temples, 173, *174*, 233
Reid, Gilbert, 147
Rennie, David Field, 46–47
revenue raising, 10, 67, 68
Richard, Timothy, 145, 146, 147
Ritchie, W. W., 309–10
Rocher, Louis, 126, 158
Rongfahe hong, 207
Royal Mail, British, 4–5
Russell, Earl, 49

Harvard East Asian Monographs
(most recent titles)